# TEACHING THINKING:

## An Agenda for the Twenty-First Century

# TEACHING THINKING:

# AN AGENDA FOR THE TWENTY-FIRST CENTURY

Edited by
**CATHY COLLINS**
*Texas Christian University*
**JOHN N. MANGIERI**
*University of New Orleans*

**LEA** LAWRENCE ERLBAUM ASSOCIATES, PUBLISHERS
1992    Hillsdale, New Jersey                    Hove and London

Lawrence Erlbaum Associates, Inc., Publishers
365 Broadway
Hillsdale, New Jersey 07642


Library of Congress Cataloging in Publication Data

Teaching thinking : an agenda for the twenty-first century / edited
  by Cathy Collins, John N. Mangieri
        p.   cm.
    Includes bibliographical references and indexes.
    ISBN 0-8058-0867-1. — ISBN 0-8058-0868-X (pbk.)
    1. Thought and thinking—Study and teaching—United States.
  I. Collins, Cathy.   II. Mangieri, John N.
  LB1590.3.T53 1991 1992
  370.15′2—dc20                                          91-26961
                                                          CIP

Printed in the United States of America
10  9  8  7  6  5  4  3  2  1

To the memory of Dr. John W. Arnn, Jr., a friend in the truest sense
of the term and the epitome of professionalism;
and,
In honor of our mothers, JoAnn Neva Zinke and Rose Marie Mangieri,
for the love, understanding, and encouragement which
they have always given to us.

# Contents

# Preface

For most people, thinking represents a true contradiction. These individuals know how to think, but know little about what thinking is, how they learned to think, and whether or not they are *good* at thinking. They would agree that it is a crucial ability, but yet these same persons are not concerned that they know so little about thinking.

Why this is so is certainly a matter of conjecture. Consider if you will, however, the following circumstances. Most adults received little or no education or training in how to think. The teaching of thinking per se is not part of the preparation process for either elementary or secondary teachers. The majority of school curricula do not significantly address the topic. Most people probably have more erroneous, than correct, ideas about thinking.

At present, thinking is the purview of neither parents nor educators. Parents know little about thinking, and assume that if it needs to be formally taught, then the schools will handle it. Some parents also incorrectly believe that thinking can't be taught. They would contend that either a person has or does not have the ability to think well.

Educators similarly operate with a false set of assumptions. Many teachers know little about thinking. It has not been part of their own education, and they are unsure as to which content area *owns* thinking. Also, because in most schools thinking is not taught as a separate entity, some individuals then feel it is not meant to be taught in the schools. Others may contend that since it is not taught as a discipline, then every teacher probably deals with some dimensions of thinking. Regrettably, even if this were true, what is frequently everyone's business becomes no one's business. Thus, the teaching of thinking does not occur in a concerted, logical fashion. Rather, it is taught in a fragmented way, and the skills provided and the methods employed may or may not be compatible.

Fortunately, this lamentable situation does have some rays of hope. We now know more about thinking than at any point in our history. Numerous research investigations using diverse populations have been conducted and have yielded positive and consistent results relative to the efficacy of teaching thinking. You will read more about these results in several chapters in this volume.

Also, teacher preparation programs are increasingly beginning to include content and pedagogical practices about the development of thinking in children and other learners. These programs will result in the next generation of educators being better prepared to teach thinking than their predecessors.

The teaching of thinking is now beginning to become a part of the curriculum in both elementary and secondary schools. Educators are no longer equating the development of thinking skills as being purely a maturational process. Instead, they are using teaching techniques that can foster the thinking abilities of individuals. If you wish to teach thinking in your school, but are unsure how to do it, the authors offer numerous excellent ideas and strategies to develop thinking in students.

Publishing companies are also providing impetus to the thinking movement. Formerly, many companies did not publish instructional materials designed to promote thinking development in individuals. They adopted a "wait and see" attitude. Each wanted a competitor to take the first step (and the related expense), and if the venture proved successful, then the competing companies would develop comparable products. Fortunately, this situation too is now changing. Materials designed for classroom use to develop thinking skills are currently being produced and/or are being planned by several publishing companies.

Finally, the previously discussed research investigations are resulting in a significant corpus of knowledge about thinking. This information is not only being presented in classroom materials but in professional textbooks such as this one. We hope these books will lead to an increased dissemination of knowledge about thinking to educators as well as to a heightened interest in the field of thinking. The resultant effect of the aforementioned will be more and better research regarding thinking.

This volume was truly a collaborative venture. When planning it, we discussed its proposed content with numerous colleagues throughout the country. These individuals included elementary and secondary teachers and administrators as well as university educators. Due to the number of these individuals, it is impossible to name them here. They know who they are, however, and to each our heartfelt thanks for their contribution.

This volume consists of 16 chapters and a concluding discussion. For purposes of reader convenience, they have been divided into three categories: elementary school; middle school, high school, and adult learners; and, general material related to the teaching of thinking in children, adolescents, and adults.

Each chapter has been written by a person or persons nationally recognized for their knowledge of that particular segment of thinking, and each chapter is preceded by an introduction by a colleague with an equally esteemed reputation in the field about which they have written. To both sets of authors, we publicly acknowledge what we have privately conveyed to them—our thanks for taking such a significant portion of time from their busy lives in order to contribute to this volume.

Finally, we wish to share a personal message to the reader. The editing of this volume was truly "a labor of love" for us. It was a real joy to read each contribution and to learn about the ideas and research conveyed by the authors. Although some chapters may at initial impression have more interest for you than others, we would urge you to read all of them. The content of the entire volume can provide you with a gestalt of the wide-ranging, complicated process known as thinking.

It was our pleasure to serve as volume editors. Our goal will be realized if you derive as much information and enjoyment from reading this book as we did while editing it.

**John N. Mangieri**
**Cathy Collins**

# Introduction to
# Chapter 1

*James Voss, Professor of Psychology and
Political Science and Associate Director of the
Learning Research and Development Center,
University of Pittsburgh*

Chapter 1 by Isabel Beck and Janice Dole makes two quite
general and yet quite substantial contributions to the issue of
how reading and comprehension relate to the teaching of
thinking. First, the authors, quite appropriately in this writer's judgment, point to the need to consider reading and
comprehension skills as being related to the goals of the
individual, and the context in which the individual is processing the discourse. While not phrasing their position in
these terms, they do state thinking is more than reading
comprehension and they subscribe to the position that thinking involves going beyond the information given, with individuals elaborating upon the discourse, and, in a sense,
providing an interpretation of the discourse contents in relation to what they already know. Readers thus provide a
context for the purpose of interpretation.

The importance of this orientation should not be under-
estimated. Literacy is a function of the person and the context. A political scientist reading an editorial typically will
evaluate the article's contents virtually as the reading takes
place. A novice will focus on what the "writer is saying."
Because there has been so much preoccupation in the teaching of reading with the idea of comprehending "what is
written," we have neglected the study of how "what is
written" can be interpreted by different individuals. "What
is written," moreover, is not an inkblot, but an opportunity
for a person to provide an interpretation or meaning to
what is read.

Two matters that Beck and Dole discuss then follow
logically from this position. One is that a person's prior
knowledge will influence the nature, form, and complexity

1

of the interpretation. The other is that the structure of the discourse will influence the nature of the interpretation and the level of understanding that the individual develops. The authors underscore these points by illustrations indicating how prior knowledge does not only facilitate thinking but also can interfere with it, and how text coherence can and should be improved if students are to have the opportunity to learn from the text contents and to use such contents for thinking about the issues. In addition, the important point is made that if one is to think effectively it is important to not only have the knowledge but to also be able to use such knowledge.

While the authors present their empirically supported view on the importance of prior knowledge and text coherence in a forceful and convincing manner, the other general contribution of this chapter is even greater. This effort, perhaps surprisingly, rests upon what the authors suggest or imply rather than what is explicitly stated. The contribution is their attempt to deal with the issue of what they term engagement. Becky is "engaged," as she describes the text contents in her own words, while Carol is not "engaged" as she recalls "what the text said." Near the end of the chapter, the authors relate engagement to motivation, but this effort only is scratching the surface of what constitutes engagement. Nevertheless, the authors' acknowledgment of engagement as a critical thinking process is thought-provoking and should lead others to further investigate this nebulous factor that permeates the intellectual life of children and adults. The authors' recognition of engagement as a critical aspect of comprehension, a place "where the action is," should raise the awareness of readers interested in developing a better understanding of the processes of comprehension and thinking.

# 1 Reading and Thinking with History and Science Text

Isabel L. Beck
*University of Pittsburgh*

Janice A. Dole
*University of Utah*

As reading researchers, our interest is in thinking with, and about, text. Our focus is on reading and thinking with expository texts, specifically in the areas of social studies and science. These texts represent the major subject matter domains in the elementary school, and "are the ones that convey new information and explain new topics" (Black, 1985, p. 249). Since much of social studies and science content is taught through these texts, it makes sense to examine them carefully and to consider how learners read and think about the material in these texts. Towards this end we draw from two programs of research, one by Beck and her colleagues at the University of Pittsburgh and one by Dole and her colleagues at the University of Utah.

A major position taken in this chapter is that although thinking with social studies and science texts is related to what has been traditionally called reading comprehension, it is more than that. What we have in mind by thinking with subject matter text is closer to what Resnick (1987) refers to as higher order thinking, which is a complex process that involves, "elaborating, adding complexity, and going beyond the given" (p. 42).

When considering higher order thinking, it is important to point out that the terms thinking and higher order thinking, as well as problem solving, reasoning, and critical thinking, are difficult to differentiate from each other. In Nickerson, Perkins, and Smith's (1985) review of investigators' use of the terms, they suggest that thinking tends to be considered the broadest term, as it encompasses both reasoning and problem solving with problem solving and reasoning used interchangeably. Psychologists tend to use the terms problem solving and reasoning, and educators usually speak about critical thinking and more recently higher order thinking. In terms of definitions, Nickerson et al. have noted that "formal definitions are of little help in understanding a concept, especially one that is . . . abstract" (p. 2). Resnick (1987) has elaborated on this point:

> Thinking skills resist the precise forms of definitions we have come to associate with the setting of specified objectives for schooling. Nevertheless, it is relatively easy to list some key features of higher order thinking. When we do this we become aware that, although we cannot define it exactly, we can recognize higher order thinking when it occurs. (p. 2)

So while we can't define the abstraction precisely, we "know it when we see it," and it is highly valued and important for understanding and learning. Since the terms that label the abstraction are often used synonymously, for our purposes here, we use higher order thinking or thinking well (Norris & Phillips, 1987).

## COMPREHENDING AND THINKING WELL

To point to some differences between comprehending and thinking well, consider two 5th grade proficient readers' recalls after reading a passage from a 5th grade social studies textbook. The passage, which was about the Intolerable Acts that the British imposed on the Colonists during the American Revolutionary period follows:

> The British were very angry! Within a few months, they passed what the colonists called the Intolerable Acts. Intolerable means 'unbearable.' These acts were meant to punish the people of Boston. The port of Boston was closed. No self-government was allowed in Massachusetts. British troops had to be housed by the Massachusetts colonists.
>     Colonial leaders in Boston acted quickly. Letters were sent telling people in the other colonies what was happening in Boston. The other colonies sent help and supplies. People wondered if their colony would be the next to feel the anger of Great Britain.

First, consider Carol, whose standardized reading comprehension score is at the 99th percentile, and her response when asked to tell everything she could remember:

> It was about the Intolerable Acts, [they] were like unbearable acts. Since the [people of] Boston threw over the tea, [the British] closed all the ports in Boston. And they said all the British soldiers had to be housed and fed in the Massachusetts homes.

Although Carol recalled only information from the first paragraph, her comprehension of that material can be considered more than adequate. Becky (whose standardized reading comprehension score at the 81st percentile is good, but not as good as Carol's) also recalled only information from the first paragraph, but her recall is qualitatively different from Carol's:

> Britain got very mad, 'this is intolerable, this is not right.' Then they said, 'Okay, just a minute, we have to have something done with Boston, they must be punished because they humiliated us and we are bigger than them.' Then they closed up the Boston port; that way no ships could get through. But this is the really stinky part, the soldiers had to live with the poor people who weren't even getting any more food, they had to like give up their bed, give up some of their food, and still keep the house warm . . .

In our view Becky's recall of the passage represents what Resnick (1987, p. 42) suggests is involved in higher order thinking. Specifically, Becky engaged in a complex process that involved, at the least, elaborating on key ideas, ". . . this is intolerable, this is not right," adding complexity, "they must be punished because they humiliated us and we are bigger than them," and going beyond the given, "this is the really stinky part . . . they had to give up their bed, their food, and still keep the house warm."

What accounts for the differences between these two proficient readers' responses to the same text? One factor could be differences in prior knowledge. Although we do not know whether Becky was more familiar with the content than Carol, it is our guess that she was. Beyond prior knowledge, though, we also see in Becky's response a disposition to become engaged with the material and a tendency to make text information meaningful for herself. As an additional illustration of this engagement, consider the difference between Carol and Becky's answer to a question about information in the second paragraph of the passage, information that neither student spontaneously included in her recall:

What did the people of Boston do about the Intolerable Acts?

*Carol:* They wrote to the other colonies and asked them for help.

*Becky:* They started writing letters to other colonies and said, 'Help, we're in trouble here, we're starving to death.'

Variation in background knowledge alone would not seem to account for the differences in the two responses. Rather, Carol simply responded with something very close to the text's statement, but Becky, by drawing inferences about, and elaborating upon, the information presented in the text, transformed a simple statement into a vivid event. We see this kind of disposition to engage with the information in text as an important and often overlooked component of thinking well with textual material.

# THE PROBLEM OF INADEQUATE TEXTS

It is important to point out that although Becky and Carol comprehended the Intolerable Acts passage, many students did not (Beck, McKeown, Sinatra, & Loxterman, in press). In fact, this text was judged far from adequate for helping students comprehend, even at a minimal level, the events described, let alone to think through those events and understand their significance. And, this is a serious problem in that students cannot think well about events and concepts that they do not understand.

The Intolerable Acts passage was taken from a 5th grade textbook which was examined in a program of research on learning from history texts. The research was initiated with an analysis of four widely used elementary social studies textbook series (Beck, McKeown, & Grommoll, 1989). From the analysis the investigators concluded that the text presentations generally lacked the kind of information that connected events and ideas and that explained their role in a historical chain of events. Because of the narrative nature of history, making connections is particularly important since historical events have causes and consequences, and people's reactions to events and their consequences often cause subsequent events (Stein, 1986). Hence, a key to history understanding lies in the learner's appreciation of the chain of events.

The salient issue here is that it is not enough for young learners to be presented with the elements of the chain—statements of causes, events, and consequences—as was the case with most of the textbooks examined by Beck et al. (1989). To affect thinking well about history content, learners need to know how these elements are related to each other. This notion relates to a large body of research about causal sequences which suggests that the construction of a coherent interpretation requires making connective inferences, assisted by stated connections (Trabasso & Sperry, 1985; Trabasso & van den Brock, 1985).

In light of the above, Beck et al. (1989) concluded that young students are unlikely to be able to engage in higher order thinking and reasoning about historical events from the kind of text presentations found in the social studies textbooks analyzed. The investigators proposed that, for students to build meaningful historical knowledge and to understand the significance of that knowledge, the presentation of the information must expose the reasoning that connects a cause to an event and an event to a consequence. In order to do so, the presentation needs to be oriented toward what they termed a causal/explanatory style because explanations provide the connections among historical events that are key to making instructional content meaningful. The important point here is that students are unlikely to engage in thinking about historical material, [i.e., "make elaborations," "add complexity," and "go beyond what is given" (Resnick, 1987, p. 2)] when that material fails to help students see the basic relationships and connections between events.

Less than adequate texts have also inhibited students' abilities to engage in higher order thinking about science content. Dole and Smith (1987, 1989) and Dole and Niederhauser (1989) found many of the same kinds of problems in science texts that were identified by Beck and her colleagues in history texts (see also, Anderson & Armbruster, 1984; Roth, 1985). Generally, Dole and her colleagues found that science texts, like their social studies counterparts, fail: to make important points clear, to make important causal links explicit, and to expose the underlying conceptual frameworks which hold ideas together. For example, in the following excerpt from a 5th grade science textbook, notice that the most important idea—that cells help the body repair a cut by growing new cells—is buried in conceptually dense text:

> Cells also help repair the body of an organism. For example, blood cells rush to a cut. Some blood cells form a scab to keep out bacteria and dirt. Other blood cells, such as the ones shown here, destroy any bacteria that entered through the cut. Underneath the scab, other healthy cells produce new cells that take the place of the damaged ones. The scab falls off after the new cells are in place. Cells usually take a few days to repair a cut.

It is unlikely that novice learners will get the crucial point—that cells repair a cut by reproducing new cells—since the causal link between fixing a cut and growing new cells is never made clear, and that the main point is never explicitly stated.

A particularly serious problem found in some science texts is that the underlying conceptual framework that is needed to bring together the information in a passage is missing. Consider the following example:

> A cell is the smallest living part of an organism. A tiny cell on the tip of your nose carries on the same life activities as your whole body. Cells get energy from food. They use this energy to grow and to respond to their surroundings. Cells also reproduce—or make more cells of the same kind.

Without any statement of the underlying conceptual framework, (i.e., a single cell can do all of the things that a living organism can do, such as getting and using energy, responding to the environment, and reproducing), the passage is very problematic. The first sentence could be misleading because young learners might infer that the passage is about parts of an organism. The second sentence appears to be unrelated to the first; it is unclear what "cell on . . . your nose" has to do with the cell as a part of an organism, or what "carries on the same life activities" means. Further, there is no apparent relationship between the last three sentences; they could well be three disparate ideas.

Such problems probably account for the fact that the passage was incomprehensible to many novice learners (Dole & Smith, 1987, 1989). In contrast, the investigators found that the passage was quite comprehensible to adults with expertise in science and who understood the underlying conceptual framework—that a single cell can do all of the things that a living organism can do. Novice learners do not have control of such understanding.

Less coherent texts can sometimes cause students to learn the wrong information. In this regard, Dole, Hayes, and Niederhauser (1990) traced proficient readers' thinking related to cell and body growth. The following is the text read by the students:

> Cells help organisms grow. A puppy does not grow just because its cells get bigger. Instead, muscle cells produce more cells to make longer and stronger muscles. Also, skin cells produce more skin to make the skin larger. The number of cells becomes larger as the puppy gets older. The number of cells stops getting larger once the puppy becomes an adult dog.

The essential point of this paragraph is that cells help organisms grow by producing more cells. This point, however, is obscurely embedded in the next to the last sentence. Further, the phrase, "the number of cells becomes larger as the puppy gets older" was confusing for students; many of them understood it as the cells themselves getting bigger, rather than the number of cells increasing. For example:

> Tell me what you have learned about cells.
> *Tammy:*   . . . when we get bigger our cells get bigger.
> *John:*   . . . a cell grows bigger each time you grow.
>
> How did you come up with that answer?
> *Tammy:* From this paragraph here (points to paragraph above).
> *John:* In this part here (points to paragraph above).

Both Tammy and John were proficient readers whose comprehension of the cells passage was otherwise quite reasonable. What they understood from this particular paragraph, however, would inhibit subsequent learning about cells. While the recognition of less than comprehensible texts is not new to educators, research about the attributes of text that can cause people difficulty is relatively new (see, for example, Black & Bern, 1981; Haviland & Clark, 1974; Just & Carpenter, 1987; Kintsch & Vipond, 1979). Much of the research indicates that the coherence of texts affects their comprehensibility. Also, in the last 10 years or so researchers have begun to create more coherent texts and examine the effects of those texts on young learners' comprehension and thinking.

## THE NEED FOR COHERENT TEXTS

In a study mentioned earlier, Beck et al. (in press) revised four passages drawn from a 5th grade social studies textbook and examined students' comprehension of the original texts and their revised counterparts. The content of the passages involved the period leading to the American Revolution. The revisions focused on presenting the material in a way that makes the nature of events and ideas and their relationships apparent. Thus, the emphasis was on developing coherent text.

Coherent text is especially necessary for novice learners who need easy access to unfamiliar content. If textual information is fragmented and not explicitly connected to main ideas, it is unlikely that novice learners will be able to understand the relationships among pieces of text information. Therefore, it is highly questionable as to whether students will gain the content knowledge they need to think well about the ideas.

Coherence, however, must arise from the content that is to be communicated; we do not believe that it is a structural component of the text that is something separate from the content. As an illustration, consider the original and revised passage about the Boston Tea Party from the Beck et al. (in press) study. The information the original passage provided was that the British kept a small tax on tea; the colonists were angry about the tax and boycotted British tea. Even after Parliament lowered the price of the tea itself, the colonists continued to refuse to buy it and responded with protests, one of which was throwing tea from a ship in Boston Harbor.

The problem with the presentation of the Boston Tea Party information in the original text was that even though the actual events were presented, the motivations for those events and how they related to one another were conspicuously absent. Thus, most of the revisions for this passage involved motivating and explaining actions and reactions, and explicitly connecting causes to events and events to consequences. For example, the colonists' anger over the tax was explicitly portrayed as the cause of their refusal to buy tea, which in turn was presented as the motivation for the British lowering the price of tea. The tax that remained despite the lower price was explicitly discussed as the cause of the colonists' strong reactions to the new situation.

As an illustration of how the connections between events were implemented, consider the following excerpts from, first, the original and then the revised texts:

(Original) Boatloads of tea were sent to America. Since it was cheaper than ever, the British thought that surely the colonists would buy tea now! They were wrong. Tea was burned. Tea was left to rot.

(Revised) Since it was now cheaper than ever, the British thought that surely the colonists would buy tea! So they sent boatloads of it to the colonies. But, because the tea still had the tax on it, the colonists were as angry as ever. To show their anger, the colonists burned some of the tea. They left some to rot.

Thus, the primary goal of the revisions of the Boston Tea Party text was to help readers understand the colonists' actions as motivated by their objection to the taxes.

Results showed that students who read the revised text recalled a significantly greater percentage of content and answered significantly more questions than students who read the original text. Qualitative analyses of transcripts of students' recall protocols revealed that students who read the revised text were more likely to make elaborations and draw inferences about the central themes of the passages (Beck et al., in press).

An additional analysis emerged during the scoring of students' recalls that involved an examination of student language which might reflect their awareness of the causal sequence of events in the text. The wording of students' recalls was examined for evidence that they may have established a causal link among events portrayed in the text. Specifically, the recalls were examined for the appropriate use of explicit connectors such as: because, so, since, if/then. On average, the recalls of students in the revised group included twice as many explicit causal connectors, and this difference was significant.

Previously cited research supports the fact that readers are assisted by stated connections. In addition, we would assert that there is a second clear advantage of making explicit causal connections between events. This advantage is that information that is connected is much more likely to be permanent, as well as more understandable, than isolated facts since it is well known that information having many connections to other information is more memorable (e.g., Graesser, 1981; Kintsch & van Dijk, 1978; Lehnert, 1978, 1982). As such, connected information is much more likely to be available for application and further learning.

Positive effects of more coherent text were also found by Dole and Niederhauser (1989) who rewrote science text passages to improve their coherence along many of the same lines as Beck et al. (1990). In addition to examining the effects of their revised text on student learning of science concepts, Dole and Niederhauser studied the transfer of that learning to real-world problems. Results of the revisions indicated that students who read the revised text made significantly more changes in their thinking from intuitive to more scientifically accurate conceptions about the two topics studied (cells and matter) than students who read the original text passages. Further, students who read the revised text made significant gains in their abilities to apply what they had learned to new situations and topics.

Beyond the obvious advantage for students of enhanced comprehension from coherent text, there is an additional potential advantage as well. Well-written and coherent texts may provide students with models of coherent, causally connected reasoning in subject matter domains. Such models may serve as "prototypes" of thinking that students eventually adapt into their own repertoires and apply to understanding complex information that they are asked to learn and remember

# COHERENT TEXT IS NOT ENOUGH

Although we see coherent text as a helpful ingredient, it is certainly not a sufficient condition for thinking well. Much more is needed, and high on the list of what is needed is encouragement and support to use what one knows to arrive at a reasonable conclusion based on all the information available.

As an illustration for what we have in mind, let us describe students' inconsistent responses to three questions about Britain's tax laws and the colonists' reaction to them [from Beck et al., (in press)]. For two of the questions ("What does it mean that the colonists were not members of Parliament?" "What does 'No Taxation without Representation' mean?"), students who read the revised text showed a striking advantage in understanding the issues underlying the colonists' discontent. Yet, for the third question ("Why were the colonists upset about the taxes?") which might be considered an application of the issues underlying the colonists' discontent, very few students used what they appeared to know and offered intuitive solutions instead.

In response to the question, "What does it mean that the colonists were not members of Parliament?" 38% of those students who read the revised text responded that this meant the colonists had no representation (e.g., "they didn't have anybody to vote for and the British did"), while only 8% of those students who read the original text noted these representational issues. In response to the most direct question regarding the issue of voice in government, "What does 'No Taxation without Representation' mean?" more than three times as many students in the revised group than in the original group (51% versus 15%) responded that this meant that the colonists had no voice in government.

It is not surprising that so many students in the revised text condition showed some understanding of representation because the revised text gives an explanation of this concept whereas in the original text the meaning would have to be inferred from very obtuse text statements. However, when students were specifically asked, "Why were the colonists upset about the taxes?", most students in both groups responded that it was simply a matter of money (e.g., "cause they didn't think that they should have to pay extra money to buy the stuff"). Only 16% of the revised group and 5% of the original group stated that the colonists were upset because they were not represented in the decision leading to the imposition of the taxes.

Why didn't those students who seemed to have the knowledge use it? Even though information about the concept of taxation without representation was available to them to think through their responses, the revised group tended to base their responses instead on a more familiar notion—that taxes meant paying money, and no one favored that. The concept of representation is much more complex and novel for these students, so they may have responded from a more accessible notion. In a subsequent study (McKeown, Beck, Sinatra, & Loxterman, 1991), it was decided that those students who responded that the colonists' distress was because of the money involved in taxes should be given another opportunity to consider the question, and encouragement to use what they had learned from reading the text.

In this subsequent study (McKeown et al., 1991), 48 students read all four passages, recalled them, and answered questions. Twenty-six of those students answered the question about why the colonists were upset about the taxes by pointing to money issues. Half of these students (13) were then told that " . . . the tax was very small, equal to what would be about a penny today, and it really wasn't having to pay extra money that bothered the colonists. So take a little time and think about that question again." The remaining 13 students were asked to simply go back and think again about why the colonists were upset.

In the first condition which directly refuted the students' original answer, three students changed their answers to having no voice in the tax laws as the cause of the colonists being upset. In the second condition, which simply asked students to reconsider their answer, three students changed their responses to the representation issue. Thus, when challenged or asked to give additional thought to the question, almost a quarter of the students (6 out of 26 or 23%) upgraded their answers and apparently used knowledge that was available to them. (The numbers are too small to conclude anything from the similar findings in both conditions.)

These data suggest both good and not so good news about changing learners' beliefs. The good news in the McKeown et al. (1991) study is that under the circumstances, 23% can be considered significant movement because both the reconsideration and the refutation conditions were weak implementations—they were added to a study whose primary purpose was not the investigation of changing students' thinking. But, even these weak implementations of recon-sideration and refutation did produce indications of better thinking.

Some other good news comes from a study reported earlier by Dole and Niederhauser (1989). These investigators rewrote science textbook chapters with two types of revisions. In the first type of modification, as described earlier, the investigators developed coherent text. There was, however, a second type of revision which involved adding statements that identified students' most common incorrect ideas about the topics of the texts and then directly refuted those ideas. For example, subsections of the revised text about cells began with statements such as the following:

> Many people think that, if you have a cut, your body repairs it by growing a scab. Other people think that your skin grows back. But the scab and the skin do not heal a cut.

This second type of revision, often referred to as a "refutation text," can be considered a stronger implementation of challenging students' ideas than the simple oral challenge provided in the McKeown et al. (1991) study. Also, this stronger implementation produced significant improvements in students' thinking and learning of the science material they were asked to read. As a matter of fact, students' thinking and application of science concepts improved significantly more for those students who read the second type of revision (the refutation text) than for those who read the first type of revision (the coherent text).

So, the good news is that coherent text and text that specifically refutes students' most likely naive or incorrect ideas help them learn and apply information better than the less than coherent texts so prevalent in elementary subject matter textbooks. However, as we mentioned earlier, there is some not so good news as well. Many students' thinking in the two previously cited studies did not seem to be influenced by information that conflicted with their original ideas.

For example, in the McKeown et al. (1991) study, of the 13 students who were specifically challenged and confronted about their answer that having to pay money was the reason the colonists were upset (i.e., "It wasn't having to pay the extra money that bothered the colonists. The tax was really very small, equal to what would be about a penny today."), only three students changed their answers. The other 10 ignored the confrontation and reiterated the money issue, with some of them trying to justify their thinking by describing situations of deep poverty, (e.g., "Because some of them didn't even have enough money to feed their family," "Maybe they weren't working").

In the Dole and Niederhauser (1989) study, findings were similar. Although students who read the refutation text made significant changes in their thinking over students who read the coherent or original text, 65% of the students in the refutation group continued to maintain their original naive ideas from pre to post test. Thus, well over half the group were not influenced by the direct refutation, and therefore did not learn from the material.

## COMPREHENDING AND THINKING: THE ROLE OF PRIOR KNOWLEDGE

The McKeown et al. (1991) and Dole and Niederhauser (1989) studies add additional support to the large body of research that underscores the importance of prior knowledge in comprehending and thinking from text (see, for example, Beck, Omanson, & McKeown, 1982; Chiesi, Spilich, & Voss, 1979; Pearson, Hansen, & Gordon, 1979; Spilich, Vesonder, Chiesi, & Voss, 1979). Additionally, findings from the McKeown et al. and Dole and Niederhauser studies that point to students' resistance to changing their ideas are very consistent with recent science research (Driver, Guesne, & Tiberghien, 1985; West & Pines, 1985) and also with a growing body of research in reading (Alvermann & Hynd, 1988; Alvermann, Smith, & Readence, 1985; Lipson, 1982; Maria, 1987; Marshall, 1988).

A variety of labels have been used to characterize students' existing knowledge in science—alternative frameworks, intuitive conceptions, preconceptions, and misconceptions (Driver & Erickson, 1983; Linn, 1986; Nussbaum & Novick, 1982). Regardless of the label used, and regardless of whether students' ideas consist of an isolated belief about something (e.g., spiders have six legs), or a well developed and cohesive conception about something (e.g., a Newtonian conception of motion), the problem of the tenacity of those ideas in the face of contradictory evidence is a serious one that educators have just begun to appreciate.

Even when students appear to comprehend new information from text, the tenacity of their original knowledge shows itself. Dole, Hayes, and Niederhauser (1990) presented students with a series of pretest questions to determine their knowledge and understanding about cells and matter. Two weeks later, the students read two science textbook chapters on cells and matter and answered questions about the textual material. To examine whether and how students' thinking had changed as a result of reading the text, the pretest questions were readministered as a posttest, 2 weeks later.

Consider Tom's responses from pretest through the posttest. We start with his response to one pretest question.

*Pretest question:* Where in your body is food used?
*Tom:* In your stomach. I really don't know.

Tom's response to this question was the most common answer given by students, most of whom thought that food is used in their stomachs rather than throughout their bodies.

Now consider the text passage that could have helped Tom with a more scientifically accurate response, and then note his response to a related question asked immediately after reading:

Food must be broken down into particles before it can reach your blood. First, your teeth grind food into small pieces. Second, your stomach and intestines work to break the pieces into particles. Then, the particles move into the cells of the intestines. Finally, the food particles move from these cells into your blood . . . Blood carries these nutrients to all your body cells. Nutrients move from the blood into the cells.

*After-reading question:*
How do food and water get to your cells?
*Tom:* Well, it gets ground up and the little particles of water get up into water particles and it gets carried through the blood to the cells and they take care of it and what happens with the food is that it gets ground up in the stomach and it breaks it up into food particles and the same thing happens.

Tom's comprehension of the passage was quite reasonable as evident from his response to the after-reading question, and as such, most would agree that he comprehended what he read. Now examine his response to the posttest question about food use, 2 weeks after he read the text:

*Posttest question:* Where in your body is food used?
*Tom:* Your stomach. It grinds up food.

Tom's repetition of the phrase "grinding up food" from his after-reading response to his posttest response would seem to indicate that he connected at some level the relationship between the after-reading question about how food and water get to your cells and the posttest question about where food is used. Tom's posttest response, however, clearly indicates that he maintains his earlier scientifically naive knowledge.

The pattern of returning to one's prior knowledge exhibited by Tom was typical of many students in the Dole, Hayes, and Niederhauser (1990) study. As a matter of fact, of the 15 good readers that were studied, almost half of them (6) returned to their naive prior conceptions despite scoring quite high on the comprehension questions asked after reading. Thus, the role of prior knowledge is quite strong.

Students' prior knowledge about the many concepts studied by them seems to serve as a filter through which they interpret and understand new information. It must be pointed out that prior knowledge is a double-edged sword. Part of what we saw in Becky's recall of the Intolerable Acts was in all likelihood the use of accurate prior knowledge to help engage in higher order thinking about an historical topic. However, what we saw in Tom was prior knowledge that consisted of a scientifically naive, or at best incomplete, conception. This incomplete conception may not have affected his comprehension of the to-be-learned material, but it certainly did affect his learning. Thus, *when prior knowledge consists of naive ideas or wrong information, students often have difficulty thinking well because they fail to reconcile the new and conflicting information with what they already know.*

## COMPREHENDING AND THINKING: DISPOSITIONS TOWARD ENGAGEMENT

At the beginning of this chapter, we identified two of the major components involved in reading and thinking well—(1) appropriate prior knowledge and, (2) a disposition to engage with the content of the text. We have shown how important prior knowledge is, especially when it consists of intuitively appealing notions that are hard to abdicate. Additionally, though, we believe that a disposition to engage in, and to make sense of, the material is crucial. Becky's responses about the Intolerable Acts show a willingness to engage in thinking. Although Carol comprehended what she read, there was little evidence of engagement.

Dole, Niederhauser, and Hayes (1990) found that students varied in their willingness to engage in thinking about the content of what they had read. Qualitative analyses of transcripts revealed that, in general, proficient readers were willing to engage with the textual material and to use it as a resource for their thinking. Poor readers, on the other hand, often appeared to be unwilling to engage in any discussion of the content presented in the text and they did not use the text to help them answer questions. Instead, they often ignored the text completely and were unwilling to go back to the text to help them think through answers to questions.

This difference between dispositions toward engagement can be seen by contrasting two students' responses to questions about the topic of matter. First, consider the way Jamie, a proficient reader, responded to the following after-reading questions about a passage she read:

How is a solid different from a liquid?
*Jamie:* Solids you can't pour and they're hard and liquids you can pour and they are usually runny. Oh (looks back to her reading packet, points to the word "molecules"). Oh, it's also the liquids have molecules and are farther apart than the solids.

How did you come up with that answer?
*Jamie:* Here in the text . . .
Can you show me where?
*Jamie:* Here on lines 46–52.

What did you think about this idea before?
*Jamie:* Oh, I just thought that it was that solids are hard and liquids are runny. I just remembered that part in the packet about the molecules.

The first part of Jamie's response was a description of the differences between a solid and a liquid and not an explanation of those differences. Her response is a common one given by elementary students. However, in Jamie's case, she used the text to help her think through the question and to provide an explanation of the phenomenon at a molecular level.

Now compare Jamie's willingness to consider the text with Tony's unwillingness:

How is a solid different from a liquid?
*Tony:* A solid—it does not move and a liquid it moves and that's all.

How did you come up with that answer?
*Tony:* I just thought of it.
Did any information in the text help you?
*Tony:* No.

Do you want to go back into the text to see if there might be something to help you?
*Tony:* No.

What did you think about this idea before?
*Tony:* Nothing.

In addition to the spartan responses Tony offers, his nonverbal behavior (e.g., looking away, shrugging) indicated that he did not see the text as helpful to him, and he did not wish to engage in the material. Many poor readers gave similar nonengagement responses. When asked whether there was any information in the text that might help them answer a question, they most often said, "No." Further, when interviewers asked them if they wanted to look back in the text for information to help them, they said no again.

At this point, we can only speculate as to why these students did not engage with the material. All of them could *decode* the words on the page, and so serious decoding problems did not seem to be an issue for any of the students in the study. Less coherent text may have been a problem for some of the students in the study as they read text from the original commercially produced science texts. Other readers, however, read the coherent and refutation revisions of the chapters. Yet, some of these readers also were unwilling to think through the questions and use the text as a resource for answering them.

There is some evidence that students who thought they knew the answers to the questions relied on their prior knowledge and did not see the text as providing any new information, even when their prior knowledge contradicted what was said in the text. For example, one student responded to a question asked before and after reading, "Tell me what you know about a cell" with, "Just the same thing I said before." When probed more, she responded, "[I got this idea] from what I learned in science class, I guess I already knew everything that [the text] said." This pattern was repeated throughout the interviewer's line of questions, e.g., "I knew it before . . . I remembered it from last year."

Thus, *some students may ignore new information because they believe that they already have the needed information. But there were other students like Tony who simply refused to engage with the material, and simply gave up.* This giving up tendency is consistent with tangential findings from other reading research. For example, Alvermann and Hynd (1988) reported losing several adult subjects who simply refused to learn some difficult material. Marshall (1988) also reported losing several adult subjects for similar reasons. It is clear that having a disposition to engage with textual material is essential for learning many things, let alone learning to think well.

## SUMMARY AND COMMENTS

This chapter drew from two research programs designed to examine social studies and science texts and to see how young learners interact with these texts. We have made the point that thinking well about social studies and science content is more than simply comprehending the material. Rather, thinking well is a matter of having a disposition toward making sense out of textual material. And, to do so requires integrating new information gleaned from text with appropriate prior knowledge. *Toward developing thinking, we target coherent text, the appropriate use of existing knowledge, and a disposition toward engaging in and thinking about the content as three of the essential ingredients.*

We believe that coherent text is a necessary condition towards helping students to think well in subject matter domains. Unfortunately, we found existing materials from elementary social studies and science textbooks to often be less than coherent. In general, they do not provide novice learners with the necessary causal links between ideas and do not make explicit the relationships among chains of events. Although this is especially true for social studies text, it is also an issue for science text.

Additionally, many texts do not make main points explicit, but embed them in ways that make their importance obtuse. This is particularly problematic for novice learners who find it difficult to differentiate the most important information from less important information. It is especially true for science texts, but it is also a serious issue for social studies texts. Further, science texts often do not make apparent the underlying conceptual frameworks that hold ideas together. While expert science readers can infer such frameworks, novices can not. Thus, for novice readers, many subject matter texts lack the coherence that might help them to understand new information. As such, it is unlikely that novice learners can learn to think well about the content with such texts.

Revisions can be made to social studies and science texts to improve novice learners' comprehension of these materials. It is important to note that the revisions made to improve text coherence in the Beck et al. (in press) and Dole and Niederhauser (1989) studies arose from the content to be communicated. We do not believe that coherence should be viewed as a structural component of text that is separate from the content. In this way, we see content and structure as inseparable. Attempts to improve the coherence of texts in both the Beck et al. and Dole et al. programs of research were successful in enabling a higher percentage of novice learners to comprehend and learn subject matter material.

Thinking well depends on not only the reader but also the text. Thus, we targeted the appropriate use of existing knowledge as an essential element toward thinking well in subject matter domains. The reader needs to have available some knowledge that can be related to the to-be-learned content, and that knowledge should not conflict with the information presented in the text. In all probability, Becky had the appropriate existing knowledge about the Intolerable Acts, and she used that knowledge to make the text come alive. Some students in the McKeown et al. (1991) study appeared to have the appropriate knowledge, but they did not use it. Many students in the Dole, Niederhauser, and Hayes (1990) study did not have the appropriate knowledge. To the contrary, these students, and students in the Beck et al. (in press) study as well, had naive conceptions or fragmented knowledge about the topics they studied, and this knowledge may have interfered with their learning the material (see also McKeown & Beck, 1990). This interference occurred for students who successfully comprehended the material as well as for students who did not.

A third and critical factor in thinking well and learning from subject matter texts is a disposition to engage in the material. We believe this is an important element often overlooked in reading research [see, for example, Zajonc's (1980) discussion of "cold cognition"]. In the Dole, Niederhauser, and Hayes (1990) study many students appeared to be unwilling to engage in, and think about, the content of the text. These findings are consistent with what many educators know to be true. Motivating students to engage in academic tasks is hard work; motivating them to engage in difficult academic tasks is even harder. Thus, attitude and motivation towards a task are nontrivial variables (Brown, 1988).

The willingness to engage in the task of making sense out of difficult material is a component of higher order thinking that we are just beginning to appreciate. Although researchers in psychology have addressed the issue of motivation for decades, it is still not a well-understood construct in education. Nevertheless, as we think about developing coherent text and helping students think well about the content in text, we must consider how to engage students in wanting to construct meaning from those texts. Sternberg (1986) reminds us that motivation must be considered, "especially for instruction based on cognitive theories . . . [which] are wholly cognitive and hence contain no direct implication for how students can be motivated to learn . . ." (p. 381).

As we think about developing higher order thinking of difficult content, we realize the importance of motivation and attitude. In all likelihood, these constructs will turn out to be at least as important as prior knowledge. Thus, we see that understanding the role that motivation and attitude play in thinking well will be one of the most important areas of research for the 21st century.

## ACKNOWLEDGMENTS

The history portion of this chapter was supported by a grant from the A. W. Mellon Foundation to the Learning Research and Development Center, University of Pittsburgh. The opinions expressed do not necessarily reflect the position or policy of the Mellon Foundation, and no official endorsement should be inferred.

## REFERENCES

Alvermann, D. E., & Hynd, C. R. (1988, December). *Study strategies for correcting misconceptions in physics: An intervention.* Paper presented at the meeting of the National Reading Conference, Tucson.

Alvermann, D. E., Smith, L. C., & Readence, J. E. (1985). Prior knowledge and comprehension of compatible and incompatible text. *Reading Research Quarterly, 20*, 420–436.

Anderson, T. H., & Armbruster, B. A. (1984). Content area textbooks. In R. C. Anderson, J. Osborn, & R. J. Tierney (Eds.), *Learning to read in American schools* (pp. 193–226). Hillsdale, NJ: Lawrence Erlbaum Associates.

Beck, I. L., McKeown, M. G., & Gromoll, E. W. (1989). Learning from social studies texts. *Cognition and Instruction, 6*, 99–158.

Beck, I. L., McKeown, M. G., Sinatra, G. M., & Loxterman, J. A. (in press). Revising social studies text from a text-processing perspective: Evidence of improved comprehensibility. *Reading Research Quarterly*.

Beck, I. L., Omanson, R. C., & McKeown, M..G. (1982). An instructional redesign of reading lessons: Effects on comprehension. *Reading Research Quarterly, 4*, 462–481.

Black, J. B. (1985). An exposition on understanding expository text. In B. K. Britton & J. B. Black (Eds.), *Understanding text: A theoretical and practical handbook for analyzing explanatory text* (pp. 249–267). Hillsdale, NJ: Lawrence Erlbaum Associates.

Black, J. B., & Bern, H. (1981). Causal coherence and memory for events in narratives. *Journal of Verbal Learning and Verbal Behavior, 20*, 275–290.

Brown, A. L. (1988). Motivation to learn and understand: On taking charge of one's own learning. *Cognition and Instruction, 4*, 311–321.

Chiesi, H. L., Spilich, G. J., & Voss, J. F. (1979). Acquisition of domain-related information in relation to high and low domain knowledge. *Journal of Verbal Learning and Verbal Behavior, 18*, 275–290.

Dole, J. A., Hayes, M. T., & Niederhauser, D. S. (1990, April). *Good readers' text processing strategies and their conceptual change learning from science text*. Paper presented at the meeting of the American Educational Research Association, Boston.

Dole, J. A., & Niederhauser, D. S. (1989, December). *The effects of considerate and refutation text on learning conceptually easy and difficult science topics*. Paper presented at the meeting of the National Reading Conference, Austin, TX.

Dole, J. A., Niederhauser, D. S., & Hayes, M. T. (1990). *Comprehension and conceptual change learning from science text* (Unpublished manuscript).

Dole, J. A., & Smith, E. L. (1987, December). *When prior knowledge is wrong: Reading and learning from science text*. Paper presented at the meeting of the National Reading Conference, St. Petersburg, FL.

Dole, J. A., & Smith, E. L. (1989). Prior knowledge and learning from science text: An instructional study. In S. McCormick & J. Zutell (Eds.), *Cognitive and social perspectives for literacy research and instruction* (pp. 345–352). Chicago, IL: National Reading Conference.

Driver, R., Guesne, E., & Tiberghien, A. (1985). *Children's ideas in science*. Philadelphia, PA: Open University Press.

Driver, R., & Erickson, G. (1983). Theories-in-action: Some theoretical and empirical issues in the study of students' conceptual frameworks in science. *Studies in Science Education, 10*, 37–60.

Graesser, A. C. (1981). *Prose comprehension beyond the word*. New York: Springer-Verlag.

Haviland, S. C., & Clark, H. H. (1974). What's new? Acquiring new information as a process in comprehension. *Journal of Verbal Learning and Verbal Behavior, 13*, 512–521.

Just, M. A., & Carpenter, P. A. (1987). *The Psychology of Reading and Language Comprehension*. Newton, MA: Allyn and Bacon.

Kintsch, W., & van Dijk, T. A. (1978). Towards a model of text comprehension and production. *Psychological Review, 85*, 363–394.

Kintsch, W., & Vipond, D. (1979). Reading comprehension and readability in educational practice and psychological theory. In L. G. Nilson (Ed.), *Perspectives on memory research* (pp. 325–365). Hillsdale, NJ: Lawrence Erlbaum Associates.

Lehnert, W. G. (1978). *The process of question answering*. Hillsdale, NJ: Lawrence Erlbaum Associates.

Lehnert, W. G. (1982). Plot units and narrative summarization. *Cognitive Science, 4,* 293–331.

Linn, M. C. (1986). Science. In R. F. Dillon & R. J. Sternberg (Eds.), *Cognition and instruction* (pp. 155–204). San Diego, CA: Academic Press.

Lipson, M. Y. (1982). Learning new information from text: The role of prior knowledge and reading ability. *Journal of Reading Behavior, 14,* 243–261.

Maria, K. (1987, December). *Overcoming misconceptions in science: A replication study at the fifth grade level.* Paper presented at the meeting of the National Reading Conference, St. Petersburg, FL.

Marshall, N. (1988, December). *Overcoming problems with incorrect prior knowledge: An instructional study.* Paper presented at the meeting of the National Reading Conference, Tucson.

McKeown, M. G., & Beck, I. L. (1990). The assessment and characterization of young learners' knowledge of a topic in history. *American Educational Research Journal, 27,* 688–726.

McKeown, M. G., Beck, I. L., Sinatra, G. M., & Loxterman, J. A. (1991). *The contribution of prior knowledge and coherent text comprehension.* (Submitted for publication).

Nickerson, R. S., Perkins, D. N., & Smith, E. E. (1985). *The teaching of thinking.* Hillsdale, NJ: Lawrence Erlbaum Associates.

Norris, S. P., & Phillips, L. M. (1987). Explanations of reading comprehension: Schema theory and critical thinking theory. *Teachers College Record, 2,* 281–306.

Nussbaum, J., & Novick, S. (1982). Alternative frameworks, conceptual conflict, and accommodation: Toward a principled teaching strategy. *Instructional Science, 11,* 183–200.

Pearson, P. D., Hansen, J., & Gordon, C. (1979). The effect of background knowledge on young children's comprehension of explicit and implicit information. *Journal of Reading Behavior, 11,* 201–209.

Resnick, L. B. (1987). *Education and learning to think.* Report. Washington, DC: National Academy Press.

Roth, K. (1985, April). *Conceptual change learning and student processing of science texts.* Paper presented at the meeting of the American Educational Research Association, Chicago.

Spilich, G. J., Vesonder, G. T., Chiesi, H. L., & Voss, J. F. (1979). Text processing of domain-related information for individuals with high and low domain knowledge. *Journal of Verbal Learning and Verbal Behavior, 18,* 275–290.

Stein, N. L. (1986). Knowledge and process in the acquisition of writing skills. In E. Z. Rothkopf (Ed.), *Review of research in education* (Vol. 13, pp. 225–258). Washington, DC: American Educational Research Association.

Sternberg, R. J. (1986). Cognition and instruction: Why the marriage sometimes ends in divorce. In R. F. Dillon & R. J. Sternberg (Eds.), *Cognition and instruction* (pp. 375–382). San Diego, CA: Academic Press.

Trabasso, I., & Sperry, I. I. (1985). Causal relatedness and importance of story events. *Journal of Memory and Language, 24,* 595–611.

Trabasso, I., & van den Brock, P. (1985). Causal thinking and the representation of narrative events. *Journal of Memory and Language, 24,* 612–630.

van Dijk, T. A., & Kintsch, W. (1983). *Strategies of discourse comprehension.* New York: Academic Press.

West, L. H. T., & Pines, A. L. (1985). *Cognitive structures and conceptual change.* Orlando, FL: Academic Press.

Zajonc, R. B. (1980). Feeling and thinking: Preferences need no inferences. *American Psychologist, 35,* 151–175.

# Introduction to
# Chapter 2

*Donna Alvermann, Professor of Education,
University of Georgia, and President of the
National Reading Conference*

By all estimates, diversity among students enrolled in
schools in the United States will increase as we move toward the year 2000. This diversity promises challenges of
many types. One of those challenges, developing students'
problem-solving abilities, is the topic of Donna Ogle's
thought-provoking chapter.

In this chapter, preliminary field work with a problem-
solving strategy which had its origin in mathematics classes
was applied successfully to reading and thinking about stories. Although many students of all ability levels demonstrated improved thinking with the problem-solving strategy
introduced here, several issues will need to be addressed if
the strategy is to have widespread applicability.

First, students' background of experiences vary greatly
and are expected to widen even further. If we are to ensure
that all students have equal access to knowledge, we must
abolish practices such as tracking that promote inequality in
course assignments, teaching materials, and instructional
methods. The problem-solving strategy described by Ogle
is a step in the right direction.

Second, the curriculum of most middle schools in the
United States fosters a subject-centered approach to teaching and learning. One of the arguments against this approach is that it fragments the curriculum and inhibits the
probability that teachers and students will see links across
the various subject areas. In fact, it was this issue that
nearly precluded the problem-solving strategy used in mathematics classes from being used in story reading. When
Ogle noted the similarities in processing required of problem-solving in mathematics and language arts classes, how-

ever, teachers and students were quick to see the relevance of the strategy.

Finally, thinking takes time. If students are to become problem solvers, they must be afforded the time to think both during instruction and in follow-up evaluations. Presently, in most states, writing assessments are far more likely to be cognizant of this factor than are reading assessments. The problem-solving strategy presented in this chapter holds promise relative to the development of new approaches in reading assessments.

# 2 Developing Problem-Solving Through Language Arts Instruction

Donna M. Ogle
*National-Louis University*

The need to develop better thinking among America's school children has been well documented. The National Assessment data from both reading and mathematics have highlighted the problem that has emerged from an overemphasis on skill instruction and multiple-answer testing. Students can select the correct answer when options are provided, but lack the ability to explain why they choose their answers or to substantiate their thinking about the choices they make. In the report issued by the National Assessment of Educational Progress (1988, p. 11) the authors expressed "increased concern about the critical reading abilities of our nation's students."

Considered more broadly, one of the goals of our educational system is to develop citizens who can contribute intelligently to the resolution of the issues confronting our society, citizens who can think critically and help to solve problems in local communities as well as in the national and international arenas. Pragmatically, there is also concern about the adequacy of the problem-solving abilities of our students who are graduating and taking their places in the world of work (Berryman, 1988). Business has raised a loud call for workers who can work on teams to solve problems. Even blue collar jobs now require problem-solving abilities, which employers are not finding well developed in their new employees.

This state of affairs is particularly troubling and challenging to individuals involved in literacy education since literacy instruction provides an ideal context for the development of children's thinking. Reading IS a thinking process. Readers regularly must focus and set goals, make inferences, suspend judgments, make predictions, test ideas against text, and construct meanings for whole units of text. Writing, too, is a natural context for the development of thinking.

Flowers and Hayes (1978) have, in fact, defined mature writing as problem solving including all the basic processes that any problem-solving situation requires.

Two assumptions underlie this chapter. First, there is a need to coordinate thinking skills instruction if it is going to be effective. Children will only become better thinkers if they have numerous opportunities to practice the approaches to thinking to which they are introduced. It is not easy to instill a thoughtful approach to learning. Beyer (1987), who has devoted much attention to the development of better thinkers, forcefully expresses the need for rich and elaborated instruction and frequent applications of thinking skills and strategies. He also argues that students need to use those skills and strategies in a variety of contexts and across content areas so they can really make them their own. According to Beyer:

> To be proficient in a thinking skill or strategy means to be able to use that operation effectively and efficiently on one's own in a variety of appropriate contexts. To develop such proficiency requires more than simply introducing the thinking skill or strategy and practicing it in a single context. It also requires instruction and guided practice in how and when to transfer the thinking skill or strategy from the context in which it was initially learned to the widest variety of contexts possible. (p. 163)

The second assumption is that we should focus on a few thinking strategies that are most useful and transferrable from one area to another so that students will be likely to use the skills and strategies regularly. With the wide variety of thinking programs available, it is important that students not be given so many series of strategies that they become overwhelmed. With over 30 different programs outlined in the ASCD publication *Developing Minds,* it would not be difficult for teachers to become overwhelmed, too. More is not necessarily better.

Given the tremendous need to develop thinking and the potential within reading and writing instruction for that to occur, this chapter presents some ideas as to how thinking might be developed more fully. In the chapter, one thinking skill or strategy, problem solving, is highlighted. It has been selected for several reasons. First, problem solving is central to critical thinking and has tremendous real world applications. Second, it is found frequently in thinking skills programs. Third, problem-solving strategies have been widely implemented by teachers in the current mathematics programs. As explained in Chapter 4, since students have already been introduced to problem solving in one content area, it is a likely strategy to be extended in another area. Finally, problem solving is also central to much of the literature children read, both in terms of the content and the way we read.

The basic question I address is how we can maximize the potential within literacy instruction to facilitate the development of student thinking. As you read the examples provided, and reflect on the issues that are raised, I hope you will be stimulated to find other ways to further develop students' thinking through literacy instruction. The best effort of all concerned—teachers, researchers, program developers, and teacher educators—is certainly needed if we are going to significantly impact instruction. Both better research and clearer instructional priorities and directions are needed.

## READING AS PROBLEM SOLVING

Why should we consider reading as a good setting for teaching problem solving? Stories provide an ideal context for developing students' abilities to engage in good problem solving. Often, stories provide examples of how characters solve the problems they face and offer realistic "thinking aloud" about resolving conflicts that students can follow. Many excellent books and short stories exist that provide clear examples of problem solving—stories like *Bridge to Terebithia* (Paterson, 1977), *Dicey's Song* (Voight, 1983), *The Cay* (Taylor, 1969), and *Number the Stars* (Lowry, 1989). These novels place children as protagonists in situations that require real problem solving. Mysteries provide particularly good examples of problem solving by detectives like Encyclopedia Brown. Children love to read and predict how mysteries will be resolved. Perhaps this is one of the reasons Nancy Drew and the Hardy Boys have been so popular for so long.

Rather than providing simple, laboratory type examples or problems, stories have the advantage of developing deeper elaboration and real life contexts that makes the transfer to students' own lives more possible. Students can identify with the situations and dilemmas characters face. They can think along with the protagonists as they grapple with their choices of action.

Stories provide not only good models of problem solving but also examples of contexts in which some characters do not use good strategies and get in trouble. Think, for example, of the problem Chicken Little gets into by misinterpreting her experience and overreacting. The Little Red Hen does not think of options in resolving her dilemma and is not successful as a problem solver. At upper grade levels Fox's (1984) *The One-Eyed Cat* and Zindel's (1969) *The Pigman* illustrate the outcomes of poor problem solving. These stories can be used to help readers think through better ways of resolving problems, and thus, go beyond the texts.

Reading also offers students the opportunity to engage in problem solving. During the reading of some kinds of texts active readers are invited to solve problems. When readers pause after reading just a portion of a text to predict how they think the issue facing the characters will be resolved they become active problem solvers. The reading of mysteries may be the easiest experience with which most of us can identify. As we read to find out who has committed the crime, we have to first identify the crime, then take into account the important clues that a detective, and we surrogate detectives, need to use in resolving the mystery. In doing so we formulate various hypotheses about what might have happened and how the crime was committed. As we read further, we generally eliminate some options and focus on others that have confirming evidence. We keep going back in our thinking to reaffirm our hypotheses and often rethink our probable solutions. We actively try to resolve the problem before the author reveals the climax. (For example, I am currently reading the Tony Hillerman detective novels and often put down my book and take a break before reading the conclusion just so the author doesn't reveal too much to me before I have figured out my own sense of what has really occurred. I need more time to think through the problem than continued reading permits!)

## A FRAMEWORK FOR ENCOURAGING PROBLEM SOLVING

In my own work with teachers, we have been experimenting with a reading–writing framework to help students utilize their reflective abilities better. I began with the DR–TA (Stauffer, 1979) that has been used by teachers for many years. This process encourages students to make predictions about what they are reading, both initially and then periodically during the reading of the story. Students' predictions should be based on the information provided by the author and by the picture clues. After making predictions students read and then discuss if their predictions were verified or not. Teachers are encouraged to ask, "Can you prove it?" thus redirecting students to the text for evidence. The predict, read, prove cycle models interactive, thoughtful reading–thinking behavior. It does not, however, provide enough time for more reflective use of a problem-solving strategy to figure out how characters can resolve problems.

After trying to engage students in deeper and more extended discussions of possible options for resolving problems without much regular success, we decided to apply the problem solving steps that students had been successfully employing in mathematics classes to their thinking about stories. Many teachers with whom I work have been using a model of math problem solving based on Polya's (1957) work (see Fig. 2.1). The strategy guide shown in Fig. 2.2 was on the wall of a school classroom as a reminder for students to use in mathematics. Interestingly, before I raised the possibility of linking mathematics and reading problem solving, none of the teachers had tried to extend the math model beyond that content area. (This limited use of the strategy spoke to me of the need for educators to be more self-conscious in thinking about the applicability of the strategies we teach students.) However, as soon as I made the suggestion, several teachers and some of their students immediately made the connection and have

POLYA'S MODEL

HOW TO SOLVE IT

| I. | Understand the problem |
| II. | Devise a plan |
| III. | Carry out the plan |
| IV. | Look back and explain the solution |

FIG. 2.1.

# Understand Math Problems

1. Restate the problem

2. Clarify the question

3. Organize information

4. Solve the problem
   - find and solve the hidden problem
   - draw a picture or diagram
   - use easier numbers or estimate
   - find a pattern

5. Check your solution

FIG. 2.2.

found it to be quite transferable, with some modifications necessary depending on the stories being read.

We have also found in other work (Ogle, 1986) that providing a writing component increases student commitment to thinking and helps each student take a more personal role. Therefore, we developed a problem-solving worksheet to be used by pairs of students. This worksheet makes the steps in the strategy clearer and helps students work at their own pace.

An example from a story we have used with middle grade students may help clarify the process. The story, *The Princess and the Admiral* (Pomerantz, 1974) is a Vietnamese folktale about a young princess leader of a small peace-loving country faced with a major problem. Just as they are about to celebrate 100 years of peace her advisors bring the warning that an enemy fleet is approaching the harbor. What can they do? The country lacks military weapons so the Princess is forced to engage in creative problem solving. She thinks about her resources and calls in her astrologers to find out the position of the moon for the next few nights.

Before giving the students the story they were asked to review the steps in problem solving and were introduced to this reading–thinking activity. Several words from the tale were listed on the board and the students activated what they knew about them and what these words suggested about the story. (Included on the list were: admiral, kingdom, tides, harbor, princess, poor farmers, advisors, and fleet.)

Students then were given the first part of the story to read independently. After completing the text they worked with their partner to identify the main problem in the story and the information the author had provided that would be useful in resolving the problem. They were also encouraged to draw on their prior experiences and knowledge in thinking about how the Princess and the kingdom might proceed. They were asked to identify any additional information they would need to resolve this problem. With this work done student teams then generated three possible solutions the characters might pursue. Their final task was to evaluate those solutions to determine which seemed best. Their ideas were represented on the worksheets completed by each pair. (See Fig. 2.3 for examples of worksheets.)

When they were finished problem solving the students were given the remainder of the story to read. All students eagerly read the story ending, purposefully involved now in wanting to find out if they had solved the problem as the Princess had. The next day, as a follow-up activity, the class discussed their feelings about the story, the options they had proposed, and the actual resolution of the folktale.

Many students have found this new *stance* as a reader–problem solver energizing and motivating. The eagerness with which students return to read the stories has been convincing evidence to teachers that additional time used to reflect on the problems is worthwhile. The depth of discussions during and after reading adds further evidence that the students are thinking deeply.

Name _Darla_

Name _Maria_

Story _The Princess + The Almond_

PROBLEM-SOLVING THINK SHEET

1.  WHAT IS THE MAIN PROBLEM THAT THE CHARACTERS HAVE TO
    SOLVE? * no soldiers * no weapons * no experience in war
    But there were ships coming to attack them + they
    had to do something.

2.  AS YOU THINK ABOUT HOW YOU MIGHT SOLVE THIS PROBLEM,
    WHAT INFORMATION HAS THE AUTHOR GIVEN YOU THAT MIGHT
    BE IMPORTANT?

    A. the position of the moon + sun
    B. cut down the tall trees
    C. sent out fishing boats to tease the war ships

3.  WHAT ELSE DOES THE CHARACTER (OR CHARACTERS) NEED TO
    KNOW TO MAKE A GOOD PLAN?

    how they are going to carry out the plan

4.  WITH ALL THIS INFORMATION AND GOOD THINKING WHAT DO YOU
    THINK ARE THE MOST LIKELY WAYS TO SOLVE THIS PROBLEM?

    A. so the fisherman can distract the warships.
    while the people back home can make weapons to
    B. defend themselves. The moon can help them
    out
    C. The warships won't suspect the people working
    at night by the moonlight

FIG. 2.3a.

After using this approach to reading several students reported that they had
never before taken adequate time to think about solutions to the story problems.
They normally just made quick guesses about what might happen, then read to
find out what the author unfolded. Some children found the activity frustrating
because it slowed them down and interfered with their regular reading. Others
really enjoyed the opportunity to become more actively involved in the problems
and think through resolutions.

Some classrooms have altered the basic worksheet to make it reflect their own
approaches to problem solving and to particular stories. For example, in one

Name _Corie_

Name _Donovan_

Story _The Princess and the Admiral_

### PROBLEM-SOLVING THINK SHEET

1. WHAT IS THE MAIN PROBLEM THAT THE CHARACTERS HAVE TO SOLVE?

    *How to stop the war because they don't have soldiers or weapons*

2. AS YOU THINK ABOUT HOW YOU MIGHT SOLVE THIS PROBLEM, WHAT INFORMATION HAS THE AUTHOR GIVEN YOU THAT MIGHT BE IMPORTANT?

    A. *cut down trees*

    B. *Kingdom has no soldiers*

    C. *they have fishing boats*

3. WHAT ELSE DOES THE CHARACTER (OR CHARACTERS) NEED TO KNOW TO MAKE A GOOD PLAN?

    *How many people they are on each boat*

4. WITH ALL THIS INFORMATION AND GOOD THINKING WHAT DO YOU THINK ARE THE MOST LIKELY WAYS TO SOLVE THIS PROBLEM?

    A. *You don't need war to compremize*

    B. *Talk to each other*

    C. *Both college can talk the princes can send one of her people across the ocean to send a letter of peace to the other college to compremize.*

FIG. 2.3b.

classroom, students immediately made the connection to their math thinking. Students suggested that the sheet should have an additional component. They felt they should define the criteria they would use to select one or another option as a possible solution. That is, criteria such as "Would be easy to implement" or "Wouldn't seem natural" or "Would require too much skill" would be provided by the students to evaluate most likely options. The teacher developed a new

Name_____

Name_____

Story_____

### PROBLEM-SOLVING THINK SHEET

1. WHAT IS THE MAIN PROBLEM THAT THE CHARACTERS HAVE TO SOLVE

2. AS YOU THINK ABOUT HOW YOU MIGHT SOLVE THIS PROBLEM, WHAT INFORMATION HAS THE AUTHOR GIVEN YOU THAT MIGHT BE IMPORTANT?

3. WHAT ELSE DO YOU ALREADY KNOW THAT MAY BE HELPFUL IN FINDING A WAY TO SOLVE THE PROBLEM? WHAT ELSE DOES THE CHARACTER NEED TO KNOW TO MAKE A GOOD PLAN?

4. WITH ALL THIS INFORMATION AND GOOD THINKING WHAT DO YOU THINK ARE THE MOST LIKELY WAYS TO SOLVE THIS PROBLEM? FIRST LIST THREE GOOD OPTIONS?

    A.
    B.
    C.

5. WHAT CRITERIA CAN YOU USE TO CHOOSE THE BEST PLAN TO SOLVE THE PROBLEM FROM THE LIST OF OPTIONS ABOVE? (i.e., it won't hurt anyone else; it can be done easily; it won't require extra tools or equipment.)

    A.
    B.
    C.

USING THE ABOVE CRITERIA CIRCLE THE OPTION FROM QUESTION 4 THAT YOU THINK WILL WORK BEST TO SOLVE THE PROBLEM.

FIG. 2.4.

worksheet to incorporate this idea (see Fig. 2.4). Another group of 3rd grade readers wanted a space to write the actual resolution of the problem so they could have closure on the process. That was added to their sheet (see Fig. 2.5).

## ISSUES TO CONSIDER

As we have worked with this application of problem solving to story reading, several issues have emerged. First, many stories do provide rich bases for students to identify or engage in thinking together to solve problems. However, teachers have not customarily used them for this purpose. Therefore, there is a need to work with teachers to explore the best ways to use stories for problem solving. Second, the stories in many basal readers, particularly at the middle

Name_____

Name_____

Story_____

## PROBLEM-SOLVING THINK SHEET

1. What is the problem the character has to solve?

2. What information did the author give you that was important?

3. What could the characters do to solve the problem?

    A.
    B.
    C.

4. How did the characters actually solve the problem?

FIG. 2.5.

grades, contain such short snips that they no longer retain interesting problems. In the middle grades we often have had to turn to full novels and biographies to find real problem solving situations. This difficulty in locating interesting stories for middle grade readers poses an issue that deserves further exploration. It also raises the possibility of using the quality of problem posed and the nature of the resolution as a criteria for evaluation of stories students are asked to read. It certainly seems justifiable to insist that some stories and articles middle grade readers are given engage them actively in thinking through problems and provide examples of how others deal with real life issues.

Third, the way the problem solving strategy is conceived must be flexible; different stories and problem situations require variations on the basic framework. For example, during a lesson I was teaching using *The Princess and the Admiral* many students could not seem to get involved. As I talked with them, it became apparent that they lacked the necessary schemata to make sense of the clues the author had provided. When I brought the class back together and helped them draw a picture of the setting and include the information the author had provided they were then able to proceed in their thinking. They had to visualize the situation in order to come close to solving the problem. This step was not included on the worksheet but was necessary since they did not have enough background knowledge of villages located on a harbor, nor of the effect of tides on the level of the water in the ocean, to enter into problem solving using the clues the author had provided.

Experiences such as the aforementioned underscore Beyer's (1987) discussion of the need for thinking strategies to be conceived of as flexible because "they are also very much shaped by the subject matter, disciplines, or content with which they are used" (p. 164). Putting the set of steps in a strategy on the board for students or constructing a worksheet to facilitate team or group interaction should be viewed in a flexible fashion rather than as a rigid prescription for students to follow while engaging in problem solving. Both teachers and students should not become too rule-bound and feel a need to follow step-by-step through counterproductive processes. It should be emphasized that the strategies should serve the thinkers, not the other way around.

This piloting of a problem solving process in reading has also raised an issue relative to the role of the teacher. It was clear in the classes where the folktale was being used that, had I stayed in the background at the time students were confused, they probably would not have found the key to unlocking that story problem. As I took the same story to another class of precocious readers I was interested in determining how they would handle the story problem. This group also lacked the schemata to resolve the story. However, I did not intervene. As a result, they did not come nearly as close to resolving the problem as did the first class, of less able students. Examples in Fig. 2.3 from the less able class reflect the difference that teacher guidance made. Students were finally able to develop possible solutions that made sense relative to the story.

In this example teacher guidance was needed to help the class develop more adequate schemata for the story content. The influence of schemata on comprehension has been well established (see Beck and Dole, Chapter 1). Our work with classrooms has supported this reality; students' ability to solve problems is very closely related to their depth of understanding of the variables and constraints inherent in the story situations. Teachers can be sensitive to students' inadequate schemata and intervene. However, in many real world situations such a bridging "teacher" is not available to identify gaps in knowledge. Even in school situations teachers and texts often assume more knowledge than novice learners possess. Can we help students become more metacognitively aware so they can identify when they lack adequate knowledge to solve problems and learn to search out information to fill the gaps?

For example, in another class rather than assume a "teaching role" I supplied additional reading material for students to use that would help extend their knowledge on relevant topics. I provided articles on the effect of the moon on tides from science textbooks and encyclopedias and some pictures of harbor villages. I asked students to read those along with the folktale. While some students were not eager to read more, others did use information from their resources to help clarify the situation.

Much can still be done to help students learn to use multiple resources to build schemata. I found the groups with which I have tried this approach enjoyed it, but are totally unfamiliar with using multiple resources for problem solving or even for building understanding. Here, too, is another area needing elaboration if students are to become independent thinkers and problem solvers. How can teachers model and provide students with adequate support to help them think deeply about their reading, and yet still develop the requisite independence? What would happen if students used a problem solving strategy over time that included periodic discussions focused on the adequacy of their knowledge to resolve the problems? Could students learn to identify, locate, and use needed additional resources—and thus become more independent learners?

The final issue that this pilot work has raised is how to evaluate the effectiveness of the approach. In the first explorations assessment has been primarily the students' ability to summarize the stories they have read, either immediately after reading or 2 days later, as an indication of the processing it has stimulated. We have also interviewed students to ascertain their own reactions to the "interrupted reading" format. However, the caution raised by Lockhead and Whimbey (1987) is important:

> Unfortunately, classroom teachers who try to encourage their students to employ (such) habits generally have been disappointed with the results. There is a good reason for this. Recent studies of cognitive processes strongly suggest that expertise in problem solving takes approximately ten years to acquire and that expert reasoning patterns learned in one area do not transfer easily to other areas (Hayes, 1981). Thus, we can not expect measurable results in the time frames normally available in conventional instruction. (p. 74)

If we want to measure not just the improvement in story comprehension and enjoyment but also the development of thinking, we need to develop new measures and indicators. These measures may also require a longer time frame. Can our assessments become more sensitive to the effectiveness of our efforts to encourage better thinking by students?

## FITTING THIS PILOT WORK INTO THE LARGER BODY OF WORK ON THINKING IN LANGUAGE ARTS

A review of the literature shows that at present very little research has been reported and few articles have been written about how to develop problem solving in reading and language arts instruction. Flynn (1989) describes her application of Bransford's IDEAL (1986) strategy to reading. Flynn placed students in cooperative groups where they learned to work together to solve problems in stories. Using an article dealing with a realistic problem, she made copies and then cut them into sections. "Each student was responsible for reading one section of the article to the group . . . I kept the fifth section which provided the solution . . . The students worked together, first identifying the problem, then defining it more clearly, etc." (p. 667). She reports that mysteries, human relations and social problem articles from journals and social studies texts, short stories, novels, and newspaper articles all were excellent texts with which students practiced using the IDEAL strategy.

Brown (1986) used Bloom's classification system to help prioritize higher levels of thinking and more complex processes like decision making and problem solving. She explained four ways she had developed better thinking with her students using children's literature:

1. providing children with a problem-solving guide (developed for an educational television program for children, "Think About") to use in thinking about problems of characters in stories;

2. modeling problem-solving behavior and using examples from literature to demonstrate how characters resolve problems;

3. brainstorming ideas and showing how characters in books also brainstorm;

4. role playing and using creative drama based on story situations.

Although no evaluation data was provided, nevertheless, Brown thought the students had gained from her focus on thinking.

In a recent article, Beck (1989) argues that "literature is enormously rich" in opportunities to engage in problem solving (p. 679). She suggests that teachers have students read part of a story until a problem has been established and then ask what the problem is and how it might be solved. After reading a story, the teacher should ask questions that focus on the problem–solution framework. The discussion can be extended to encourage more creative solutions by giving students a new problem for the character to solve. In the third step, Beck suggests the teacher propose a difficult problem for students to solve, thus extending their thinking to a more "decontextualized situation."

Raphael Kirschner, and Carol Englert (1988), Jones, Amiran, and Kalims (1985), and Taylor (1982) have done significant research in the area of text structure and macro frames. They have demonstrated that when students learn to identify these organizing structures they read and retain more information. These same frames also provide structure for students' writing. The problem–solution frame is one of the basic structures that most researchers have included in their work—either asking students to learn to identify structures in reading or to use them in writing their own compositions. However, recognition of structures or even use of them can be fairly low level tasks, depending on how they are executed by the learners and on the quality of teacher guidance.

## CONCLUSION

It seems clear that many research opportunities lie before us. We know little about how students problem solve when reading. We have a few suggestions for ways of helping students become better problem-solvers in their reading and writing—by using models in stories and by involving them in activities that engage them more deeply with problems and characters. At present we are unsure about the effects of some systematic attention to problems in stories, if or how students can learn to transfer strategies learned in one context to others, nor do we know why teachers have not done more to develop problem solving or to link instruction in thinking across content areas. A rich array of challenges lie before us.

We particularly need more dialogue among those developing thinking skills strategies and programs and those working directly with students. Rather than focusing on the differences in the content applications of strategies for thinking, a first step is to get teachers to experiment with possible applications of strategies in their teaching. They should be our first resources in answering the questions of the possibility of generalizeable strategies or of the content specificity of strategies.

Because written text provides such a rich resource for thinking it seems especially unfortunate that so little work has been done to link language arts and reading instruction to the development of strategic thinking, generally, and problem solving, specifically. Perhaps this decade will be the time when we accept the challenges and find ways to facilitate better thinking and to document that achievement.

# REFERENCES

Berryman, S. (1988). *The educational challenge of the American economy.* Paper prepared for a forum of the National Education Association, October 7, 1988. Washington D.C.

Beck, I. (1989). Reading and reasoning. *The Reading Teacher, 42*(9), 676–682.

Beyer, B. (1987). *Practical strategies for the teaching of thinking.* Boston, MA: Allyn and Bacon.

Bransford, J., & Stein, B. (1984). *The ideal problem solver.* New York: W. H. Freeman.

Brown, L. (1986). Developing critical thinking and problem-solving skills with children's books. *Childhood Education, 63*,(2), 102–107.

Flowers, L. S., & Hayes, J. R. (1978). Problem solving strategies and the writing process. *College English, 39,* 449–461.

Flynn, L. (1989). Developing critical reading skills through cooperative problem solving. *The Reading Teacher, 42*(9), 664–668.

Fox, P. (1984). *The one-eyed cat.* Scarsdale, NY: Bradley Press.

Jones, B. F., Amiran, M. R., & Kalims, M. (1985). Teaching cognitive strategies and text structures within language arts programs. In S. F. Segal, S. F. Chipman, & R. Glaser (Eds.), *Thinking & learning skills: Relating instruction to research, 1.* Hillsdale, NJ: Lawrence Erlbaum Associates.

Lockhead, J., & Whimbey, A. (1987). Teaching analytic reasoning through thinking aloud pair problem solving. In J. Stice (Ed.), *Developing critical thinking and problem solving abilities.* San Francisco, CA: Jossey-Bass.

Lowry, L. (1989). *Number the stars.* Boston, MA: Houghton-Mifflin.

*National Assessment of Educational Progress* (1988). U.S. Department of Education: Washington, D.C.

Ogle, D. (1986). KWL: A teaching model that develops active reading of expository text. *The Reading Teacher, 39,* 564–570.

Paterson, K. (1977). *Bridge to terebithia*. New York: Crowell.

Polya, G. (1957). *How to solve it*. Princeton, NJ: Princeton University Press.

Pomerantz, C. (1974). *The princess and the admiral*. Reading, MA: Addison-Wesley.

Raphael, T. Kirschner, B., & Englert, C. (1988). Expository writing program: making connections between reading & writing. *The Reading Teacher, 41,* 790–795.

Stauffer, R. (1979). *Directing reading maturity as a cognitive process*. New York: Harper & Row.

Taylor, B.M. (1982). Test structures and children's comprehension and memory for expository material. *Journal of Educational Psychology, 74,* 323–340.

Taylor, T. (1969). *The cay*. Garden City, NY: Doubleday.

Voight, C. (1983). *Dicey's song*. New York: Antheneum.

Zindel, P. (1969). *The pigman*. New York: Harper & Row.

# Introduction to
# Chapter 3

*John A. Dossey is Distinguished University
Professor of Mathematics, Illinois State
University, and Past President of the National
Council of Teachers of Mathematics*

The 1980s will long be remembered as a period of foment in American public education. There were fervent calls for reform and many simplistic solutions proposed. Quietly hidden beneath this politically charged, publicity driven arena of outcry, mathematics education was coming of age in a systematic fashion. The programs of research in mathematics education focusing on learning, curriculum, and teaching variables which had their roots in the mid-1960s were beginning to bear fruit.

These products, combined with the united backing of all of the members of the mathematical sciences community, led to the proposing of new standards for school mathematics at the close of the 1980s. These recommendations for what students should know *and* be able to use have focused major renovations in the structure of mathematics education from primary grade activities through graduate and inservice education programs for faculty development.

In the following chapter, Thomas Romberg carefully outlines the major shifts underlying the reform effort in mathematics education. He does so by first considering the nature of the recommended changes in the learning environment. The related instructional changes, if effected in practice, bring concomitant changes in the use of technology, modes of evaluation, and organization of the classroom and school. Romberg's analysis in the subsequent chapter of the changes in goals, conceptions of knowledge, characterizations of the actions of both teachers and students, and use of a wide range of technological support places the reforms suggested by the National Council of Teachers of Mathematics' *Curriculum and Evaluation Standards for School Mathematics* (1989), in perspective.

The research base for the *Standards* is strong. It includes work in mathematics education, but it also includes work in educational psychology, sociology, and a number of other fields. Romberg shows the integration of this work in the following chapter. It is this integration of work from various areas that is enhancing our knowledge of children's conception of mathematics and the activities that promote their continued mathematical growth. This integration is also necessary if we are to view schools as places where students confront interesting problems in cooperative learning settings and work, both individually and as social groups, to apply problem-solving strategies and technology to resolve the issues at hand.

This broader view of mathematics education is reflected in the goals set for school mathematics by the *Standards*. They call for the following outcomes for all students:

1. Learning to value mathematics.
2. Becoming confident in one's own ability.
3. Becoming a mathematical problem solver.
4. Learning to communicate mathematically.
5. Learning to reason mathematically.

It is the combination of these affective and cognitive goals, and the processes and content knowledge supporting them, that will mark mathematical literacy in the coming decade. Success in attaining these goals will be marked by a change in schools to perceiving mathematics as a "doing" activity, rather than a "remembering" activity. Progress will also be marked by growth in the use of technology to explore and address problems posed by the curriculum. Both of these marks of advancement must also be accompanied by expanding access to the study of advanced mathematics to all students regardless of gender or racial/ethnic background.

Romberg provides a strong base for understanding the matrix of ideas that undergird the advances made in mathematics education in the past decade. It remains for all involved in mathematics education and schooling to work with these ideas in shaping strong curricula, continuing the development of supportive patterns of schooling, and nurturing the continued development of a precious natural resource—our children's mathematical development. To do so will call for a cooperative effort to confront the issues of conceptions of mathematics, methods of teaching, structure of schooling, methods of assessment, and structure of curriculum in a unified way, adjusting all of the factors which impact the system in such fashion that they move together to provide a strong infrastructure for learning, teaching, and thinking about mathematics.

# 3 Mathematics Learning and Teaching: What We Have Learned in Ten Years

Thomas A. Romberg
*University of Wisconsin—Madison*

Ten years is a very brief period of time in the history of American education. However, for mathematical sciences education, the decade of the 1980s has been a period of controversy, reflection, and productive research that has culminated in calls for radical reform in the content and methods of instruction in mathematics classrooms. I have chosen to focus on this decade because it began with the publication of *An Agenda for Action* (National Council of Teachers of Mathematics, 1980), which was the initial call for reform, and ended with the publication of *Curriculum and Evaluation Standards for School Mathematics* (National Council of Teachers of Mathematics, 1989), which presents a vision of mathematics learning and teaching for the next century. The purpose of this chapter is to highlight what has been learned that has led to the reform effort during the past hectic decade. Furthermore, I argue that the implications of what we have learned, if followed, would change the public's view of mathematics, as well as the way mathematics is taught and learned in school. To organize my argument, I have chosen to contrast classroom instruction in mathematics as traditionally practiced with the vision of authentic classroom instruction that is now being advocated. With that contrast as a point of departure, I examine the changes in epistemological thinking and cognitive research that underlie the calls for reform. The chapter concludes with a summary of the implications of these changes and a series of questions that need to be addressed.

## Traditional Classroom Instruction

Wayne Welch, in a set of case studies funded by the National Science Foundation in the 1970s, found:

> In all math classes I visited, the sequence of activities was the same. First, answers were given for the previous day's assignment. The more difficult problems were worked by the teacher or a student at the chalkboard. A brief explanation, some-

43

times none at all, was given of the new materials, and problems were assigned for the next day. The remainder of the class was devoted to working on the homework while the teacher moved about the room answering questions. The most noticeable thing about math classes was the repetition of this routine. (Welch, 1978, p. 6)

Furthermore, the picture drawn from a survey of elementary school mathematics instruction practices found:

The "median" classroom is self-contained. The mathematics period is about 43 minutes long, and about half of this time is written work. A single text is used in whole-class instruction. The text is followed fairly closely, but students are likely to read, at most, one or two pages out of five pages of textual materials other than problems. It seems likely that the text, at least as far as the students are concerned, is primarily a source of problem lists. Teachers are essentially teaching the same way they were taught in school. (Conference Board of the Mathematical Sciences, 1975, p. 77)

Herbert Kliebard (1972) argues that this instructional pattern is based on an industrial production metaphor in which students are seen as "raw material" to be transformed by "skilled technicians."

In traditional classrooms, the work of the teacher is to "transmit" knowledge and the job of the student is to receive it, regurgitating on demand. In fact, the real work of the student is often a passive routine, meeting expectations sufficiently to pass through the system (Skemp, 1979). Clarke (1984) quoted a student's description of a mathematics classroom as follows:

She tells us what we're gonna do. And she'll probably write up a few examples and notes on the board. Then we'll either get sheets handed out or she'll write up questions on the board. Not very often. We mainly get a textbook. We'll get pages. She'll write up what work to do, page number and exercise. And that's about what happens. (p. 22)

The traditional situation described is organized, routine, controlled, and predictable—an unlikely environment for creative thinking and knowledge formation.

## In Contrast: Authentic Classroom Instruction

Consider a mathematics classroom where instruction is focused on a problem situation. In the class, a group of six 5th-grade students views a videotape of the 100-meter dash from the 1984 Olympics. Their task is to count the number of steps, estimate the length of each step (noting the variability), and estimate the time for each step for the winner, Carl Lewis. Then they compare number, average length of steps, and average time per step of Lewis' performance with similar data for the second- and third-place finishers. Another group of students watches a video of Olympic diving competition and discusses details of how the scoring is carried out. They then devise a scoring routine (judgment procedures and rules) and compare their results with the official scores. Other groups are similarly engaged. All of the activities are related to measurement and grow out of scaling Olympic sporting events. The work on these activities continues for several days with numerous opportunities for the groups to report and discuss findings. Also, the teacher occasionally raises questions (such as how the scaling of diving and gymnastics activities are similar and different), points out distinctions (e.g., nominal, ordinal, interval, and ratio scales), and judges the strategies individual students use and the kinds of arguments they give to justify their conclusions.

This description is no pipe dream for I saw these activities being used in a classroom in Melbourne, Australia, in 1986 as a part of the MCTP project (see Lovitt and Clarke, 1988, pp. 31–74 for a description of this set of activities). Nor is this a description of a completely foreign or isolated instructional activity. Similar descriptions of instruction involving students working on complex problem situations are described in several other recent reports: for example, *Thinking Through Mathematics* (Silver, Kilpatrick, & Schlesinger, 1990), *Knowing, Doing, and Teaching Multiplication* (Lampert, 1986), and *Learning and Testing Mathematics in Context—The Case: Data Visualization* (de Lange, van Reeuwijk, Burrill, & Romberg, in preparation).

## The Contrast

The two descriptions of mathematics instruction obviously differ in many ways. I have chosen to contrast them on the basis of four characteristics of instruction adapted from the sociological notions of Popkewitz, Tabachnick, and Wehlage (1982). These notions are:

1. Schools are *goal* directed. Schools for all children are historically recent and were created to transmit aspects of the culture to the young and to direct students toward and provide them with an opportunity for self-fulfillment.

2. Schools are places where conceptions of *knowledge* are distributed and maintained. One important decision that must be made by those who organize schools is selecting what to teach. This decision must grow out of a consensus as to what it is important for the young to know.

3. School is a place of *work* where students, teachers, and administrators act to alter and improve their world, produce positive social relations, and realize specific human purposes. For example, it is assumed that knowledge will be acquired by the young via some deliberately created activities organized and managed by the teacher.

4. The work in schools is carried out using an established *technology*.

*Goals.*    In traditional programs, mathematics is viewed as a fixed body of knowledge, elements of which should be understood by all. It has been assumed that some set of mathematical concepts and skills should be acquired by all students (minimal competencies). For example, the subset of mathematics that is the backbone of most elementary programs emphasizes almost exclusively arithmetic procedural skills. Generally, algebra serves a similar function in the secondary curriculum. This emphasis leaves little time for other important aspects of thinking and mathematics (e.g., measurement, statistics), relationships between concepts, using mathematics to solve realistic problems, proving assertions, and so on. In traditional programs, mathematics instruction is directed by goals that prescribe the amount of procedural knowledge to be taught under competitive conditions and time pressures.

By contrast, the Olympic measurement activities reflect a different set of goals. As articulated in the NCTM *Standards* (1989), the goals for students are

> (1) that they learn to value mathematics, (2) that they become confident in their ability to do mathematics, (3) that they become mathematical problem solvers, (4) that they communicate mathematically, and (5) that they learn to reason mathematically.
>
> These goals imply that students should be exposed to numerous and varied interrelated experiences that encourage them to value the mathematical enterprise, to develop mathematical habits of mind, and to understand and appreciate the role of mathematics in human affairs; that they are encouraged to explore, to guess, and even to make errors so that they gain confidence in their ability to solve complex problems; that they read, write, and discuss mathematics; and that they conjecture, test, and build arguments about a conjecture's validity. The opportunity for all students to experience these components of mathematical training is at the heart of our vision of a quality mathematics program. The curriculum should be permeated with these goals and experiences such that they become commonplace in the lives of students. (p. 5)

*Knowledge.*    The content of school mathematics is, of necessity, restricted. This leads to the controversy between mathematics as a science and as a school subject (Damerow & Westbury, 1985). Scientific management has resulted in hierarchical classification and taxonomies of mathematical knowledge. To develop a curriculum, one needs to segment and sequence the mathematical ideas for instruction. However, scope and sequence charts specifying procedural objectives to be mastered by students at each grade level are not appropriate. In fact, the use of behavioral objectives and learning hierarchies has separated mathematics into literally thousands of segments, each taught independently of the others. Furthermore, the student's task is to get correct answers to well-defined problems or exercises.

A major difficulty with this approach is that, while an individual objective might be reasonable, it is not seen as part of a larger network. It is the network, the connections between objectives and their processing, that is important. Fragmentation, and a corresponding emphasis on low-level thinking, is reinforced by the testing procedures often associated with curricula based on behavioral objectives. Multiple-choice questions on concepts and skills emphasize the independence rather than the interdependence of ideas and reward right answers rather than the use of reasonable thinking processes and procedures.

Stress on isolated segments essentially trains students in a series of routines, without educating them to grasp an overall picture that will ensure the use of appropriate ideas for given purposes. Mathematics as a discipline has not only internal structure, but integral and reciprocal relationships with other disciplines, especially science, and increasingly with the social sciences and humanities. The complexities of these relationships are challenging the traditional hierarchical taxonomies of content.

In the Olympic measurement activities, students see and experience the role of mathematics as a language and a science that order the universe and as a tool for representing situations, defining relationships, solving problems, and thinking. They have an opportunity to experience its language and notational system in the solution of problems in a wide variety of domains. The connectedness of ideas is critical. If students can experience mathematical lessons in this manner, they will see mathematics as a process: of abstracting quantitative relations and spatial forms from the real world of practical problems, of inventing through the process of conjecture, and of demonstrating the validity of propositions.

When mathematical knowledge, in this sense, means knowing and doing mathematics rather than knowing about mathematics, other things follow. This knowledge is both personal and communal in the sense that, while it may originate with the individual, it is validated by the community. Thus, the process of adding to mathematical knowledge through communicating is an integral part of knowing mathematics.

*The work of students and teachers.*    The work roles of students and teachers are complementary; some teach, the others learn. However, since the goals of schools are directed toward student learning, the role of the teacher should complement that of the student, rather than vice versa. Unfortunately, when knowledge is regarded as "knowing about" rather than "knowing," the vocabulary reflects a reversal of emphasis.

The Olympic measurement activities, on the other hand, demonstrate that learning need not occur only via passive reflection. Instead, research indicates that individuals approach new tasks with prior knowledge, that they assimilate new information, and construct their own meanings. Ideas are not isolated in memory, but are organized in collections of what Anderson (1983) has called "loosely structured schemas." Such schemas are associated with the natural language one uses and the situations that one has encountered in the past. This constructive notion of learning and thinking is reflected in the measurement activities.

Moreover, activities which focus on exploring complex problem situations require that students be active and constantly extend the structure of the mathematics that they know by making, testing, and validating conjectures. As long as students are making conjectures, their mathematical knowledge will always be structured, consciously or unconsciously, because conjecture cannot be created from nothing. Clearly, the work of students in such an environment is no longer a matter of acting within somebody else's structures, answering somebody else's questions, and waiting for the teacher to check the response. In the creation of knowledge, there is only that which fits the structure of mathematical knowledge already created by the student and that which does not and should, therefore, prompt conjecture.

In the traditional classroom, the primary work of teachers is to maintain order and control (Romberg & Carpenter, 1985). There is an inexorably logical sequence when the acknowledged work of teachers is to transmit the record of knowledge. The most cost-effective way to transmit the record of knowledge is through exposition to a captive audience. Consequently, that exposition cannot happen unless there is control, which is easier if children talk as little as possible and stay in one place. This simple sequence has dictated classroom practice, furniture arrangement, and architecture for the last hundred years and is the tradition that is challenged by any attempt at change. In addition, during the past quarter-century, there has been a tendency to over-specify instructions for teachers so that they can readily adopt and use new programs. Often, there are no decisions to make about what activities to use. Taken to an extreme, the teacher becomes only a conduit in a system, covering the pages of a program without thinking or consideration. Teachers are not encouraged to relate the ideas of one lesson to another. Their task is to get students to complete pages or do sets of exercises with little effort to establish relationships between ideas.

Again, by contrast, the work of teachers in the Olympic activity is quite different. Their job is to support, promote, encourage, and, in every way, facilitate the creation of knowledge and thinking by students. Their management responsibility is the creation of a collaborative learning environment in which students can explore and investigate problems. Thus, they guide, listen, discuss, prompt, question, and clarify the work of students. To do this, they must orchestrate appropriate and interesting activities as they attend to each student's needs.

*Technology.*    The technology of traditional instruction includes a basal text, which is a repository of problem lists, a mass of paper-and-pencil worksheets, and a set of performance tests. Although a few of the books include reading material, very little of it is interesting to read. Thus, workbook mathematics gives students little reason to connect ideas of "today's" lesson with those of past lessons or with the real world. The tests currently used ask for answers that are judged right or wrong, but the strategies and reasoning used to derive answers are not evaluated.

In schools of the 21st Century, rather than providing paper-and-pencil activities for students to do independently at their desks, activities will provide group problem solving at work stations. The technology will include video recordings, calculators, and computers as student tools. Evaluation will consist of the judgments of students and teachers as to the coherence of student presentations, the reasoning given, and so on.

In summary, this contrast between the stereotype of "what is" and "what could be" in terms of mathematics instruction in school classrooms should make the differences clear and the potential of a reform approach to mathematics instruction obvious. However, to have schools and teachers follow such procedures involves considerable change from current practice. Simple alterations in existing programs will not suffice.

## MATHEMATICS IN THE FUTURE

What mathematics do we want students to know? The rethinking that is taking place is a consequence of the upheavals in industry and the economy that have spurred public awareness that we are moving into a new industrial age, variously called "the information age" (Bell, 1973; Naisbitt, 1982; Toffler, 1985), "the post-industrial age" (Bell, 1973), or "the super-industrial age" (Toffler, 1985). This, in combination with the geometric growth of knowledge, particularly in the mathematical sciences, is the force behind this rethinking. The impact of these changes promises to be as dramatic as the shift from an agrarian society in the 1800s to an industrial society in the 20th Century. Economically, the consequences of the revolution are only now being realized as market rivalries evolve from within-country competition to between-country competition. Jennings (1987) has recently argued that this economic competitiveness represents "the Sputnik of the 80s" in educational reform.

The works of several authors (Naisbitt, 1982; Provenzo, 1986; Shane & Tabler, 1981; Toffler, 1985; Yevennes, 1985) suggest the attributes of the new age. Naisbitt's (1982) key points characterize the shift to an information society:

1. It is an economic reality, not merely an intellectual abstraction.

2. The pace of change will be accelerated by continued innovation in communications and computer technology.

3. New technologies, which will be applied first to traditional industrial tasks, will soon generate new processes and products.

4. Basic communication skills will become more important than ever before, necessitating a literacy-intensive society.

5. Concurrent with the move from an industrial society to a society based on information is awareness of the change from a national economy to a global economy.

Information has value only if it can be controlled and organized for a purpose. To tap the power of computers, it is obligatory first to communicate efficiently and effectively, to be both literate and numerate. In addition, in an environment of accelerating change, the approach of training for a lifetime occupation must be replaced by learning power, which also depends on the abilities to understand and to communicate. This change is accompanied by the perception that the United States and other advanced societies of the West are losing their industrial supremacy. Mass production is more cheaply accomplished in the less developed parts of the world. Toffler (1985) envisioned the change as a series of waves, in much the same framework as Frederick Jackson Turner characterized the westward movement of the frontier in North America. Thus, just as industrial society replaced agrarian society and then began to push out, so the new postindustrial age will replace industrial society in the West and gradually expand.

The Mathematical Sciences Education Board (1990a) has summarized the impact of these changing conditions for school mathematics as follows:

First, as the economy adapts to information-age needs, workers in every sector—from hotel clerks to secretaries, from automobile mechanics to travel agents—must learn to interpret intelligent computer-controlled processes. [As James Duffy (Chapter 12 in this book) and Jones, Tinzman, and Pierce (Chapter 10) confirm, most jobs now require analytical rather than merely mechanical skills]. . . . so most students need more mathematics in school as preparation for routine jobs. Similarly, the extensive use of graphical, financial, and statistical data in daily newspapers and in public policy discussions suggests a higher standard of quantitative literacy and thinking for the necessary duties of citizenship. [See Gross's discussion of this point on pp. 135–143.]

Second, in the past quarter of a century, . . . not only has much new mathematics been discovered, but the types and variety of problems to which mathematics is applied have grown at an unprecedented rate. Most visible, of course, has been the development of computers and the explosive growth of computer applications. Most of these applications of computers have required the development of new mathematics in areas where the applications of mathematics were infeasible before the advent of computers (Howson & Kahane, 1986). . . .

Third, computers and calculators have profoundly changed the world of mathematics. They have affected not only what aspects of mathematics are important, but also how mathematics is done (Rheinboldt, 1985). It is now possible to execute almost all of the mathematical techniques taught from kindergarten through the first two years of college on hand-held calculators. This fact alone . . . must have significant effects on the mathematics curriculum (Pea, 1987). Although most developments at the forefront of a discipline cannot generally be expected to have a major effect on the early years of education, the changes in mathematics brought about by computers and calculators are so profound as to require readjustment in the balance and approach to virtually every topic in school mathematics.

Fourth, as mathematics has changed, so has American society. The changing demographics of the country and the changing demands of the workplace [are not reflected in similar changes in school mathematics (MSEB, 1989).]. . . . In the early years of the next century, when today's school children will enter the workforce, most jobs will require greater mathematical skills than are required at present (Johnston & Packer, 1987). At the same time, white males—the traditional base of mathematically trained workers in the United States—will represent a significantly smaller fraction of new workers (Oaxaca & Reynolds, 1988). Society's need for an approach to mathematics education that ensures achievement across the demographic spectrum is both compelling and urgent (Office of Technology Assessment, 1988, pp. 1–3).

These points make the argument that a complete redesign of the content of school mathematics and the way it is taught are urgent. Unfortunately, schools and the mathematics taught in their classrooms are products of the past industrial age. What is being argued is that we need an authentic curriculum that will provide students an opportunity to learn the practical mathematical concepts and skills needed for everyday life, for intelligent citizenship, for vocations, and for human culture in an age centered on information rather than on industrialization.

## HOW DO WE BEGIN THE CHANGE?

First, many nonmathematicians such as sociologists, psychologists, school administrators, and even curriculum generalists see mathematics as a static, bounded discipline (Barbeau, 1989). "To most non-mathematicians, it is a cold and austere discipline which provides no scope for judgment or creativity" (p. 2). That these views are limiting is a serious problem since persons with such views often influence the decisions about school mathematics. Fortunately, during this decade, a large number of books about mathematics have been published for a non-technically-educated audience [for example, *The Mathematical Experience* (Davis & Hersh, 1981), *Descartes' Dream* (Davis & Hersh, 1986), *Mathematics and the Unexpected* (Ekeland, 1988), *Speaking Mathematically* (Pimm, 1987), *Innumeracy* (Paulos, 1988), *Capitalism and Arithmetic: The New Math of the 15th Century* (Swetz, 1987)].

In addition, there have been several books about mathematics written for policy makers, general educators, and administrators in response to the current calls for reform in mathematics teaching and learning. These books include: *Mathematics Counts* (Committee on Inquiry into the Teaching of Mathematics in Schools, 1982), *Renewing US Mathematics: Critical Resource for the Future* (Commission on Physical Sciences, Mathematics, and Resources, 1984), *Perspectives on Mathematics Education* (Christiansen, Howson, & Otte, 1986), *Mathematics, Insight, and Meaning* (de Lange, 1987), *Cognitive Science and Mathematics Education* (Schoenfeld, 1987), *Mathematics Tomorrow* (Steen, 1981), *Everybody Counts* (MSEB, 1989), *Curriculum and Evaluation Standards for School Mathematics* (NCTM, 1989), *Reshaping School Mathematics* (MSEB, 1990a), and *On the Shoulder of Giants* (MSEB, 1990b).

Second, a new view about mathematics must be developed, one that is more than just the difference between "knowing what" and "knowing how." If "knowing what" is stressed, then the student is treated as a "piece of registering apparatus, which stores up information isolated from action and purpose" (Dewey, 1916, p. 147). And, if "knowing how" is emphasized, then the student is seen as an active constructor of knowledge "operating in important ways on his environment" (Bourne, 1966, p. 36). These different psychological views about how one learns are important and are addressed more fully later in this chapter. However, it must be noted that instruction in current classrooms emphasizes "knowing what," and the reform proposals emphasize "knowing how."

Third, mathematics, like all disciplines, must begin to be understood as the social product it is. Mathematical objects have both been created in response to social problems and have contributed to the development of contemporary society. In fact, "next to the invention of language itself, . . . mathematics is without doubt the most subtle, powerful, and significant achievement of the human mind" (Schaaf, 1966, p. iii). The primary objective of all mathematical work, then, must be to help humans make sense of the world around them. Today it is impossible to determine the overall impact of mathematics on contemporary culture because quantification and mathematical modeling permeate almost all aspects of society, and their influence is growing.

For example, to illustrate this interdependence, Frank Swetz (1987) traced the development of capitalism in Western society to the adoption of Hindu-Arabic arithmetic by the merchants of Venice in the 15th Century. Out of the interaction of this set of mathematical symbols and the rules for their use in confronting the growing problems faced by commercial entrepreneurs, modern mercantile capitalism evolved.

However, the adoption of Arabic arithmetic was gained at a cost. Ray Nickerson (1988) provided an illustration of this fact when he compared several ancient systems of representing numbers with the Arabic system now in common use throughout the world. He suggests that "the Arabic system is a superior vehicle for computing . . . bought at the cost of greater abstractness. Numbers in the Arabic system bear a less obvious relationship to the quantities they represent than do numbers in many earlier systems" (p. 181). Hence, for many, the computational algorithms we now use are mysterious routines only to be memorized.

Fourth, as Ubriatan D'Ambrosio (1985), Jean Lave and her colleagues (Lave, Smith, & Butler, 1988), Analucia Schliemann and Nadja Acioly (1989), and many others point out, schools must begin to present different cultural uses of mathematical thinking. Presently, schools emphasize the formal mathematics of collegiate mathematicians, but not the mathematics developed and used by farmers, carpenters, tailors, and others. Each of these social groups has, of necessity, developed its own mathematical language and thinking procedures independent of and separate from its formal education. This separation in application keeps students from developing mathematical habits of mind.

Finally, the conflicts between the culture of school mathematics and the culture of mathematics must be resolved. Jahnke (1986) argues that while most teachers believe that "school mathematics and scientific mathematics are essentially identical, and that they differ merely with regard to the level and degree of difficulty" (p. 85), this is a naive and false belief. He goes on to argue that schools have a social responsibility to educate that is expressed in terms of societal goals described "in terms of methodological attitudes and philosophical beliefs" (p. 85). A merely scientific view of mathematics is inadequate. The consequence is that school mathematics bears little resemblance to what mathematicians do or how mathematics is used.

## MATHEMATICAL THINKING: A LOOK INTO THE NEXT CENTURY

Throughout this book, we have argued that students, at all levels and in all subjects, need to learn by active participation. However, as Collins (Chapter 4 in this volume) and Jones, Tinzmann, and Pierce (Chapter 10) also affirm, simply developing a collection of interesting activities is not sufficient. The knowledge gained must lead somewhere. Thus, what is constructed by any individual depends to some extent on what is brought to the situation, where the current *activity* fits in a sequence leading toward a goal, and how it relates, in this case, to mathematical knowledge. Thus, the suitability and effectiveness of selected learning activities is an empirical problem. It depends on both the student's prior knowledge and the student's expectations.

This view of learning is an outgrowth of the revolution in psychology that has become dominant during the past decade.[1] Research on human information processing leads to the following eight notions of how the mind works. Every mathematics lesson, now and in the future, should work with or actively use these eight components.

1. The key components of the mind and how they are assumed to be related are summarized in Fig. 3.1. Thinking processes begin with an experience. Information from the experience is filtered by an executive control mechanism which involves deciding what to do with the information and the beliefs and attitudes held with respect to that information. Next, mediated information is organized and stored in memory. This critical aspect of cognitive theory distinguishes

---

[1]See Phillips and Soltis (1985) for a brief introduction to cognitive psychology, Gardner (1985) for a history of the revolution, Calfee (1981) or Greeno (1987) for the implications of the revolution for education, and Romberg and Tufte (1987) for its implications for the learning of mathematics.

between three types of memory: Working memory (the limited amount of information or chunked, related knowledge that one processes at a particular point in time), short-term memory (knowledge used in a relatively short period of time), and long-term memory (information storage).

2. While humans are capable of remembering a great deal, they have an extremely limited capacity to think about many different things at any one time. As a consequence, information stored in long-term memory must be well organized. The mind naturally organizes repeated similar experiences in long-term memory into what psychologists call *schema*. These are complex networks of concepts, rules, and strategies, not isolated facts or algorithms. For example, one typically organizes the experiences of eating in restaurants into a *restaurant schema*. The general features of past experiences are organized into a network of related facts (e.g., waiters, tablecloths, menus) and relationships (e.g., sequence of ordering, serving, paying). Having information stored in this way helps an individual cope with new experiences. For example, when one is in a new city and sees a sign for a restaurant, one *knows* what to expect based on past experiences. Such *schema* develop over long periods of time and by continual exposure to related contextual events.

3. New experiences either use one's existing *schema* (called assimilation), or force a change in particular *schema* (called accommodation). For example, if one had never been to a Chinese restaurant, such an experience (e.g., shared dishes, chopsticks, and so forth) would force one to add new features about restaurants to one's schema.

4. Naturally occurring *schema* are idiosyncratic to the individual, who is usually unaware of the organization. For example, each individual's restaurant *schema* differs from others because of different restaurant experiences, but one

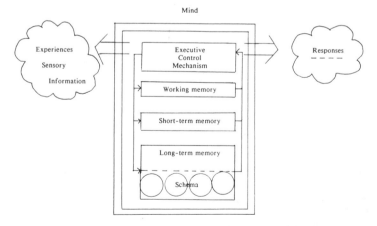

FIG. 3.1.   Key components of the mental processing of information.

rarely thinks about the consequences of persons having different *schema* related to the same general phenomena.

5. While most learning occurs through the natural assimilation and accommodation of experiences, it can also occur via pre-organized and structured experiences. Much of what is presented in school should have this character. For example, learning the common names and features for geometric figures on the basis of natural experience is unlikely (e.g., isosceles, parallel, perpendicular). Learning the formal language, signs, and symbols, properties, and principles associated with any mathematical domain is no easy matter. Instructional activities should serve as the means of connecting one's informal, natural experiences with the formal aspects of mathematics. The assumption is that students will reorganize their informal quantitative and spatial *schema* as a consequence of interacting in such activities.

6. Coherent instructional activities which are designed to promote conceptual reorganization in an individual's *schema* should have a three-part sequence. First, there should be an *exposing event* which encourages students to use and explore their own conceptions in an effort to understand the event. This is followed by a *discrepant event* which serves as an anomaly and produces cognitive conflict. It is hoped that this will lead the students to a state of dissatisfaction with their current conceptions. A period of *resolution* follows in which the alternative conceptions are made plausible and intelligible to students, and in which the students are encouraged to make the desired conceptual shift (Nussbaum & Novick, 1982). This sequence should be seen as a negotiation process between students and instructors. The objective is for students to develop well-organized *schema* which reflect current notions about mathematics. It is also argued that the encoding, comprehension, and retrieval of new information are aided when material is presented in a form that has structure and when the student is cognizant of that structure. In particular, these processes are facilitated when the information can be related to existing schema of the learner. Thus, when information is presented in a familiar contextual setting, the transitions, concepts, and procedures are likely to be remembered. Some psychologists call this a generic story shell for the *schema*.

7. *Schema* are never fixed. They continually change over time as the individual grows and has additional experiences. In fact, there is general agreement that the evolution of one's thinking goes through several cyclic stages. Several developmental psychologists have proposed similar theories which trace children's development from early psycho-motor reactions to logical thinking (e.g., Biggs & Collis, 1982; Case, 1985; Fischer, 1980). The common ideas in these theories enable us to use their insights as a sound basis for identifying key elements in understanding and competence during the school years.

(a) Two phenomena are involved in determining the level of an individual's response to an experience, the *mode* of functioning, which is determined by the level of abstraction of the elements utilized, and the complexity of the *structure* of the response within that mode.

(b) There are at least four modes of functioning. The elements involved in the "sensori-motor mode" are the objects in the immediate physical environment and the operations on them are concerned with their management and coordination. In the "iconic mode," the elements become signifiers (words, images) which stand for objects and events; the operations involve the manipulation of these signifiers to establish oral communication, to make links between affect and image, and to make perceptually based qualitative judgments. In the "concrete-symbolic mode," the elements are not just signifiers, but concepts that are manipulated using a logic of classes and equivalences, both elements and manipulations being directly tied to the empirical world. This mode enables the concrete world to be interpreted through symbolic systems such as written language and the signs and symbols of mathematics. Finally, in the "formal mode" the elements become abstract concepts and propositions and the operations on them are concerned with determining the actual and deduced relationships between them; neither the elements nor the operations need a real world referent.

(c) The modes progress from concrete actions to abstract concepts and principles, and the emergence of one mode does not supplant its predecessor. The modes, in fact, accrue the later developing modes existing alongside the earlier modes. The implications of this last statement are that as an individual matures physiologically, the modes developed earlier continue to develop as a consequence of both physical development and experiences and, as the modal repertoire available increases, multimodal functioning becomes the norm.

For school age children, it is important to note that they do not, as yet, think like adults. They are more likely to respond in an iconic or concrete-symbolic mode to new information. Only in later grades do they begin to build formal relationships between disparate experiences, and, as yet, they do not think in terms of composite, abstract concepts.

8.  Students who have formed initial and not well-organized *schema* actively search for experiences that will provide them structure. However, people resist change in well-developed *schema* because such *schema* have great assimilative power. What is supposed to be a new view may be assimilated by the old. It is difficult for teachers to distinguish between assimilation and accommodation. People whose important beliefs are threatened will attempt to defend their positions, dismiss objections, ignore counterexamples, keep logically incompatible *schema* segregated, and so forth.

In summary, cognitive psychologists have provided the concept of "well-organized *schema*" to explain how people impose an order on and think about experiential information. Assimilation, accommodation, and mode of functioning in response to new information are important in our enterprise of schooling. Without some *schema* into which new information can be assimilated, experience is incomprehensible, and, therefore, little can be learned from it. However, the *schema* by which a student assimilates a lesson may not be assumed by teachers or mathematicians. This fact can easily escape detection since the student will often be able to repeat segments of the text and lecture even though she or he understands them in terms on an incorrect, incomplete, or inconsistent framework. Indeed, students may develop specialized frameworks for maintaining the particular identity of lesson material in order to cope with the demand for veridical reproduction. *Schema* use must be a dynamic, constructive process, for it is not the case that people have stored a *schema* to fit every conceivable situation. In this view, acquisition of knowledge implies *schema* change, not just the mere aggregation of information.

Furthermore, since children have had sufficient experiences to have formed some frameworks to make sense of certain mathematical situations, instruction should start by nurturing those frameworks. Then, teachers need to create instructional activities that give students new experiences. For example, most American 1st-grade mathematics textbooks only include join (result unknown [a + b = [ ]) and separate (result unknown [a − b = [ ]) problems.[2] This provides children a limited perspective on addition and subtraction which restricts their ability to apply their arithmetic skills to the solution of problems. Furthermore, it encourages them to use superficial problem-solving strategies such as looking for key words to decide "is this a plus or is this a take away?" Teachers must provide children with a variety of different problem types within each of the four basic classes and negotiate meanings with each child from those experiences so that well-organized *schema* are developed. Also, note that symbols should be introduced to represent concepts that children already know. One should never start with the symbols +, −, or = and then attempt to give them meaning. Unfortunately, in most classrooms, as Ernst von Glasersfeld (1987) points out: "Rarely, if ever, is there a hint, let alone an indication, of what one must do in order to build up the conceptual structures that are to be associated with the symbols" (pp. 13–14).

If our future instructional experiences do not build on existing *schema,* new *schema* are developed that are seen by children as being unrelated to their prior experiences. For example, Romberg and Collis (1987) found that 3rd-grade children who were capable of performing addition and subtraction calculations

---

[2]Stigler, Fuson, Ham, and Kim (1986) compared the number of addition and subtraction problem types in four prominent American textbooks with those included in a Soviet textbook. They found that the distribution of word problems across the problem types was extremely uneven in the American books, with two thirds of all problems being of only three simple one-step types. The Soviet text included a more even distribution of problems, and many more complex two-step problems.

with two- and three-digit numbers failed to see any connection between their calculation skills and solving word problems in an interview situation. They solved word problems with large numbers using known facts and counting skills. When asked if they could have calculated, most saw no reason for doing so, although their teachers were confident that all would calculate to find answers to the problems.

It is equally important to note that the development of well-organized *schema* can only be accomplished over a long period of time. This implies that teachers must regularly assess each child's knowledge and the processes used to solve different problems. For addition and subtraction, the strategies that children use initially correspond to the action or relationships described in the problem. Physical objects or fingers are used to directly model the action or relationships described in each problem (the iconic mode). Then direct modeling strategies are replaced by more abstract counting strategies, which are later replaced by the use of number facts (operating in the concrete-symbolic mode). Finally, as the numbers get larger, children write sentences and use algorithms. The problem of growth over time also can be explained developmentally. For example, suppose a required skill is based in the concrete-symbolic mode (e.g., two-digit subtraction). Many children may be working in the iconic mode. They might solve problems within their usual environment by using their highly developed iconic procedures, but they have not joined in the new concrete-symbolic "game" of arithmetic. On the other hand, while they be competent at this "game," they may be unable to extend beyond the concrete-symbolic mode to the formal mode where the abstractions of algebra become the beginning of a new "game." Researchers have also demonstrated that the strategies do not have to be taught explicitly, but can develop in a problem-solving environment. If children discuss the strategies they use and are able to validate their own thinking, they become confident in their work and may influence the thinking of other children. Providing children with the opportunity to discuss their strategies encourages the accommodation of new experiences.

Finally, current research focuses on the problem of choosing the right activities to evoke changes in students' strategies. The assumption is that problem situations can be designed to cause a student to make a transition to a new strategy. Even if such dynamically created problems cause a specific change in strategy, this is not sufficient. Children need to generalize the precondition in which the strategy is applicable so that it is used whenever appropriate and opportunities are not missed. Furthermore, each child must be appropriately challenged so that accommodation happens. To accomplish this, current work focuses on mechanisms, such as goal-posting (Singley, 1987), or problem-solving traces (Brown, 1985); or on helping students to reflect on and monitor their problem-solving strategies (Collins & Brown, 1988; Davis, 1985; Schoenfeld, 1985; Schwartz, 1989). In fact, teacher and student self-monitoring is critical, for both need to be held accountable for making needed changes. Nevertheless, choosing the right problems to evoke changes in the strategies students use and holding them accountable for those changes is a difficult task.

Although there is no doubt that many interesting activities exist or can be created, "Do they lead anywhere?" is a serious question. An activity approach could lead to "no mathematics at all." Christine Keitel (1987) has argued that the problem is one of relevance. Too often, a problem situation is judged to be relevant through the eyes of adults, not children. Also, that vision is undoubtedly a Western, middle-class, static one. The use of concrete situations by themselves provides no guarantee that students will see their relevance to their own worlds, nor that the situations will be relevant for *all* students, or prepare them to deal with a changing, dynamic world.

## CONCLUSIONS AND QUESTIONS

At the beginning of this chapter, a contrast was made between the way in which mathematics has been taught traditionally and an example, using Olympic measurement, of how mathematics can be taught. The Olympic example reflects what has been learned during the last decade. To summarize the argument for change, three questions are addressed.

### What Is Mathematics?

Too many people view the subject as a large collection of concepts and skills to be mastered. Not enough people see mathematics as a human activity or a cultural product. As Arthur Jaffe (1984) has pointed out:

> Mathematics is an ancient art, and from the outset, it has been both the most highly esoteric and the most intensely practical of human endeavors. As long ago as 1800 B.C., the Babylonians investigated the abstract properties of numbers, and in Athenian Greece, geometry attained the highest intellectual status. Alongside this theoretical understanding, mathematics blossomed as a day-to-day tool for surveying lands, for navigation, and for the engineering of public works. The practical problems and theoretical pursuits stimulated one another; it would be impossible to disentangle these two strands. (p. 117)

Also, mathematics is both a body of knowledge and something people do. Curricular reformers are now advocating a shift so that all students learn to value mathematics and to reason mathematically.

### What Mathematics Do We Want Students To Know in the 21st Century?

The authentic teaching of mathematics begins with the vision of school mathematics presented in NCTM's *Curriculum and Evaluation Standards for School Mathematics* (1989). This vision includes:

- mathematical power for all in a technological society;
- mathematics as something one does—solve problems, communicate, reason;
- a curriculum for all that includes a broad range of content, a variety of contexts, and deliberate connections;
- the learning of mathematics as an active, constructive process;
- instruction based on real problems;
- evaluation as a means of improving instruction, learning, and programs. (p. 255)

This Utopian vision assumes that the authentic teaching of mathematics has an inescapable social context that requires the redefinition of mass literacy from basic training to the universal empowerment of human potential. Thus, a radically different, but strongly supported, picture of mathematics teaching is envisioned. Succinctly, the vision requires teachers to create situations in which students can explore problems, generate questions, and reflect on patterns. It requires teachers with their academic and pedagogical knowledge to provide flexible approaches, encouraging informal and multiple representation while fostering the gradual growth of mathematical language and thinking.

### How Do Mathematics and Thinking Interrelate?

Knowledge about related concepts, skills, and contexts is organized in a student's memory in what psychologists call *schema*. These *schema* develop over long periods of time and by continual exposure to related contextual events. They appear to guide, organize, and direct both the search for a problem solution and the retrieval of expository details. For example, if students in Grade 1 have developed a "measurement *schema*" for measuring lengths with a variety of properties (units are arbitrary, common units are useful for communication, big units yield a small number and small units a big number, tools are useful, error is always involved), then it should be possible to create problem situations for new attributes (weight, area, volume, acceleration, value). The Olympic measurement activities assume that students are aware of the general properties of measurement and can use them in the activities of that unit.

In conclusion, the quality of instruction in the classrooms of this nation has always been a reflection of society at large. Change will only happen if society adopts a different perception of mathematics, of appropriate student activities based on how students learn, and of teacher roles. However, the changes being proposed by the mathematical sciences education community will not be easy to implement. There are many reasons to anticipate probable difficulties. The proposed changes will take time to implement, will demand considerable resources, and will require the concerted effort and commitment of a large number of persons during the coming decade.

## ACKNOWLEDGMENTS

The research reported in this paper was supported by the Office of Educational Research and Improvement of the US Department of Education and by the Wisconsin Center for Education Research, School of Education, University of Wisconsin-Madison. The opinions expressed in this publication are those of the author(s) and do not necessarily reflect the view of the OERI or the Wisconsin Center for Education Research.

## REFERENCES

Anderson, J.R. (1983). *The architecture of cognition*. Cambridge, MA: Harvard University Press.

Barbeau, E. J. (1989, September). *Mathematics for the public*. Paper presented at the meeting of the International Commission on Mathematical Instruction, Leeds University, England.

Bell, D. (1973). *The coming of post-industrial society: A venture in social forecasting*. New York: Basic Books.

Biggs, J. B., & Collis, K. F. (1982). *Evaluating the quality of learning: The SOLO taxonomy*. New York: Academic Press.

Bourne, L. E., Jr. (1966). *Human conceptual behavior*. Boston: Allyn and Bacon.

Brown, J. S. (1985). Process versus product: A perspective on tools for communal and informal electronic learning. *Journal of Educational Computing Research, 1*, 179–201.

Calfee, R. (1981). Cognitive psychology and educational practice. In D. C. Berliner (Ed.), *Review of research in education* (pp. 3–74). Washington, DC: American Educational Research Association.

Case, R. (1985). *Cognitive development*. New York: Academic Press.

Christiansen, B., Howson, A. G., & Otte, M. (1986). *Perspectives on mathematics education*. The Netherlands: D. Reidel Publishing Co.

Clarke, D. (1984). Secondary mathematics teaching: Towards a critical appraisal of current practice. *Vinculum, 21*(4), 1–22.

Collins, A., & Brown, J. S. (1988). The computer as a tool for learning through reflection. In H. Mandl & A. Lesgold (Eds.), *Learning issues for intelligent tutoring systems*. New York: Springer-Verlag.

Commission on Physical Sciences, Mathematics, and Resources. (1984). *Renewing United States mathematics: Critical resources for the future. Report of the Ad Hoc Committee on Resources for the Mathematical Sciences*. Washington, DC: National Academy Press.

Committee on Inquiry into the Teaching of Mathematics in Schools (CITMS). (1982). *Mathematics counts*. London: Her Majesty's Stationery Office.

Conference Board of the Mathematical Sciences. (1975). *Overview and analysis of school mathematics, grades K–12*. Washington, DC: Author.

D'Ambrosio, U. (1985). *Socio-cultural bases for mathematics education*. Boston: Birkhauser.

Damerow, P., & Westbury, I. (1985). Mathematics for all: Problems and implications. *Journal of Curriculum Studies, 17*(2), 175–186.

Davis, R. (1985). *Learning mathematics: The cognitive science approach to mathematics education*. Sydney, Australia: Croom Helm Ltd.

Davis, P. J., & Hersh, R. (1981). *The mathematical experience*. Boston: Birkhauser.

Davis, P. J., & Hersh, R. (1986). *Descartes' dream*. New York: Harcourt Brace Jovanovich.

de Lange, J. (1987). *Mathematics, insight, and meaning*. The Netherlands: University of Utrecht.

de Lange, J., Van Reeuwijk, M., Burrill, G., & Romberg, T. A. (in preparation). *Learning and testing mathematics in context—The case: Data visualization*. Madison: National Center for Research in Mathematical Sciences Education.

Dewey, J. (1916). *Democracy and education*. New York: Macmillan.

Ekeland, I. (1988). *Mathematics and the unexpected*. Chicago: University of Chicago Press.

Fischer, K. (1980). A theory of cognitive development: The control and construction of hierarchies of skills. *Psychological Review, 57,* 477–531.

Gardner, H. (1985). *The mind's new science: A history of the cognitive revolution*. New York: Basic Books.

Greeno, J. G. (1987). Mathematical cognition: Accomplishments and challenges in research. In T. A. Romberg & D. M. Stewart (Eds.), *The monitoring of school mathematics: Background papers. Vol. 2: Implications from psychology; outcomes of instruction* (pp. 3–26). Madison: Wisconsin Center for Education Research.

Howson, G., & Kahane, J. P. (1986). *The influence of computers and informatics on mathematics and its teaching*. Cambridge: Cambridge University Press.

Jaffe, A. (1984). Appendix C. Ordering the universe: The role of mathematics. In Commission on Physical Sciences, Mathematics, and Resources (Ed.), *Renewing US mathematics: Critical resources for the future. Report of the Ad Hoc Committee on Resources for the Mathematical Sciences* (pp. 117–162). Washington, DC: National Academy Press.

Jahnke, H. N. (1986). Origins of school mathematics in early nineteenth-century Germany. *Journal of Curriculum Studies, 18*(1), 85–94.

Jennings, J. F. (1987, October). The Sputnik of the eighties. *Phi Delta Kappan, 69*(2), 104–109.

Johnston, W. B., & Packer, A. E. (1987). *Workforce 2000: Work and workers for the Twenty-First Century*. Indianapolis: Hudson Institute.

Keitel, C. (1987). What are the goals of mathematics for all? *Journal of Curriculum Studies, 19*(5), 393–407.

Kliebard, H. M. (1972). Metaphorical roots of curriculum design. *Teachers College Record, 73,* 403–404.

Lampert, M. (1986). Knowing, doing, and teaching multiplication. *Cognition and Instruction, 3*(4), 305–341.

Lave, J., Smith, S., & Butler, M. (1988). Problem solving as an everyday practice. In R. Charles & E. Silver (Eds.), *The teaching and assessing of mathematical problem solving (Vol. 3,* pp. 61–81). Reston, VA: National Council of Teachers of Mathematics.

Lovitt, C., & Clarke, D. (1988). *The mathematics curriculum and teaching program. Professional development package. Activity bank (Vol. 1)*. Canberra, Australia: Curriculum Development Centre.

Mathematical Sciences Education Board (MSEB). (1989). *Everybody counts: A report to the nation on the future of mathematics education*. Washington, DC: National Academy Press.

Mathematical Sciences Education Board. (1990a). *Reshaping school mathematics*. Washington, DC: National Academy Press.

Mathematical Sciences Education Board. (1990b). *On the shoulders of giants*. Washington, DC: National Academy Press.

Naisbitt, J. (1982). *Megatrends: Ten new directions transforming our lives*. New York: Warner Books.

National Council of Teachers of Mathematics. (1980). *An agenda for action: Recommendations for school mathematics of the 1980s*. Reston, VA: Author.

National Council of Teachers of Mathematics. (1989). *Curriculum and evaluation standards for school mathematics*. Reston, VA: Author.

Nickerson, R. (1988). Counting, computing, and the representation of numbers. *Human Factors, 30*(2), 181–199.

Nussbaum, J., & Novick, S. (1982). Alternative frameworks, conceptual conflict, and accommodation: Toward a principled teaching strategy. *Instructional Science, 11*, 183–200.

Oaxaca, J., & Reynolds, A. W. (1988). *Changing America: The new face of science and engineering* (Interim Report). Washington, DC: Task Force on Women, Minorities, and the Handicapped in Science and Technology.

Paulos, J. A. (1988). *Innumeracy: Mathematical illiteracy and its consequences*. New York: Hill and Wang.

Pea, R. D. (1987). Cognitive technologies for mathematics education. In A. H. Schoenfeld (Ed.), *Cognitive science and mathematics education* (pp. 89–122). Hillsdale, NJ: Lawrence Erlbaum Associates.

Phillips, D. C., & Soltis, J.F. (1985). *Perspectives on learning*. New York: Teachers College Press.

Pimm, D. (1987). *Speaking mathematically: Communication in mathematics classrooms*. London: Routledge and Kegan Paul.

Popkewitz, T. S., Tabachnick, B. R., & Wehlage, G. G. (1982). *The myth of educational reform: A study of school responses to a program of change*. Madison: University of Wisconsin Press.

Provenzo, E. F. (1986). *Beyond the Gutenberg galaxy: Microcomputers and the emergence of post-typographic culture*. New York: Teachers College, Columbia University.

Rheinboldt, W. C. (1985). *Future directions in computational mathematics, algorithms, and scientific software*. Philadelphia, PA: Society for Industrial and Applied Mathematics.

Romberg, T. A., & Carpenter, T. P. (1985). Research on teaching and learning mathematics. In M. C. Wittrock (Ed.), *Handbook of research on teaching* (3rd ed., pp. 850–873). New York: Macmillan.

Romberg, T. A., & Collis, K. F. (1987). Different ways children learn to add and subtract. *Journal for Research in Mathematics Education: Learning to add and subtract (Monograph No. 2)*. Reston, VA: National Council of Teachers of Mathematics.

Romberg, T. A., & Tufte, F. W. (1987). Mathematics curriculum engineering. Some suggestions from cognitive science. In T. A. Romberg & D. M. Stewart (Eds.), *The monitoring of school mathematics: Background papers. Vol. 2: Implications from psychology; outcomes of instruction* (pp. 71–108). Madison: Wisconsin Center for Education Research.

Schaaf, W. L. (1966). *What is contemporary mathematics?* Stanford, CA: School Mathematics Study Group.

Schliemann, A. D., & Acioly, N. M. (1989). Mathematical knowledge developed at work: The contribution of practice versus the contribution of schooling. *Cognition and Instruction, 6*(3), 185–221.

Schoenfeld, A. H. (1985). *Mathematical problem solving*. New York: St. Martin's Press.

Schoenfeld, A. H. (1987). *Cognitive science and mathematics education*. Hillsdale, NJ: Lawrence Erlbaum Associates.

Schwartz, J. (1989). Intellectual mirrors: A step in the direction of making schools knowledge-making places. *Harvard Educational Review, 59*(1), 51–61.

Shane, H. I., & Tabler, M. B. (1981). *Educating for a new millennium: Views of 132 international scholars*. Bloomington, IN: Phi Delta Kappa Educational Foundation.

Silver, E. A., Kilpatrick, J., & Schlesinger, B. (1990). *Thinking through mathematics*. New York: College Entrance Examination Board.

Singley, K. (1987). *The effect of goal posting on operation selection*. Proceedings of the Third International Conference on Artificial Intelligence and Education, Pittsburgh.

Skemp, R. R. (1979). *Intelligence, learning, and action*. New York: John Wiley.

Steen, L. A. (1981). *Mathematics tomorrow*. New York: Springer-Verlag.

Stigler, J. W., Fuson, K. C., Ham, M., & Kim, M. S. (1986). *An analysis of addition and subtraction word problems in US and Soviet elementary mathematics textbooks* (Unpublished manuscript). Chicago: University of Chicago School Mathematics Project.

Swetz, F. J. (1987). *Capitalism and arithmetic: The new math of the 15th century.* LaSalle, IL: Open Court.

Toffler, A. (1985). *The adaptive corporation.* New York: McGraw-Hill.

von Glasersfeld, E. (1987). Learning as a constructive activity. In C. Janvier (Ed.), *Problems of representation in the teaching and learning of mathematics* (pp. 3–17). Hillsdale, NJ: Lawrence Erlbaum Associates.

Welch, W. (1978). Science education in Urbanville: A case study. In R. Stake & J. Easley (Eds.), *Case studies in science education* (pp. 515–533). Urbana: University of Illinois.

Yevennes, M. (1985). The world political economy and the future of the United States labor market. *World Futures, 21,* 147–157.

# Introduction to
# Chapter 4

*Judith L. Irvin, Professor, Florida State University, and Director, Center for the Study of Middle Level Education*

The middle school, indeed, is coming of age. It is not difficult to document that hundreds of middle schools have reorganized throughout the nation to meet the needs of young adolescents. Interdisciplinary team organization, the presence of advisor/advisee programs, and a commitment to exploration pervades many middle schools; the spirit of restructuring has renewed many tired teachers and administrators. At the heart of this reorganization is the attempt to build a school organizational structure that is consistent with the nature and needs of young adolescents.

Left untouched in many schools, however, is the curriculum handed down from the very departmentalized high school and instructional methods that leave students uninterested and unattached to learning. But, middle schools are coming of age, and the next decade will bring exciting new curricular and instructional changes for young adolescents.

Among these changes will be a curriculum that enhances thinking. The organization of middle schools lends itself to opportunities to enhance and expand the thinking abilities of students. Organizing teachers and students into interdisciplinary teams naturally (but not always) leads to integrated instruction. Organizing instruction around themes, especially those that are of interest to young adolescents, helps students see relationships between concepts and enables the applicability of new ideas across disciplines.

One caveat is in order. Many middle level students have not yet reached an abstract level of thinking, a few may never do so. Some students can solve problems and apply new knowledge to new situations impressively one day and react concretely, even literally, the next day. The challenge for middle level educators is to find ways to introduce students to abstract thinking in a success oriented way. Relating to the world of a young adolescent, however, is not always palatable to educators. Connecting with their world, their interests, and their perspective is the key to enhancing their thinking ability.

Challenges of the 21st century that we cannot image will face the youth of today: the ability to solve problems, apply knowledge to new, and probably yet unknown, situations will be imperative. As Dr. Collins describes in Chapter 4, we know more now about how people learn and think and solve problems. The pieces of school organization are in place; it is time to use these pieces to promote the thinking abilities of young adolescents.

# 4 Thinking Development Through Intervention: Middle School Students Come of Age

Cathy Collins
*Texas Christian University*

The middle school can be defined as an institution for individuals from age 10–15, designed to meet educational needs in unique ways. While middle schools began less than 25 years ago, to date, 22 innovative instructional programs, and 29 different types of grade level combinations exist (Epstein & MacIver, in press). Concurrent with the developing nature of middle schools, a commonly agreed upon best or essential curriculum has not been established.

The purpose of this chapter is to suggest that during the 21st century, middle school educators should develop new curricula to enhance adolescent's thinking. The first section of the chapter contends that such curricula should become a major component in middle school education. The second cites research where advances in thinking for middle school students have resulted from such changes in curricula. The chapter concludes with plans of action that can move us toward providing adolescents with more advanced cognitive skills.

## THINKING DEVELOPMENT THROUGH INTERVENTION

There are several reasons why middle school curriculum should include thinking developmental activities. First, the historical evolution of middle schools make it advantageous to do so. Because middle schools have less tradition than elementary and high schools, curriculum can be more easily modified to include thinking development course work than can other educational institutions.

Second, middle school students are at a point in their development when thinking can most easily expand. Middle school students are just beginning to learn how to think deeply (Collins, 1989a; Dorman & Lipsitz, 1981). Because young adolescents have budding capacities to analyze their own thoughts, and they are aware of only a few ways of thinking, if they are taught powerful thinking strategies, they will more automatically reuse them than will older students. These strategies would be among the first thinking tools young adolescents will have used successfully and independently to solve personal and scholastic problems.

They want to be shown how to execute their, first, often fragile, deep thoughts, just as they sought guidance in the difficult process of learning to walk. Without such support, many adolescents must continue to "crawl," avoiding deep thinking. Equally important, 10- to 15-year-olds experience rapid change physically, socially, emotionally, and intellectually. Adolescents need assistance to comprehend the complexities in each of these dimension of their changing lives. This assistance can come from instruction.

A third reason is that middle school students have to reach responsible decisions earlier in our society than in the past. Instead of a "sweet sixteen and never been kissed" society (in which most of us lived as young adolescents), today's youth, by ages 10 to 15, reach a point where they "have their last best chance to choose a path toward productive and fulfilled lives" (Carnegie, 1989, p. 20). In the process, they are tempted, if not pressured, to experiment with drugs and alcohol; may live in neighborhoods where they are afraid to walk to school; and experience sexual urges they do not understand (Blos, 1979; Dorman & Lipsitz, 1981). Without developmental thinking activities, and being surrounded by equally confused peers, many will make poor choices with harmful consequences (Carnegie, 1989). As Hahn, Dansberger, and Lefkowitz (1987) found, significant correlations exist between adolescents' inability to think on higher levels and their use of destructive means to fulfill a need for power and importance. Similarly, as Eichhorn (1966) discovered, patterns of inadequate thinking, developed during this period, are left unaltered in adulthood. It appears that unless we help middle school students learn to think, they may be forced to use identification with peers, emotional disengagement, and defense mechanisms as their only problem-solving strategies.

A fourth reason to include thinking developmental activities is that, through them, middle schools could become a distinct component in students' educational history. By the 21st century, middle schools could become the educational institution with primary responsibility for teaching students to choose among goals; persevere; meet challenges and enjoy transforming them to positive purposes; make decisions; attain a success-oriented personality; and achieve a level of intellectual behavior that has several dimensions. We must develop a curriculum that assists our youth to think and to see the virtues of being a good thinker. We can no longer afford to just "tell them to say no" or "say no to them." We must give them methods of building more effective standards for our society, and of generating more successful choices.

Last, in a pragmatic vein, young adolescents, of all human beings, have the most time to learn how to think. Csikszentmihalyi and Larsen (1984), and Worell and Danner (1989) found today's adolescents spend 40–50% of their time in leisure activities. Not only is this percentage more than they will have later in life, but presently this time is not used to build thinking ability. Because becoming a better thinker takes time, and adolescents have time, we, as educators, need to examine what we can do to use this time more effectively.

Before we consider making changes in middle schools, let's analyze their present features. To do so, we will assume we are young adolescents. Let's examine how we interact in the existing middle school program.

## A TYPICAL DAY IN A 1990S MIDDLE SCHOOL

To begin, as young adolescents, we feel as if we are in perpetual motion, bombarded with change (Coles, 1989). One day, as we prepare for school, we have a self-perception similar to sophisticated socialites; the next day we take our small stuffed animal to school or wear our baseball cap as our security blanket. We are self-critical and self-conscious, more so than people of other ages. Furthermore, every cognitive development and classroom activity must occur in a "kaleidoscope of our changing emotional states" (Csikszentmihaly & Larson, 1984, p. 211).

When we arrive at school, we enter an average (mean, not mode) homeroom (compiled from statistics by *Teacher*, April 1990; Carnegie Foundation, *Turning Points*, 1989; John, O'Malley, & Bachman, 1988; Lefstein, 1986). As we take our seats, 25 students are in the room. Among our group we have:

 6 who are poor;
 8 who live with only one parent;
13 whose parents are unmarried, illiterate, and/or less than 20 years of age; or, who will become teenage parents themselves;
 6 who have parents who will divorce in the next 6 years;
 4 who are mentally or physically handicapped;
 3 who speak English as a second language;
 7 who go home after school with no one there to greet them;
 5 who will not finish high school;
13 who have tried, or are still using cigarettes, alcohol, and/or illicit drugs; and,
 8 who are one or more grade levels below their peers, academically.

Thus, as we reach out to these, our peers, to develop cognitively and break our psychological attachment to parents, as a group, 73 negative factors effect our thinking daily. Moreover, we find that the typical 50 minute class period is so short that it is difficult to get into a problem-free state of mind to think.

Trying to put these problems out of mind, our homeroom begins. Throughout this period, as in all our classes, we have difficulty maintaining eye contact, making requests of others, and stating preferences and independent thoughts (Drash, 1980; Irvin, 1990; Worell & Danner, 1984). Presently, in our schools we have two choices for dealing with problems. We can develop our own coping devices, without instruction; or we can become more sophisticated in our use of strategies to avoid thinking. By the middle school years many of us will have developed a complex repertoire of such avoidance behaviors. As one of us illustrate, "I'm always scared the teacher is going to call on me. I'll fool around . . . and she tells me to shut up . . . you can do that or act sick or something [to avoid having to think]. Most of the time I just get the answer from Andrea" (Brozo, 1990, p. 324). Other strategies include "mock" participation, such as deceiving teachers so that they believe we are thinking. We do so with appropriate head nodding, and proper eye gaze (Johnston & Markle, 1986).

We also purposely forget to bring materials to class, sit in the front row (to give the impression that we are interested), and become "a good listener" by knowing the teacher well enough to know when to pay attention. When asked what we want (and ultimately need) we will tell you that we want *less external supervision, stimulation intellectually, cognitive challenges, advanced information, positive thinking models, encouragement to commit to meaningful life goals, decision-making tools to build our responsibility, and a middle school environment that provides autonomy* (Collins, 1990a.)

Passing period begins, and, as with all such periods, our pattern of consciousness is disrupted. For some of us passing periods become our most pleasurable time of day, interludes when we can discuss our problems and share jokes with friends. For others, switching classes frequently scrambles our mood, making us sometimes more and sometimes less receptive to thinking and learning. Frequent, repeated contacts with friends, however, consistently prevents us from becoming deeply engrossed in serious scholarship (Csikszentimihaly & Larsen, 1984).

Aside from our personal difficulties, lack of thinking instruction, and the disruption of frequent passing periods, as young adolescents we have another problem concerning our ability to think. Dorman and Lipsitz (1981) found that the quality of our thinking is significantly correlated to the types of lesson we are asked to complete. Best lessons are informal, employing high levels of thinking, with dense but sequenced information, such as small group discussions, and individual goal setting activities that push us to exceed our past performances. Through such lessons our enjoyment, personal engagement, energy, and idealism will rise above people at other age levels, and our thinking abilities will develop rapidly (Siegler, 1989). With other types of lessons, such as when we "*have* to do uninteresting things" (Collins, 1990b), or listen to the teacher, our minds wander to our insecurities, and little thinking occurs.

As we pass through the day, in at least one of our classes, we will feel overwhelmed by the cognitive demands of the course content. This overpowered feeling, derived from emotional, physical, and social instability, creates disproportionate fears. Because of these fears, when we become confused, we will not ask the teacher for help (as we often did in elementary school) or ask for help from parents/peers (as we will in high school). Instead our confusion will build into anxiety, worry, agitation, panic, and anger, (e.g., "In Chemistry listening to Mr. Molitor is causing me to go insane" (Csikszentmihalyi & Larson, 1984, p. 234). Similarly, our unstable self-concepts make it impossible to accurately evaluate our abilities. Therefore, we often *truly* panic over a homework assignment that, after great psychological effort, is begun, and once started, easily completed in only 20 minutes.

Equally devastating is when we leave this too difficult class, and enter the next, where the teacher requires us to work alone for long periods of time. In such classes, because the gap between gaining knowledge and our ability to obtain it is so large, we will mask our inabilities by either faking disinterest, or trying to convince our teachers that the information to be learned is "beneath us." (Collins, 1990b; Siegler, 1988).

We need teachers who take a genuine interest in us and their subjects. Ones who are intrinsically motivated and model this motivation so we see that reasoning and planning are better than random activity and pleasure seeking, which we know are short lived. We don't like flamboyant or passive teachers because we depend on their adult judgments to learn to extend our trust to other adults. Furthermore, when they are the type of people we want to become, we will less likely fear becoming adults ourselves (Collins, 1989b). The best teachers teach us how they developed their own hard-won thinking habits, and we see them model these mature decision-making abilities. They also provide cognitive work that develops our individual talents. They offer specific praises. When we receive such intrinsic and extrinsic rewards, we experience the autonomy we need.

## RESEARCH WITH MIDDLE SCHOOL STUDENTS
## WHERE ADVANCES IN THINKING ARE OCCURRING

This section of the chapter describes data relative to adolescents' thinking development and the innovative practices that produced these increases. While interest in expanding students' thinking increased in the 1980s, relatively few studies have examined variables in instructional settings that stimulate such growth (Resnick, 1989). Resnick (1989) stated that before such changes can occur, substantial research is needed to identify approaches that actually improve reasoning in academic disciplines and practical situations. Although data suggest that high school students' reasoning abilities can be increased through the infusion of thinking development strategies in science, mathematics, and social science classes (Baron & Sternberg, 1987; deBono, 1970), relatively few studies have analyzed the impact of lessons to expand thinking development upon middle level students.

One study by Epstein and MacIver (in press) analyzed data from 1400 middle schools in the United States. The study analyzed 13 programmatic factors to discern most from less successful schools. Data suggest that many factors, including the specific grade level span of middle schools, their size, and whether they are labeled "middle schools" or "junior high schools" do not influence the levels of students' academic success or adolescents' value for education. Epstein and MacIver found that the most significant contributor to high achievement and positive student attitudes is the presence of practices that respond positively to the unique needs of early adolescents. Epstein and MacIver also found that holding a middle school counseling/advisory small group discussion concerning how to solve personal problems once a week lowered the dropout rate 1%; and rewarding improvements by using written statements concerning individual student talents on report cards reduced the drop out rate by 1.7% for young adolescent males.

In ongoing studies by Collins (1989a, 1990a, 1991, in press) the effects of lessons, designed to expand thinking development for young adolescents, have been analyzed. Lessons were created, following a review of taxonomies and descriptions of the different types of thinking competencies (Beyer, 1987; Baron & Sternberg, 1987; Collins, in press-a; Gardner, 1990; Marzano et al., 1988; Paul, 1990). Eight types of lessons have been used, reflecting the dimension of thinking, described next, and depicted in Fig. 4.1.

Division 1: *basic cognitive operations,* including the ability to clarify ideas, examine relationships, see errors, summarize, and remember.

Division 2: *thinking processes* that call upon more than one operation, including inferencing, interpreting, thinking like experts, and making multiple comparisons. In dimension 2, concepts, literal elaborations, and connections are formed.

Division 3: *decision-making abilities* where one must select from competing alternatives that may or may not be obvious to the decision maker, use decision-making tools, and recognize critical points when making a decision will eliminate problems before they begin.

Division 4: *ability to solve problems,* resolving perplexing situations, assessing the quality of ideas, eliminating biases, establishing criteria, and judging the credibility of sources.

Division 5: *metacognitive thinking,* involving control of self; assessing one's current knowledge relative to individual tasks; and identifying barriers that interfere with one's talents, projects, and goals.

Division 6: *creative and innovative thinking,* including shifting frames of reference; and using models, metaphors, substitutions, humor, risk-taking, curiosity, as well as forecasting to create new thoughts and products.

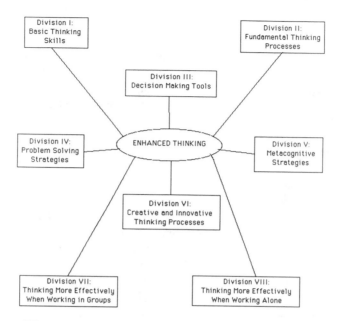

FIG. 4.1. Thinking dimensions developed through instruction. Eight categories of cognitive development.

Division 7: *thinking effectively in groups,* understanding the nature and quality of thinking in group setting; exercising power/authority/influence appropriately; using talents interactively; and developing analytical listening abilities.

Division 8: *ability to think effectively when alone,* set goals, establish redirection, take action, and elicit self-motivation to increase productivity.

While a more complete description of the 11 week treatment appears in Collins (1991b, in press). The thinking developmental activities used in the experiment reported in this chapter appear below.

*Division 1: Building Basic Reasoning Skills.* Students learned to ask eight types of questions to reason through confusions as they read, listened, and completed homework assignments. They also analyzed incidents where main characters asked clarification questions, and the effects such questions had upon events that followed.

*Division 2: Building Thinking Processes.* Students learned to recognize patterns and principles. Students listed principles, values, and justifications that protagonists used to address problems. Students described common and dissimilar thinking patterns between themselves and protagonists. Students also described how they could use patterns and principle recognition to solve problems in their lives.

Students used pattern recognition skills in two ways to perform *Ann Landers* type activities for elementary school students. They received anonymous letters from elementary school students about problems they faced. Students then divided these letters into groups so similar problems could be researched simultaneously. They also identified common patterns in the solutions to these problems that were recommended in their reading and through interviews with adults. Once a pattern between suggestions was discerned, three member groups wrote a return letter to each student. This letter contained a solution to the problem that student faced, the rationale for that solution, and a list of books for the student to read concerning the problem.

*Division 3: Building Decision-Making Abilities.* Students were taught how to analyze decision-making processes and to use decision-making tools. Students were taught how to list attributes, weight characteristics, scan barriers, set objectives, and make nature analogies. Students also compared a decision they would have made to a decision made by real historical figures. Students also interviewed community leaders to identify decision making tools they used.

*Division 4: Using Problem-Solving Strategies.* Teachers described strategies they used to solve scholastic and real world problems. Matrices, backward reasoning, and imagry were three problem-solving strategies taught.

*Division 5: Using Metacognitive Skills.* Students became more aware of their talents by reading a biography/autobiography about a famous person born on their birthdate. After comparing their strengths to that famous person, they wrote what it would be like to be that person's best friend, creating activities the two would enjoy in the student's community. Students then wrote their own autobiographies, paired with a friend, and wrote a biography of their friend's strengths, without conferring with each other. These two students compared their autobiographies and biographies to each other, reasoning why differences in perceptions and self-perceptions existed.

*Division 6: Developing Creative and Innovative Reasoning Abilities.* Students learned how to adapt, rearrange, modify and substitute parts of ideas as they summarized and predicted. Among the activities they completed was to create a proverbial statement explaining an authors reasons for writing a chapter or book.

*Division 7: Thinking More Effectively in Group Settings.* Students were taught how to mediate, collaborate, and consolidate ideas, by using current events. Pairs of students mediated, collaborated, and consolidated their ideas to reach a consensus. These students then met with other students pairs to renegotiate a plan of action. This process continued until groups of 8 had collaborated, and developed a 3-page, position paper concerning unresolved issues surrounding a current event. Other activities in this division included students developing content and thinking objectives for content area units. Students set content related and thinking development objectives they wanted to achieve. They then projected what might interfere with their goals, and identified a talent each student would contribute to the goals. They assessed their success on their objectives at the end of each unit.

*Division 8: Thinking More Effectively When Alone.* Students learned to establish priorities for 3 consecutive weeks, and completed journal entries concerning their thinking development. They learned to suspend judgment by reading first person narratives, where they were not allowed to see the title or any pictures in the writing. As they read, they identified who the narrator was, and told their teacher. Each student marked the point in the story where they had enough details to make an identity. Then students wrote the thought process they followed in selecting the narrator they did. The first three students to correctly identify the narrator explained the thinking processes they used. Students then wrote about different occasions in their life when they will suspend judgments and attend to details so as to make their lives more successful and fulfilled.

When lessons designed to build these dimensions of thinking were incorporated into one period of a traditional middle school program, benefits to young adolescents were significant (Collins, 1990b, 1991b). A group of 84 7th graders were taught for 33 days, over 11 weeks, and compared to the same number of 7th graders who were taught another type of new curriculum that did not include thinking development. The experimental subjects significantly outperformed untrained adolescents in many ways.

While pretesting of experimental and control groups found no significant differences between groups on the following standardized subtests, experimental subjects scored significantly higher on the posttest for reading comprehension posttest (RCOMP) of the Iowa Test of Basic Skills, $F = 91.49$, $p < .001$. The experimental group also scored significantly higher than the control group on vocabulary (VOCAB) and Total battery scores (TOTAL), $F = 42.47$, $p < .001$, and $F = 12.65$, $p < .001$, respectively. The means and standard deviations between groups appear in Table 4.1.

As you notice in Table 4.1, there were no significant differences between groups on Total Language Subtest scores. Scores on this subtest were derived from items that measured grammar term recognition, spelling skill, punctuation knowledge, and capitalization error recognition. These skills were more basic than, and unrelated to, the thinking dimensions taught in the study, as students

TABLE 4.1
Mean Scores and Standard Deviations on the Iowa Test of Basic Skills

| | Subscales | | | |
| --- | --- | --- | --- | --- |
| Group | RCOMP* | VOCAB* | LANGTOT | TOTAL* |
| Control | 27.52 | 15.71 | 75.23 | 255.91 |
| | (8.1) | (7.3) | (24.0) | (65.24) |
| Treatment | 51.08 | 29.62 | 81.39 | 328.23 |
| | (4.8) | (3.3) | (14.0) | (42.90) |

*$p < .001$.

had to rely upon memory capacities and exposure to direct instruction to perform well on this subtest. The fact that neither group outperformed the other on this subtest is viewed as further evidence of the effects of the experimental treatment upon thinking development.

One of the most crucial outcomes of the study occurred in post writing samples. These writing samples were unprompted journal entries, completed two weeks after the study's end. All experimental and control subjects were allowed to write on subjects of choice. Once writings were completed, 21 samples from the experimental and 21 samples from the control group were randomly selected for analysis. Without being told that the writings were a part of the study, experimental subjects included 13 types of thinking in their writings. These types came from 7 of the 8 dimensions of thinking of the experimental treatment.

Except for three single sentences, from a total of 195 statements, control subjects' writing samples were composed of factual statements, where students used only first dimensional thinking. Of the three exceptions, one was an inference, the second was an elaboration (which are level two types of thought), and the third was a statement reflecting a dimension 7 thought. The fact that experimental subjects demonstrated self-selected thinking in 7 of the 8 levels of thought is educationally significant. The differences in slopes between groups was statistically significant.

There is need for future study of such thinking development lessons upon students' self-generated thinking. The floor effect for the control group in this study creates needs for larger sample size. Moreover, it seems that middle schools students' self-generated ability to establish criteria and solve problems (RE, PS in Fig. 4.2, which were the only types of dimension 4 types of thought included in the study) may require longer periods of instruction to develop than other levels of thinking. In this research, experimental subjects, when unprompted, did not initiate statements that evidenced dimension 4 of thinking competence.

In the third measure of this study, the self-esteem scores of the experimental subjects in social competence, behavior in groups, appearance, and physical competence (as measured by the Harter Self-Perception Profile for Children; Harter, 1985) were compared to self-esteem scores in control groups. Although there were no significant differences between groups on pretest measures, experimental subjects scored significantly above control subjects in their self-perception of social competence, behavior in groups, appearance, and physical competence (Collins, 1991a).

Similarly, when five raters viewed tapes of the last lesson in experimental and control classes, all raters ranked subjects in experimental classes as better thinkers than subjects in control classes. These raters also identified 12 differences between interactions which occurred in experimental versus control groups:

- experimental subjects did not interrupt the person talking;
- they asked each other questions;
- they made fewer random comments during discussion;
- they built upon each others' answers;
- they volunteered ideas, evidence, and rationale to help classmates' thinking;
- they gave each other sufficient time to answer questions;
- students were more interested in the class, and its tasks, until the end of the period;
- students used terms to describe their thinking;
- they used jargon less frequently;
- the noise level was lower; and
- teachers engaged a greater number of students in discussions.

In like manner, 62% of experimental subjects and 0% of control subjects described at least one specific incident where they had used a thinking strategy, taught during class, in situations outside school. These very positive results

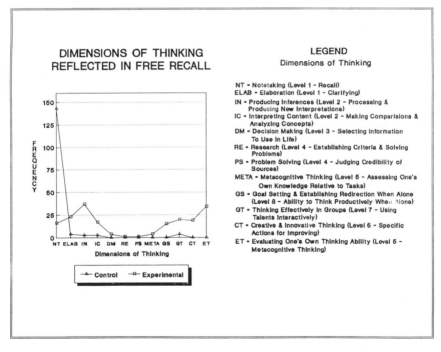

FIG. 4.2.  Dimensions of thinking reflected in free recall. Specific cognitive skills evidenced in posttests of control and experimental subjects.

emanated from only 33 days of instruction, in only one curriculum area. Their success certainly would justify incorporating thinking intervention lessons into a year long curriculum.

Other studies are underway which demonstrate the effect of a thinking development curriculum upon young adolescents. The first is codirected by the Technical Education Research Center (Cambridge, MA), the National Science Foundation (Washington, D. C.) and the National Geographic Kids Network (Washington, D. C.). In this study, analyses are being made concerning the cognitive development of middle school students who are problem solvers on an adult, scientific team. These students are collecting information about global issues, such as acid rain, weather, and the ozone layer and comparing it to data from around the world.

In a different study, Siegler (1989) found that teaching adolescents how to use backup strategies increased these students' accuracy in reading, and in recalling addition, and subtraction facts. Kerkman and Siegler (in preparation) are in the process of determining if this increased accuracy will sustain 6 months after instruction ceased.

Howard Gardner, in his Arts Propel Project (Pittsburgh, PA), has designed community service projects in which students serve as active leaders. The home base for these projects is the school campus, which is open from 7:00 A.M. until 6:00 P.M. The middle school students involved in this project have increased their problem-solving skills. Data relative to long-term effects are being collected.

The positive results from these studies suggest that we can enhance the thinking of young adolescents in very specific ways. In the next section we suggest specific actions we can take. These actions hold the potential of preparing our youth for happier, more successful lives in the years ahead.


## ADMINISTRATIVE AND INSTRUCTIONAL ACTIONS TO PREPARE FOR THE TWENTY-FIRST CENTURY

There are several steps that can be taken to develop thinking during the middle school years. Most do not require substantial changes in organization or in instructional structures. Most require only a catalyst for change.

1. We need to add thinking development activities, like those described in this chapter, to our middle school curriculum. In addition, in each class we need to ensure that we do one of the following actions to convince students that there is *not* only one correct answer or path of thinking. As McGarvey (1990) reported, in one test of creativity thinking, 84% of kindergarteners ranked high. By 2nd grade, however, only 10% sustained a significant level of creativity. The reasons behind this dramatic drop was that students quickly come to believe that there is only right answer, and they stop looking and thinking as soon as they come up with their first answer.

As Graves and Stuart (1985) report, there are many things, in and out of school, to convince students that there is only one correct answer, and that answers to problems should be simple. Students see that "all you need is one grand shootout at the O. K. corral at high noon and all this complex fuss that they have watched for three hours will be over" (p. 32). As another example, observed by Paul Messier, when kindergarten children go to cut a string, before they come to school they cut it wherever they wish. After they come to school they begin to realize that there is only *one* middle and they work feverishly to cut each string exactly where "it's supposed to be cut" (Messier, personal communication).

To change this condition, students should be asked to generate, instead of shun, alternatives as they work. As Graves and Stuart state (1985), "Since the assumption is that there is only one right answer and many wrong ones, children soon discover that it is very easy to be wrong. The underlying message is that someone else knows and you don't. Another underlying message is that your information is only valuable if it fills some else's blank" (p. 32). To alter these messages, we need to consistently ask for more than one solution to written answers, or in the case of mathematics and science where a single answer is correct, ask students to explain two different thinking processes that could lead to the answer. We also need to challenge middle school students to reconsider and restructure their "incorrect" answers.

2. In every class we can improve students' thinking by discussing problems and omissions in the textbook. When we do, we not only provide added time to develop problem-solving skills, but we address the issue raised by Beck and Dole in Chapter 1: overcoming the tenacity of original knowledge. As Beck and Dole discussed, in the face of contradictory evidence, many students will refuse to engage in thinking and learning, initially, as they believe they already have the needed information. Our job is to assist them by illustrating how even their textbooks contain inadequate reasonings. We also need to introduce different frames of thinking, as Clarke (1990) presented. The following concept map depicts the paths of thoughts that students can have to solve a problem (see Fig. 4.3). To increase the benefits of these diagrams for students, we need to offer them the opportunity to select the one they wish to use. Once they make their choice, students can spend a few minutes describing, most often in writing, why they chose the thinking frame they did. Students can also meet in small groups and discuss the types of thinking frames that resulted in most positive benefits.

3. We can spend time each week, if only for a 15 minute period, introducing students to a thinking strategy, and providing time for small group discussions concerning its application. Such discussion will be guided by the thinking development objectives we set, from the 8 dimensions, and assessed by us and the students upon completion of the study. During discussion periods, we have the opportunity to learn what, how, and how well our students think. Realizing that many middle school teachers have as many as 120 students a day, sitting with one student during this time, and then sitting with a small group the next will enable us to know each of our students better and to know them as strong thinkers.

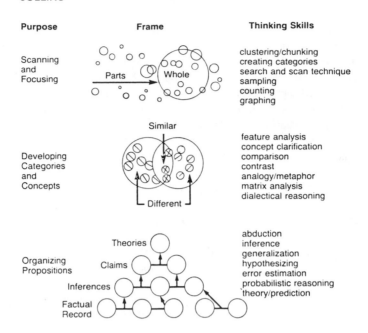

| Purpose | Frame | Thinking Skills |
|---|---|---|

Scanning and Focusing — Parts → Whole — clustering/chunking, creating categories, search and scan technique, sampling, counting, graphing

Developing Categories and Concepts — Similar / Different — feature analysis, concept clarification, comparison, contrast, analogy/metaphor, matrix analysis, dialectical reasoning

Organizing Propositions — Theories, Claims, Inferences, Factual Record — abduction, inference, generalization, hypothesizing, error estimation, probabilistic reasoning, theory/prediction

FIG. 4.3.  Thinking frames students can be taught and encouraged to use independently as they study and solve real world problems. Samples taken from lessons used in division 4. These frames were taken from John H. Clarke, *Patterns of Thinking: Integrating Learning Skills in Content Teaching.* Copyright (1990), Allyn and Bacon, p. 61. Reprinted by permission.

4. Interdisciplinary teaching teams need to be used in middle schools. These teams can require students to transfer a thinking strategy, taught in one content area to other content areas throughout a week. In this way students are reminded and asked to strengthen one thinking tool throughout an entire day. During interdisciplinary planning sessions, teams can target 1 of 8 dimensions of thinking during a reporting period. Teams can formulate coordinated activities between subjects, similar to the connection between math and language arts that Ogle reported in Chapter 2. These interdisciplinary units can be built around concepts middle school students enjoy such as courage, immortality, modesty, shyness, heroes, imperishable beauty, leadership, and philosophical, ethical, and political issues (e.g., abortion, affirmative action, and the death penalty).

5. Students can be guided to develop the ability to find important problems, and reduce myopic perceptions when they become involved in community related issues, such as helping the homeless, and recycling lunchroom waste, through programs that they design, implement, and evaluate. For example, in San Francisco, during the summer of 1990, the school board and teachers asked students, ages 12–18, to assist in directing the summer school program (Heath, 1990). Students recruited teachers, and made the content units for grades K–3. A

second illustration is to build extramural programs where students can practice their thinking. Such programs can be offered from 3:00–6:00 P.M., and students lead other students, and community members, to apply the thinking strategy they have studied the previous week (Collins, in press).

6. At the beginning of the year, establish a year-long goal to improve one specific aspect of students' thinking. To begin, identify parts of the school that are "so terrific" no one wants to change them. Then the school staff identifies one type of thinking students are not doing. Together, through backward reasoning, develop a specific year-long plan of action to assist the students in reaching that type of thinking.

7. When middle school students use technology daily at school, and share their data with others around the world, they will see the importance of and practice deep thinking. By the 21st century, with proper thinking development at the middle school level, high school students could become our planet's monitors, preparing and comparing summaries from around the world, discerning fundamentals, judging completeness, reasoning inductively and deductively, learning how experts in a field think (mentoring through telecommunications), making multiple comparisons, and asking questions to clarify and establish accurate information.

8. Middle school students can begin to assist adults, by contributing more idealistic thinking patterns in projects and planning to create new inventions. They can serve one period a day, or once a week, as a member of an adult "creative thinking team" at a local business or community agency.

As we close our discussion, we all realize that it is impossible to anticipate what adolescents will need to know in the 21st century. However, we have learned in the last few years that by teaching young adolescents to think deeply we can give them the ability to take control of certain things in their lives and to have thinking repertoires to meet new challenges. When middle school students gain the confidence that they can solve problems, they report that they feel as if they have "better control in their lives" (Collins, 1991b), and they learn to value thinking, as Lauren B., a 7th grader in our study volunteered, "Thinking is like a good friend."

In summary, we now know that we can help middle school students to think more effectively and productively. We have described 8 steps we can take to do so. When do these innovations need to be in place to benefit our youth in the 21st century? They need to be in the curriculum within the next 2 years. In 1993 students who have enrolled in 6th grade will graduate from high school in the year 2000. I invite each of us to take a first step, this year, to better prepare our youth for the future they face.

## REFERENCES

Baron, J., & Sternberg, R. (1987). *Teaching thinking skills: Theory and practice*. New York: W. H. Freeman.

Beyer, B. (1987). *Practical strategies for the teaching of thinking*. Boston, MA: Allyn and Bacon.

Blos, P. (1979). *The adolescent passage: Developmental issues*. New York: International Universities Press.

Brozo, W. G. (1990). Hiding out in secondary content classrooms: Coping strategies of unsuccessful readers. *Journal of reading, 33*(5), 324–328.

Carnegie Council on Adolescent Development (1989). *Turning points: Preparing American youth for the 21st century*. New York: Carnegie Foundation.

Clarke, J. H. (1990). *Patterns of thinking*. Boston, MA: Allyn and Bacon.

Coles, R. (1989). Grade eight students cope with today and get ready for tomorrow. In K. S. Goodman, Y. M. Goodman, & W. J. Hood (Eds.), *The whole language evaluation Book*. Portsmouth NH: Heinemann.

Collins, C. (1989a, December). *A new approach to middle school reading: Expanded thinking*. Paper presented at the annual conference of the National Reading Conference, Austin, TX.

Collins, C. (1989b). Administrators hold the key to thinking development. *REACH, 3,* 139–147. Austin, TX: Texas Education Agency.

Collins, C. (1990a, May). Reasoning through reading: Vignettes that produce engagement. Paper presented at the annual conference of the International Reading Association, Atlanta, Georgia.

Collins, C. (1990b). Administrators can promote higher level thinking skills. *NASSP Bulletin, 74* (526), 102–109.

Collins, C. (1991). Reading instruction that expands thinking ability. *Journal of Reading, 34*(6) April, 540–550.

Collins, C. (in press) *Expanding thinking through the language arts*. Englewood Cliffs, NJ: Prentice Hall.

Collins, C. (1991b). Don your critical thinking caps. *The school administrator,* 48(1), 8–14.

Csikszentmihalyi, M., & Larsen, R. (1984). *Being adolescent: Conflict and growth in the teenage years*. New York: Basic Books.

deBono, E. (1970). *Lateral thinking*. New York: Harper and Row.

Dorman, G., & Lipsitz, J. (1981). Early adolescent development. In G. Dorman (Ed.), *Middle grades assessment program*. Carrboro, NC: Center for Early Adolescence.

Drash, A. (1980). Variations in pubertal development and the school system: A problem and a challenge. In D. Ster (Ed.), *The emerging adolescent characteristics and educational implications*. Columbus, OH: National Middle School Association.

Eichhorn, D. (1966). *The middle school*. New York: The Center for Applied Research in Education.

Epstein, J. L., & MacIver, D. J. (in press). *Education in the middle grades: Overview of national practices and trends*. Columbus, OH: The National Middle School Association.

Gardner, H. (1990). *Restructuring America's schools*. Telecommunications broadcast, May 24, 1990.

Graves, D., & Stuart, V. (1985). *Teachers who write*. Portsmouth, Heineman.

Hahn, A., Dansberger, J., & Lefkowitz, B. (1987). *Dropouts in America: Enough is known for action*. Washington, D. C.: Institute for Educational Leadership.

Harter, D. (1985). *Harter self-perception profile for children*. Boulder: University of Colorado.

Heath, S. B. (1990, June). Language and Socialization Skills. Speech delivered at the Annual Meeting of the Fort Worth Literacy Conference.

Irvin, J. L. (1990). *Reading and the middle school student*. Boston, MA: Allyn and Bacon.

John, L. D., O'Malley, P. M., & Bachman, J. G. (1988). *Illicit drug use, smoking and drinking by America's high school students, college students, and young adults: 1975–1987* (DHHS Publication No. ADM 89-1602). Washington, D. C.: U.S. Government Printing Office.

Johnston, J. H., & Markle, G. C. (1986). *What research says to the middle level practitioner*. Columbus, Ohio: National Middle School Association.

Kerkman, D., & Siegler, R. S. (in preparation). Lower-class children's strategy choices in arithmetic and reading.

Lefstein, L. M. (1986). *Portrait of young adolescents in the 1980s*. Carrboro, NC: Center for Early Adolescence.

Marzano, R., Jones, B. R., Brandt, R., et al. (1988). *Dimensions of thinking.* Alexandria, VA: Association for Supervision and Curriculum.

McGarvey, R. (1990). Creative thinking. *USAir,* June 1990, pp. 34–41.

Paul, R. (1990). *Critical thinking: What every person needs to survive in a rapidly changing world.* Rohnert Park, CA: Sonoma State University.

Resnick, L. (1989). *Educational and learning to think.* Washington, D.C.: National Academic Press.

Siegler, R. S. (1988). Individual differences in strategy choices: good students, not-so-good students, and perfectionists. *Child Development, 59,* 833–851.

Siegler, R. S. (1989). Strategy diversity and cognitive assessment. *Educational Researcher, 18*(9), 15–19.

*Teacher.* (1990). Who our students are. April, 4. New York, NY: Teacher.

Worell, J., & Danner, F. (1989). *The adolescent as decision maker: applications to development and education.* San Diego, CA: Academic Press.

# Introduction to
# Chapter 5

*David C. Berliner is Professor of Curriculum and Instruction and of Psychology in the Schools in the College of Education at Arizona State University. He is a former President of the American Educational Research Association, and a Fellow of the Center for Advanced Study in the Behavioral Sciences.*

This chapter opens with two statements that some may consider outlandish: conventional wisdom about helping low income students succeed in school is wrong, and there is not now available a general thinking skills program that works. Each of these claims needs to be seriously and sympathetically examined.

As we consider Professor Pogrow's arguments we need to be clear that the deficit displayed by many low income students, declared to be "at-risk," is a deficit in school thinking, not everyday thinking, and that they bring many strengths to school situations that are not used or valued. Professor Pogrow points out that the children with whom he works are as smart as any others, but that they need to learn the forms of discourse *in school settings*. He contends that the way to teach them are through group and social experiences, with a competent adult mediating a rich learning environment. Dr. Pogrow's work may "mentor" to children learning a new culture—the American school culture and its standards of success. His program takes about 2 years of daily practice, about what you would expect if you were to estimate how long it would take you to learn to pass as an Afganistani, to be successful in that culture in settings in which you have not been taught explicitly how to act. If he is successful, as I think he may be, then he is one of the few people that has found ways to help the nonnatives learn to achieve like natives, in a culture that is not quite compatable with their own. This is a formidable achievement.

The evidence for student achievement that is presented in this chapter is certainly worth considering seriously, though I believe it is incumbent upon us to remain skeptical. I claim that the evidence in this chapter is certainly worth considering seriously. The claims of the success of Madeline Hunters' Elements of Effective Instruction have been challenged by hard-nosed research. The claims of the people that educate according to theories of brain dominance have proved untenable. The claims of the teaching machine advocates, the individualized instruction folks, the promoters of LOGO for young children, the instrumental enrichment believers, and those associated with many other educational innovations lead us to be suspicious of the claims made by anyone—including those of Professor Pogrow. I have a strong belief that he is doing work of profound importance for educators to consider. He has a remarkable aptitude for building and refining learning modules and discourse patterns that result in teaching/learning processes that are of a remarkably high level. They have all the appearances of first rate educational encounters and I would value them even if the results on achievement tests did not indicate that transfer had taken place.

Good educational encounters in traditional classes with ordinary students are hard to find. In the classes of at-risk students, they are even more rarely found. The processes advocated by Professor Pogrow certainly are rich in providing opportunity to think, and for that alone I am pleased that the HOTS program exists and is spreading around the nation. I am troubled, however, that the big private and government funding agencies do not set out to seriously examine this program. Someone other than a program's developer must attest to its utility.

When a claim was made that fusion could occur at room temperatures a few score of studies, a few hundred investigators, and hundreds of thousands of dollars were spent rapidly to examine that claim. When a claim for superconductivity was announced the same thing happened. When Pogrow claims that 5 years growth on standardized tests can occur in one year, no one in our field seems to notice. He may have developed the educational equivalent of cold fusion, or superconductivity, and we will not be sure.

I am convinced that something is happening here that should be seriously, sympathetically, and thoroughly investigated. Perhaps we are seeing, in the next chapter, the first general thinking skills program that works.

# 5 A Validated Approach to Thinking Development for At-Risk Populations

Stanley Pogrow
University of Arizona

## INTRODUCTION

There is a renewed interest among practitioners, policy makers, and researchers in developing the thinking skills of at-risk students. This interest is accelerating because of a growing realization that: (a) the *drill and kill* approach hasn't worked, and (b) even if this approach were able to raise basic test scores, that outcome, by itself, is insufficient to prepare students for a more sophisticated world of work.

While this current interest in thinking skills provides an opportunity to develop more innovative forms of curricula for at-risk students, this is no guarantee of successful development or implementation of such curricula. There is a great danger that failure to generate effective approaches for developing the problem-solving ability of at-risk students will result in the thinking skills movement becoming yet another innovation which widens learning gaps. Those who are already successful learners will do even better, and the students who were staring at the teacher before will continue to do so. Indeed, thinking development approaches tried in the 60s in the form of discovery learning failed, and the resulting disillusionment led to two decades of increasing routinization and trivialization of the curriculum.

The only hope to significantly improve American education for at-risk students is through the phenomenon of *transfer*. Transfer means that an intervention designed to develop skills in one area produces gains simultaneously in other areas. It is essential because we do not have the resources to attack each education problem individually. Transfer is to education what fusion is to the field of energy, a force that embodies the primary, perhaps *only*, hope for the future.

87

The fundamental question, therefore, becomes: "Do we know how to develop the thinking skills of at-risk students in ways which transfer to improvements in academic learning?" The answer is clearly: "no"! Indeed, research results have been so pessimistic that most researchers glibly proclaim that transfer doesn't exist—or at least that you cannot produce transfer from general thinking skill development. In addition, the track record of American education in producing gains with at-risk students in grades 4–8 even on basic measures is dismal. This does not bode well for producing sophisticated forms of learning gains.

The focus of this chapter is to share the basic conclusions that have been reached about the development of thinking skills in at-risk students from my work with these students over the past 7 years. The goal is to share a series of principles that can guide the development of more effective thinking skill approaches. Many of these principles are counter-intuitive, and most run against the grain of conventional wisdom.

One important caution to readers. **These principles for developing thinking skills are only applicable to the at-risk student.** In many cases, the approach for developing the thinking skills of high-performing students should be very different.

## WHAT IS HOTS?

For the past 9 years I have been developing the Higher Order Thinking Skills (HOTS) program (Pogrow, 1989; Pogrow, 1990b). This program replaces supplementary remedial activities for Chapter 1 students in grades 4–7 with general thinking activities. The goal was to design thinking skill activities that could replace *all* the supplemental remediation and content instruction and still: (a) enhance thinking skills, (b) improve self-confidence, and (c) produce even larger gains in standardized test scores, preferably in both reading and mathematics. The HOTS general thinking activities (i.e., those not tied to classroom content) were developed to measurably enhance content learning by increasing the conceptual ability of at-risk students to learn classroom content the first time taught—a form of transfer.

All indications are that the project has successfully achieved its ambitious goals. In data validated unanimously by the Program Evaluation Panel of the National Diffusion Network, HOTS students achieved spring to spring gains on standardized test scores that were 67% higher in reading and 123% higher in mathematics than national averages. These results were generated with an earlier, less refined version of the model. Second-year gains were also greater than national averages. These continued gains indicate that the results were not Hawthorne effects. Since then, we have not been able to do another systematic study, but schools are now reporting results that substantially exceed the best gains reported in the earlier study. Students in one site gained 5.6 years on the

Stanford Diagnostic Reading test (fall to spring) in the first year, and 20% of the 5th and 6th grade Chapter 1 students posttested beyond the high school level. Tapes of these students reveal them to be highly articulate and sophisticated learners, an indication that the extent of the gains was not a statistical fluke.

The gains in mathematics, with no supplemental remediation or re-teaching of classroom content suggest that a form of transfer occurred from the general thinking activities. There are no additional indications. On Detroit Public School's own criterion reference test, students trained in the same HOTS general thinking skills curriculum achieved 2.5 times the mastery of mathematics objectives as control Chapter 1 students who were drilled in the specific criteria. (Tests of statistical difference were not calculated.) The primary difference between the groups was on the problem-solving scales. Other indicators of transfer include: (a) In one of the 12 schools in the original study, 36% of the Chapter 1 students made the honor role, (b) at a newer site, Chapter 1 students outperformed gifted students in the quality of science inventions produced in two of the three grade levels that used the HOTS program, and (c) a majority of the gains in standardized test scores appear to be coming from the comprehension and problem-solving sections. The latter suggests that the general problem-solving techniques used in the HOTS program are being applied in other contexts. As such, it appears to be possible to design general thinking activities for at-risk students in ways that lead to even greater gains on standardized test scores, an outcome that appears to be a form of transfer.

Another goal was to determine not only if it was possible to simultaneously produce multiple learning effects from a general thinking skills program, but whether it could also be done on a large scale—a necessary condition if the approach was to be a viable national policy option. As this is being written, the HOTS program has grown to being used as *the* Chapter 1 program in over 1300 schools, ranging from inner-city districts to one-school rural districts, serving approximately 40,000 students in 47 states. The number of sites is doubling each year. The success of the program on a large-scale is important. This means that the conclusions about the nature of the learning process that have formed the basis of this program have been validated on a large-scale. They have also worked with a wide variety of racial and ethnic groups.

## CONCLUSIONS ABOUT THE DEVELOPMENT OF THINKING SKILLS IN AT-RISK STUDENTS

CONCLUSION #1: *The at-risk student is very bright.*

The HOTS curriculum consistently challenges students at very high levels. The work is designed to be difficult, but also interesting. At-risk students' performance on these difficult tasks constantly surprises me. It is clear that once the *right* type of intervention is provided, all accepted conventions about what the students can be expected to achieve, or about what activities are appropriate to particular grade levels, are gross underestimates of what is really possible. After designing curricula for these students over the past 9 years, I still have no idea of what the upper limit is of the complexity of ideas and tasks which they can be successful. In addition, we have received a number of reports from around the country of Chapter 1 students outperforming gifted and average students.

CONCLUSION #2: *The primary reason that at-risk students have trouble learning after the 3rd grade is that they do not understand "understanding."*

At-risk students do not seem to know how to deal with unstructured types of learning or with ambiguity. They seem incapable of: (a) dealing with more than one concept at a time, (b) having a conversation about ideas, (c) thinking in terms of general principles instead of specific examples, or (d) thinking ideas through. They view each piece of information as a discrete entity that only applies to the context in which it was learned. They do not seem to understand how to generalize, or that they are even supposed to generalize. They simply do not know how to work with ideas, or even what understanding is. The best way to capture this almost total naivete they have about what one does with ideas and conversation is that they do not understand "understanding."

To teachers, this phenomenon manifests itself as students' inability to even begin the process of internalizing abstract ideas. When faced with this phenomenon, teachers are reduced to making the age-old request: "Please think!" This request usually elicits blank stares. This failure to communicate is all the more tragic because each party desperately wants to communicate with the other—yet neither is capable.

It is only after the curriculum becomes more complex after the third grade that this understanding deficit manifests itself. It also explains why so many basic techniques help the at-risk student up to the 3rd grade, and are then unable to stop a precipitous plunge of their scores thereafter. Basic interventions can help students learn the simpler curriculum of the first three grades but offer no help thereafter.

Once the curriculum becomes complex, reteaching content (remediation) inhibits the formation of the linking skills needed for advanced learning, and for even retaining the information that is being taught. This produces a vicious cycle wherein the more remediation that is provided the less is learned, less emphasis is placed on linking skills, and the less students are able to apply what is learned. It is equivalent to trying to put out a fire by pouring gasoline on it—and then complaining that the fire could be put out if only there was more and better gasoline. Remedial approaches suppress the development of students' intellectual potential and knowledge bases after the 3rd grade—regardless of whether in-class or pullout models are used. Indeed, the students' failure accelerates precisely because they do what we mistakenly tell them to do.

If this is correct, we must face the possibility that the monies spent to solve the learning problems of at-risk students are inadvertently making them worse. (More than one commentator has wryly noted that the more money we spend on education the worse things seem to become.) Nor will efforts to develop better remedial approaches help. This is not an argument against drill, rote learning, or direct instruction of content. The argument is that one cannot do these things **all** the time and have the at-risk student develop intellectually. As such, the *supplemental* help provided *after the 3rd grade* should be of a different, more sophisticated, type of learning experience.

That at-risk students do not understand "understanding" is not their fault. Nor is it an indicator of a problem with their intellect, or a function of their race, ethnicity or economic class. Rather, it probably results from the adults in their lives not modeling the thinking processes for them. Such modeling has typically been done through sophisticated conversation at the dinner table and in school. Such conversation, however, is increasingly rare. Given the growing number of students coming from single working parent households, there is almost no conversation in the home lives of most at-risk children—let alone conversations about constructing meaning.

CONCLUSION #3: *The best way to overcome the understanding deficit is through general thinking experiences not tied to classroom content. It appears to take 2 years of sophisticated general thinking activities in small group settings for at least 35 minutes a day to overcome this deficit. This is what I label the 35 minute principle (Pogrow, 1990a).*

The understanding deficit is profound. Overcoming this will require a very sophisticated learning environment that is consistently maintained over an extended period of time. The notion that asking an occasional thinking question, or that all teachers can design effective approaches, or that general strategies such as cooperative learning or whole language instruction can overcome the understanding deficit is romantic fiction. For example, HOTS teachers have consistently found that it takes close to 4 months of daily modeling before students even come to understand the difference between guessing and using a strategy when dealing with the symbols of school.

The belief that occasional thinking experiences can overcome the understanding deficit is unrealistic. Producing major cognitive change is a complex process. Overcoming a major physical trauma requires highly specialized intensive care. Similarly, overcoming an understanding deficit requires highly specialized intensive services.

At the same time, it doesn't take forever to overcome the key deficit with the right intervention. After 2 years of almost daily specialized help, most of the students appear to be very different cognitively.

CONCLUSION #4: *At-risk students must first be placed in general thinking activities for 1–2 years before being put into sophisticated thinking-in-content activities. (This is the Theory of Cognitive Underpinnings.)*

Students who have major problems in constructing meaning will not be able to succeed in sophisticated problem-solving content. Research presently underway by

Charles Brainerd and Valery Reyna, at the University of Arizona establishes that rote learning and thinking are independent learning processes that are antagonistic. Thus, energy devoted to one of the forms of learning detracts from the other. If this research proves valid, it makes sense, at some point, to provide self-contained help in automating the basic thinking processes that all content learning assume that students have. It is only when such processes have been automated that they do not interfere with acquiring content knowledge.

From a practical point of view, individuals who watch videotapes of HOTS students in the early stages of the program are amazed at how primitive their reasoning skills are. There is simply no way that these students can successfully engage in sophisticated thinking-in-content activities at that stage of development. Even the best classroom teacher cannot cope with a substantial number of students who have understanding deficits in his or her classroom.

## CONCLUSION #5: *The best approach to developing general thinking skills is a social experience approach as opposed to "teaching" thinking strategies.*

The best way to visualize the problem is to view the at-risk student as someone who has a powerful engine in his or her mind that simply isn't turning over. How can it be started? The worst thing you can do is step on the gas. Similarly, at-risk students are not organizing incoming information into internal associative networks. How to get that process started? Simply teaching thinking strategies will not work. It is the equivalent of feeding more gas to a flawed engine. These strategies will, like all the other information in the student's mind, be stored as disjointed ideas.

The HOTS thinking skills model does not "teach" thinking or have the teacher model what thinking is. Rather it is a social-process approach to thinking. The HOTS curriculum creates situations where the students come to experience the need to think, and begin to share their perceptions of the thinking process with each other. While it is much harder to create this type of curriculum it is believed that a social-experience approach to thinking is more appropriate for students who do not understand understanding. This type of curriculum is consistent with the theories of L. S. Vygotsky (1989), who argues that problem-solving must first be practiced in social settings before it is integrated into the cognitive structure of the mind. In essence, the HOTS curriculum recreates dinnertable conversation around the setting of a computer screen.

Recreating the social processes of dinner table conversation in curricular form requires directed and mediated conversation. In such conversation, how the adult talks and responds to the child's ideas serves as an indicator of how adults use information. A major component of this conversation is to create situations around which problems can be posed and student efforts to respond can be critiqued in a coaching, nurturing way. It is important that the situations be such that students come to realize on their own the need to clarify a particular process or piece of information in order to respond to a given problem posed by an adult. This is done through the development of situations in which students are motivated to solve problems and come to realize the value of, and need for, understanding relevant processes and information. Accomplishing this requires activities that are of high interest to students—a requirement made easier with the use of technology.

The goal is to create an ongoing, powerful learning environment in which students begin to discover thinking through the social process of having adults react to their ideas. It is not a process of adults teaching something, but rather of reacting to students' ideas and students' attempts to construct meaning. By experiencing adults reacting to their ideas in a consistent way, students slowly begin to get a sense of what it means to understand something. Such accumulated social experiences causes the engine of the mind to start to turn over spontaneously. Once an engine starts to turn over, it continues to run as long as it gets gas. Similarly, once the mind starts to spontaneously construct complex networks, it probably is relatively easy to keep that process going—a process which is the very basis of transfer.

CONCLUSION #6: *The ability of students who do not understand "understanding" to benefit from computers is a function of the sophistication of the surrounding conversation.*

Computers, or any other technology, probably have little effect by themselves on the ability of at-risk students to learn. The most powerful and most underused technology in American society is sophisticated conversation between student and adult. Without adequate modeling of understanding through social interaction with adults, students will not develop intellectually. This is not a criticism of the use of technology. Indeed, technology represents a creative and powerful environment around which to organize the needed forms of conversation.

Unfortunately, most of the training and curricular design currently involving computers is focused on the use of the technology as opposed to the design and implementation of sophisticated conversation. Conversation is not viewed as a "technology issue." Yet, conversation is what determines whether technology will have effects until students acquire the ability to construct meaning on their own.

Conversation is developed in HOTS through a combination of detailed curriculum and a carefully specified system of Socratic probing. Conversations between teachers and students were studied over a 5-year period to determine the types of situations in which teachers reduce the degree of difficulty and ambiguity in interacting with students. These results were used to organize Socratic interaction into specific techniques for the types of conversation situations that were problematic. HOTS teachers then undergo a weeklong training in the use of these techniques.

CONCLUSION #7: *There is no single, universally true, best rule for developing thinking skills. Different approaches work better at different developmental points.*

There is no one approach for developing the thinking skills of at-risk students that works best. Asking: "Should thinking be taught as a process or in content?" is the wrong question. It appears that different approaches are needed at different points in the student's development. There are key developmental points in the schooling process where inability to learn content results from a content knowledge deficit (and supplemental drill and thinking-in-content are needed and appropriate) and others where an inability to learn content is a symptom of the students' not understanding "understanding" (and intense general thinking experiences are needed). The real question is how to sequence the different approaches.

The best guess at this time is that schools which are faced with students who have both knowledge and understanding deficits should first work on developing a knowledge base through at least the second grade. This should then be followed by two years of general thinking activities for part of each day. Thereafter, students should be placed in at least one sophisticated thinking-in-content course. It is hoped that future research will provide more detailed insight into the proper mix of the different approaches.

CONCLUSION #8: *Theory plays a very small, but important, part in creating an effective thinking skills environment. The larger role is played by metaphor and implementation details, which are more important.*

The general conception is that one should use theory and research to develop more effective instructional models. Basic research findings did, indeed, drive some of the key decisions in developing the HOTS program. For example, research suggested that the conversations in the program be organized so that students indirectly engage in the key thinking skills of: (a) metacognition, (b) inference from context, (c) information synthesis, and (d) decontextualization. At the same time, research could only help with about 15% of the curricular and implementation decisions that had to be made. Ultimately, most of the decisions in the design of a complex learning environment must be driven by either intuition, metaphor, or a combination of the two.

In the case of HOTS, we got lucky and picked the metaphor of dinner table conversation on which to model the curriculum. If good parents are able to develop thinking and literacy skills through general table conversation, and if the absence of such interaction about ideas with adults is a major contributor to the learning problems of at-risk students, then it makes sense to develop a learning environment that imitates that social process.

Indeed, it is possible that a general thinking program that is predicted on a different metaphor will have less effect—even if it is based on the same theory. For example, Instrumental Enrichment, the first general thinking environment developed for at-risk students, has many of the same theoretical propositions as HOTS. Yet, that program seems to be based more on the metaphor that if the container that is the brain is missing some specific perceptual skills, they should be put into the container. With this metaphor the program doesn't seem to provide general linking skills for most at-risk students. At the same time, I suspect that Barbara Preisseisen of Research for Better Schools, was correct in speculating that with this metaphor as its base, Instrumental Enrichment will probably be more effective than HOTS for students with specific perceptual problems such as dyslexia.

The use of dinner table conversation as the key metaphor helped us make most of the curricular decisions. For example, the goal of imitating how parents intuitively talk to children suggested that scope and sequencing weren't important. Rather, it was important to talk in a consistent way for a sufficient period of time until students began to imitate the articulation patterns. We hoped that this imitation would impact general cognitive development. This parallels the process of how parents "teach" their children to talk.

Even if one uses the appropriate theory and metaphor, the program will still be ineffective unless the details of training and dissemination are carefully worked out. Maintaining a complex learning environment, that is interesting and challenging to students, over a long period of time on a large-scale, is far more difficult than most people realize. It is easy to disseminate ideas and training. It is much more difficult to disseminate an alternative effective learning environment in a way that maintains quality control.

It is critical that implementation details and strategies not be based on idealized views of schools. There are only so many teachers capable of using sophisticated pedagogical techniques. There are limited minutes in the day. The trick is to push schools and districts to organize themselves so as to focus available resources in the hands of those teachers most likely to produce results, and then allow these teachers to work intensively with small groups of students for the time needed to produce cognitive change. Bob Calfee and Art Costa in Chapter 8 and 9, have suggestions for such organizational structures.

The final sad reality is that existing marketing mechanisms in education are insufficient for distributing intensive types of interventions. As such, the developers of the types of interventions that have the potential to be effective are also probably going to have to disseminate them.

This section has focused on general implications of the success of the HOTS program. Those interested in more specific information about the techniques used in HOTS to meet these challenges, and the background of the techniques should read *HOTS: Using Computers to Develop the Thinking Skills of Students at Risk,* Pogrow (1990c)—a book published by Scholastic which describes the HOTS system.

## WHY RESEARCHERS HAVE CONCLUDED THAT THINKING SHOULD BE DONE IN CONTENT

Of all the above conclusions, the most controversial is probably the Theory of Cognitive Underpinnings (conclusion #4), i.e., that sophisticated general thinking should precede sophisticated thinking-in-content activities. Reviews of the existing literature generally conclude either that: (a) there is no such thing as general thinking skills, and/or (b) general thinking skills do not transfer. There is almost unanimous agreement that even if general thinking skills do exist, they must be developed in content. For example, while Perkins and Salomon (1989) are in the minority in concluding that general thinking skills exist, they argue that the skills should be developed in content. Why is the research community so strongly committed to the opposite position from what has been readily apparent from experience with the HOTS project?

There are two main problems with the research base on developing thinking skills. The first is that the literature has focused on totally different types of students. The literature is heavily skewed towards studying the development of higher levels of thinking, as used by experts in their beginners in a field. This research tradition evolved in a time when schooling was designed to provide quality education for the elite and only minimal literacy for the masses. As such, it was important to find ways to develop the expertise of this elite group to provide the knowledge resources to build a modern economy. The classical research concern that emerged was how to convert this well-educated elite into experts. In almost all cases, the novices used in these research studies are college students (i.e., successful, even sophisticated learners.)

At-risk students are not even close to being novices in the classic research sense. Unfortunately, researchers act as though conclusions from the traditional novice-expert research are generalizable to the newer problem of developing thinking skills in students who have few, if any, formal learning skills with the types of symbolic ideas used in school.

Not only has the classic research been conducted with more sophisticated students, it has also been conducted with older students. There is little research focusing on the question of transfer and general thinking skills with at-risk students—particularly long-term studies at the critical grades of 4–7. At these grade levels, learning disparities between at-risk and high-performing students widen dramatically, and present efforts to help the former have little effect on standardized test measures. Alexander and Judy (1988) noted that most studies of problem-solving have been conducted with older students.

While researchers have been busy extrapolating results from older and much more sophisticated learners to the young at-risk student, there have been very few studies of thinking development in the at-risk student. In their review of the literature on the existence of general thinking effects and transfer, Perkins and Salomon (1989) found only enough studies involving the at-risk student to devote only 3 of 83 paragraphs to this population.

The second problem with the current research literature is that the evidence for the priority of thinking-in-content activities is based on indirect evidence. The evidence for in-content problem-solving approaches appears to rest on the apparent inability of individuals with low levels of domain knowledge to transfer. For example, Alexander and Judy (1988) conclude that training in general problem-solving will be of benefit only after students have achieved high levels of domain knowledge because students in their study with low levels of biology knowledge failed to benefit from instruction in a general problem-solving technique.

The fundamental problem with this conclusion is that it is unrealistic to expect the type of simplistic general thinking intervention used in studies such as this to produce transfer. Studies such as this use an intervention of one week to one month in duration. As already discussed, the understanding deficit is so large that it takes 1 to 2 years of daily, well designed activities—far better designed than those used in the typical research project—to produce an effect. In addition, "teaching" general thinking strategies, as is typically done in the research studies, is probably the wrong way to go about developing the skills that the researchers presume they are trying to develop.

The overall result is that the researchers fail to produce effects from overly-simplistic general thinking development tools, and then conclude that the lack of effects from these tools means that thinking should be done in content. It is the equivalent of physicists using an inadequate tool such as a 10 volt cyclotron and concluding that the smallest particle of matter is a speck of dust. There is no reason to expect that the primitive types of general thinking, or any type of simplistic intervention, will produce important cognitive effects in at-risk students. Furthermore, other than Instrumental Enrichment, HOTS is the only case where a carefully designed general thinking environment has been sustained over an extensive period of time. As such, until now, the effects of a general thinking approach for at-risk students have never been properly tested.

As a result, the reality is that there is no direct evidence that thinking-in-content produces effects with at-risk students. Therefore, there is no real basis at present for concluding that thinking skills should be introduced in content for at-risk students.

## SO WHAT? WHO CARES?

The questions of whether general thinking skills precede the development of thinking-in-content skills and whether it is possible to produce transfer are not esoteric. They have major implications for the success of reform efforts to deal with the problems of the at-risk learner.

For example, reformers are presently advocating eliminating tracking across the board and upgrading the curriculum across the board. All these proposals presume that the at-risk student should be immediately placed into an upgraded problem-solving oriented curriculum, i.e., thinking-in-content. If, as previously suggested, at-risk students need to first be placed into sophisticated general thinking activities, these calls for reform by highly prestigious groups will not only fail the at-risk student, they will widen learning gaps.

Another example of the importance and implications of thinking development issues is the resolution from the National Council of Teachers of Mathematics (NCTM) to increase the amount of problem-solving in mathematics at the expense of content coverage. If transfer is possible, however, the call to reduce content coverage is misguided. Indeed, what is striking about mathematics education is how little content is covered. Transfer means that it is possible to develop a form of instruction in which increased problem-solving results in increased learning of content.

The perspective that at-risk students do not understand understanding also refutes another contention of thinking-in-content advocates. Mathematics educators, for example, have generally concluded that the reason that at-risk students have trouble in mathematics problem-solving is that they do not understand the underlying concepts. Therefore, they recommend better approaches to creating understanding about the underlying ideas, a perspective probably shared by other disciplines. Yet, if at risk students, in fact, are unable initially to construct understanding around symbolic ideas, attempts to develop understanding around underlying concepts will also fail.

The goals of the reformers are not undesirable, or even unachievable. It is just that if the goals are pursued in the ways the reformers advocate, they will fail. Alternatively, policy based on the recommendations from the HOTS experience would first place the at-risk student in sophisticated general thinking experiences for part of the day as part of a 3–4 year thinking development plan. Only after students had internalized a sense of understanding would they be put into substantially upgraded content courses (i.e., content courses with a high percentage of complex problem-solving requirements). The ends are the same; the means are different.

Implementation of an approach wherein *all* at-risk students are first placed in general thinking environments has been initiated in ten urban schools/regions during the 1990–91 school year. For example, Washington D.C. will implement HOTS in all the elementary schools feeding into a particular junior high on a pilot basis. Over a two-year period, plans will be made to upgrade areas of the junior high's curriculum to prepare for the arrival of these elementary students with 2 years of HOTS experience. In the urban districts involved, the focus of the phasing-in of thinking-in-content will occur in middle schools. All the first-year at-risk students in a given middle school will be placed into HOTS for a period of 2 years, and then have at least one upgraded content course ready by the second year. Ongoing research will be conducted on the relative effectiveness of these models of reform.

At this point, I suspect that there is no need to upgrade all the content courses that formerly at-risk students are exposed to—even if it was possible to do so, which it isn't. At the same time, research is needed to determine how much thinking-in-content experience is necessary once students have had prior general thinking experience.

Two initiatives from the HOTS project will assist the pilot projects in developing exemplary middle school/junior high school thinking-in-content experiences. The first is a survey of exemplary curricula in different content areas. The second is the development of an innovative 2-year thinking-in-mathematics curricula.[1] (Both initiatives are supported by the Edna McConnell Clark Foundation.)

---

[1]The approach for this mathematics course was designed around the conception of an at-risk student as someone with limited experience in constructing understanding. As a result, instead of teaching students mathematical algorithms, students will be provided with a wide variety of technological tools to help generate a pattern of results which they will analyze to derive the algorithms on their own.

# CONCLUSION

There appear to be identifiable reasons why previous reform efforts have failed to help the at-risk student—even when such efforts have been based on the consensus of what constitutes best practice by reformers and researchers. Such efforts, though guided by good intentions, have been based on incorrect assumptions. The research community is not yet adept at understanding the implications of basic research for practice. In addition, the relationship between research and practice appears to be even more complex than generally realized.

There is a reason why neither the basic skills or thinking skills movements have been able to impact the problem of the at-risk student. Both of these movements have misunderstood the fundamental nature of the learning problem and what the fundamental need is. Pushing the wrong approach to thinking development is no better than pushing remediation or promoting the elimination of pullouts as solutions. The well-intentioned misunderstanding on the part of experts in these movements is satirized in the postscript.) The critical need is for the thinking skills movement to stop focusing (initially) on trying to develop thinking-in-content across the curriculum. It simply cannot be done substantively. Even if it could, such an approach would not help students who do not understand "understanding."

At the same time, this does not mean that any general thinking program will be effective. There are hundreds of possible variations of how to provide general thinking skills, of which probably only a few will be effective. Hopefully, this chapter provides guidance as to some of the key design elements that should be built into thinking skills programs.

The experience with the HOTS program indicates that it is possible to design a class of interventions that can dramatically change the intellectual and academic performance of at-risk students. This can also be done within available funding and organizational capability. Doing so, however, requires us to give up the comfort of conventional wisdoms and basic instincts that have been reinforced by decades of advocacy. The techniques that have evolved in the HOTS program go against all conventional wisdoms—yet they work powerfully. Instead of blaming parents or students when our inadequate and inappropriate school interventions fail, we need to provide the types of sophisticated conversation experiences that are lacking and needed. It can be done.

# REFERENCES

Alexander, P., & Judy, J. (1988). The interaction of domain-specific and strategic knowledge in academic performance. *Review of Educational Research,* Winter.

Perkins, D. N., & Salomon. (1989). Are cognitive skills context-bound? *Educational Researcher,* January-February, 16–25.

Pogrow, S. (1989). Learning dramas-an alternative curricular approach for using Computers with At-Risk Students. *Educational Leadership*, February.

Pogrow, S. (1990a, March). "The Effects of Intellectually Challenging At-Risk Students: The 35 Minute Principle and other Findings from the HOTS Program. *Phi Delta Kappan.*

Pogrow, S. (1990b). *HOTS (Higher Order Thinking Skills): Using computers to develop the thinking skills of students at-risk.* New York: Schoolastic, Inc.

Vygotsky, L. S. (1989). *Mind in society: The development of higher cognitive processes.* In M. Cole, V. John-Steiner, S. Scribner, & E. Souberman (Eds.), Cambridge, MA: Harvard University Press. 1989.

# POSTSCRIPT

## Suppose We Used Modern Pedagogy to Teach Kids to Talk

(Since many techniques in HOTS parallel the instinctive wisdom used by parents to help their children to talk, it is interesting to speculate on the converse, i.e., what if parents used modern pedagogical techniques to teach their children. Here's one possible scenario.)

Johnny reached the 11 month stage and still hadn't said a word. In a total panic the parents call in a diagnostic specialist who concluded that the child was indeed at-risk to be a late talker. The specialist, however, assured the parents that the problem could be solved by hiring several additional specialists, one to help the child practice regular words and another to practice number words (a "number-talk" specialist). When the parents ask why two specialists were needed, they were assured that the National Association for Infant Math Education had concluded that insufficient exposure to number words early on was the most important contributor to later mathphobia.

At the first coordinating meeting, the primary issue discussed was whether to talk to the child while he was in the crib (hereafter referred to as an in-crib model), or whether to take him out first (hereafter referred to as the pullout approach). Since the specialists had recently not had success with the pullout approach, they recommended that an in-crib model be used. Johnny who missed his mother's voice, reacted to all the strangers leaning into his crib and talking to him by constantly crying. The diagnostic specialist 'diagnosed' the crying as an indication that the non-talking was caused by some deep emotional problem and recommended hiring a therapist.

The parents took out a loan to hire a therapist who coordinated his work with that of the talk specialists under the direction of the diagnostic specialist.

Finally, in the thirteenth month, success was achieved and Johnny said his first words. The fact that the first words were spoken at a time when all the specialists were leaning over the crib, without the parents in the room, was taken as an indication of the effect of the specialized help. At the same time, the specialists, particularly the number talker, were puzzled by the significance of the first words that Johnny chose to speak which were: "Get lost!"

Whereupon the specialists raised their fees and submitted a research grant to study how infants decide what words to say first.

# Introduction to Chapter 6

*Arthur N. Applebee, Director, Center for the Learning and Teaching of Literature, University of Albany, State University of New York.*

Fred Newmann's analysis of the level of thoughtfulness in high school classes highlights both the problems and the possibilities in recent attempts to redress the balance in emphasis on specific content versus ways of knowing and doing in the school curriculum. Though he focuses on Social Studies, he rightly poses the issues as one that applies across the curriculum.

Two points that Newmann's study makes are particularly important in the broader context of educational reform. One of the most important is the suggestion that the most successful teachers—those who were best able to structure a classroom environment that prompted thoughtfulness— were able to do so *for students of all ability levels.* This finding parallels results from studies of the teaching of English sponsored by the Literature Center, which also suggest that an emphasis on students' own meaning-making abilities will produce more effective classrooms for all students (see Judith A. Langer, *Literary Understanding and Literature Instruction,* Technical Report No. 2.11, Albany, NY: Center for the Learning and Teaching of Literature, 1990). Such findings are critical if we are to keep the current interest in promoting higher level thinking skills from becoming an elitist and ultimately divisive effort at reform. They help counter a commonsense wisdom that reserves intellectual endeavors for the academically talented, and relegates other students to a skill- and fact-oriented curriculum that is dull for students and teachers. Unfortunately, Newmann also finds this belief that thoughtfulness is the prerogative of the academically talented at work even in the highly select group of schools and classrooms he studied (reflected in an overall correlation between an emphasis on thoughtfulness and the ability level of the class).

The second particularly encouraging finding in Newmann's results is left implicit in his discussion; this is the finding that teachers are in fact successful in aligning what occurs in their classrooms with the goals they set—and they are successful within a variety of organizational frameworks. In other words, teachers do make a significant difference. Such a belief in the professionalism of teachers underlies recent national efforts to reform teacher education, departmental efforts to reform curriculum, and the efforts of the various subject matter organizations to develop new frameworks for teaching and learning within specific disciplines. At the same time, Newmann's findings highlight how difficult reform may turn out to be. A shift in emphasis toward more thoughtful classrooms will require changes in deeply held beliefs about the importance of breadth and coverage, and about the need for a well-developed body of knowledge before meaningful thinking about that content can begin. Left unchallenged, such beliefs will frustrate even the most ambitious efforts at reform, not because teachers are intransigent or incapable, but because they do not accept some of the fundamental principles on which the efforts at reform are based.

# 6 The Prospects for Classroom Thoughtfulness in High School Social Studies

Fred M. Newmann
*University of Wisconsin-Madison*

Can American high schools teach students to think, to use their minds to solve complex problems? Or, are American schools destined to follow the familiar path of passing on numerous fragmented bits of information that students memorize, but soon forget? In spite of persistent injunctions that American schools ought to teach reasoning, problem solving, critical thinking and creative use of the mind, many studies confirm the conspicuous absence of attention to these goals in classrooms.

Research suggests that the failure to emphasize higher order thinking may be due to several obstacles: difficulties in defining higher order thinking and in evaluating student performance; class size and teaching schedules that prevent teachers from responding in detail to students' work; curriculum guidelines and testing programs that require coverage of vast amounts of material; students' apparent preferences for highly structured work with clear, "correct" answers; and, teachers' conceptions of knowledge that emphasize the acquisition of information more than interpretation, analysis and evaluation.

Such problems lead to two central questions that we have pursued through a long-term study: To what extent is it possible for American high school social studies departments to promote higher order thinking? and, How are the apparent barriers overcome in the more successful departments? This chapter summarizes findings on these questions through three steps. First, we present a framework for observing classroom thoughtfulness as a tool for assessing the extent to which higher order thinking is promoted across diverse social studies classes. Next, we describe the extent to which levels of classroom thoughtfulness are associated with student background characteristics, differences between schools and differences between teachers. Finally, we summarize qualities that distinguish between the most and least successful teachers and departments in promoting classroom thoughtfulness. We conclude with a review of findings that suggests both optimistic prospects and substantial challenges to the promotion of classroom thoughtfulness in high school social studies.

## A FRAMEWORK FOR THE ASSESSMENT OF CLASSROOM THOUGHTFULNESS

Based on a review of philosophical, psychological, and educational literature, we have defined higher order thinking as *the interpretation, analysis, or manipulation of information to answer a question that cannot be resolved through the routine application of previously learned knowledge* (Newmann, 1988). According to this definition, higher order thinking occurs whenever students respond to nonroutine intellectual challenges. However, the mere posing of higher order challenges offers no assurance that students will meet the challenges successfully. A useful pedagogical conception of thinking should identify the kinds of *resources* that students need to resolve higher order problems competently and what teachers can do to help students develop the resources. Consistent with other literature, we have explained elsewhere the need for three types of resources: in-depth knowledge, intellectual skills, and dispositions of thoughtfulness (Newmann, 1990a).

The main points of this perspective seem reasonably well accepted among researchers and informed practitioners (see, for example, Walsh & Paul, 1987). Controversy rages, however, over how to translate these general ideas into curriculum, pedagogy, and assessment. Disagreement occurs on at least two levels. First, how much emphasis should be given to developing each of the three central resources—students' knowledge, skills and dispositions? Second, regardless of one's position on this issue, to what extent must knowledge, skills or dispositions—and pedagogies appropriate for each—be specified in detailed technical categories, as opposed to being conceived in more general, global terms? These issues can be summarized as the problem of priorities among central resources and the problem of level of specificity. We discuss each of these problems and explain how our approach to assessing classroom thoughtfulness tries to resolve them in a way that is likely to advance practice.

### Priorities Among Central Resources

Consider a teacher trying to help students answer the question, "Were the American colonists justified in using violence to secure their independence from England?" To enhance students' success in addressing this problem, how much attention should teachers give to developing students' knowledge, skills, and dispositions? Building on our previous review of literature (Newmann, 1990a), we summarize here key arguments that can be made for each of these as the most critical resource.

*The Knowledge Argument.*   Regardless of what side the student takes, a successful answer to this question demands in-depth knowledge of the circumstances of colonial life under British rule, including colonial grievances, British responses, principled arguments dealing with inalienable rights, taxation without representation, and ethical reasoning related to the destruction of property and the taking of human life. Beyond substantive knowledge about the historical period, students will need analytic knowledge; for example, on elements of a well-reasoned argument, distinctions between empirical and normative issues, and criteria for judging the reliability of evidence. Metacognitive knowledge may also be important, such as having a systematic approach for organizing one's thinking or an awareness of how one's thought processes and perceptions of others in a discussion might lead to error. The behavioral manifestations of some of these points might be labeled skills or dispositions, but they may all be considered knowledge in the sense that they all can be represented as cognitive beliefs. Skills and dispositions may facilitate the application of knowledge, but these points suggest that knowledge itself is the most critical foundation of understanding.[1]

*The Skills Argument.*   Knowledge is undoubtedly important, but for the purposes of the teaching of thinking, skills are critical, because they are the tools that permit knowledge to be used or applied to the solution of new problems. Some skills may be specific to the domain under study, and others more generic. To intelligently address the foregoing problem, for example, one must be able to detect bias in the documents of colonial history and logical fallacies in inferences and arguments over the justification of the American revolution. One must be able to distinguish important from irrelevant information, to anticipate and to respond to arguments in opposition to one's own, and to state one's views clearly and persuasively. Skills themselves may be construed or labeled in a variety of ways, but the main point is to recognize their role as cognitive processes that put knowledge to work in solving problems according to criteria for critical inquiry. In practice, knowledge is usually only transmitted from teacher to student without expecting the student to manipulate the knowledge to solve a higher order challenge. Unless the essential processes of using knowledge, i.e., skills, are stressed as central goals of education, higher order thinking is likely to be neglected and the knowledge transmitted to remain inert. Perhaps for this reason

---

[1]Various points in the argument for the centrality of knowledge have been made by Glaser (1984), McPeck (1981), and Nickerson (1988).

many educational reformers prefer not to advocate the teaching of thinking, but instead the teaching of thinking *skills*.[2]

*The Dispositions Argument.*    Without dispositions of thoughtfulness, neither knowledge nor the tools for applying it are likely to be used intelligently. Those who argue for dispositions suggest several traits: a persistent desire that claims be supported by reasons (and that the reasons themselves be scrutinized); a tendency to be reflective—to take time to think problems through for oneself, rather than acting impulsively or automatically accepting the views of others; a curiosity to explore new questions, and the flexibility to entertain alternative and original solutions to problems. Thoughtfulness thereby involves attitudes, personality or character traits, general values and beliefs or epistemologies about the nature of knowledge (e.g., that rationality is desirable; that knowledge itself is socially constructed, subject to revision and often indeterminate; and that thinking can lead to the understanding and solution of problems.) Knowledge and skills will be important for the mastery of particular challenges, but without dispositions of thoughtfulness, knowledge and skills are likely to be taught and applied mechanistically and nonsensically. Of the three main resources, dispositions have attracted the least attention in professional literature, but a strong argument can be made that dispositions are central in generating both the *will* to think and in developing those artistic, ineffable qualities of judgment that lead knowledge and skills in productive directions.[3]

Our approach to the assessment of classroom thoughtfulness recognizes the legitimacy of each of the three resources, and we believe it is not possible to establish a defensible hierarchy among them. Thus, the observation scheme presented later is an attempt to capture the promotion of thoughtfulness through teachers' efforts to develop knowledge, skills and dispositions, without giving center stage to any one resource.[4] At the same time, we deliberately refrain from trying to assess the precise kinds of knowledge, skills and dispositions being promoted. The reasoning behind this choice relates to our conclusion on the next major issue.

## Level of Specificity

The main issue here is the degree of precision and differentiation that is needed or useful in identifying the kinds of knowledge, skills, and dispositions to guide

---

[2]Various points in the argument for skills as the most central resource have been made by Beyer (1987), de Bono (1983), Herrnstein, Nickerson, De Sanchez, and Swets (1986), Marzano et al. (1988).

[3]Various points in the argument for dispositions as a central resource have been made by Cornbleth (1985), Dewey (1933), and Schrag (1988).

[4]Those who emphasize interaction and interdependence among these resources include Bransford, Sherwood, Vye, and Rieser (1986), Ennis (1987), Greeno (1989), Perkins and Salomon (1989), and Walsh and Paul (1987).

instructional goals and pedagogy. At one end of the continuum is an orientation that seeks ever increasing levels of specificity. At the other end is a perspective that strives for synthesis, integration, and holistic awareness.

Approaches to curriculum, instruction, assessment, and research itself seem to reflect tendencies toward increased specificity. For example, to determine whether students are engaged in higher order thinking about issues of violence in the American revolution, one might identify the particular knowledge they need to understand the Stamp Act controversy, the different intellectual skills they should employ in evaluating destruction of property in that event, and the dispositions that would be required for reflective examination of this controversy. Then, one might develop a curriculum to teach the specific knowledge, skills and dispositions that have been identified as critical for understanding of this specific problem.

This approach seems systematic and reasonable, but it suffers from at least two serious inadequacies. First, by attempting to specify in advance the precise knowledge, skills and dispositions needed to solve particular problems and then teaching these directly, we risk overprogramming students for success. Challenges that initially require original thought to manipulate information thereby become reduced to a series of mechanistic steps leading to solutions. Ironically, if carried to its extreme, this degree of programmed precision could actually reduce demands on the student for higher order thinking.

Second, such an approach escalates the specialization and balkanization of curriculum, teaching and assessment into countless specific tasks and many distinct types of knowledge, skills, and dispositions necessary for success on each. The resulting enormous collection of instructional units may serve as a rich bank of resources, but this level of specialization also makes it ever more difficult to synthesize resources into frameworks for curriculum and assessment that can be used across different instructional settings.[5] Balkanization of curriculum into fragmented lists of knowledge and skills also reinforces recitation and drill which inhibits coherent discourse about the subject of study.

This critique is not intended to suggest that we should always avoid programming students for success in specific tasks, or that we should cease research on the teaching of specific topics. It is offered only to point out problems that have resulted from striving for increasing specificity in curriculum goals and in prescribed teacher behavior.

To minimize these problems, we searched for another model. Our work with history and social studies teachers indicates that calls for specific types of thinking (e.g., critical, inductive, moral) are unlikely to generate widespread consensus for any particular type. Instead, social studies teachers are likely to support a

---

[5]The high degree of specificity that can occur in the naming of thinking skills is illustrated in Marzano et al. (1988) which notes twenty one different core thinking skills, including such items as defining problems, setting goals, observing, ordering, inferring, summarizing, establishing criteria.

plurality of types of thinking, but even these will be grounded primarily in the teaching of their *subjects*. Thus, a broad conception of thinking, adaptable to a variety of content and skill objectives, is more likely to generate serious interest among a diverse population of high school teachers.

Rather than translating thinking into specific knowledge problems, skills, and attitudes for students, we began by asking what observable qualities of classroom discourse would be most likely to help students achieve depth of understanding, intellectual skills, and dispositions of thoughtfulness within the many domains of social studies. Thus, we move from a consideration of the nature of thinking in individual students to the problem of promoting thoughtfulness in classrooms. Assessing general qualities of classroom discourse rather than highly differentiated behavior helps to avoid fragmentation in teaching, which itself can undermine student thinking. A more general, global approach may also hold more promise for transfer, both for students facing new problems and for teachers anticipating new lessons.

A broad conception can strike at the heart of an underlying malady identified by many studies. At best, much classroom activity fails to challenge students to use their minds in *any* valuable ways; at worst, much classroom activity is nonsensical or mindless. The more serious problem therefore, is not the failure to teach some specific aspect of thinking, but the profound absence of thoughtfulness in classrooms. Even programs designed to teach thinking skills can fail to promote thoughtfulness. A general conception of thinking can address this basic issue. Ultimately, of course, teachers must focus on specific activities to develop understanding of subjects, but the point here is to arrive at a general framework through which these can be interpreted as promoting or undermining higher order thinking.

## Indicators of Classroom Thoughtfulness

In devising indicators of classroom thoughtfulness responsive to the points above, we used the following guidelines intended to maximize the utility and generalizability of the research tool:

- The indicators should be able to be observed in the teaching of a variety of subject matter, skills, and dispositions within social studies.
- The indicators should refer to teacher behavior, to student behavior, and to activities involving both teacher and student.
- The indicators should allow for judgments on a continuum from less to more, rather than merely discrete categorical values.
- The indicators should be conceptualized in ways that might later be used to help teachers reflect on their practice.

We rated lessons on 15 possible dimensions of classroom thoughtfulness, summarized in Table 6.1.[6] After examining them from a theoretical point of view and with an awareness of some empirical qualities (distributions and correlations), we chose six as most fundamental.[7] Presumably, all of these 15 dimensions could contribute to thoughtful discourse. To respect the many ways in which thoughtfulness could conceivably be shown, but also to develop a simple scheme that could be used in different classrooms, we created a minimal set of dimensions. Each dimension seemed so essential that one could not imagine judging a lesson "thoughtful" unless the criterion were met. Since we were not able to find analytic or empirical literature that conclusively justified a few key criteria, we put each of many dimensions to the following test: Based on the conception of higher order thinking outlined earlier, could a lesson conceivably score low on this dimension, yet still be considered a highly thoughtful lesson? If the answer was "yes," then the dimension was not considered critical or a minimal criterion. If the answer was "no," the dimension was judged as being minimally necessary, though perhaps not a sufficient, criterion for thoughtfulness.

The six minimal dimensions are described next. Each was used to make an overall rating of observed lessons on a five point scale. That is, the criterion for thoughtfulness indicated by the dimension was judged from 1 = "a very inaccurate" to 5 = "a very accurate" description of this lesson.

*Dimension 1.   There was sustained examination of a few topics rather than superficial coverage of many.*

Mastery of higher order challenges requires in-depth study and sustained concentration on a limited number of topics or questions. Lessons that cover a large number of topics give students only a vague familiarity or awareness and, thereby, reduce the possibilities for building the complex knowledge, skills and dispositions required to understand a topic.

*Dimension 2.   The lesson displayed substantive coherence and continuity.*

Intelligent progress on higher order challenges demands systematic inquiry that builds on relevant and accurate substantive knowledge in the field and that works toward the logical development and integration of ideas. In contrast, lessons that teach material as unrelated fragments of knowledge, without pulling them together, undermine such inquiry.

---

[6]The development of these indicators is described more fully in Newmann (1990a; 1990b). See also Schrag (1987, 1989).

[7]Illustrative reasoning on the selection of the final six is presented in Newmann (1990b).

TABLE 6.1
Nature of Discourse in 287 High School Social Studies Lessons (16 High Schools)

| | | 1 | 2 | 3 | 4 | 5 |
|---|---|---|---|---|---|---|
| *1 FEWTOP | In this class, there was sustained examination of a few topics rather than a superficial coverge of many. | 8 | 17 | 24 | 26 | 24 |
| *2 SUBCOH | In this class, the lesson displayed substantive coherence and continuity. | 8 | 26 | 29 | 26 | 11 |
| *3 TIME | In this class, students were given an appropriate amount of time to think, that is, to prepare responses to questions. | 0 | 1 | 8 | 36 | 54 |
| *4 TCONS | In this class, the teacher carefully considered explanations and reasons for conclusions. | 25 | 37 | 23 | 12 | 4 |
| *5 TCHAL | In this class, the teacher asked challenging questions and/or structured challenging tasks (given the ability level and preparation of the students). | 4 | 19 | 25 | 29 | 23 |
| 6 TSOC | In this class, the teacher pressed individual students to justify or to clarify their assertions in a Socratic manner. | 53 | 32 | 11 | 2 | 3 |
| 7 TORIG | In this class, the teacher tried to get students to generate original and unconventional ideas, explanations, or solutions to problems. | 38 | 37 | 18 | 4 | 3 |
| *8 TMOD | In this classroom, the teacher was a model of thoughtfulness. (Principal indications are: the teacher showed appreciation for students' ideas and appreciation for alternative approaches or answers if | 4 | 24 | 36 | 24 | 11 |

based on sound reasoning; the teacher explained how he (she) thought through a problem, the teacher acknowledged the difficulty of gaining a definitive understanding of the topic.)

| | | 1 | 2 | 3 | 4 | 5 |
|---|---|---|---|---|---|---|
| 9 SCRIT | In this class, students assumed the roles of questioner and critic. | 19 | 25 | 25 | 16 | 15 |
| *10 SEXPL | In this class, students offered explanations and reasons for their conclusions. | 20 | 21 | 25 | 23 | 13 |
| 11 SORIG | In this class, students generated original and unconventional ideas, explanations, hypotheses, or solutions to problems. | 12 | 17 | 49 | 20 | 2 |
| 12 SARTI | In this class, student contributions were articulate, germane to the topic, and connected to prior discussion. | 2 | 16 | 29 | 36 | 16 |
| 13 TALK | What proportion of students were active participants? | | 0-25% 4 | 25-50% 15 | 50-75% 35 | 75-100% 47 |
| 14 DISC | What proportion of time did students spend engaged in thoughtful discourse with each other? | 0% 54 | 1-25% 30 | 25-50% 8 | 50-75% 6 | >75% 2 |
| 15 INVO | What proportion of students showed genuine involvement in the topics discussed? (Cues include raising hands, attentiveness manifested by facial expression and body-language, interruptions motivated by involvement, length of student responses.) | | 25% 19 | 25-50% 28 | 50-75% 26 | >75% 24 |

Classes were rated from 1-5. 1 = "very inaccurate" description of class; 5 = "very accurate." Findings are reported as the percent of lessons receiving each rating.

*These variables are considered minimal requirements for a thoughtful lesson.

*Dimension 3. Students were given an appropriate amount of time to think, that is, to prepare responses to questions.*

Thinking takes time, but often recitation, discussion, and written assignments pressure students to make responses before they have had enough time to reflect. Promoting thoughtfulness, therefore, requires periods of silence where students can ponder the validity of alternative responses, develop more elaborate reasoning, and experience patient reflection.

*Dimension 4. The teacher asked challenging questions and/or structured challenging tasks (given the ability level and preparation of the students).*

By our definition, higher order thinking occurs only when students are faced with questions or tasks that demand analysis, interpretation, or manipulation of information; that is, non-routine mental work. In short, students must be faced with the challenge of how to use prior knowledge to gain new knowledge, rather than the task of merely retrieving prior knowledge.

*Dimension 5. The teacher was a model of thoughtfulness.*

To help students succeed with higher order challenges, teachers themselves must model thoughtful dispositions as they teach. Of course, a thoughtful teacher would demonstrate many of the behaviors described above, but this scale is intended to capture a cluster of dispositions likely to be found in any thoughtful person. Key indicators include showing interest in students' ideas and in alternative approaches to problems; showing how he/she thought through a problem (rather than only the final answer); and, acknowledging the difficulty of gaining a definitive understanding of problematic topics.

*Dimension 6. Students offered explanations and reasons for their conclusions.*

The answers or solutions to higher order challenges are rarely self-evident. Their validity often rests on the quality of explanation or reasons given to support them. Therefore, beyond offering answers, students must also be able to produce explanations and reasons to support their conclusions.

The six dimensions were combined into single scale (CHOT) which served as the indicator of classroom thoughtfulness for an observed lesson. Items on the scale have reasonably high level of internal consistency (Cronbach alpha = .82). Exploratory factor analysis and LISREL modeling also identified these dimensions as a distinct construct of thoughtfulness.[8]

---

[8]Such analyses for a sample of select departments were reported in Newmann (1990b). Preliminary analyses for the entire sample of lessons show similar results.

# STUDY DESIGN AND METHODOLOGY

Between the fall of 1986 and the spring of 1990, the project conducted almost 500 lesson observations, and in-depth interviews with 56 teachers, social studies department chairs and principals in sixteen demographically diverse high schools. The main goal was to discover how some departments may be able to overcome barriers that others have not. Thus, rather than concentrating primarily upon differences between individual teachers, this study explored the problem of institutionalization: what is required for departmental-wide promotion of higher order thinking? The strategy was to identify exemplary social studies departments (i.e., those that make a serious departmental-wide effort to emphasize higher order thinking) and then, by contrasting these departments with others, to draw inferences about barriers and opportunities for success.

Through national searches which involved nominations, phone interviews, and site visits, we identified three different sets of social studies departments: (a) those that place special emphasis on higher order thinking, but that organize instruction according to familiar patterns in the comprehensive high school (henceforth the five "select" departments); (b) those that make no special departmental-wide efforts toward higher order thinking and are also conventionally organized (henceforth the seven "representative" departments); (c) those that involve a departmental emphasis on higher order thinking and, in addition, have made significant changes in the organization of instruction (henceforth the four "restructured" departments). Initial evidence of departmental emphasis on higher order thinking was drawn from statements of the department chair, examination of course syllabi, and classroom observations and staff interviews completed in a 1-day, two-person site visit.

Since we sought an estimate of the highest levels of classroom thoughtfulness, the strategy was to concentrate on those teachers in each department who most emphasized higher order thinking. However, we also wanted evidence that opportunities for thoughtfulness were available to all students, not restricted to the high achievers. The department chair at each school selected three main courses, taught by different teachers, to be observed at least four times over the school year. The three classes were to illustrate as much higher order thinking as possible, but they were also to include (a) a class with a substantial proportion of lower and middle achieving students; (b) a history course with a diverse range of students; and, (c) any other class that best illustrated an emphasis on higher order thinking (which usually comprised high achievers). Our analyses are based on four lesson observations from each of these three classes, plus six other lessons observed in each department drawn from at least two additional teachers.[9] With-

---

[9] Lessons from at least two additional teachers were observed to gain a more representative sampling of teaching within each department. Analyses of departmental differences in lesson thoughtfulness, therefore, incorporated at least five teachers per department. Analyses of teachers relied primarily upon the three teachers per department for whom we had at least four observations and interview data, and whose classes were selected to insure student diversity along comparable criteria across schools.

in scheduling constraints, teachers were encouraged to select for our observation those lessons that placed most emphasis on higher order thinking. In addition to recording ratings on the 5-point dimensions, observers also wrote descriptive notes, especially to elaborate on high-scoring dimensions.[10]

Teachers, departments chairs, and principals completed at least two hours of interviews.[11] These probed their written responses to questionnaires which explored their conceptions of and commitment to higher order thinking as an educational goal, the factors they perceived as necessary to accomplish it, the barriers that stand in the way, and the kind of leadership devoted to it within the school. Students were interviewed and/or surveyed and also tested in the representative and restructured schools, but findings on students will be reported in future reports.

At this writing, data analysis has not been completed. In some cases, therefore, the findings reported below will be based on only some of the schools, lessons, teachers, department chairs, or principals studied.[12]

## LEVELS OF CLASSROOM THOUGHTFULNESS AND DIFFERENCES DUE TO TEACHERS, DEPARTMENTS AND STUDENT BACKGROUND

### Overall Levels

How much thoughtfulness was actually observed across all schools? Table 6.1 presents frequencies on 15 dimensions.[13] Some dimensions occurred very rarely, especially Socratic reasoning (6), teacher encouraging originality (7), and students participating in thoughtful discourse with each other (14). Others showed high frequencies, such as teachers allowing enough time for students to respond (3) and students participating in class (13). Frequencies on the six minimal dimensions of thoughtfulness showed considerable variance, except for time, which was consistently high.

In general, the select and restructured departments showed levels higher than

---

[10]To estimate inter-rater reliability, 87 lessons were observed independently by different pairs of raters drawn from a team of six researchers. Considering the six dimensions in the CHOT scale, each scored from 1 to 5, the two observers agreed precisely in 64% of the ratings, they differed by one point or less on 96% of the ratings, and the overall average correlation between two raters was .76.

[11]Principals in the representative schools were interviewed for 1 hour.

[12]Later reports of this study (e.g., Newmann, forthcoming) will include specific findings related to the relationship of classroom thoughtfulness to student engagement, to student achievement, and barriers to the promotion of classroom thoughtfulness.

[13]To facilitate comparability among schools we included here and in subsequent analyses 18 lesson observations per department, comprised of 4 lessons from each of three teachers identified as most likely to promote higher order thinking, plus six other lessons from at least two other teachers in the department.

the representative departments, as indicated in Fig. 6.1 and Table 6.2 (school names are fictitious) which are discussed in more detail later. We expected the five select departments and four restructured departments to score higher, because they were included in the study on the basis of their apparent commitment to promoting higher order thinking for all students. However, site visits during the selection process, did not allow enough classroom observations to determine actual levels of thoughtfulness on the specific dimensions in our framework. It was important to learn, therefore, not only whether these departments surpassed representative ones, but also to get an estimate of the highest levels that exemplary departments achieve. Since the mean of the four highest scoring departments is below 4, we concluded that, even among the most successful departments there was considerable room for improvement.

## Teachers Differences

Up to this point, we have described overall levels of thoughtfulness among lessons, but have not asked about the extent to which differences between lessons can be attributed to differences between teachers (whose levels of thoughtfulness may be relatively consistent across lessons) or to differences within teachers

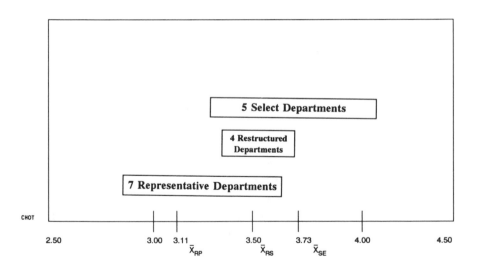

$\bar{X}_{RP}$ = mean of 7 representative departments

$\bar{X}_{RS}$ = mean of 4 restructured departments

$\bar{X}_{SE}$ = mean of 5 select departments

FIG. 6.1.  Distribution of departmental means on classroom thoughtfulness (CHOT = 1-5).

TABLE 6.2
Departmental Means and Standard Deviations on Classroom Thoughtfulness According to
Sample Set

| | Mean | St. Dev. | Departmental Rankings | |
|---|---|---|---|---|
| **Select Departments (N = 90 lessons):** | | | | |
| Grandville | 4.05 | (.57) | Grandville | 4.05 |
| Carlsberg | 4.04 | (.47) | Carlsberg | 4.04 |
| Arnold | 3.85 | (.65) | Arnold | 3.85 |
| Bradley | 3.48 | (.75) | Williams | 3.72 |
| Scarborough | 3.22 | (.56) | Vander Meer | 3.63 |
| All select depts. | 3.73 | (.33) | Carter | 3.56 |
| All lessons | 3.73 | (.68) | Bradley | 3.48 |
| | | | Nelson | 3.36 |
| **Representative Departments ( N = 125 lessons):** | | | Newcombe | 3.35 |
| | | | Shaw | 3.35 |
| Vander Meer | 3.63 | (.84) | Scarborough | 3.22 |
| Newcombe | 3.35 | (.84) | Mathewson | 3.13 |
| Mathewson | 3.13 | (.96) | Pierce | 2.94 |
| Pierce | 2.94 | (.83) | Wadsworth | 2.93 |
| Wasdworth | 2.93 | (.98) | Downing | 2.92 |
| Downing | 2.92 | (.41) | Erskine | 2.88 |
| Erskine | 2.88 | (.88) | | |
| All representative departments | 3.11 | (.26) | | |
| All lessons | 3.11 | (.86) | | |
| **Restructured Departments (N = 72 lessons):** | | | | |
| Williams | 3.72 | (.68) | | |
| Carter | 3.56 | (.51) | | |
| Nelson | 3.36 | (.90) | | |
| Shaw | 3.35 | (.78) | | |
| All restructured departments | 3.50 | (.15) | | |
| All lessons | 3.50 | (.73) | | |
| Total among depts. | 3.40 | (.38) | | |
| Total among lessons | 3.40 | (.82) | | |

(whose lessons for a given class may vary considerably in thoughtfulness). It is conceivable that levels of thoughtfulness in lessons may be distributed randomly among teachers, each of whose lessons vary greatly in thoughtfulness over a school year. We explore this issue first by summarizing the means and standard deviations of the 48 teachers who were designated as the three within each department most likely to promote higher order thinking in the types of classes we chose to observe.

As shown in Table 6.3, teachers vary from a high mean of 4.63 to a low of 2.21, and several teachers are represented at different points in the distribution. Regression analysis indicated that differences between teachers accounted for 51% of the total variance among lessons. About 30% of the total variance was

TABLE 6.3
Teacher Means and Standard Deviations on Classroom Thoughtfulness (CHOT)*
(N = 48)

| Mean Range | # Teachers | Std. Dev. Range | # Teachers |
|---|---|---|---|
| 2.75 - 3.00 | 12 | .00 - .10 | 2 |
| 3.01 - 3.25 | 4 | .11 - .20 | 1 |
| 3.26 - 3.50 | 6 | .21 - .30 | 9 |
| 3.51 - 3.75 | 7 | .31 - .40 | 6 |
| 3.76 - 4.00 | 7 | .41 - .50 | 7 |
| 4.01 - 4.25 | 5 | .51 - .60 | 9 |
| 4.26 - 4.50 | 4 | .61 - .70 | 6 |
| 4.51 ➞ | 3 | .71 - .80 | 3 |
|  |  | .81 - .90 | 3 |
|  |  | .91 ➞ | 2 |
| minimum    2.21 |  | .00 |  |
| maximum    4.63 |  | .98 |  |
| grand mean  3.53 |  | .49 |  |

*Means and standard deviations are based on four observations per teacher, CHOT scale ranges from 1-5.

due to differences between teachers within a school, and 20% was due to differences between schools. The remaining variance in lesson thoughtfulness (49%) might be attributed to variance within teachers, plus other factors.[14]

How consistent are teachers in classroom thoughtfulness across several lessons within a class? The standard deviations for each teacher across lessons can be considered a measure of teacher consistency—the lower the standard deviation, the greater the number of lessons scoring close to the teacher's mean. As shown in Table 6.3 the teachers vary in lesson consistency from a standard deviation of .00 to one of .98, but only 16% are higher than .7, more than half are .5 or below, and the average standard deviation is .49 which indicates that ratings on lesson thoughtfulness tend to fall within half a point (+ or −) of the teacher's mean rating on the 5-point scale.

To obtain another estimate of teachers' consistency across lessons, we computed Cronbach's alpha, a measure of internal consistency which can be constructed as an indicator of the extent to which the several lessons of each teacher measure something in common, rather than either distinct or random phenomena. This statistic varies from 0 to +1, and will increase with the number of

[14]To estimate the amount of lesson variance associated with differences between teachers, CHOT for each lesson was regressed on teacher entered as a dummy variable (adjusted r square = .51). To estimate lesson variance associated with differences between teachers due to their membership in different schools, CHOT was regressed on the mean CHOT for each school (adjusted r square = .21). It follows that about 30% of the variance is due to teacher differences within schools. The design of the study did not permit regressions that would estimate the extent to which school differences in lesson thoughtfulness are due to schools' policies for attracting particular types of teachers versus distinctive aspects of school climate and leadership that affect the quality of teaching.

items in the scale (which in this case are lesson observations). Using samples of teachers from different types of schools, with different numbers of lesson observations, we found that the Cronbach alpha ranged from .70 to .92.

We conclude that teachers vary considerably from one another in the levels of classroom thoughtfulness they promote, and that most teachers are rather consistent in the extent to which they promote thoughtfulness across several lessons within a class. The research did not assess the consistency of individual teachers in teaching different types of classes such as Advanced Placement, "regular" or "basic" tracks, but we see later that higher ability classes generally showed higher levels of thoughtfulness.

## Departmental Differences

Even with considerable variation among teachers, is it possible that some social studies departments have more thoughtful lessons than others? If so, analysis of the properties of the more successful departments might lead to strategies to enhance thoughtfulness. For example, if major departmental differences were found to exist in classroom thoughtfulness, then further analysis would be necessary to learn whether higher scoring departments reflect common approaches to organizational structure, programs, culture and leadership that distinguish them from less successful ones. On the other hand, if only minuscule amounts of the variation in lesson thoughtfulness can be attributed to differences between departments, organizational analysis would be less useful.

As shown in Table 6.2, departmental means range from 2.88 to 4.05. The difference between the means of departments in the highest quartile (3.92) and lowest quartile (2.92) is 2.6 times the overall departmental standard deviation (.38) or 1.2 times the overall standard deviation among lessons (.86). Departmental standard deviations (which reflect the degree of consistency in lesson thoughtfulness within departments) also vary. As indicated in Fig. 6.1, there is overlap between the three groups of select, representative, and restructured departments, but the means of these groups differ considerably. The difference between the select and representative departments is more than twice the representative departments' standard deviation; the restructured–representative difference is 1.5 times the representative standard deviation; and the difference between the select and restructured departments is more than 1.5 times the standard deviation within restructured departments.

In relative terms, these represent large differences between departments and between sets of departments in the promotion of classroom thoughtfulness. Regression analysis indicates that these differences account for about 21% of the total variance in thoughtfulness among lessons (Table 6.4, model 1).[15] The

---

[15]To estimate the impact of departmental differences, we initially regressed CHOT on each department entered as a dummy variable. Using the department's mean level of thoughtfulness as the independent variable in the regression produces the same results and is more convenient to report.

TABLE 6.4
Regression of Lesson Classroom Thoughtfulness of Departmental Mean Thoughtfulness and on Lesson Background Characteristics
(N = 287 Lessons)[1]

| | Mean | Std. Dev. | Model 1 | | Model 2 | | Model 3 | |
|---|---|---|---|---|---|---|---|---|
| | | | B | Beta | B | Beta | B | Beta |
| Departmental Thoughtfulness (DCHOT) | 3.40 | .38 | 1.00 (.11) | .46** | | | 1.03 (.12) | .48 |
| Required Courses (REQ) | .74 | .44 | | | -.02 (.11) | .00 | -.25 (.10) | -.13* |
| Class Grade Level (CGRADE) | 10.11 | 1.37 | | | .07 (.03) | .11* | .02 (.03) | .03 |
| Class Ability Level (CABIL) | 2.09 | .58 | | | .32 (.09) | .22** | .34 (.08) | .24** |
| Percent African American | 19.36 | 25.25 | | | .00 (.00) | -.08 | .00 (.00) | .01 |
| Percent Variance Explained (adjusted R²) | | | | .21 | | .07 | | .28 |

[1]The dependent variable of classroom thoughtfulness (CHOT) has a mean of 3.40 and standard deviation of .82.

DCHOT = departmental mean of 18 lessons on classroom thoughtfulness (CHOT = 1-5).

REQ = course required = 1, not required = 0.

CGRADEAV = mean grade level of students in the class, based on teacher report of percent of student at each level, grades 9 - 12.

CABIL = mean ability of students in the class, based on teacher report of percent of students in the lowest (1), middle (2) and highest (3) thirds of school achievement, 1 - 3.

CAFAM = % of students in the class who are African American, based on teacher report.

B = metric regression coefficient.

( ) = standard error.

Beta = standard regression coefficients.

*p < .05.
**p < .001.

actual significance of departmental differences on lesson thoughtfulness, however, may depend in part on the influence of background features of each class.

## Student Background Features of the Class

Would teachers assume that older students are more capable of higher order thinking, and therefore, emphasize higher order thinking more frequently in 12th grade than 9th grade classes? Would classes with a preponderance of high achieving students offer consistently higher levels of thoughtfulness than classes with large proportions of low achievers? Would the proportion of African-American students in a class tend to decrease the level of thoughtfulness? Are elective courses more likely to promote thoughtfulness than required courses? We examined these issues by regressing CHOT on the relevant variables.

For each lesson, teachers indicated the percentage of students enrolled in the 9th, 10th, 11th, and 12th grades; the percentage of students whose grade point average placed them in the lowest, middle, and highest one-third of the school achievement distribution; the percent of African-American students; and whether the class was required or elective. Means and standard deviations of these variables are given in Table 6.4.

Results of the regression in Table 6.4 (model 2) show that when these background factors are simultaneously controlled, the ability level of the class (and only this variable) has a sizeable association with lesson thoughtfulness. If a casual relationship were to be inferred, the hypothesis of teacher expectations would make sense: teachers perceive higher ability groups as more capable of participating in thoughtful discourse, and therefore they offer such groups more opportunities. This finding was expected, and is further evidence that classes with higher percentages of low-achieving students are deprived of educational opportunities. On the other hand, the variance in lesson thoughtfulness explained by background features is low, only 7%, which supports the more hopeful prospect that other variables (perhaps unmeasured) have far more impact than student background.[16]

---

[16]Regressions within each of the groups of select, representative, and restructured departments did not show results uniformly consistent with the analysis of all lessons pooled. For example, for model 2, in neither the select or restructured schools was ability level of class significantly associated with lesson thoughtfulness, but other background features were. In the select schools a negative association was found with percent African American students and in the restructured schools there was a negative association with required courses. When the regression model controlled for departmental differences in classroom thoughtfulness within each group (model 3), however, these findings changed. Since the number of schools within each group is so small, we consider it more meaningful to direct most of our attention to the overall findings.

## The Relative Influence of School and Background Features

Having seen that levels of classroom thoughtfulness vary according to both the department (school) and to the ability of the class, we must ask how they function independently of one another. If we hold class ability level stable, for example, what impact do departmental differences have on the level of classroom thoughtfulness? If some departments perform consistently better than others at all grade levels, ability levels and percentage of minority students, we would certainly want to learn more about those schools. Model 3 in Table 6.4 gives the results. When department is held constant, classroom thoughtfulness increases with the ability level of the class and decreases somewhat in required courses. The good news is that neither race nor age of the students seems to determine levels of thoughtfulness, and that the department has twice the impact of the most important background feature. The strong impact of the department in relation to background features offers hope, because, in contrast to background characteristics of students (age, race, prior school achievement), features of departments can conceivably be changed for the better.

We examined model 3 also within each of the groups of select, representative and restructured departments. In the select group, departmental differences had by far the most powerful effects, and background variables had no effect. The variance in classroom thoughtfulness explained by the full model was also highest in the select group (24%), compared to 21% for representative schools and 15% for restructured schools. In both the representative and restructured samples, among all the variables in the model (including departmental differences), ability level of the class had the largest association with classroom thoughtfulness.

Because of the small number of schools in each group, we must be cautious about generalizing from differences in the regression models between the groups. At the same time, we should be alert to a potentially major implication of these findings; namely, that the select departments were most successful not only in promoting classroom thoughtfulness, but also in delivering it most equitably to classes of students with different background characteristics! In considering qualities critical to success in the promotion of thoughtfulness in the pooled sample of 287 lessons, we should, therefore, be mindful of other ways in which the select departments might distinguish themselves.

## QUALITIES CRITICAL TO SUCCESS

Differences in thought and practice between the most and least successful teachers and departments can suggest possible factors that need to be changed to increase classroom thoughtfulness. First, we compare aspects in the thinking of individual teachers, and then we compare the kinds of leadership and institutional contexts that appear to promote thoughtfulness.

## Teachers' Thinking

In the sample of select social studies departments, Onosko (1989) studied differences in the thinking of teachers whose lessons scored in the highest one-third versus lowest one-third classroom thoughtfulness. While the sample was small—five teachers in each group—interesting differences emerged in teachers' instructional goals, their thoughts on the problem of depth versus breadth of content coverage, and their conceptions of thinking.

In contrast to lower scorers, high scorers were more likely to identify student thinking as their highest priority goal, and they found the development of students' thinking more interesting than exposing students to subject matter content. When asked what gave them satisfaction as a teacher, they tended (more than lower scorers) to identify student behaviors closely associated with thinking (e.g., "seeing students start to make connections," "students wrestling with values and making links," "teaching students to generalize from data"). High scorers' open-ended goal statements were lengthier and more detailed, with a more impassioned focus on thinking.

On the issue of depth versus breadth of content coverage, both groups felt persisting conflict. Higher scorers attributed the pressure to external sources such as state tests and curriculum guidelines, whereas lower scorers said the main pressure came from within themselves. Lower scorers, which included four who had taught Advanced Placement United States history courses, felt that broad coverage helped to promote students' thinking, but high scorers believed that breadth of coverage inhibited thinking. Lisa, a lower scorer, explained:

> If I had to make a choice I would choose coverage because it is perhaps their only experience and probably a concluding experience with history. I really feel an obligation to at least expose them to some of the pressing issues of our time. Not to get to the 1950s and 1960s, the Cold War. . . is unconscionable.

Harold, a high scorer, feels too much coverage pressure from the state curriculum guidelines and test:

> I do not preoccupy myself with finishing the curriculum. Instead, I attempt to teach whatever I teach well and select classroom topics and materials very carefully. . . I don't emphasize content coverage. It's ludicrous to attempt to cover 100 years of history in a month or two. I focus on concepts or ideas.

We asked teachers two questions to explore their conceptions of thinking: Do you have a conception of thinking that guides your teaching (If so summarize its main aspects)? Consider your best thinkers, what distinguishes them from other students? In contrast to lower scorers, high scorers placed more emphasis on dispositions and skills. Hugh illustrates the importance of dispositions:

> A good thinker isn't afraid if someone challenges a position. . . is willing to take a look at someone else's hypothesis or theory even if it's 180 degrees apart from his own. . . .I'd like kids to always be questioning, to always be probing. You should always be on edge, never comfortable, no matter how well you've digested the material.

The main skills mentioned by high scorers dealt with understanding, analyzing, manipulating and generalizing from data; understanding the relevance of data to a central theme, formulating hypotheses and conclusions; and relating learning to one's own life experience or to current affairs.

Higher scorers had more to say about the nature of thinking. They included points of clarification and subtle distinctions between their own views and possible alternative conceptions. For example, Hans challenged the notion that Bloom's cognitive skills should be viewed hierarchically, Hilary argued that students' intellectual curiosity should not be equated with inherent cognitive capacity, and Hanson asserted that the development of students' thinking should not be divorced from the development of students values. Elaboration of this sort was missing in the brief statements of lower scorers.

Whether the differences we found in teachers' thought between higher and lower scorers in select departments are sustained in forthcoming analysis of teachers in the representative and restructured schools remains to be seen. And even if differences in teachers' thought are associated with differences in practice (i.e., in their levels of classroom thoughtfulness), this alone does not establish a causal link from thought to practice. Nevertheless, these findings are consistent with previous research which highlights a connection between teachers' thought and practice, and they suggest that it may be useful to help teachers reflect more systematically on their goals, conceptions of thinking, and management of the dilemma of depth versus coverage. Other strategies for helping individual teachers to promote higher order thinking are summarized in Newmann, Onosko, and Stevenson (1990).

## Leadership

A main purpose of our study was to understand the extent and determinants of differences at the school or departmental level. Having found that departments do in fact differ in the levels of classroom thoughtfulness they promote (Tables 6.2 and 6.4), we asked about the extent to which differences in school leadership and organizational structure might account for differences in classroom thoughtfulness. The most successful schools were defined as those scoring more than one standard deviation (.38) above the mean level of classroom thoughtfulness for all schools (3.40). From Table 6.2, these include three select schools: Grandville, Carlsberg, and Arnold. The least successful were those scoring more than one standard deviation below the mean, which involves four representative schools: Erskine, Downing, Wadsworth, and Pierce.

Based on observations and staff interviews regarding the nature of departmental and principal leadership, we found differences between the top scoring and bottom scoring schools related to goals, curriculum, pedagogy, and school culture.[17] In the top schools, department chairs, with support from principals, worked to develop a focus within the social studies department on the goal of promoting students' thinking. The three top schools varied considerably in their approach to higher order thinking, but in contrast to the bottom schools—all of whom lacked a coherent departmental focus on thinking—social studies departments in the top schools each aimed toward a common vision for promoting students' thinking. Grandville used a modified version of Bloom's taxonomy to structure generalizations, concepts and themes in all courses. Carlsberg adopted a common procedure for each lesson: first posing an evaluative question at the beginning that required students to take a stand and to offer supporting evidence and second, structuring teacher-centered discussion to answer the question. Arnold presented students with a central question or issue that framed each unit and asked them to create metaphors, analogies, and other sources of evidence and insight to achieve understanding.

The common goals were reinforced and implemented by the department heads' active participation in curriculum development with colleagues in the department who worked in teams who teach the same course. The top departments varied in resources allocated for curriculum development, but all three schools worked on curriculum during the school year and/or summers. The main objective was not simply to update course content, but to do so in ways that would operationalize the department's approach to developing students' thinking. At two of the top schools, principals provided special support for curriculum development. In contrast, low scoring schools participated in curriculum development, but it tended not to be focused on a common departmental vision of thinking.

Department heads made special efforts in the top three schools to comment in considerable detail on their colleagues' teaching, and to support peer observation and discussion of specific pedagogy that promotes thinking. At Carlsberg, the department head taught demonstration lessons with colleagues observing and offering constructive critique afterwards. Department meetings there have been used to view videotapes of colleagues' teaching and to jointly plan lessons. The principal at Carlsberg also took an active role in detailed observation and clinical

---

[17]The analysis of leadership is based on McCarthy and Schrag (1990) and King (1990).

supervision of teaching. In the lower scoring schools, department heads' and principals' attention to pedagogy involved only perfunctory required visits for purposes of organizational evaluation.

The efforts of department heads and principals in the high scoring schools to shape goals, curriculum and pedagogy toward an emphasis on thinking seems to have nurtured the kind of collegial faculty culture in these schools that has been found in other research to contribute to school effectiveness (e.g., Bryk, Lee, & Smith, 1990; Rosenholtz,1989). These schools show how leadership can build such a culture by helping teachers to develop and to keep their sights on a common instructional mission, by directing technical assistance both from within and outside the system on this goal, and by providing material and emotional support for teachers to help one another approach the work critically.

## Organizational Features

Some teachers may be committed to the promotion of higher order thinking, but find too many obstacles in the existing organizational structure of high schools. Discussions on the restructuring of education suggest that major organizational changes may be needed to assist teachers in the promotion of higher order thinking; for example, increased opportunities for team planning among teachers to generate curriculum oriented toward thinking; smaller classes and student load to allow for teachers to respond more thoughtfully to students' work; and, changes in the scheduling of instruction to allow for more sustained inquiry than is possible in short class periods. How important are structural features such as these?

To investigate the importance of organizational features, we examined four social studies departments that we perceived in the selection process as indicating a sincere emphasis on higher order thinking but also operated in schools with organizationally innovative structures along the lines just mentioned. Each of the four used extensive team planning, and in three of the schools this occurred across different subjects. Three of the four included classes well below 25 students, and three of the four included scheduling changes that permitted more flexibility in the conduct of instruction.

The previous discussion of leadership and earlier information in Table 6.2 shows that although the restructured departments scored above the representative departments and above overall mean, none of the restructured departments scored highly enough on classroom thoughtfulness to be included in the top group. Furthermore, the highest scoring schools did not differ substantially in structural features from the lowest scoring ones, except that in two of the three highest scoring schools, the department chair taught only one class per semester—a structural feature that allowed considerable time to exercise program leadership. How might we explain the finding that innovative structural features do not seem critical to achieving high levels of classroom thoughtfulness?

In examining the influence of organizational features on higher order thinking, Ladwig (1990) distinguishes between organizational structures and organizational programs. Structures include the amount of time available to teachers for planning and sharing ideas with colleagues; the amount of time that teachers and students work together in classes and the degree of flexibility in how the time is spent; the number of students in a class and the total number taught by teachers; the degree of authority teachers have individually and collectively to make important decisions about curriculum and teaching. Organizational programs could include departmentally coordinated curriculum design and revision; staff development activities using both outside authorities and collegial expertise to develop common goals and curriculum; an organized program of peer observation and critique of individual teaching.

Organizational structures and programs are logically independent of one another. For example, having innovative structures does not necessarily entail having any particular instructional program. One would expect the highest levels of classroom thoughtfulness to occur in schools which combined a strong programmatic focus on higher order thinking with the innovative organizational structures that seem to facilitate it. The restructured schools we studied, however, did not manifest strong organizational programs aimed at promoting higher order thinking. These departments expressed a clear interest in the goal and worked to implement it in several classes. In this sense they distinguished themselves from, and scored higher than, the representative schools. On the other hand, their programmatic efforts for higher order thinking were not as focused and as comprehensive as the highest scoring three departments located in conventionally organized schools.

The select high scoring departments in conventional schools had focused programmatic agendas for higher order thinking. In contrast, staff in the restructured schools were concurrently engaged in several programmatic activities which usually encompassed a number of educational goals beyond the promotion of higher order thinking. These efforts included individualizing and personalizing school experiences for students, empowering faculty to develop curriculum and school policy, reducing negative consequences of tracking and ability grouping, creating interdisciplinary curriculum, building special experiences for students at risk, and developing new methods of assessment. It is possible that having to deal with such a variety of issues tended to dilute the programmatic concentration that might otherwise have been channeled to the promotion of higher order thinking.

Within the group of restructured schools it is interesting to note that the two highest scoring departments are part of efforts to restructure the entire school, the next is a restructured program within a traditionally structured school, and in the lowest scoring of these departments, restructuring occurs primarily within individual courses. The sample is too small to allow generalization about the process of restructuring in a larger more diverse set of schools, but this finding suggests that school-wide efforts to restructure may offer more potential for reinforcing organizational programs for higher order thinking than restructuring aimed only at parts of the school (i.e., at individual courses or "schools within schools"). School-wide initiatives could offer more of the support that teachers need from administrators and colleagues to emphasize student thinking, and depth of understanding, rather than absorption of knowledge fragments, and coverage information.

The relative position of restructured schools (in Fig. 6.1 and Table 6.2) illustrates several points: (a) Innovative structural features alone offer no advantages. Strong program design may be more important. (b) Conventional school structures do not preclude reasonably high levels of classroom thoughtfulness. (c) It is possible that schools that combine significant restructuring with a strong programmatic emphasis on higher order thinking will achieve levels of classroom thoughtfulness higher than we have yet been able to observe.

## CONCLUSION: PROSPECTS FOR THE FUTURE

Previous research has documented the general absence of high level cognitive work in American high schools (e.g., Goodlad, 1984). To learn more about prospects for improvement, this project searched for and studied social studies departments which seemed most committed to, and successful in, promoting higher order thinking. We found such departments in both conventionally structured and "restructured" schools, and we compared them with departments in representative schools which claimed no major departmental emphasis on higher order thinking. All departments were encouraged to show us their best, for we asked to observe and to interview only those teachers most likely to promote student thinking.

To assess teachers' and departmental success in promoting higher order thinking, we developed a set of observable dimensions of classroom thoughtfulness, and rated almost 300 lessons in 16 high schools. The results indicated tremendous variation between lessons, teachers and departments. Some teachers showed consistently high levels of thoughtfulness, but even in the most successful departments, the mean level barely reached 4 on a 5-point scale, and we rarely observed teachers engaging in Socratic discussion, encouraging students to generate original ideas, or arranging for students to talk thoughtfully with one another. These results indicate that some teachers and departments do promote higher order thinking, but there is much room for improvement, even for those apparently committed to the goal.

What seems to contribute to the level of classroom thoughtfulness in a lesson?

As might be expected, classroom thoughtfulness is associated with consistencies within, and differences between, teachers. Teachers who succeed seem to have conceptualized the nature of thinking more carefully; they emphasize it more in their goal statements—where they give attention to skills and dispositions as well as to knowledge; and they prefer depth over coverage in their approach to knowledge. Classroom thoughtfulness also depends on the school or department in which the teachers work. The most successful departments evidence strong leadership which helps to develop and sustain a focused departmental vision, with collegial support for curriculum development and pedagogical critique aimed at higher order thinking.

The most successful departments in this study functioned within conventional school structures, and their structural conditions did not differ substantially from the least successful departments. At the same time, restructured departments chosen for their emphasis on higher order thinking were more successful than a set of conventionally structured schools which espoused no similar departmental commitment. This led to our conclusion that the strength of organizational program is a more powerful determinant of lesson thoughtfulness than innovative organizational structure, but that the highest levels of thoughtfulness may be achieved when strong programs are combined with innovative structures.

Concerned that opportunities for higher order thinking might be restricted to high-achieving students, older students, and White students, the study investigated the association between these student background characteristics and levels of classroom thoughtfulness. When the characteristics were considered together, achievement level of the class had a significant association with classroom thoughtfulness, but its association accounted for only a small portion of the variance in thoughtfulness and the impact of the school was twice as large. Within the select group of departments, student background characteristics had no relationship to classroom thoughtfulness. These findings demonstrate that teachers and departments have been successful in promoting higher order thinking in classes composed of lower-achieving, younger, and minority students. Though some teachers believe it is easier to promote thinking among older and higher-achieving students, the findings indicate that levels of classroom thoughtfulness need not be determined by student background.

Having found that some teachers and departments do succeed in promoting thoughtfulness with all types of classes, and having identified some dimensions of success in teacher thinking, departmental leadership and program emphasis, we have grounds for optimism about prospects for the future. At the same time, the data indicate that even when given the opportunity to show their best efforts in the promotion of thinking, the level of classroom thoughtfulness remains low for many teachers and departments. The challenge posed by this research is how to help these teachers and departments develop the characteristics of their more successful counterparts.

## ACKNOWLEDGMENTS

This paper was prepared at the National Center on Effective Secondary Schools, supported by the U.S. Department of Education, Office of Educational Research and Improvement (Grant No. G-008690007-89) and by the Wisconsin Center for Education Research, School of Education, University of Wisconsin-Madison. The opinions expressed in this publication are those of the author and do not necessarily reflect the views of the supporting agencies. Major contributions to this work have been made by Dae-Dong Hahn, Bruce King, James Ladwig, Cameron McCarthy, Joe Onosko, Francis Schrag, Robert Stevenson, and the cooperative staff and students in sixteen high schools.

## REFERENCES

Beyer, B. (1987). *Practical strategies for the teaching of thinking.* Boston: Allyn & Bacon.

Bransford, J., Sherwood, R., Vye, N., & Rieser, J. (1986). Teaching thinking and problem solving. *American Psychologist, 41*(10), 1078–1089.

Bryk, A. S., Lee, V. E., & Smith, J.B. (1990). High school organization and its effects on teachers and students: An interpretive summary of the research. In W. Clune & J. Witte (Eds.)., *Choice and control in American education* (Vol. 1, pp. 135–226). Philadelphia: Falmer Press.

Cornbleth, C. (1985). Critical thinking and cognitive processes. In W. B. Stanley (Ed.), *Review of research in social studies education: 1976–1983.* Boulder, CO: ERIC Clearinghouse for Social Studies/Social Science Education.

de Bono, E. (1983). The direct teaching of thinking as a skill. *Phi Delta Kappan, 64*(*10*), 703–708.

Dewey, J. (1933) *How we think.* Boston: D. C. Heath.

Ennis, R. H. (1987). A taxonomy of critical thinking dispositions and abilities. In J. B. Baron and R. J. Sternberg (Eds.), *Teaching for thinking.* New York: Freeman.

Glaser, R. (1984). Education and thinking: The role of knowledge. *American Psychologist, 39,* 93–105.

Goodlad, J. I. (1984). *A place called school: Prospects for the future.* New York: McGraw Hill.

Greeno, J. G. (1989). A perspective on thinking. *American Psychologist, 44*(2), 134–141.

Herrnstein, R. J., Nickerson, R. S., De Sanchez, M., & Swets, J.A. (1986). Teaching thinking skills. *American Psychologist, 41*(11), 1279–1289.

King, M. B. (1990, April). *Leadership efforts to promote higher order thinking in social studies.* Paper presented at annual meeting of the American Educational Research Association, Boston, MA.

Ladwig, J. G. (1990, April). Organizational features which promote classroom thoughtfulness in secondary social studies departments. Paper presented at annual meeting of the American Educational Research Association, Boston, MA.

Marzano, R. J., Brandt, R. S., Hughes, C. S., Jones, B. F., Presseisen, B. Z., Rankin, S. C., & Subor, C. (1988). *Dimensions of thinking: A framework for curriculum and instruction.* Alexandria, VA: Association for Supervision and Curriculum Development.

McCarthy, C. & Schrag, F. (1990). Departmental and principal leadership in promoting higher order thinking. *Journal of Curriculum Studies, 22*(6), 529–543.

McPeck, J. E. (1981). *Critical thinking and education.* New York: St. Martins.

Newmann, F. M. (1988, May). Higher order thinking in the high school curriculum. *NASSP Bulletin, 72*(508), 58–64.

Newmann, F. M. (1990a). Higher order thinking in social studies: A rationale for the assessment of classroom thoughtfulness. *Journal of Curriculum Studies.* 22(1), 41–56.

Newmann, F. M. (1990b). Qualities of thoughtful social studies classes: An empirical profile. *Journal of Curriculum Studies, 22*(3), 253–275.

Newmann, F. M. (forthcoming). Higher order thinking and prospects for classroom thoughtfulness. In F. M. Newmann (Ed.), *Student engagement and achievement in American high schools.* New York: Teachers College Press.

Newmann, F. M., Onosko, J., & Stevenson, R. B. (1990, Summer). Staff development for higher order thinking: A synthesis of practical wisdom. *Journal of Staff Development, 11*(3), 48–55.

Nickerson, R. S. (1988). On improving thinking through instruction. In E. Z. Rothkopf (Ed.), *Review of Research in Education, 15,* (pp. 3–57). Washington, DC: American Educational Research Association.

Onosko, J. (1989). Comparing teachers' thinking about promoting students' thinking. *Theory and Research in Social Education, 17*(3), 174–195.

Perkins, D. N., & Salomon, G. (1989). Are cognitive skills context-bound? *Educational Researcher, 18*(1), 16–25.

Rosenholtz, S. J. (1989). *Teachers' workplace: A social organizational analysis.* White Plains, NY: Longman.

Schrag, F. (1989). *Evaluating thinking in school.* Madison, WI: National Center on Effective Secondary Schools.

Schrag, F. (1988). *Thinking in school and society.*London: Routledge & Kegan Paul.

Schrag, F. (1989). Are there levels of thinking? *Teachers College Record, 90*(4), 529–533.

Walsh, D., & Paul, R.W. (1987). *The goal of critical thinking: From educational ideal to educational reality.* Washington, DC: American Federation of Teachers.

# Introduction to
# Chapter 7

*Paul Messier, Acting Director of the Division of Society and Education, US Department of Education; and Director, National Learning Foundation, Washington, D.C.*

Dr. Gross's chapter introduces a new perspective concerning adult thinking. I agree with Dr. Gross that we, as adults, have never had as much power and information to use in reshaping our lives and increasing our thinking as is presently available. As one example, neuroscience has gained more insights into the mental and cognitive functions of the brain in the past two decades than had hitherto been known. Neuroscientistis have also expanded our understanding of how adults engage in successful thinking, use multiple dimensions of intelligent behavior, and create unique methods of expanding their mind sets.

Among the most startling points Dr. Gross makes is that in the 21st century, even the basic phases of adult life will pose challenges that require advanced thinking and fresh learning. He suggests that thinking together, learning how we can improve our own thinking abilities, and using technology to expand our intelligence are the most important thinking developmental activities adults will engage in the coming years.

Dr. Gross establishes 10 megatrends, and he challenges adults to become deeper thinkers. As you read his chapter, I encourage you to identify ways to respond to so that your present and future lifestyles and thinking development are strengthened. While emphasizing the diversity and integrity of the individual, Dr. Gross's general thrust is that each person has the possibility of a greater range of intellectual and learning capabilities.

As I read the chapter, I became increasingly aware of the need to initiate new measures of adult thinking and to improve opportunities for adults to learn more about how they think. I wish to assist adults to become more active in improving their own thinking abilities.

# 7 Lifelong Learning in the Learning Society of the Twenty-First Century

Ronald Gross
*Columbia University*

In previous chapters, we have described new strategies to advance thinking for children and young adults. It is our intent, in this chapter, to emphasize the need for these strategies from a different perspective. I argue that young adults, who have increased their thinking competencies in formal education, can and must continue to develop those capacities throughout their lives.

By the time adolescents graduate, they must realize that the quality of their lives will be determined by their own thinking abilities, just as much by other circumstances and conditions. While they will require good information from sound sources to survive and grow, their own capability to process such input will be crucial. Second, young adults must understand that adult learning requires that they work to increase their thinking competencies as well as their adeptness in learning new information. If young adults understand these concepts, and the fact that learning is a continuous, never-ending process, they will succeed in the 21st century, as this century already promises to bring with it "the learning society."

In my book, *The Great School Debate* (Gross, 1985), I project that in America, particularly, adults are being propelled into a new way of thinking about education. I have identified 10 "mega-trends" that exist. By "mega-trend" I mean a distinctive, locally observable, pervasive, significant change in the way we learn and think. These are tendencies which we already see all around us, feel in our own lives, and find auspicious for the future. In this chapter, I describe how each will influence adult education, thinking development for adults, and adult life styles, in the future.

# TEN MEGA-TRENDS IN ADULT
# THINKING DEVELOPMENT

Ten mega-trends in American society are propelling us towards a new way of thinking, and of thinking about adult education. Each of us can feel these mega-trends impelling us as we cope with information overload, acquire new skills, and seek to reshape our lives and our organizations. New strategies to assist our thinking, learning, growing, questioning, and self-directed change are already becoming an integral part of our lifestyle. For example:

- a troubled couple enters therapy together to clarify problems with a skilled mediator;
- a harried executive acquires time-management skills through a video tape;
- a mother on welfare attends a literacy class, which is required by the federal government;
- a doctor subscribes to a cable television channel to receive the newest research in his practice;
- a retired policeman and his wife attend Elderhostel programs in five states during their summer vacation;
- a firm of architects refines their collective techniques by de-briefing and learning from each assignment via a "reflective practice" thinking strategy;
- a gay clerical worker modifies his lifelong pattern of behavior to protect himself against AIDS, as an example of changing conditions in our world that make ongoing learning and thinking as an adult a "live-or-die" necessity;
- an amateur astronomer communicates and questions with colleagues around the world via computer bulletin boards; and,
- a handicapped person who failed to graduate from high school 20 years ago, earns a GED, then a BA, and is now working on a Master's Degree, enabling her, though deaf, to contribute to society at a high level.

These new kinds of learning are reshaping our thinking, our lives, and our society. Americans are discovering that continuous learning, and facility with higher level cognitive tasks have become a *sine qua non* of successful living, indeed of simple survival now and in the future. In reviewing the 10 mega-trends leading us to lifelong learning, I indicate how we can respond to each trend, on levels ranging from the personal to social policy.

## Mega-trend #1: We Will Learn Throughout Our Lives

The "front-end load" concept of education is obsolete. Otherwise known as the "innoculation" theory of education, this model posits that the individual "gets" his or her education during childhood and youth, then graduates and shifts from learning to work, with only occasional returns to learning.

This model is defunct. No longer can we expect our formal schooling, even if it extends to graduate or professional study, to serve us for a lifetime. "In a world that is constantly changing," declares futurist John Naisbitt (1982) in *Megatrends,* there is no one subject or set of subjects that will serve you for the foreseeable future, let alone for the rest of your life. The most important skill to acquire now is learning how to learn."

As Jim Duffy describes in chapter 12, the half-life of knowledge in many fields is already 5 years, meaning that after this amount of time, half of what one has learned will be obsolete. Moreover, the conditions of occupational and even personal life change rapidly nowadays. Most Americans can anticipate switching occupations half a dozen times during their careers, and very likely changing spouses and life styles.

In such a volatile era, there is constant alteration in what one needs to know, to understand, and be able to do. Even the basic stages and phases of adult life pose challenges that require advanced thinking and fresh learning. Suddenly, the midlife professional realizes that he or she wants to learn some profound things about relationships, child-rearing, or spiritual growth. Therefore, learning opportunities must be available at every age. Our recognition of this is further reflected in the burgeoning of adult and continuing education, and of nontraditional programs in postsecondary education, over the past 25 years. Such programs are reviewed in my report prepared for the Ford Foundation, entitled *Higher/Wider Education* (Gross, 1976).

The promotional efforts of colleges and universities each fall and spring provide a useful reminder and stimulation to adults to make some fresh educational plans. The next step should be to inject a healthy dose of "consumerism" into the system. Adult learners should be encouraged to become more selective and demanding customers in the lifelong learning marketplace. They should be empowered to do more analysis of their own needs, comparison-shopping, and product-appraisal.

## Mega-trend #2: We Will Learn in a Rich Array of Organizations, Institutions, Associations, and Networks

We are moving out of an historic era in which schools and colleges had a virtual monopoly over the provision of learning opportunities. Such a monopoly has not been the norm through the ages. As we return to more diffuse, society-wide system of education, we will be restoring an ideal with deep roots in our cultural tradition.

In classical times, Socrates noted that "not I but the city teaches." In the early days of our nation, Jefferson and other founding fathers—like John Dewey later on—contended that what educated the citizenry was a free press, robust political life, and voluntary social institutions. Currently, we are seeing a diffusion of learning throughout major social institutions, primarily business, the professions, and the media, including television and computerized communications. Already, the education and training enterprise, within American business and industry, dwarfs the entire postsecondary education system in numbers of learner and dollars spent (Gross, 1985).

For example, consider how profoundly educative the activities of major national associations in every profession and occupation are, with their panoply of courses, programs, standard-setting, certification, conferences, seminars, and special interest networks. Through these associations, adults share their thinking, develop technical as well as ethical standards, and develop new data. From a practical point of view, adults should consider getting involved in an appropriate organization as a prime way to advance and stimulate their thinking. In such settings, thinking and learning are so intertwined that they are often more engaging and serviceable than thinking and learning that occurs through classes. Such involvement will be particularly rewarding for adults whose learning *styles* make such gregarious, sociable learning congenial (see Mega-trend #4, p. 139).

Significantly, as new population groups are included in our emerging "lifelong learning society," it will probably be through such "non-formal" settings and modes. For example, the current movement to involve America's 27 million disabled adults, pioneered by the new National Association for Adults with Special Learning Needs, focuses on nonformal ways these people can learn and grow. My own work takes me into Catholic Charities Senior Centers where I stimulate elders in their 80s and 90s to enjoy and benefit from learning.

In summary, I direct policy makers to become keenly aware of the educative function of virtually every social institution, a position supported by recent studies, such as the work conducted by Ray Oldenburg (1989) in *The Great Good Place: Cafes, Coffee Shops, Community Centers, Beauty Parlors, General Stores, Bars, Hangouts, and How They Get You Through the Day*.

### Mega-trend #3: We Will Focus Learning on Real Needs

In the 21st century, we will focus more of our thinking and learning on our real needs. For centuries we have equated what's worth knowing with major academic and scientific subjects. Now, we are enlarging our perspective to include a wider range of learning needs. Research studies in the "natural" learning reveal that traditional academic subjects play a relatively minor role in adult education (Gross, 1985). Most of the actual learning which adults find enjoyable and useful focuses on practical life-needs: coping skills, hobbies, and more passionate enthusiasms, understanding themselves and others, enhancing their lifestyle or their community (Gross, 1977).

Even within the realm of academically based learning, the traditional disciplinary demarcations are being transcended by interdisciplinary studies in fields like holistic health, the study of the future, conflict resolution, and ethnic studies. New technical and professional fields are also emerging, such as development communications or semeiotics. Moreover, as educational levels in our society rise to historically unprecedented levels of advanced training, more and more people will discover that they have a "calling" to scholarship or science even though they do not pursue it as their occupation. They are "independent scholars"—individuals pursuing advanced intellectual work, but not based in academe. This phenomenon is documented in my two books on such "high learners," and their interests are not represented by a new organization, the National Coalition of Independent Scholars (Gross, 1990; and 1985). From a practical and policy point of view, adult learning can and should be driven by the life-needs and life-goals of learners. The planning and conduct of lifelong learning should be an individual enterprise, derived from each person's unique configuration of objectives. Although for many people, most of the time, such learning will be focused on the concerns of practical life, the independent scholars have demonstrated that there is no limit to the heights to which such self-directed learning may aspire.

## Mega-trend #4: We Will Learn with our Whole Brains

Insights into the ways in which our brains function have generated tremendous excitement in scientific and educational circles over the past decade. It is now apparent that learning can be enlivened and strengthened by activating more of the brain's potential. We can accelerate and enrich our learning, by engaging the senses, emotions, imagination, memory, and associative capacities.

The studies of Roger Sperry and Ned Hermann (Hermann, 1988), on the right–left brain specialization, Howard Gardner and Robert Sternberg on multiple intelligences, as presented by Tsantis and Keefe, in chapter 14, and dozens of theories on learning styles, have pointed the way. Systems like Superlearning or Peak Learning can heighten the experience in ways that transcend the linear, verbal, analytic mode of the traditional classroom. "Mental gyms" are opening in storefronts in major cities already, using electronic devices that directly stimulate the brain. For adults to reach their full cognitive capacities, they should seek out, and providers should offer, a much wider range of thinking and learning modalities. Adults can and should learn through simulations, creative problem solving, discussion and dialogue, apprenticeship and internships, computer communications, visualization and fantasy, paradox and insight, in ways very similar to those presented in the first section of this book.

## Mega-trend #5: We Will Learn Together

Our image of learning has been one of the loner-learner: the individual student competing against his fellows, or the solitary scholar in her carrel. But learning in the 21st century and in our world today usually occurs in groups, from the family to the problem-solving task force in business or the professions. Increasingly, we are recognizing and rewarding collaborative thinking and learning. Consider this hard-edged example: Under the heading "Two Heads are Better than One," the Business Council on Effective Literacy recently reported that pairs of low-literate worker manifested a substantially higher work-place literacy capacity than either of them individually. "One of the major differences between the schools and the workplace is that the latter permits employees to work together on tasks," quoted the Council from the report by Thomas Sticht of Applied Behavioral and Cognitive Sciences. "If one person does not know how to do something, he or she may ask someone else for information."

## Mega-trend #6: We will Learn via Multiple Media, Technologies, Formats, and Styles

In the 21st century, we will learn via multiple media, technologies, formats, and styles. The Where, When, and How of learning will be transformed by the imminent integration of communications media—telephonic, computer, and video—offering instantaneous and affordable access to knowledge on a global basis. Already, we can assemble for ourselves, via videotape, a finer faculty than could be commanded by any university. Already, adults can study economics with Milton Friedman, Art with Sir Kenneth Clark, Mythology with Joseph Campbell, Astronomy with Carl Sagan, and Science with Joseph Bronowski. As interactive media become more readily available and lower in cost, we can foresee the actualization of Buckminster Fuller's and Ted Nelson's (inventor of hypertext) prophetic vision: We will all participate actively at the forefront of intellectual life. High-tech and high-touch can be combined as we draw from world-wide resources, while establishing intimate contact with kindred spirits.

"The Invisible University" is the term I suggest for this emergent system of world-wide access to learning. It ranges from small-scale technology like audio-cassettes for use while driving, to interactive video teleconferencing and the new virtual reality technologies, such as videodiscs and high resolution television broadcasting.

## Mega-trend #7: We will Direct our Own Thinking and Learning

In the future, we will direct our own thinking and learning by more freely selecting the topics we will explore. The pioneering research of Allen Tough (1979) at the Ontario Institute for Studies in Education showed that when *all* of the learning that goes on in the lives of adults is put under the microscope, only about 20% is the result of someone teaching it to someone else. The rest is self-directed. Adults themselves set the goals, marshall the resources, conduct the thinking processes, and evaluate 80% of the learning they do. Since Tough's revelatory finding, enterprising practitioners have developed a repertoire of techniques for directing one's own learning more effectively. Through books such as Robert Smith's (1982) *Learning how to Learn,* many self-directed methods can be mastered. Technology has also been adapted to serve learners working on their own. One of the prototypes or technologically assisted exploration exists at the innovative Personal Learning Lab, Georgia Center for Adult Education, Athens, Georgia.

## Mega-trend #8: We will Learn by Teaching

In our increasingly well-educated and specialized society, everyone tends to know things worth teaching. Moreover, the experience of teaching is wonderfully educative for the teacher. We never know our own subject quite as well as when we are called upon to teach it.

Learning by teaching and interpretive thinking processes will perform more crucial roles in learning in the 21st century, as more adults routinely find themselves in instructive roles in their occupation, leisure life, families, and citizenry. Educators will find a new role here, too. In the next century, certified teachers will function as orchestrators of teaching resources in their community. Already many leading deans and directors of adult and continuing education across the country make it a major part of their work to find and recruit people from the community to share what they know.

## Mega-trend #9: Our Systems of Formal Education— Schools and Colleges—will Change Radically (if slowly) to Support the Ideal of Lifelong Learning and a Learning Society

The new model of adult thinking development—lifelong learning in a learning society—offers schools and colleges the opportunity to shift to a new paradigm. They can finally take seriously the mission they have always claimed to have: teaching students *how* to learn, rather than merely "covering" a fixed curriculum. Already, the stated *objectives* of most schools and colleges is to instill the love of learning and provide students with the attitudes, tools, thinking strategies, and techniques to continue their education on their own after graduation. However, in *practice,* most formal education is still mired in the obsolete "front-end load" paradigm (as discussed in Mega-trend #1). Therefore, many present educators feel compelled to convey everything that students need to know about their subject. They place less emphasis upon motivating, empowering, and impelling students to become independent learners.

Once individuals and our society take seriously the idea that formal schooling is merely the beginning of thinking development and lifelong learning, teachers will be relieved of the compulsion to *cover* so much material. They will also be relieved of a number of other problems that often sabotage their work (i.e., compelling students' attention to subjects for which they are not yet attracted, forcing all students to learn in the same way, and imposing a uniform curriculum on everyone). Instead, future classrooms will become devoted to the celebration of each student's capacity to think and learn. Formal instruction will focus on instilling in young people the joy of learning, the power of knowledge and analysis, and the tricks of the trade.

If such a vision of the future seems utopian, consider how dramatically our postsecondary system has advanced toward this goal in the last 30 years. In 1950, college was exclusively for 18–22 year olds. If a person failed to go directly from high school to college, his or her opportunity for higher education was virtually closed. Millions of Americans who had missed that "window" in their lives, were relegated to inferior status despite their capacity and willingness to learn. Today, in dramatic contrast, we take for granted the availability of "nontraditional" degree programs. At any age, in any circumstances, adults can begin working towards a college degree. In fact, 18–22 year-old "Joe College" stereotype is no longer the norm on most campuses. The average student is over 25; the grandmother getting her degree hardly merits a headline. Thus does the provision of learning opportunities transform our image of education.

## Mega-trend #10: We will Learn How to Learn

Leading futurists point out that learning how to learn is the master skill of the coming era. Alvin Toffler, author of *Future Shock,* has declared that tomorrow's illiterate will be the person who has not learned how to learn.

In the future "learning how to learn" will have four components. First, adults must adapt a pro-active *attitude* towards their own growth and development. Adults will become more aware that they have the responsibility for acquiring the thinking skills and knowledge they need to achieve their life goals. Second, in the next century, adults' awareness of their own learning styles, on a variety of dimensions, will become automatized. Already, adults tend to know their preferences regarding time-of-day when their minds work best (e.g., "larks" vs. "doves"). Such self-knowledge and understanding will become wider and deeper, as adults discover their thinking strategy preferences and aversions. Third, future adults will exercise a fuller range of *options and resources* for learning because they will know how to do so. These adults will be more sophisticated about the alternative ways they can go about thinking, problem solving, and learning. For example, they will become more selective knowledge consumers, weighing learning opportunities according to such criteria as convenience, cost, and congeniality with their thinking and life style-preferences. The last component in the adult "learning how to learn" model is the possession of more specialized thinking *strategies and learning techniques*. Future adults will acquire their own repertoire of thinking skills to facilitate the learning process, including techniques for accessing and organizing information, storing and displaying data, setting goals and objectives, monitoring progress and evaluating results.

## IMPLICATIONS FOR TODAY'S EDUCATORS

What can teachers, administrators, policy makers, and citizens concerned about education, start doing today that will move American education towards launching lifelong learners?

1. Reconsider the goals of each school, school system, college or university. Is preparation for lifelong learning one of the chief goals? If not, should it be?

2. Review each program, offering, and course to determine whether it addresses that goal, and how might it better do so.

3. Encourage such an emphasis on learning-how-to-think in the reward system for both teachers and students.

4. Provide plentiful opportunities for students and teachers at every level to set their own learning and thinking goals, respond to differences in style, acquire a repertoire of learning skills and thinking skills, and produce significant products from their learning.

5. Expand opportunities and resources for lifelong thinking development throughout the lifespan by significantly increasing allocations to appropriate institutions, agencies, and programs—even if that involves a re-allocation of limited resources.

## REFERENCES

Aslanian, C., & Brickell, H. (1980). *Americans in transition: Life changes as reasons for adult learning*. Princeton, NJ: College Entrance Examination Board.

Faure, E., et al., (Eds.). (1972). *Learning to be*. Paris: UNESCO.

Gross, R. (1976). *Higher/wider education: A report on open learning*. New York: The Ford Foundation.

Gross, R. (1977). *The lifelong learner*. New York: Simon and Schuster.

Gross, R. (1982). *The independent scholar's handbook*. Reading, MA: Addison-Wesley.

Gross, R. (1985). *The great school debate*. New York: Simon and Schuster.

Gross, R. (1990). *Peak learning*. Los Angeles: Jeremy Tarcher.

Herrmann, N. (1988). *The creative brain*. Lake Lure, NC: Applied Creative Services.

Naisbitt, J. (1982). *Megatrends*. New York: Warner Books.

Oldenburg, R. (1989). *The great good place*. New York: Paragon House.

Smith, R. (1982). *Learning how to learn*. Chicago, IL: Follett.

Tough, A. (1979). *The adult's learning projects*. Austin, TX: Learning Concepts.

# Introduction to
# Chapter 8

*John I. Goodlad, Director, Center for
Educational Renewal and author of* A Place
Called School,
*and* Teachers For Our Nation's Schools.

By the close of the school reform decade of the 1980s,
policymakers and grassroots reformers appeared to have
reached at least rhetorical agreement on the school unit as
the center for efforts to change. Policymakers spoke of restructuring; grassroots reformers of renewal. Both groups
would grant more freedom to principals and teachers to
engage in the necessary restructuring or renewing. Neither
group took adequate cognizance of the fact that teachers are
trained to function independently in classrooms, with little
or no expectation and preparation to redesign the regularities of schooling in concert with their colleagues.

For some years, Robert Calfee has immersed himself in
the total ecology of individual schools. Perhaps intuitively,
he seems to have been aware that teachers do not take readily
to renewing their schools, however much they perceive the
need to change regularities that impede their efforts in the
classroom. They take much more readily to strategies
focused directly on their daily preoccupations of teaching
children to read, write, and spell. The Calfee approach, *The
Inquiring School*, addresses these preoccupations directly
through processes of inquiry that appear to be precisely those
required for productively engaging in renewal of the total
school. But even if teachers do not get to this larger task, as
frustrated reformers so frequently find to be the case, they get
to the very essence of what elementary schools must do—
develop in children critical literacy. Calfee's hypothesis—
both promising and intriguing—is that, as an accompani-
ment of this focused effort, the entire school community
increasingly becomes a center of inquiry where all practices
ultimately become the subject of scrutiny.

# 8 The Inquiring School: Literacy for the Year 2000

Robert Calfee
*Stanford University*

## INTRODUCTION

The last 30 years have seen frenetic policy activity in American schools: Sputnik in the 1950s ("Bring in the experts!"), the Great Society in the 1960s (a blend of "Equal education for all" and "Teacher-proof curricula"), the turbulence of the 1970s ("Power to the people," "Relevance to the individual"), and finally the rapid succession of waves during the 1980s (Murphy, 1990), starting with *A Nation at Risk* (National Commission on Excellence in Education, 1983; "Shape up! Excellence above all"), followed by a variety of school-based models (effective schools, teacher centers, restructured schools, site-based schools, among others). The contemporary scene is chaotic, a blend of new waves, sporadic whitecaps, and deep swells. Most of this activity is superficial; the daily classroom routines that make up the deep structure of schooling are but slightly affected by the tempests at the top (Cuban, 1990). Midway through these decades, a single note sounded, with clear tones, then drifted away:

> [W]e can no longer afford to conceive of schools as distribution centers for dispensing cultural orientations and information. . . . The intellectual demands upon the system have become so enormous that the school must become much more than a place of instruction. It must become a center of inquiry—a producer as well as a transmitter of knowledge. . . . Not only our need for new knowledge but also our responsibility for the intellectual health of teachers suggests this conception. . . . [Otherwise], teaching resembles employment as humdrum as an educational sales clerk.
>
> [Instead, the school must become the model] of an institution characterized by a pervasive search for meaning and rationality in its work. . . , [and students] simi-

larly encouraged to seek a rational purpose in their studies. The school conceived as a center of inquiry is now a vision, but we have the economic resources, the manpower, and the knowledge to make the vision a reality. All we require is the will and the wit to make it so. (Schaefer, 1967, pp. 1–5)

Schaefer's remarks to the John Dewey Society had little impact at the time. Twenty-five years later, they turn up with increasing frequency in discussions of school change and reform. Schaefer laid out a brilliant vision. He saw the social sciences (psychology, anthropology, and sociology) as providing the necessary concepts and tools for inquiry. He viewed institutional structure and governance as critical to fundamental change. He did not, however, spell out the pragmatics for realizing the dream.

This chapter sketches my experiences over several years with a program, *The Inquiring School,* that aspires to Schaefer's vision. The model builds on curricular bedrock; its foundation is the teaching of reading and writing in the elementary grades. I begin with a portrayal of this elemental curriculum, a conception of classroom instruction in literacy that contrasts sharply with current practice. I then make a sharp turn and connect the classroom with three school-wide issues: the task of school reform, the professionalization of teaching, and the restructuring of schools.

## CRITICAL LITERACY: TWO PROPOSITIONS

Readers of this volume on thinking development, puzzled on encountering the title of this chapter, may now be even more confused. What have basic literacy skills to do with reforms to advance thinking? The link comes from two propositions that are at the heart of my argument. Both build on the concept of *critical literacy,* which I define as "the capacity to use language in all its forms as a tool for thinking, problem solving, and communicating" (Calfee, 1982, in press; Calfee & Drum, 1986):

> *Proposition 1:* Critical literacy is the core curriculum for elementary education, the "engine" that drives effective education in all other domains of knowledge and skill.
> *Proposition 2:* Critical literacy is the foundation for the vision of the school as center of inquiry; in both the 1st-grade classroom and the faculty meeting, effective use of language is critical to the goals of democratic engagement of a community.

There is more to these two themes than meets the eye. Proposition 1 entails a major reconceptualization of elementary reading and writing, a radical departure from the centuries-old emphasis on basic skills and toward a "literacy of thoughfulness" (Brown, 1987). Present practices, especially in schools serving children most at risk, start the curriculum with behavioral competencies in decoding and vocabulary. Only after students have mastered these basics are they allowed access to more challenging "good stuff"—literature, essays, poetry. Many children never move beyond the basics; virtually all trudge through these dull and pointless preliminaries lacking any sense of purpose and devoid of interest.

In Proposition 1, I envisage a curriculum in which the acquisition of elementary literacy takes shape as a challenging, meta-cognitive achievement from kindergarten onward. The emphasis from the outset in this model is on purpose, understanding, problem solving, and communication. It calls into question the "learn to read; read to learn" model (e.g., Chall, 1983) that currently guides both policy and practice. Psychologists currently debate whether thinking takes shape as a general set of multipurpose strategies or as subject-specific algorithms (Resnick, 1989). In the concept of critical literacy, I propose a reconciliation of these views; the literate use of language can serve as a broadly applicable set of systematic strategies grounded in the most fundamental of subject matters, reading and writing.

The shift from basic skills to critical literacy requires a fundamental change in the teacher's role. Numerous observers have commented on the "assembly-line" character of elementary schooling, the "egg-crate" isolation of teachers, and decision making responsibilities more akin to those of postal clerks than full-fledged professionals (Apple & Junck, 1990). In Proposition 2, I suggest that the curriculum shift to critical literacy for students requires an equally significant change in the thinking and communication patterns among adults. In addition, I emphasize the potential of the concepts and strategies of critical literacy to support that goal. The isolation of the egg-crate school springs from many sources, but one reason is the lack of technical language. Might the commonplaces of the reading lesson serve as the foundation for school restructuring—that is exactly what I am proposing. Schools for tomorrow must incorporate reflective language in every aspect of their being. Resnick (1987) argues that academic work should reflect realities of life after school. Let me suggest further that interactions among school professionals can and should mirror the best that we know about language use, whether at work or play, whether in public or private exchanges. By joining the goals for schoolchildren and those for adults, the school achieves a degree of coherence, of "vertical integration," that seldom appears in present practice.

What does critical literacy embody as a curriculum? How does it influence instruction and thinking development? What does it imply for assessment? Let me describe a 6th-grade graduate of the program. First, the youngster possesses an array of *tools for analyzing language* in all its forms, tools to "see below the surface," a capacity for x-ray vision. In contrast, existing programs emphasize superficial understanding. The point can be illustrated by the three sentences that you have just read. A superficial analysis yields as key words *6th-graders, tools,* and *details.* A critical reading focuses instead on *first point* (more will follow, prepare for a list), and *in contrast* (the author is converting the list to a matrix or *semantic weave*).

Second, critical literacy is *metacognitive;* our 6th-grader can talk about thought and language. He or she possesses a technical vocabulary for reflection. In the previous example, the student can explain the task of parsing the three sentences, employing words like *weave* (in kindergarten) or *matrix* (by 6th grade).

Third, critical literacy allows the student to connect with others familiar with the same language. Like Mr. Spock in Star Trek, students virtually come to read one another's minds. Indeed, a key element in critical literacy is the capacity to explain yourself to others—going beyond surface understanding to the underlying comprehension.

Finally, the critically literate 6th-grader has acquired a strategic "habit of mind," an automated approach to the thoughtful use of language in reading, writing, speaking, and listening. These routines come from years of purposeful application with guidance, scaffolding, and feedback from teachers and other students, starting with kindergarten and filling each day of the 7 years of elementary school. If this image of the literate 6th-grader permeates the school, then this level of achievement can be attained by virtually every student, even those from home and family backgrounds usually correlated with risk of academic failure.

## ACHIEVING FUNDAMENTAL REFORM IN SCHOOLS

U.S. schools have experienced tidal waves of reform for more than a century. The present alarums have distinctive facets: problems associated with declining student demographics and increasing needs for human capital, new tensions in educational policy and practice, and calls for fundamental change in elementary education.

### Problems

Dissatisfaction with American schools runs broad and deep, in one believes public reports. A complete compilation would fill volumes; Murphy (1990) presents the litany in comprehensive and readable form. Let me dissociate myself from the Cassandras. American public schools are doing many things quite well. Parents trust their children for 180 days each year, for most waking hours, for a baker's dozen years, to the care of another adult. This confidence is generally fulfilled. U.S. schools guide most youngsters to a level of achievement far above most other national efforts.

On the other hand, demands on our schools have changed dramatically in the past 30 years. "Inputs" are different; today's students receive less home support than a generation ago. The school has become the primary center of advocacy for children; education is only one of many needs met by the school (Hodgkinson, 1989; Reed & Sauter, 1990). "Outputs" have been moved steadily upward. A level of attainment once reserved for the elite has become the standard for all (Grant, 1988; National Center for Education and Economy, 1990). The push for equity has joined the need for a capable workforce and an involved citizenry (Knapp & Shields, 1990), as discussed in greater depth in chapters 10 and 12. Schools can no longer simply *grade* students; they must help them *grow*.

## Tensions

American schools are a nexus of persisting tensions. Teachers aspire to *professional status;* the commonplaceness of the task downgrades the role to *technician*. "Teachers don't git no respect." As mentioned in the previous chapter, Jeffersonian tradition emphasizes the role of highly *educated* citizens in a dynamic democracy, but practicalities lead schools to stress *training*. Textbooks and instructional materials flood schools with a deluge of "*paper*" unmatched by any other nation; the ineffectiveness of these teacher-proof programs reveals schooling to be an inherently "*people*" business. Finally, *locus of control* in the neighborhood school encompasses several tensions: the long tradition of local control, a quarter-century of top-down mandates by state and federal governments, and emerging support for site-based decision making.

## Changes

Attempts to reform a large, diffuse system like the public schools are easily frustrated by these tensions, especially when efforts are kaleidoscopic and piecemeal. The newest buzzword is *restructuring*. As noted by Newmann in Chapter 6, meanings for this term vary widely, as reform advocates try to cover all bases (Lewis, 1989; Educational Leadership, 1990a, 1990b). McDonnell (1989) identifies four recurring themes: (a) decentralized authority (governance), (b) greater accountability (evaluation), (c) curriculum and instruction (substance), and (d) connections to parents and community (responsiveness). Cohen (1988), in a lucid presentation, joins these basic elements in a matrix that analyzes implications for states, districts, and schools. Most treatments, however, resemble a *piñata* approach—keep swinging hard and high, and maybe you will hit the prize. "Each of the major strategies addresses a different part of the educational system. . . . Few efforts are being made to design any type of comprehensive strategy. . . . Proponents do not even talk to each other on a regular basis. . . . A disjointed enterprise" (McDonnell, 1989, p. iii).

Despite the scattershot appearance of this educational *perestroika,* the movement captures the notion that dramatic transformations are both possible and essential. Discussions of restructuring often imply the concept of *fundamental change* (SRI, 1987; also cf. CED, 1987). Incremental improvement, emphasized from 1970–1985, sought to upgrade schools through investments aimed toward immediate, widespread, albeit limited impact. Fundamental change, in contrast, explores state-of-the-art breakthroughs inspired by a vision of substantial and permanent transformations. In the SRI analysis, the two strategies differ in several dimensions: *investments* that are modest but continuing (incremental), versus larger and constrained in time (fundamental); *response times* that are gradual versus abrupt; *organizational resistance* that is obvious (fundamental) rather than subdued (incremental); *content and approach* (what is taught and now to teach it) remain the same (incremental), versus "radical restructuring" (fundamental); *personnel* retrained (incremental) or replaced (fundamental); *dissemination* through broad distribution of packaged programs (incremental) versus creation of working prototypes (fundamental).

Some facets of the school system resist rapid change—buildings, people, resources, and the routines of schooling are as fixed as the Maginot line. Child care is an important reality; so are "human" services. Machines are unlikely to replace teachers in these areas.

What might change—*fundamentally*—and why? My experience with the *Inquiring School* model leads me to the propositions that begin the chapter. I believe that restructuring of elementary schools can most effectively occur through transformations in:

- the way that educators understand the concept of literacy, in what is taught and how it is taught; and
- the way that educators think about the organization of the school, and in how they interact to define and realize the goals of schooling for students.

These statements do not appear radical. They are not flamboyant. They call for change in conceptualization and in social interaction; they do not require new people or additional resources. Nonetheless, I think that they form a workable and trustworthy basis for fundamental change in schools that will lead to enhanced thinking development. An anecdote illustrates the subtlety of the transformation:

A teacher explains to visiting colleagues how she finds time to plan and make decisions, now that she has assumed professional responsibility for the reading–writing curriculum. Doesn't this mean increased day-to-day work? She responds: "At first it did take a lot of time. I spent hours with [the support manual] and lessons felt awkward. But now, now it's all up here" [pointing to her head].

This teacher's directness and articulateness are not typically observed in practitioner dialogues (e.g., Fraatz, 1987). Nor are these characteristics tapped by teacher evaluation methods, which tend to emphasize performance more than understanding (Millman & Darling-Hammond, 1990). Fundamental change in teaching will place new demands on school faculty, but also those who prepare, select, and support teachers (Goodlad, 1990).

## THE PROFESSIONALIZATION OF TEACHING

In Schaefer's (1967) vision, the school had become a collective of "scholar-teachers in command of the conceptual tools and methods of inquiry requisite to investigating the learning process in their own classrooms. Why should our schools not nurture the continuing wisdom and power of such scholar-teachers? (p. 5.) . . . what could be more engaging than inquiring into the myriad mysteries of the child's world?" (p. 59). The last several years have seen an outpouring of articles on professionalization. In virtually every instance, possession of a technical language and communication with colleagues are marks that distinguish professionals from technicians.

### To Be a Professional Educator

What does it mean to define teaching as a profession? This question has been explored by academics, policy makers, and professional associations. Recent offerings (Goodlad, 1987; Joyce 1990; Lieberman, 1988; Rosow & Zager, 1989; November 1988 *Educational Leadership)* converge on three themes:

- To achieve and sustain status as a profession, teachers must distinguish their knowledge and skill from that which others gain simply through school attendance.
- The teaching community must develop and champion standards for competence, growth, and communication typical of other professions.
- Teachers must establish levels of articulateness, leadership, and collegiality that mark them as knowledgeable.

The task is challenging. Schools cannot be shut down while the staff undergo professional development. With more than 2 million teachers in the present force, even a modest per-person investment represents a significant overall expenditure. Some observers question the benefits. Is professional status worth the costs? Others see the drive for professional status as another top-down mandate of questionable merit: "In the final analysis, there is no professional culture for teachers save what is conferred through their students" (Cooper, 1988, p. 64). The following sections of this chapter examine professionalization through two lenses—the teacher in the classroom, and the teacher as a colleague. The analysis accepts the position taken by Devaney and Sykes (1988): "[The] case for all teachers being professional exists. It is clear and potent. It derives from two sources: economists' and demographers' portrayal of a markedly different economy and society for which our public schools must prepare the young, and cognitive scientists' recent findings on how human intellectual ability develops" (p. 9).

## The Teacher as Classroom Professional

What does a teacher need to know to operate as a professional in the classroom? At the risk of offending both sides of the science-versus-art debate (Eisner, 1991; Gage & Needels, 1989), I propose that a clearcut domain of knowledge and procedures exists in answer to this question. Defining the domain requires no empirical justification. The argument is partly intuitive, but the basic principles can be clearly explicated.

To be sure, I am treading where angels are advised to be cautious. For instance, Reynolds (1989) compiled a volume for the American Association of Colleges for Teacher Education on *The Knowledge Base for the Beginning Teacher*. The text attempts to formulate a "stable curriculum . . . [like] medicine with its base of scientific knowledge, or law with its analytic methods" (p. ix). Unfortunately, the AACTE volume is a complex and inchoate collection, likely to puzzle both beginning teacher and experienced teacher educator. Let me attempt a simpler answer (Calfee & Shefelbine, 1981).

## ESSENTIAL KNOWLEDGE AND SKILL

At the technical core of classroom education are three basic elements: curriculum, instruction, and assessment. Hardly a novel idea, but let me examine more carefully the first element, curriculum. What are reasonable achievement goals within the "literacy of thoughtfulness?" Many observers believe that the cart presently drives the horse. For 3 decades, assessment based on the technology of standardized testing has defined reading as a piecemeal collection of behavioral objectives. Writing, which has defied such operationalization, has fallen through the curricular cracks. Instruction has followed suit.

How else might we define curriculum? Shulman (1987), in a "Back to the future" move, has reminded us that teacher knowledge of a subject matter is different from expert knowledge. Hatano (1982), from another perspective, contrasts routine and adaptive experts. The former is very good at what he or she can do; the latter is equally competent, but can also adopt the novice's perspective.

## The Curriculum of Critical Literacy

Now to the matter of reading and writing in the early grades. Assuming that these processes are two faces of the same coin, what is the curriculum for this domain? My answer springs from 10 years of experience with Project READ, a staff development program designed to improve reading and writing instruction in the elementary grades (Calfee, Henry, & Funderburg, 1988).

A *curriculum* is a *course* of study. Both words derive from the Latin *currere: to run.* Imagine a race course—not the simple high school track, but the more complex marathon from Athens to Sparta. You need to think about where you want to end, where you will start, and a few benchmarks along the way. Let us begin at the end. The young person leaving the middle grades requires full command of language in order to handle the challenges of high school and life thereafter: "Learning depends greatly on communication. . . . The social contexts we create and inhabit are not simply the background against which life plays out. They are both shaped by, and the shapers of, our language and learning" (Florio-Ruane, 1989, p. 163). This perspective shifts from the view of reading and writing as "basic skills for handling print" to the perspective of *critical literacy:* the capacity to use language in all of its forms as a tool for problem solving and communication.

This change in conception may appear subtle, but the implications are substantial. It breaks the grip of the stage-model on teacher thinking; phonics is no longer the entry way to literacy, but rather part of a "tool kit." Student discussion is no longer ancillary to instruction, but an essential constituent. Comprehension is not satisfied when students simply supply answers to literal questions; instead, the task is to reconstruct the text and connect it to personal meanings. Composition is no longer an optional task inserted when convenient, but a critical element of the curriculum from the earliest grades. A child need not be facile with paper and pencil; composing is a communicative act.

The first foundation stone for effective communication comes from the *rhetoric,* a set of conventions devised by the ancient Greeks to shape dis*course* (the same root as curriculum) in the Forum. These techniques now appear in college composition texts and "How to communicate" seminars. Psychologists have applied the techniques in recent years for the study of structures of knowledge: story grammars and expository forms, for instance (Calfee & Drum, 1986; Chambliss & Calfee, 1988).

A second principle arises from the *constancies* of human thought and language (Calfee & Nelson-Barber, in press). Teachers see individual differences among students; they are less aware of the similarities. For instance, all kindergartners enter school (the start of the course) with a fully operational linguistic system: rich semantic networks and well-formed story grammars (see Salinger, Chapter 16, this volume). They do not realize that they possess these resources, they lack a meta-language for talking about knowledge and language, and they are not strategic about learning. They vary enormously in the match of their experiences and styles with the conventions of schooling. The curriculum of critical literacy assumes that, despite these differences, every child has the potential to acquire the skills to use language for problem solving and communication.

A third principle springs from cognitive psychology. The human mind has virtually infinite potential to store experience in long-term memory, but the attentional capacity of short-term memory is quite limited (Calfee, 1981). Hence the K.I.S.S. principle—"keep it simple, sweetheart." This principle has intuitive appeal, but "simple ain't easy." The basal curriculum is inordinately complicated; "mess" is an appropriate label for the typical scope-and-sequence chart. On the other hand, whole-language methods often resist any form of analysis, an approach that can easily become a "lump" (Goodman, Smith, Meredith, & Goodman, 1987). The romantic notion that "you learn to read by reading," that literacy naturally emerges from exposure to *Charlotte's Web* or through journal writing, is a luxury that many students can ill afford.

Our alternative to messes and lumps builds on the concept of short-term memory "chunks." The mind can handle about half a dozen distinctive pieces of information (chunks) at any given time. Selecting workable units becomes the key to effective use of intellectual resources. What elements can serve as the foundation for an integrated language-literacy curriculum? In Project READ we shaped an answer around the linguistic analysis of oral language into phonology, semantics, and discourse. The parallel building blocks of critical literacy—decoding and spelling; vocabulary and concept formation; comprehension and composition of narrative and expository texts—are benchmarks for deciding what to teach from kindergarten onward.

In the curriculum of critical literacy, each major component is subdivided into a few "sub-chunks." The decoding-spelling strand, for instance, breaks along two dimensions: language origin and level of analysis. English is a layered language, with elements from Anglo-Saxon, Romance, and other sources. The spelling patterns in each layer have distinctive features at both the letter-sound and morphological (word part) levels (Balmuth, 1982). In kindergarten, the word-part strand leads children to examine compound words from Anglo-Saxon: "You know *doghouse* and *raincoat;* what do you think about *rainhouse* and *dogcoat?*" In 6th grade, students explore Romance combinations: "See what you can make from these prefixes, roots, and suffixes—*inter-, bi-; -nation-, -system-; -al, -ness.*" Some combinations (*international*) are "real," while others (*intersystemness*) have not yet entered the language. The curricular goal in both examples is to engage students in perceiving the structure of complex words. This understanding supports word analysis through an "X-ray" capacity to see the elements in *peregrinations* and to write *nononsenseness* with confidence.

A fourth principle centers on lesson design. Basal reading lessons are a collage of curricular skills and scripted activities. We devised a simple lesson plan that provided students with structures and strategies for independent thought and productive social interaction. Lesson design in Project READ meets two criteria: (a) clarity in curricular goals, and (b) dependence on students' collective knowledge to achieve the goal. The first criterion is supported by the lesson *opening* and *closing,* the second criterion by the *middle* activities.

In the opening and closing, a brief statement focuses attention on the *content, process,* and *structure* of the lesson. The content is the topic, process is the means of analysis, and structure is the "picture" that synthesizes. The middle activities guide students in exploring the topic, with the teacher as facilitator.

Here is an example. A 1st-grade class starts a lesson on *food*. The topic is familiar but provides numerous opportunities for problem solving and communication; grocery stores and menus both depend on the principle of categorization (Barton & Calfee, 1989). The teacher opens the lesson: "We all know something about food; let's see what's on your mind. We'll do this by webbing; let's first see what you know about the topic, and then we'll organize the information. What comes to mind when you think about 'food?' I'll write your ideas down." This brief statement is the opening; it states the topic (food), identifies the process (free associations and clustering), and lays out the structure (a web).

The move to the middle happened quickly and you may have missed it. "What comes to mind. . . "—the teacher's request for associations is genuine, and opens discussion. The move to structure is equally direct. Once students have generated an array of associations, the next step is to cluster the array; "What are some ways in which we can make bunches of words?" The emphasis throughout the lesson is on students' thoughts, rather than a compilation of correct answers. The lesson employs familiar *content* to assist students in acquiring high-level *structures* and *strategies* of broad applicability; "high road" transfer is an integral part of the basic design (Salomon & Perkins, 1989; Calfee, Avelar La Salle, & Cancino, in press).

Explicitness is a fifth principle in this curriculum. Teaching rhetorical devices like the topical web, and giving the devices explicit names, allows students to talk about language and thought. Genuine questions are open-ended and probe for explanations. "What comes to mind when you think about food?" is an authentic question, more so than "What goes with ice cream?" Equally important, any answer is an opportunity for the student to make his or her reasoning a public matter: "Pickles and peanut butter are an unusual combination. How did you come up with that!" Research on meta-cognition—reflecting about one's thoughts, *and talking* about these reflections—reveals the importance of a high level of articulateness. The meta-instructional strategies of READ place this capacity at the heart of the lesson.

## The Teacher's Role in Critical Literacy

In critical literacy, the classroom professional possesses a deep understanding of curriculum goals, and hence enjoys substantial freedom in adapting a lesson or project to a particular context. He or she is able to lay out a broad framework for thinking, and then allow students free rein to explore a topic within that framework. The teacher's conceptual knowledge (again, an "x-ray vision") allows him or her to assess the process of student learning, and to furnish guidance and support as necessary. In this reconceptualization of reading and writing, teacher judgment becomes the critical ingredient in deciding about classroom activities. Teaching becomes genuine inquiry.

While the conceptualization of the curriculum of critical literacy has certain distinctive features, the notions of meta-level learning, engaging instruction, and authentic assessment can be found elsewhere in current literature. An example from Duckworth (1987) is especially pertinent; it complements earlier points, it is wonderfully rich, and it leads naturally to my next point. Here is Duckworth's account of her efforts to help novice teachers examine student learning rather than focusing solely on content:

> I love to teach teachers, . . . to find ways [to] catch everyone's interest; to find out what people think about things and ways to get them talking about what they think; . . . to build their fascination with what others think, and with the light that other people's thinking sheds on their own. . . [Teaching] puts students into contact with phenomena in the area of study, [leads them] to explain the sense they are making, and to understand [that] sense" (p. 123).

Duckworth contrasts the primary and secondary tasks of a lesson, a distinction akin to the earlier contrast between content (e.g., food) and strategy (e.g., webbing). In one project, she assigns student teachers to observe the moon for several weeks (the secondary task). They then investigate how classmates understand the moon's phases. When students balk at the assignment ("How is looking at the moon going to make me a better teacher?"), Duckworth points to several outcomes of the exercise:

a.  by explaining their thoughts to others, teachers achieve greater clarity in their own understanding;

b.  they gain skill at formulating questions that foster explanation;

c.  they develop independence of thought and problem solving;

d.  they appreciate the "powerful experience of having your ideas taken seriously";

e.  they learn how much they can learn from one another; and

f.  they come to recognize knowledge as a "human construction" (p. 130–131).

Duckworth's (1987) examples lead to a significant insight about the development of professional expertise: As a class member expressed it, "My biggest problem in this class [is] forgetting about being a teacher and relearning how to be a learner" (p. 126). Most people view the teacher as possessor-of-knowledge and transmitter-of-information. Duckworth suggests that expertise can actually be a barrier to effective instruction: "[During the moon exercise], more knowledgeable class members sometimes get impatient [because they already know how the moon works]. I invite them to put their efforts into trying to elicit and understand someone else's explanation—to join me in practicing teaching by listening rather than explaining" (p. 129). This assessment applies directly to the elementary teacher, who is clearly "expert" at reading and writing, and hence may be impatient when a 1st-grader struggles with the printed page.

Becoming a master teacher, from this perspective, means going against the grain of wellworn traditions and memories. The experienced teacher bears a greater burden than the novice, and the college graduate inherits almost two decades of conventional teaching. Shifting paradigms takes time, practice, feedback, and the opportunity to reflect, as Art Costa describes in the next chapter. This process can take 2 to 3 years, *assuming a supportive environment*—which I will take as a lead to examine the school as a professional environment.

## THE RESTRUCTURING OF SCHOOLS

### The Teacher's Role as Colleague

The roles of professional in the classroom and the school often appear quite distinctive. Scholarly reports seldom connect the two activities. Project READ (a classroom-oriented program) began as a school-wide effort by happenstance. The principal of Graystone school, our first site, suggested I work with the entire staff, which made intuitive sense. When the project expanded to several other schools, I quickly discovered the meaning of "supportive context." I have experimented with READ in myriad situations around the nation during the past decade. Sometimes the project has taken root and flourished, but other times a promising beginning has died on the vine.

It is easy to generate hypotheses that explain these inconsistencies. Support from the school principal is crucial; unfortunately, predicting effective leadership is easier after the fact. Finding a "local champion" helps; few principals have the time, energy and knowledge to handle day-to-day support. Discovering this individual and legitimating his or her role requires buy-in from the entire staff (Little, 1987, 1988). But the real key to successful expansion of the READ model has been the engagement of a faculty cadre. Our most successful experiences came from "remote" sites, where school staff have had to build on their own resources. From these events emerged the concept of the Inquiring School.

### The "Ah-ha" Experience

In 1985 while visiting READ schools throughout California, I encountered a remarkable phenomenon. Faculties were employing READ structures and strategies (webs and weaves) for their own planning and communication. At a Southern California site, the faculty decided to simplify the cacophony of special programs (Chapter I, bilingual, special education) that were hampering efforts to implement an integrated literacy program. At their preschool retreat, faculty constructed webs around "Our ideal program" versus "What we've got now." From the webs emerged a matrix contrasting "Categorical programs now" and "Categorical programs next year." The teachers divided the task of program revision into four chunks (K.I.S.S.): curriculum, assessment, staff development, and accountability. In May they demonstrated their approach to visitors from the International Reading Association convention—they had constructed an integrated, school-wide program, 3 years before Congress authorized the concept (Williams, Richmond, & Mason, 1987).

A second example materialized at a Bay Area School. The staff first reviewed the standard approach recommended for implementation of READ: focus for several weeks on a single curriculum component (e.g., vocabulary is a universal need, so work on that for a while), then move to narrative and literature; in the spring tackle decoding and exposition (tough areas). Over the course of several meetings, the faculty developed a novel proposal in which curriculum teams would develop expertise concurrently in vocabulary, narrative, exposition, and phonics. READ became the school's central focus for the year, and every teacher became expert in a domain.

What was compelling about these and other examples was the reliance on the techniques of critical literacy to foster school-wide problem solving—by grown-ups! The results were impressive. Faculty room discussions centered on curriculum and instruction. Technical terms—matrix, episodic analysis, sequential exposition, graphic organizer—popped up frequently in small talk. Student work blossomed everywhere, on classroom walls and outside teachers' doors, by the principal's office, around the lunch room. Questions directed to me shifted from "What do you think we should do?" to "We made some changes in the project. They seem to work pretty well. What do you think?"

Suddenly came the realization that I was observing Schaefer's "community of inquiry." I should not overdramatize the events, which were relatively rare and frequently subtle. Nonetheless, two features struck me as especially significant. First, teachers were acting in concert to solve school-wide *educational* problems. Second, they were employing tools from the technical core of the enterprise: the curriculum of critical literacy. The result entailed a high degree of *vertical integration;* professional efforts focused on classroom concepts and pragmatics, rather than turning into "one more committee."

The outcome was a fundamental change in school climate. Teachers assumed the status and characteristics of genuine professionals. The organization took on a different structural "flavor." On the other hand, the engine driving this transformation was quite familiar: the core curricula of elementary schooling, reading and writing, were scarcely mysterious entities. The vision of literacy as a technology for amplifying language and thought freed teachers from the constraints of basal readers and standardized tests, but it also empowered them to overcome the barriers of time, money, and mandates that had frustrated previous efforts.

## FOSTERING AN INQUIRING SCHOOL

The preceding sketch describes one approach to the reformation of the American elementary school. What lessons can be learned from this experience? Schaefer (1967) thought that organizational change was essential to professional development and problem solving, and he had a few suggestions to offer on this topic:

> [Elementary teachers] do not possess a working technical vocabulary, concepts or propositions on teaching sufficiently precise to be shared in professional association. . . . A practitioner rarely perceives himself as having any stake in [educational research]. Fully occupied with the daily business of keeping school, he is effectively deprived of the opportunity to reflect systematically upon his experience. Unless typical organizational patterns are radically restructured, there is little possibility that the situation can be improved. ( pp. 42–43)

READ teachers turned this formulation upside down; empowered by the concepts of critical literacy, they led their schools to achieve high-level student objectives in thinking and communicating by employing the same tools for their own reflection and interaction. They became reflective about their classroom work, and began to communicate about the core of their work—which led to institutional change. One basis for establishing the school as a community of inquiry, then, rests on the core curriculum of the elementary grades: reading and writing. My experience suggests that this foundation is more than practical. It is a deeply conceptual insight, and it also connects with motivations and feelings. Teachers' chief aim is to foster the intellectual and social development of children. Pay and working conditions are not major attractions; instead, satisfaction comes from success with students and interactions with colleagues.

Besides the establishment of critical literacy as the touchstone for problem solving and communication throughout the institution, what else is needed to support the development of the Inquiring School concept? My answers are necessarily tentative. The conceptual and pragmatic issues are daunting. Research and development takes not weeks or months, but years. Nonetheless, let me propose three other elements that buttress the model: *team communication, group decision making,* and *action-oriented evaluation.* We have experimented with the first item on the list, and evidence favoring the others can be found in the literature (two other items, *personal growth* and *leadership,* have been proposed by several school cadres with whom we have discussed the topic). Remaining to be studied is the combined effect of the total configuration, when care is taken to connect the several parts into a coherent whole. Slavin (1984) has suggested that school improvement requires "doing several things well." I concur with this advice, and add the caution that what is done and how it is done is crucial.

Our experience with team communication illustrates the coherence principle.

Most people assume that a group of educated adults, if possessed of a shared purpose and a modicum of good will, can easily join forces to solve a problem. From personal experience with innumerable faculty meetings, including 4 years as a school board member, I question this assumption.

Implementation of Project READ required considerable teamwork: to plan lessons, to observe and give feedback, and to disseminate the techniques to colleagues. In the first few years of READ schools, graduate assistants handled these tasks through weekly meetings with individuals and small groups. Without realizing it, our staff was assuming responsibility for several critical matters: setting the agenda, fostering group interaction, managing the meeting, and determining next steps. As READ expanded, the importance and challenge of these tasks became increasingly apparent. Time is a scarce resource in schools, and teachers quickly lose patience when a hard-won 30-minute grade-level session starts 10 minutes late and setting an agenda takes an additional 10 minutes. The problem can be alleviated in part by "making time." For instance, we made the radical suggestion that faculty meetings be devoted to staff-development activities. But a fundamental task remained; teams came back with the question: "How do you plan a staff development meeting?"

As part of another project for school administrators, we had created a "group process" package for facilitating team meetings (Funderburg, Wippern, & Calfee, 1987). The package combined techniques for planning and conducting a meeting, opportunities for group exercises, and a technical vocabulary for discussing group process. It occurred to us that these techniques could also serve READ teachers. We simplified the package and gave it a name, *Teaming with excellence* (TWE). The initial reception in READ workshops was cool—one more item on the agenda, another set of labels and terms.

A breakthrough came when we realized that the package did not have to be designed as an add-on, but could be integrated with the concepts and strategies of critical literacy. For instance, a READ lesson is designed around two dimensions: sequence (opening, middle, closing, followup) and substance (content, process, and structure). We redesigned TWE to incorporate the same elements. Meetings are not exactly the same as lessons. The teacher "agendizes" a lesson, whereas the team leader generally consults with colleagues to plan a meeting (we recognized later the advantages of engaging students in lesson planning, but that is another story). The similarities were nonetheless substantial. Graphic organizers like webs and matrices markedly improved the middle of a TWE meeting. The concept of a closing review and assignment for followup relieved the sense of emptiness—"What did we really decide during the last hour?"—that often comes when participants are leaving a session.

The present version of TWE incorporates three distinctive components (K.I.S.S.): the *Meeting,* the *Group,* and the *Individual*. The program takes about 20–30 minutes, usually placed near the start of a READ workshop. The techniques are practiced and discussed during small-group sessions throughout the workshop. The express intent is a systematic opportunity to practice team-building as an essential ingredient in school restructuring and professionalization.

The Meeting component includes techniques for planning the schedule (including follow-up responsibilities), for organizing and analyzing the content, and for "drawing pictures" of the group's deliberations. The Group segment reviews important roles (e.g., facilitator, recorder, reporter, observer), and activities that support collaboration (initiating, clarifying, and so on). Transfer is relatively easy for teachers familiar with cooperative learning. The Individual focuses on responsibilities of team members, and portrays stereotypical roles that can either help or harm the group process (e.g., Andy Analyst, Clarence Clown).

TWE techniques are simple-minded. The parallel with READ lesson design fosters transfer from working with students in a classroom to adults working in a meeting. The program incorporates a profound concept: the importance of making explicit what we otherwise take for granted. I have discussed elsewhere the value of *explanation* as a hallmark of the school experience (Calfee, 1987). The class that creates a semantic map around the topic of *food* is dealing with a commonplace familiar to all. What can they learn from the exercise? First, individuals gain insights from the wisdom of the group. Second, they acquire facility in the process of group problem-solving, which then serves as a tool for wrestling with larger, more authentic tasks (recall Duckworth's primary and secondary tasks). The same generalizations hold for TWE. Rather than assuming that adults can approach a task as a team, TWE provides reflective experience with this process, and *names* the roles and procedures. It furnishes adults with a meta-cognitive approach to group problem solving.

The two other components mentioned earlier, evaluation and decision making, are not developed in the present version of the Inquiring School model, although we have identified some starting points. Teacher-based research is currently a "hot topic," but we are unclear about how to translate social science methods to the needs of school-site evaluation (Cochran-Smith & Lytle, 1990; Hiebert & Calfee, in press). Similarly, the move toward site-based management has led to renewed interest in decision making (e.g., Saphier, Bigda-Peyton, & Pierson, 1989). Whatever the shape of these elements in the model, it will be important to "connect" the various parts. All elements build on effective use of language; all link to the elementary reading–writing curriculum, when the latter is defined as critical literacy.

Simplicity, parsimony, coherence—these themes undergird the Inquiring School concept described in this chapter. Today's schools are often places of chaos, a melange of overlapping and conflicting programs, concepts, and languages. The vision of the Inquiring School assumes that teachers are wise and dedicated to their craft, and that with the proper tools a school faculty can create an educational experience sufficient to guide all students to their full potential. The challenge is to empower teaching communities to unite in systematic inquiry toward that end. It is with more than a small measure of delight that I close this chapter with the suggestion that the simplest and most basic entries in the curriculum—reading and writing— provide the "few powerful tools" needed to achieve this goal.

# REFERENCES

Apple, M., & Junck, S. (1990). You don't have to be a teacher to teach this unit: Teaching, technology, and gender in the classroom. *American Educational Research Journal, 27,* 227–254.

Balmuth, M. (1982). *The roots of phonics: A historical introduction.* New York: McGraw-Hill.

Barton, J., & Calfee, R. C. (1989). Theory becomes practice: One program. In Flood, J., Lapp, D., & N. Farnham (Eds.), *Content area reading-learning: Instructional studies.* Englewood Cliffs, NJ: Prentice Hall.

Brown, R. (1987). Who is accountable for thoughtfulness? *Phi Delta Kappan, 69*(1), 49–52.

Calfee, R. C. (1981). Cognitive psychology and educational practice. In D. Berliner (Ed.), *Review of Educational Research.* Washington DC: American Educational Research Association.

Calfee, R. C. (1982). Literacy and illiteracy: Teaching the nonreader to survive in the modern world. *Annals of Dyslexia, 32,* 71–91.

Calfee, R. C. (1987). Those who can explain, teach. *Educational Policy, 1,* 9–28. Also in L. Weise, P. G. Altbach, G. P. Kelly, H. G. Petrie, & S. Slaughter (Eds.), *Crisis in teaching.* Albany, NY: State University of New York Press.

Calfee, R. C. (in press). School-wide programs to improve literacy instruction for students at-risk. In B. Means & M. Knapp (Eds.), *Teaching advanced skills to educationally disadvantaged students.* San Francisco, CA: Jossey Bass.

Calfee, R. C., Avelar La Salle, R., & Cancino, H. (in press). Critical literacy as the foundation for accelerating the education of at-risk students. In H. Levin (Ed.), *Accelerating the education of at-risk students.*

Calfee, R. C., & Drum, P. A. (1986). Research on teaching reading. In M. C. Wittrock (Ed.), *Handbook of research on teaching* (3rd Ed). New York: Macmillan.

Calfee, R. C., Henry, M. K., & Funderburg, J. A. (1988). A model for school change. In S. J. Samuels, & P. D. Pearson (Eds.), *Changing school reading programs.* Newark, DE: IRA.

Calfee, R. C., & Nelson-Barber, S. (in press). Diversity and constancy in human thinking: Critical literacy as amplifier of intellect and experience. In E. H. Hiebert (Ed.), *Literacy for a diverse society.* New York: Teachers College Press.

Calfee, R. C., & Shefelbine, J. (1981). A structural model of teaching. In A. Lewy & D. Nevo (Eds.), *Evaluation roles in education.* New York: Gordon and Breach.

CED (Committee for Economic Development). (1987). *Children in need: Investment strategies for the educationally disadvantaged.* New York: Committee for Economic Development.

Chall, J. S. (1983). *Stages of reading development.* New York: McGraw-Hill.

Chambliss, M., & Calfee, R. C. (1988). Beyond decoding: Pictures of expository prose. *Annals of Dyslexia, 38,* 243–258.

Cochran-Smith, M., & Lytle, S. L. (1990). Research on teaching and teacher research: Issues that divide. *Educational Researcher, 19*(2), 2–11.

Cohen, M. (1988). *Restructuring the education system: Agenda for the 1990s.* Washington DC: National Governors' Association.

Cooper, M. (1988). Whose culture is it, anyway? In A. Lieberman (Ed.), *Building a professional culture in schools.* New York: Teachers College Press.

Cuban, L. (1990). Reforming again, again, and again. *Educational Researcher, 19*(1), 3–13.

Devaney K., & Sykes, G. (1988). Making the case for professionalism. In A. Lieberman (Ed.), *Building a professional culture in schools.* New York: Teachers College Press.

Duckworth, E. (1987). *"The having of wonderful ideas" and other essays on teaching and learning*. New York: Teachers College Press.

*Educational Leadership*. (1988). *The future of the teaching profession, 46*(3).

*Educational Leadership*. (1990a). *Creating a culture for change, 47*(8).

*Educational Leadership*. (1990b). *Restructuring: What is it?, 47*(7).

Eisner, E. (1991). *The enlightened eye: Qualitative inquiry and enhanced educational practice.* New York: Macmillan.

Florio-Ruane, S. (1989). Social organization of classes and schools. In M. C. Reynolds, (Ed.). *Knowledge base for the beginning teacher*. New York: Pergamon Press.

Fraatz, J. M. B. (1987). *The politics of reading*. New York: Teachers College Press.

Funderburg, J. A., Wippern, D., & Calfee, R. C. (1987). *The San Jose-Stanford Administrator Training Program: The language of ATP*. Unpublished manuscript. Stanford CA: Stanford School of Education.

Gage, N. L., & Needels, M. C. (1989). Process-product research on teaching: A review of criticisms. *Elementary School Journal, 89*, 253–300.

Goodlad, J. I. (Ed.). (1987). *The ecology of school renewal*. Chicago: National Society for the Study of Education.

Goodlad, J. I. (1990). *Teachers for our nation's schools*. San Francisco, CA: Jossey-Bass.

Goodman, K. S., Smith, E. B., Meredith, R., & Goodman, Y. (1987). *Language and thinking in school: A whole-language curriculum*. New York: Richard Owen.

Grant, W. T. Foundation. (1988). *The forgotten half: Non-college youth in America*. Washington DC: W. T. Grant Commission on Work, Family, and Citizenship.

Hatano, G. (1982). Cognitive consequences of practice in culture-specific procedural skills. *Quarterly Newsletter of the Laboratory of Comparative Human Cognition, 4*(1), 15–18.

Hiebert, E. H., & Calfee, R. C. (in press). Assessment for instructional decision-making. In A. E. Farstrup and S. J. Samuels (Eds.), *What research has to say to the reading teacher*. Newark, DE: International Reading Association.

Hodgkinson, H. L. (1989). *The same client: Demographics of education and social service delivery systems*. Washington DC: Institute for Educational Leadership.

Joyce, B. (Ed.). (1990). *Changing school culture through staff development*. Alexandria VA: Association for Supervision and Curriculum Development.

Knapp, M. S., & Shields, P. M. (Eds.). (1990). *Better schooling for the children of poverty: Alternatives to conventional wisdom*. Volume II: Commissioned papers and literature review. Menlo Park CA: SRI International.

Lewis, A. (1989). *Restructuring America's schools*. Washington DC: American Association for School Administrators.

Lieberman, A. (Ed.). (1988). *Building a professional culture in schools*. New York: Teachers College Press.

Little, J. W. (1987). Teachers as colleagues. In V. Richardson-Koehler (Ed.), *Educators' Handbook*. New York: Longman.

Little, J. W. (1988). Assessing prospects for teacher leadership. In A. Lieberman (Ed.). *Building a professional culture in schools*. New York: Teachers College Press.

McDonnell, L. M. (1989). *Restructuring American schools: The promise and the pitfalls*. New York: Institute on Education and the Economy, Teachers College, Columbia University.

Millman, J., & Darling-Hammond, L. (Eds.). (1990). *The new handbook of teacher evaluation: Assessing elementary and secondary school teachers*. Newbury Park CA: Sage Publications.

Murphy, J. (Ed.). (1990). *The educational reform movement of the 1980s: Perspectives and cases*. Berkeley CA: McCutchan Publishing.

National Commission on Excellence in Education. (1983). *A nation at risk: The imperative for educational reform*. Washington, DC: Government Printing Office.

National Center for Education and the Economy. (1990). *America's choice: High skills or low wages*. Washington DC: National Center for Education and the Economy.

Reed, S., & Sauter, R. C. (1990). Children of poverty: The status of 12 million young Americans. *Phi Delta Kappan, 71*(10), K1–K12.

Resnick, L. B. (1987). *Education and learning to think.* Washington, DC: Academy Press.

Resnick, L. B. (Ed.). (1989). *Knowing, learning, and instruction: Essays in honor of Robert Glaser.* Hillsdale NJ: Erlbaum.

Reynolds, M. C. (Ed.). (1989). *The knowledge base for the beginning teacher.* New York: Pergamon Press.

Rosow, J. M., & Zager, R. (1989). *Allies in educational reform: How teachers, unions and administrators can join forces for better schools.* San Francisco CA: Jossey-Bass.

Salomon, G., & Perkins, D. N. (1989). Rocky roads to transfer: Rethinking mechanisms of a neglected phenomenon. *Educational Psychologist, 24,* 113–142.

Saphier, J., Bigda-Peyton, T., & Pierson, G. (1989). *How to make decisions that stay made.* Alexandria VA: Association for Supervision and Curriculum Development.

Schaefer, R. J. (1967). *The school as a center of inquiry.* New York: Harper and Row.

Shulman, L. S. (1987). Knowledge and teaching: Foundation of the new reform. *Harvard Educational Review, 57,* 1–22.

Slavin, R. E. (1984). Component building: A strategy for research-based instructional improvement. *Elementary School Journal, 84,* 255–269.

SRI. (1987). *Opportunites for strategic investment in K–12 science education.* Menlo Park, CA: SRI International.

Williams, B. I., Richmond, P. A., & Mason, B. J. (Eds.). (1987). *Designs for compensatory education.* Washington, DC: Research and Evaluation Associates.

# Introduction to
# Chapter 9

*Barbara Z. Presseisen, Director of National Networking, Research for Better Schools, and Author of* At-Risk Students and Thinking: Perspectives from Research.

In the midst of much educational change and reform, Art Costa challenges us to consider what is a supportive environment for developing thinkers? For that matter, he raises our consciousness about the very issue *what is a community of thoughtful people* and how do our schools measure up to that definition. His discussion forces us to see that American schools are lodged in a nineteenth century factory model of education, while already facing 21st century space age problems.

Costa is both an optimist and a pragmatist. On three important aspects he says it is possible to forge an environment that can support the program which underlies, in the words of our President and Governors' national goals, "an economy in which our citizens must be able to think for a living." It is important to consider each of these issues.

That education needs to be purposeful and that such a focus needs to be commonly shared and articulated by all the persons in a school system is at least as old as John Dewey's view of schooling in a democracy. However, it should receive even more emphasis today, for all levels of our educational system seem to be fragmented and disassociated from a meaningful whole. The gaps between preschool, elementary education, secondary education, an higher education are no less felt than the chasm between liberal arts and teacher education. Yet, are learning and thinking any different across all these constituents of the educational process? A school environment that supports thinking is important to all these levels.

Costa discusses thinking as the *raison d'etre* for the educational community to come together; he proposes that developing minds, both those of the teachers and the students, are the real out-comes for which to strive. "Teachers are the bearers of civilization," said the President of Columbia University (1986), and their trust must be balanced by autonomy and freedom or the goal cannot be achieved. Freedom to explore and to make errors, so that one can learn from them as well as from discoveries, must not only be tolerated—they must be sought. Then, perchance, curriculum can entice and instruction motivate.

Finally, Costa calls for an environment in which schools and classrooms are interdependent. As restructuring efforts abound in our country, will such endeavors have the impetus to significantly alter administrative and supervisory structures? Can we communicate in our schools with the speed and flexibility of a facsimile machine? Can the supportive environments for teaching thinking be "user friendly" and interactive? Discerning what is central and what is not is the old thinking task of comparing and contrasting. Costa's chapter will make you consider what is, what is not, and what might have been—if only we understood!

# 9 An Environment For Thinking

Arthur L. Costa
*California State University, Sacramento*

> *IN THE MAIN, THE BUREAUCRATIC STRUCTURE OF THE WORK PLACE IS MORE INFLUENTIAL IN DETERMINING WHAT PROFES- SIONALS DO THAN ARE PERSONAL ABILITIES, PROFESSIONAL TRAINING OR PREVIOUS EXPERIENCE.*
> *THEREFORE, CHANGE EFFORTS SHOULD FOCUS ON THE STRUCTURE OF THE WORKPLACE, NOT THE TEACHERS.*
> —Jack Frymier, "Bureaucracy and the Neutering of Teachers,"*Phi Delta Kappan*, September, 1987, p. 10.

Many factors influence teachers' thinking as they make decisions about curriculum, instruction, and content. Their own cultural background, cognitive style, and professional values and beliefs about education all subconsciously enter their daily decision making. Knowledge of students' needs and perceptions of students' abilities and backgrounds influence teacher judgments about "when" to teach "what" to "whom." The available resources for instruction—tests, materials, equipment, textbooks, time, and space—all have an impact on teachers' instructional planning.

Less obvious influences on teacher thought, but vastly more compelling, are the norms, culture, and climate of the school setting. Hidden but powerful cues emanate from the school environment. They signal the institutional value system that governs the operation of the organization (Saphier & King, 1985).

Recent efforts to bring an intellectual focus to our schools most likely will prove futile unless the school environment conveys to the staff, students, and community that development of the intellect is of prime importance as the

169

school's goal. Efforts to enhance the staff's instructional competencies, develop curriculum, revise instructional materials and testing procedures, and pilot and adopt published programs are important components in implementing cognitive education. It is also crucial that the school climate in which teachers make their decisions be aligned with the goals of full intellectual development.

Unfortunately, schools can be intellectually depressing places, not only for students but for teachers as well. John Goodlad (1984) found that:

- Teachers are extremely isolated. They perform their craft behind closed doors and have little time within rigid daily schedules to meet, plan, observe, and talk with one another.
- Teachers often lack a sense of power and efficacy. Some feel they are at the bottom of the hierarchy while the decisions and evaluations affecting them are being made "up there" someplace.
- The complex, intelligent act of teaching is often reduced to formulas or series of steps and competencies, the uniform performance of which supposedly connotes excellence in the art and elegance of teaching.
- Information about student achievement is for political, evaluative, or coercive purposes; it neither involves nor instructs the school staff members in reflecting on, evaluating, and improving curriculum and instruction.
- Educational innovations are often viewed as mere "tinkering" with the instructional program. There are so many of them, and their impact is so limited, that teachers sometimes feel, "If I do nothing, this, too, shall pass." Instead of institutionalizing change, traditional practices and policies so deeply entrenched in the educational bureaucracy remain static. Testing, reporting, securing parent understanding and support, teacher evaluation, scheduling, school organization, and discipline procedures are seldom revised to harmonize with the overall innovation.

When such a dismal school climate exists, teachers understandably become depressed. Their vivid imagination, altruism, creativity, and intellectual prowess may soon succumb to the daily occurrences of unruly students, irrelevant curriculum, impersonal surroundings, and equally disinterested coworkers. Under such conditions, the likelihood that teachers will value the development of students' intellect is marginal.

## TOWARD A THOUGHTFUL SCHOOL ENVIRONMENT

Teachers are more likely to teach for thinking in an intellectually stimulating environment. When teachers are in school climate conditions which signal, promote, and facilitate their intellectual growth, they will gradually align their classrooms and instruction to promote students' intellectual growth as well. As teachers teach students to think, become more aware of conditions that promote student thinking, and become more powerful thinkers themselves, they will demand and create school climate conditions that are intellectually growth-producing as well. Thus, respect for intelligent behavior grows to pervade all levels of the institution.

In this chapter, I propose that three environmental conditions facilitate the intellectual growth of all the school's inhabitants. These conditions are that: (1) all participants share a common vision of the school as a home for the mind, (2) the process of thinking is the content of curriculum and instruction, and (3) schools and classrooms are interdependent communities. These conditions provide a sharper image of a climate for thinking in schools and classrooms that are dedicated to becoming homes for the mind.

## A COMMON VISION

Effective organizations are characterized by a deep sense of purposefulness and a vision of the future. Members at all levels share a commitment to that vision, a sense of ownership, and an internal responsibility for performance (Harmon, 1988). This shared vision is evident in several ways.

### Faith in Human Intellectual Potential

There must be an inherent faith that all people can continue to improve their intellectual capacities throughout life; that learning to think is as valid a goal for the "at-risk" handicapped, disadvantaged, and foreign-speaking as it is for the "gifted and talented"; and that all of us have the potential for even greater creativity and intellectual power. Students, teachers, and administrators realize that learning to use and to continually refine their intelligent behavior is the purpose of their life-long education. Such a belief is expressed in many ways.

Thinking is valued by all students, certified staff, and classified staff as well. A principal of a "thinking school" reported that a newly hired custodian constantly asked her to check on how well he was cleaning the classrooms and to tell him whether he was doing an adequate job. She decided to help him develop a clear mental image of what a clean classroom looked like and then worked to enhance his ability to evaluate for himself how well the room he cleaned fit that image.

School staff members continue to define and clarify thinking as a goal and seek ways to gain assistance in achieving it. Their commitment is reinforced when they are able to report and share progress toward installing thinking in their schools and classrooms. One superintendent reviews with site administrators their long-range goals and progress toward including the development of thinking skills in the school's mission. Teachers keep journals and portfolios and periodically share with their colleagues new insights about lessons and activities to teach problem-solving strategies, creativity and thought processes.

## Philosophy, Policies, and Practices

The vision is also expressed in the district's board-adopted mission statement, purposes, and policies. Enhancing reasoning and problem solving behavior is explicitly stated in the school district's adopted philosophy and mission. District policies and practices are constantly scrutinized for their consistency with, and contribution to, that philosophy. Evidence of their use as criteria for decision making is examined. Furthermore, procedures for continuing to study, refine, and improve district-wide practices encourage schools to keep growing toward more thoughtful practice.

Personnel practices, for example, reflect the desire to infuse thinking. Job specifications for hiring new personnel include skills in teaching thinking. Teachers are empowered to make decisions that affect their jobs. Supervision, evaluation, and staff development practices enhance the perceptions and intellectual growth of certified staff and honor their role as professional decision-makers (Costa & Garmston, 1985; Costa, Garmston, & Lambert, 1988).

Selection criteria for texts, tests, instructional materials, and other media include their contribution to thinking. Counseling, discipline, library, and psychological services are constantly evaluated for their enhancement of, and consistency with, thoughtful practice (Curwin & Mendler, 1988).

## Protecting What's Important—
## Saying "No" to Distractions

Sometimes our vision of the desired school is temporarily blurred or obscured. We are distracted from our intellectual focus by fads, bandwagons, other educational "panaceas," and by pressures from public and vocal groups to include their special interests in the curriculum. The school's purposes may be temporarily clouded by politically and financially expedient decisions. Educators must have the strength to ignore all of these distractions as irrelevant to their central issue of developing thoughtful humans.

Deciding what to omit helps sharpen a staff's conviction of what to include. If we adopt any current educational practice, material or curriculum without critically analyzing its consistency with developing thinking, we weaken our mission and our vision.

On the other hand, we need to encourage philosophical discussion because it gives voice to alternative views. Considering other perspectives creates tensions, honors divergent thinking, and expands and refines our vision. Such discussion encourages staff members to include modes of thinking and inquiring in their classroom interaction. Such discussion strengthens the staff's commitment to the principle that to learn anything—to gain cultural literacy or basic skills—requires an engagement of the mind.

Knowing that thinking is the important goal, all inhabitants of the school believe that their right to think will be protected. District leaders keep this primary goal in focus as they make day-to-day decisions. Teachers' rights to be involved in the decisions affecting them are protected, as are the rights of those who choose not to be involved in decision making. Since change and growth are viewed as intellectual processes, not events, we value the time invested in ownership, commitment, and learning.

## Communications

Embedded in an organization's communications are expressions of what it prizes. Pick up any newspaper and you see a reflection of society's values in its major sections: sports, finances, and entertainment.

As a school becomes a more thoughtful place, the vision increasingly pervades all of its communications. Report cards, parent conferences, and other progress reports include indicators of the growth of students' intelligent behaviors: questioning, metacognition, flexibility of thinking, persistence, listening to others' points of view, and creativity (Costa, 1985b).

Growth in students' thinking abilities is assessed and reported in numerous ways, including teacher-made tests, structured observations, and interviews. Students maintain journals to record their own thinking and metacognition; and they share, compare, and evaluate their own growth of insight, creativity, and problem-solving strategies over time. Parents, too, look for ways in which their children are transferring intellectual growth from the classroom to family and home situations. Portfolios of students' work show how their organizational abilities, conceptual development, and creativity are growing. Test scores report such critical thinking skills as vocabulary growth, syllogistic thinking, reasoning by analogy, problem solving, and fluency.

Parents and community members are sent magazine and newspaper articles, calendars, and newsletters informing them of the school's intent and ways they can engage children's intellect. Parent coordinators can be enlisted to inform the community of the school's goals and to describe ways parents may help and monitor their child's intellectual development (Feldman, 1986).

To inform the community, mottoes, slogans, and mission statements are visible everywhere. "LINCOLN SCHOOLS ARE THOUGHT-FULL SCHOOLS" is painted on the district's delivery trucks. "THOUGHT IS TAUGHT" is emblazoned on that school's note pads. "MAKING THINKING HAPPEN" is printed on the school's letterhead stationery. "WE'RE TRAINING OUR BRAINS" is the motto on student-made buttons. "LEARNING TO THINK/THINKING TO LEARN" is silk screened on the schools "T" shirts.

## Tangible Support

How teachers, school administrators, and other leadership personnel expend their valuable and limited resources—time, energy, and money—conveys the organization's value system. The School Board encourages school principals to spend time on curriculum development and instructionally related activities by hiring administrative assistants to provide support for principals.

Thoughtful schools allocate financial resources to promote thinking. Fulltime thinking skills resource teachers are employed. Substitutes are hired so that teachers can be released to visit and coach one another. Staff members and parents are sent to workshops, courses, conferences, and inservice sessions to learn more about effective thinking and the teaching of thinking.

Instructional materials and programs related to thinking are purchased, and time is provided to plan for and train teachers in the use of these materials and to gather evidence of their effectiveness. Consultants discuss and report new learnings about intellectual development and implications for program improvement. Vignettes and "critical incidents" are recorded, described, and analyzed as indicators of students' application of critical and creative thinking skills and dispositions.

Administrators use their time and energy to visit classrooms to learn more

### THE ART OF COGNITIVE COACHING FOR INTELLIGENT TEACHING

#### A Definition

Cognitive Coaching is the coach's application of a set of strategies designed to enhance the teacher's perceptions, decision, and intellectual functions. These inner thought processes are prerequisite to improving overt instructional behaviors which will, in turn, produce greater student learning.

#### A Visual Representation

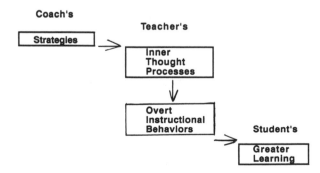

FIG. 9.1. From Costa and Gramsten (1989). *The Art of Cognitive Coaching: Supervision for Intelligent Teaching.* Sacramento, CA. The Institute for Intelligent Behavior.

about, and to coach, instruction in thinking, following the steps in Fig. 9.1. Teachers spend time planning lessons and observing each other teach for thinking. Time in classrooms, as well, is allocated to thinking skills and talking about thinking.

Thus, we see that the whole school community—students, teachers, administrators, classified personnel, board members, and parents—share a common vision of the thoughtful school. They continually work to sharpen that image, to clarify their goals, and to align daily practices with that vision of the future: the first condition for intellectual growth.

## PROCESS AS CONTENT

The process of thinking must become the content of curriculum. Development of the intellect, learning to learn, knowledge production, metacognition, decision making, creativity, and problem solving must become the subject matter of instruction. Content must be selected because of its contribution to the thinking process, and thus become a vehicle to practice these thinking processes.

### Problem Solving, Decision Making, and Open Communication

Being committed to the improvement of intellectual growth, everyone in the school is willing to discuss their curriculum and instruction strategies as well as their suggestion for improving school climate, interpersonal relationships, and the quality of their interactions and problem solving. As an example of process as content, students and school personnel practice, evaluate, and improve their listening skills of paraphrasing, empathizing, clarifying, and understanding.

Moreover, at school board, administrative, and faculty meetings, decision-making processes are discussed, explained, and adopted. At these meetings observers are invited to take field notes about thinking processes used, and growth in the group's decision making, consensus seeking, and communication skills.

As a first step, in every school board meeting, teacher's meeting, and classroom we must respect each group member's opinions and questions. Disagreements are stated without fear of damaging relationships. Debates and critical assessment of alternate points of view are encouraged. Responsibility for "errors, ommissions, and inadequacies" is accepted without blaming others. Responses are given and justified, and new ideas are advanced without fear of criticism or judgment. Group members' differing priorities, values, logic, and philosophical beliefs become the topics of analysis, dialogue, understanding, and further questions.

## Continuing to Learn—Expanding the Knowledge Base

Knowledge about thinking and the teaching of thinking is vast, complex, uncertain, and incomplete (Marzano, Brandt, Hughes, Jones, Presseissen, Rankin, & Suhor, 1987). We will never know all there is to learn about this topic, nor would we wish to reduce teaching thinking to a simplistic, step-by-step lesson plan (Brandt, 1987). In a thoughtful school, the inhabitants continually expand their knowledge base: gaining more content, learning more about learning, and thinking more about thinking. They add to their repertoire of instructional skills and strategies, seeking greater diversity rather than conformity.

Knowing that the school's mission is to develop the intellect, teachers increasingly strive to invest thoughtful learning, metacognition, and rigor into curriculum and instruction. They expand their repertoire of instructional skills and strategies to develop a wide range of reasoning, creative, and cooperative abilities in students.

Teachers increase their knowledge of the sciences, mathematics, and humanities because it helps them ask more provocative questions which invite inquiry and critical thinking. A wider knowledge base supports the transfer of concepts across several subject areas and encourages appreciation for the disciplined methodologies of great thinkers throughout history.

Teachers draw from their growing repertoire of knowledge about instructional techniques and strategies to make decisions on goals, students' characteristics, and the context in which they are working. They vary their lesson designs according to students' developmental levels, cognitive styles, and modality preferences (Jones, 1987).

While the students will expand their range of intelligent behaviors, teachers and administrators will concurrently improve their own thinking as well: pursuing course work in philosophy, logic, and critical thinking; learning how to perform specific thought processes as well as knowing what to do when solutions to problems are not immediately known; and acquiring study skills, learning-to-learn, reasoning, problem-solving, and decision-making strategies. Teachers and administrators learn about their own cognitive styles and how to cooperate with, and value, others who have differing styles. They learn how to cause their own "creative juices" to flow by use of strategies such as brainstorming, inventing metaphor, synectics, and concept mapping.

## Modeling

Thinking is probably best learned through imitation and emulation of effective thinkers. Adults in thoughtful schools try to model the same qualities and behaviors they want students to develop. Teachers and administrators share their metacognitive strategies in the presence of students and others as they teach, plan, and solve problems (Jones, 1987).

Staff members restrain their impulsivity during emotional crises. They listen to students, parents, and each other with empathy, precision, and understanding. They reflect on, and evaluate, their own behaviors to make them more consistent with the core value that thoughtful behavior is a valid goal of education.


## THE SCHOOL AS A COMMUNITY

Humans, as social beings, mature intellectually in reciprocal relationships with other people. Vygotsky (1978) points out that the higher functions actually originate in interactions with others.

> Every function in. . . cultural development appears twice: first, on the social level, and later on the individual level; first between people (interpsychological), and then inside (intrapsychological). This applies equally to voluntary attention, to logical memory, and to the formation of concepts. All the higher functions originate as actual relationships between individuals.

Together, individuals generate and discuss ideas, eliciting thinking that surpasses individual effort. Together and privately, they express different perspectives, agree and disagree, point out and resolve discrepancies, and weigh alternatives. Because humans grow by this process, collegiality is a crucial climate factor.

### Collegiality

The essence of collegiality is that people in the school community are working together to better understand the nature of intelligent behavior. Professional collegiality at the district level is evident when administrators form support groups to assist one another; and when teachers and administrators from different schools, subject areas, and grade levels form networks to coordinate efforts to enhance intelligent behavior across all content areas; and, in district policies and practices. Committees and advisory groups assess staff needs, identify and locate talent, and participate in district level prioritizing and decision making. They support and provide liaison with school site efforts; plan district-wide inservice and articulation to enhance teachers' skills; and develop an aligned, coordinated, and developmentally appropriate curriculum for students.

Selection committees for instructional materials review and recommend adoption of materials and programs to enhance students' thinking. Through district-wide networks, teachers share information and materials and teach one another about skills, techniques, and strategies they have found to be effective.

In schools, teachers plan, prepare, and evaluate instructional materials. Teachers visit each other's classrooms frequently to coach and give feedback about the relationship between their instructional decisions and student behaviors. Instructional skills teams prepare, develop, remodel, and rehearse lessons. They then observe, coach, and give feedback to one another about their lessons.

Teachers and administrators continue to discuss and refine their vision of the thoughtful school, as Fred Newmann demonstrated in Chapter 6. Definitions of thinking and the teaching and evaluation of students' intellectual progress are continually clarified. Child-study teams keep portfolios of students' work and discuss each student's developmental thought processes and learning styles. Teams explore instructional problems and generate experimental solutions. Faculty meetings are held in classrooms where the host teacher shares instructional practices, materials, and videotaped lessons with the rest of the faculty. Teacher teams sequence, articulate, and plan for continuity, reinforcement, and assessment of thinking skills across grade levels and subject areas.

## An Environment of Trust

People are more likely to engage and grow in higher level, creative, and experimental thought when they are in a trusting, risk-taking climate (Kohn, 1987). Because higher-order thinking is valued as a goal for everyone in the school, the school's climate is monitored continually for signs of stress that might inhibit complex and creative thinking. Risk taking required a nonjudgmental atmosphere where information can be shared without fear that it will be used to evaluate success or failure.

A climate of trust is evident when experiments are conducted with various lesson designs, instructional sequences, and teaching materials to determine their effects on small groups of students (or with colleagues before they are used with a group). Various published programs and curricula are pilot tested, and evidence is gathered over time of their effects on students' growth in thinking skills. Teachers become researchers when alternate classroom arrangements and instructional strategies are tested and colleagues observe student interactions.

## Appreciation and Recognition

Whether a work of art, athletic prowess, acts of heroism, or precious jewels, what is valued in society is given public recognition. Core values are communicated when people see what is appreciated. If thinking is valued, it, too, is recognized by appreciation expressed to students and to teachers and administrators as well.

Students are recognized for persevering, striving for precision and accuracy, cooperating, considering another person's point-of-view, planning ahead, and expressing empathy. Students applaud each other for acts of ingenuity, compassion, and persistence. The products of their creativity, cooperation, and thoughtful investigation are displayed throughout the school.

One form of appreciation is to invite teachers to describe their successes and unique ways of organizing for teaching thinking. In faculty meetings, teachers can share videotaped lessons and showcase the positive results of their lesson planning, strategic teaching, and experimentation.

Schools within the district receive banners, flags, trophies, or certificates of excellence for their persistence, thoughtful actions, creativity, cooperative efforts, or meritorious service to the community. Some schools have even established a "Thinkers Hall of Fame."

## Sharing, Caring, and Celebrating

Thinking skills are pervasive in schools that value thinking. They are visible in the traditions, celebrations, and everyday events of school life.

Staff members are often overheard sharing humorous anecdotes of students who display their thought processes. ("I saw two 7th grade boys on the athletic field yesterday ready to start 'duking it out.' Before I could get to them, another boy intervened and I heard him say, 'Hey, you guys, restrain your impulsivity.' ")

Teachers and administrators share personal, humorous, and sometimes embarrassing anecdotes of their own problems with thinking (tactics for remembering peoples' names, finding their car in the parking lot, or solving the dilemma of locking the keys in the car.)

At career days, local business and industry leaders describe what reasoning, creative problem solving, and cooperative skills are needed in various jobs. At school assemblies, students and teachers are honored for acts of creativity, cooperation, thoughtfulness, innovation, and scholarly accomplishments. Academic decathlons, thinking and science fairs, problem-solving tournaments, dialogical debates, invention conventions, art exhibits, and musical programs celebrate the benefits of strategic planning, careful research, insightfulness, sustained practice, and cooperative efforts.

### AN HYPOTHESIS:
### TEACHERS WILL MORE LIKELY TEACH FOR THINKING
### IF THEY ARE IN AN INTELLECTUALLY STIMULATING
### ENVIRONMENT THEMSELVES.

The three elements described herein—a common vision, process as content, and the school as a community—are not ends in themselves. We must constantly remind ourselves that the reason we construct our schools is to serve youth. These elements act as cornerstones and building blocks of school climate, which are gradually cemented into a sturdy foundation. Teachers will in turn create classrooms with corresponding climate factors that recognize and support growth in students' intelligent behaviors.

This vision of education, as the development of critical thinking abilities, will become evident as students deliberate and persevere in their problem solving, work to make their oral and written products more precise and accurate, consider others' points-of-view, generate questions, and explore the alternatives and consequences of their actions. Students will engage in increasingly rigorous learning activities that challenge the intellect and imagination. Such scholarly pursuits require the acquisition, comprehension, and application of new knowledge and activate the need for perseverance, research, and increasingly complex forms of problem solving.

Since such processes of thinking as problem solving, strategic reasoning, and decision making are explicitly stated as the content of lessons, thinking processes become the "tasks that students are on." Metecognitive processes engaged in while learning are discussed and applied to new knowledge. Thus students' thinking becomes more conscious, more reflective, more efficient, more flexible, and more transferable.

Collegiality becomes evident as students work together cooperatively with their "study-buddies" in learning groups and in peer problem solving. In class meetings, students are observed learning to set goals, establishing plans, and setting priorities. They generate, hold, and apply criteria for assessing the growth of their own thoughtful behavior. They take risks, experiment with ideas, share thinking strategies (metacognition), and venture forth with creative thoughts without fear of being judged. Value judgments and criticisms are replaced by accepting, listening, empathizing with, and clarifying, one another's ideas (Costas, 1985a).

## REFERENCES

Brandt, R. (1987, October). On Teaching Thinking Skills: A Conversation with B. Othanel Smith. *Educational Leadership, 45:* 35–39.

Costa, A., & Garmston, R. (1989). *The art of cognitive coaching: Supervision for intelligent teaching.* Sacramento, CA: Institute for Intelligent Behavior. p. S–.

Costa, A. (1985a). Teacher behaviors that enhance thinking. In A. Costa (Ed.), *Developing minds: A resource book for teaching thinking.* Alexandria, VA: Association for Supervision and Curriculum Development.

Costa, A. (1985b). How can we recognize improved student thinking? In A. Costa (Ed.), *Developing minds: A resource book for teaching thinking.* Alexandria, VA: Association for Supervision and Curriculum Development.

Costa, A., & Garmston, R. (1985, February). Supervision for intelligent teaching. *Educational Leadership.* Vol: *42*(5), 70–80.

Costa, A., Garmston, R., & Lambert, L. (1988). Teacher evaluation: A cognitive development view. In S. Stanley & J. Popham (Eds.), *Teacher evaluation: Six prescriptions for success.* Alexandria, VA: Association for Supervision and Curriculum Development.

Curwin, R., & Mendler, A. (1989). *Discipline with dignity.* Alexandria, VA: Association for Supervision and Curriculum Development.

Feldman, R. D. (1986, November 11). How to improve your child's intelligent behavior. *Woman's Day,* pp. 62–68.

Goodlad, J. I. (1984). *A place called school: Prospects for the future*. New York: McGraw Hill.

Harmon, W. (1988). *Global mind change*. Indianapolis, IN: Knowledge Systems, Inc. Published in cooperation with the Institute of Noetic Sciences, Sausalito, CA.

Jones, B. F. (1987). Strategic teaching: A cognitive focus. In B. F. Jones, A. S. Palinscar, D. Ogle, & E. Carr (Eds.), *Strategic teaching and learning: Cognitive instruction in the content areas*. Alexandria, VA: Association for Supervision and Curriculum Development.

Kohn, A. (1987, September). Art for art's sake. *Psychology Today, 21,* 52–57.

Marzano, R., Brands, R., Hughes, C., Jones, B. F., Presseissen, B., Rankin, S., & Suhor, C. (1987). *Dimensions of thinking*. Alexandria, VA: Association for Supervision and Curriculum Development.

Saphier, J., King, M. (1985, March). Good seeds grow in strong cultures. *Educational Leadership, 42,*(6), 67–74.

Vygotsky, L. (1978). *Society of mind*. Cambridge, MA: Harvard University Press.

# Introduction to
# Chapter 10

*Robert N. Ennis, Director, Illinois Critical Thinking Project, Department of Educational Policy Studies, University of Illinois.*

"Changing Societal Needs: Changing How We Think About Curriculum and Instruction" by Margaret Tinzmann, Beau Fly Jones, and Jean Pierce brings us up to date on the psychological (though not the philosophical) literature concerned with the teaching of thinking and on the infrastructure that has developed around the pursuit of this task. They then present a description of their own program, *Breakthroughs*, which is based upon significant features emphasized in this literature, including cooperative learning, metacognition, problem solving, phases of learning, and graphic organizers. The program explicitly and justifiably rejects the idea that the basic skills must be developed before the higher order learnings.

The 1- and 2-week trials (45 minutes per day) given to this program in attempts at formal assessment seem of insufficient duration to do justice to any program with such grand objectives. But even so, the authors report a statistically significant positive finding, and have various indications of success. Although more research is needed, the program has promise.

Avenues of planned further development for the program include teaching students *how to do* such higher order activities as comparing and contrasting, evaluating ideas for solving problems, and judging the appropriateness of predictions. This planned development is commendable. Without such guidance for students built into such a program, the risk is that students will be well motivated, but confused.

The chapter is interesting to read and will be helpful to many professionals.

# 10 Changing Societal Needs: Changing How We Think About Curriculum and Instruction

Margaret Tinzmann
Beau Fly Jones
*North Central Regional Educational Laboratory*

Jean Pierce
*Northern Illinois University*

## INTRODUCTION[1]

The first part of this chapter presents a broad view of problems with schooling in our nation today. Dramatic societal changes along with research from a variety of sources compel educators to rethink traditional school practices to ensure a high quality of life for all citizens. New practices must derive from a vision of learning appropriate for the 21st century.

In the second part of the chapter, we focus on curriculum and instruction in the classroom. We briefly review research and trends in critical areas and, for each area, provide an example of how we have applied this research to curriculum development work in which we have been involved over the past 2 years. This work represents our attempt to merge the best that we know about curriculum materials with the best that we know about instructional practices. In this section, we also summarize three studies that have evaluated the effectiveness of the materials.

## THE PROBLEMS

Doesn't every school in the country promote thinking? Well, yes and no. Yes, every school believes its mission is to promote thinking; indeed, schools throughout America have plans for improving student achievement. The "no" part of the

---

[1]Parts of this chapter were adapted from B. F. Jones, (1990). The importance of restructuring to promote learning. In D. S. Ogle, W. T. Pink, and B. F. Jones (Eds.), *Restructuring to promote learning in America's schools: Selected readings. Volume 1.* Columbus, OH: Zaner Bloser.

answer refers to the fact that schools are not always successful in meeting their goals. Too many students are dropping out (Wehlege & Rutter, 1987). Even some of those students who graduate with good grades and test scores cannot read with fluency, think critically, or solve problems (Anderson, Hiebert, Scott, & Wilkinson, 1985; Dossey, Mullis, Linquist, & Chambers, 1988; Kirsch & Jungeblut, 1986; McKnight, Crosswhite, Dossey, Swafford, Travers, & Cooney, 1987; National Assessment of Educational Progress, 1983, 1985, 1986). Too many students leave school unprepared to meet the demands of a changing society and to lead productive, nurturing lives.

The problem is complex and requires solutions in a variety of areas, including systemic restructuring (Goodlad, 1984; Reigeluth, 1988; Sizer, 1989), new models of staff development (Darling-Hammond, 1988; Shulman, 1987a, 1987b), a focus on at-risk students (Levin, 1988; Natriello, McDill, & Pallas, 1990), community involvement (Mid-continent Regional Educational Laboratory, 1989; Mootry, 1989; Tinzmann et al., 1990a), and other major solutions. In this chapter, we discuss one part of the problem: the vision of learning that underlies the everyday business of schooling and classroom practices. It is vital to examine this vision because it determines the nature of curriculum objectives, classroom instruction, assessment, and extends even into the very social structure of the school. If, for instance, a teacher believes that students must learn basic skills before tackling higher order skills, he or she will probably teach to that belief.

The model of learning that drives most schools today has changed little since the early years of the 20th century (Resnick, 1987). This is true, in large part, because the underlying vision of how students learn has remained remarkably static. Yet society is anything but static. Society is dynamic and changing at an increasingly rapid pace (Berryman, 1988; Hodgkinson, 1988; Johnston & Packer, 1987; Schlesinger, 1986). What is argued here is that if schools are to serve students and members of society better, they must define new visions of learning based on recent research and on the current and future needs of society.

## Traditional Model of Learning

Models of schooling typically are founded on answers to questions such as: What do individuals need to learn in order to live full and meaningful lives? How can schools best prepare students to meet the challenges of life outside school?

Most schools have addressed these questions in what has come to be called the basic skills model. In this model, educators and researchers define learning in terms of basic skills. That is, learning is essentially a matter of decoding skills in reading, computation skills in mathematics, and memorizing various facts in history and science. Additionally, this basic skills model asserts that "higher order thinking skills" are desirable objectives, but only after students have mastered "the basics."

Many have argued that this model worked well in the past for most students because it prepared them for most jobs in the work force (Berryman, 1988). It also was consistent with previous research on learning (Resnick, 1984; Resnick & Klopfer, 1989). Moreover, the fact that the model did not work as efficiently for some was considered a reflection of individual students' limitations rather than a problem with the system (Goodlad & Keating, 1990; Sinclair & Ghory, 1987).

Yet, across the land, educators, researchers, parents, and the business community are challenging these assumptions (Brown, Collins, & Duguid, 1989; Resnick, 1987; Weiner, 1989). There is growing consensus that a focus on isolated basic skills neither enriches the lives of students, nor prepares them for the tasks they will perform at home, at work, and in the community. What has brought about this change of focus?

## Challenges to the Basic Skills Model

Challenges to the basic skills model arise largely from two sets of issues. First, the United States is in the midst of unprecedented waves of change, each reflecting and causing the others. The traditional model is fundamentally misaligned with the needs of this rapidly changed and changing society (Benjamin, 1989; Berryman, 1988; Jones, 1990). Second, recent research suggests that there are richer definitions of learning than the basic skills model (Anderson et al., 1985; Jones, Palincsar, Ogle, & Carr, 1987; Resnick & Klopfer, 1989).

*Changes in Society.*   As described in Chapter 11, in the past, goods were produced by an assembly-line industrial model of manufacturing oriented to mass production of standardized products, local employment, manual work, and technology devoted primarily to machine tools and plant design. Over the decades, our economy is increasingly characterized by customized products and specialized markets such as in banking and textile manufacturing (Berryman, 1988), global production and competition (Tyler, 1990), an emphasis on providing services (Catterall, 1988), and reliance on information-processing technology (White, 1987; Zuboff, 1988).

These trends indicate that tomorrow's jobs will require "knowledge work" and problem solving (Tucker, 1988), expertise in diverse technologies, teamwork, communication skills (Parnell, 1986), critical and creative thinking (Perkins, 1986) as well as acceptance and respect for diverse perspectives (Gardner, 1987; Wolf, 1989). Some schools already teach these skills, but many, if not most, do not. Although there is much debate about the specific implications of these changes for vocational schools and junior colleges, it is clear that we should greatly strengthen what students learn in school at each level to address these needs (Resnick, 1987).

Life outside the workplace has changed as well (Berryman, 1988). Personal finance, caring for young and elderly family members, decisions about major purchases, learning about and utilizing community agencies, coping with the prevalence of drugs and alcohol, and so on, are more complicated life tasks than they used to be. They require thoughtful judgment, planning, problem solving, and flexibility, and cooperating with others.

*Changes in the Population.*    While economic trends call for a highly skilled work force, massive population changes are altering the available work force. Shortly after the year 2000, 83% of new workers will be a combination of women, minorities, and immigrants (Hodgkinson, 1988). Moreover, unprecedented concentrations of citizens will live in metropolitan areas which have declined or shown little growth (Levine & Havighurst, 1989). Based on these trends, Hodgkinson (1988) argues that student populations will increasingly be urban, nonwhite, impoverished, and limited in English proficiency.

These demographic characteristics mean that women and young persons will frequently be the breadwinners and caregivers for the very young. Further, the poverty and early family responsibilities of many students jeopardize their capability to compete even for blue collar jobs. These youth not only need access to meaningful education that builds on their strengths; they also need support services that will address the physical, financial, and emotional issues that arise from their poverty and disconnectedness. Traditional schools lack the support services needed to serve these new "clients" as well as the linkages to home and community that would help schools build on clients' strengths (Denton, 1989; Graham, 1990; James, 1989).

In sum, America is experiencing massive changes toward a world economy calling for highly skilled workers and two-income families at the same time that the work force increasingly lacks formal education. The basic skills model, devised for assembly-line jobs, does not prepare members of society to meet society's new demands. Because of this fundamental misalignment between what schools prepare students to do and the needs of a changing society, many worry that there will not be enough educated learners to fill the jobs needed in the new service industries and to function productively as individuals and community members.

## Issues from Recent Research

The need for increased emphasis upon thinking development in our schools is based on more than societal change. In the past 15 years, research concerning intelligence, knowledge, learning, and teaching has identified reasons for increased attention.

*New Conceptions of Information.*    While society is requesting workers with higher levels of thinking ability, research is changing our understanding of information and what is needed for its processing. According to Schwartz and Ogilvy

(1979), we once thought that disciplinary knowledge consisted largely of component parts and that the tasks of thinking and learning were to identify the parts and their relations. In this view, effects are preceded by causes, and the principles within a given discipline could be understood largely in terms of distinct categories.

Now we think more in terms of complex wholes and interactive, relative systems, according to Schwartz and Ogilvy. Therefore, schools must teach students how to look beyond the component parts of knowledge and to focus on its interactions.

*Recent Research on Learning and Thinking.*   Recent research concerning comprehension and intelligence suggests other ways the basic skills model minimizes learning. For example, the authors of *Becoming a Nation of Readers* argue that memorizing isolated facts fragments learning. Students may do well on objective tests, but quickly forget what they have learned (Anderson et al., 1985). Others argue that learning skills separately from real world tasks and purposes may allow students to master a school task but leave them unable to apply those same skills in new situations (e.g., Brown et al., 1989).

Research emerging from cognitive psychology, philosophy, and multicultural education provides additional support for more focused instruction and richer definitions of learning and thinking. While indepth discussion of their findings are presented elsewhere (Jones & Fennimore, 1990), the common threads among them are:

1.  Learning is most fundamentally a matter of making sense of the information at hand. This happens when learners actively participate in their own learning and work to internalize the criteria for making decisions and judgments they develop with others (Anderson et al., 1985; Brown, 1986; Lipman, in press; Resnick, 1984);

2.  Students' learning is enhanced when they develop a repertoire of strategies for thinking and monitoring the process of their own learning (Borkowski, Carr, Rellinger, & Pressley, 1990; Palincsar & Brown, 1989a, 1989b; Weinstein, Goetz, & Alexander, 1988)

3.  Learning and thinking are enhanced when students have opportunities to learn and transfer new knowledge to authentic tasks while interacting with others. This is especially true when school learning is coupled with real world tasks (The Cognition Group at Vanderbilt, 1990; Collins, Brown, & Newman, 1989; Hull, 1989; Resnick, 1987; Romberg, 1990; Usiskin, 1985);

4.  Learning is enhanced when teachers build on the strengths of what students already know. This means linking new information with familiar experiences and prior knowledge, and correcting misconceptions (Anderson et al., 1985; Bransford, Sherwood, Vye, & Rieser, 1986; Carpenter, 1985; Roth, 1990; Newmann & Thompson, 1980); and finally

5. Learning occurs when instruction is cognizant of cultural differences among students. It is necessary to understand, respect, and value the diversity of cultures in a classroom. In other words, children from different cultures learn in different ways, and children from different cultures can learn from each other (Banks, 1988; Heath, 1982; Moll & Greenberg, 1990; Weber & Dyasi, 1985).

As presented in Chapter 13, research on the nature of intelligence has increased our understanding of the nature and capacity of the human mind (Gardner, 1987). In the past, we believed that a child's intelligence consisted largely of cognitive skills, that cognitive capacity was limited to learning a few discrete items at a time, and that innate intelligence was essentially unchangeable after the first years of life (Jensen, 1969). These views were consistent with the assembly-line model of schooling.

There is also increasing consensus that intelligence is dynamic and modifiable. We now know it is possible to alter significantly the achievement of low-achieving students, and often of those with special problems, when such students are exposed to optimal learning environments and rich opportunities to engage in thinking and problem solving (Borkowski et al., 1990; Brown, Palincsar, & Purcell, 1986; Derry (1990); Derry & Murphy, 1986; Dyasi, 1989; Feuerstein, Rand, Hoffman, Epozi, & Kaiwel, 1991; Figueroa & Amato, 1989; Palincsar & Brown, 1984; Pinnell, Lyons, Young, & Deford, 1987; Weinstein et al., 1988).

*Research on Expert Teaching.*    Paralleling these changes about learning and intelligence is a renewal of the ways in which we conceptualize expert teaching and professional development. In the past, the teacher was essentially a dispenser of knowledge who worked in isolation behind closed doors with little language to conceptualize learning, classroom instruction, or problems concerning students at risk. As a matter of fact, until the last few years, more effort had been used to define standards of good breeding for animals than used to define criteria for good teaching and teacher education (Berliner, 1986).

Many researchers argue that expert teachers have the same characteristics as expert learners. They have rich knowledge bases, not only of their respective content areas, but also knowledge of learning, teaching, and classroom management (Berliner, 1984, 1986; Duffy, Roehler, & Rackliffe, 1986; Leinhardt, 1986). They have powerful repertoires of cognitive and metacognitive learning strategies, as well, to help them process information and control the process of their own learning, organizational patterns, and routines for lesson planning (Borko & Shavelson, 1990; Clark & Peterson, 1986; Lanier & Featherstone, 1988; Prawat, 1990; Shavelson, 1983; Shulman, 1987b). Moreover, teacher educators are giving increased attention to the need for teachers to learn collaboratively and to plan and assess activities for their own professional development (Schon, 1987).

To summarize, massive shifts in socioeconomic conditions, new societal demographics, and research call for changes in the way we conceptualize schools, information, learning, thinking, and expert teaching. The assembly-line model of schooling underlying traditional schools, and traditional schools of teacher education, is not aligned with these changes.

## EDUCATIONAL REFORMS AND LEARNING

Our educational system is beginning to respond to these paradigm shifts, although much remains to be done. Next, we briefly summarize four categories of reform from the lens of recent research on learning and thinking, and expert teaching.

### For Students At Risk

Significant changes in Chapter 1 legislation allow for a new focus on higher order thinking, problem solving, and critical thinking; use of Chapter 1 personnel in the regular classroom; and better coordination of pullout program curricula with regular classroom instruction (*Education Daily,* 1988; Lytle, 1988). In addition, Chapter 1 Technical Assistance Centers (TACs), which formerly were essentially extensions of the state education agencies, are now charged for the first time to be change agents to help schools implement the new Chapter 1 legislation (see TAC Request for Proposals, U.S. Department of Education, 1988). Parallel changes exist for students in special education (Jenkins, Pious, & Jewell, 1990; O'Neil, 1988). There are also numerous urban reforms targeted to improve learning for students at risk such as the Illinois State Board of Education's Urban Education Program.

These policy and funding changes are consistent with, and supported by, policy statements from the Council of Chief State School Officers (1987a, 1987b) and the National Governors' Association (1986) to guarantee at-risk students equal opportunities for a quality education and funding for support services such as counselling and transportation to enable them to take advantage of these opportunities. In fact, both agencies refer to the states' new capacity to take charge of academically and financially "distressed" schools which cannot assure quality education for students at risk. Additionally, many look upon the recent Governors' Summit, convened by President Bush to discuss the state of education, as a landmark event. Finally, there appears to be significant funding for reform in urban schools which support a focus on higher order thinking and problem solving, especially in the areas of mathematics, science, and technology, e.g., Casey Foundation, McConnel Foundation, and Piper Foundation grants.

## For Urban and Rural Education

A second area of reform focuses on the various initiatives to improve education in rural and urban contexts. Problems of rural schools center on curriculum enhancement, which usually refers to providing such courses as foreign language and science to schools with tiny student populations. Reform initiatives in urban schools often focus on extending the time and resources for basic skills courses in mathematics, science, and reading, some exceptions notwithstanding (e.g., Cooper, 1989a, 1989b).

However, these reforms tend not to focus on higher level thinking development and tend to be incremental, oriented to limited gains on standardized tests; or fragmented, oriented to change in specific areas such as teaching thinking as an adjunct program (Berman & McLaughlin, 1978; Calfee, 1988; Crandall et al., 1982). Yet, they have been useful in centering national attention on student achievement and in providing important preconditions or catalysts for change focused on learning. Thus, while we do argue for fundamental systemic change focused on learning, we do not say that schools should abandon earlier reforms. Rather, new reforms for fundamental restructuring should seek to build on the strengths of previous initiatives (Cooper, 1989b). In this way an increased focus on thinking development can be conceptualized as another step in a succession of steps toward significant improvements in student achievement.

## For Teaching Thinking

A third area of reform in recent legislation is to apply research on learning to content areas. This includes thrusts for improved learning from text, critical thinking, "higher-order thinking," process writing, using technology as a resource, and cooperative learning. Examples of these reforms include initiatives in curriculum and assessment in reading and strategic teaching (Michigan Reading Association and Michigan Department of Education, 1985; Wisconsin Department of Public Instruction, 1986, 1989); new guidelines for mathematics developed by the National Council of Teachers of Mathematics (1989); the National Science Foundation's programs to relate school curriculum to the world and real scientists, and the recent initiatives for Science, Technology, and Society (Yager, 1989); new guidelines from social studies (National Commission on Social Studies in the Schools, 1989); and seven-digit funding from NASA for students to work directly with scientists to build and use space program equipment.

Unfortunately, much of the reform toward the teaching of thinking is targeted only for above-average students. There are exceptions to be sure, e.g., the Illinois State Board of Education's Urban Education Program; Ohio Reading Recovery Program (see Pinnell et al., 1987). The result is that those who most need a higher level curriculum are excluded from its benefits. At-risk students are also often pulled out for separate instruction which may or may not focus on thinking, uses of technology, and problem solving (Allington, 1991).

## For Restructuring Schools

Fourth, there is a flourishing movement toward restructuring schools. However, most of these efforts are aimed at decentralizing school management (Levine & Eubanks, 1989), empowering teachers for professional development and advancement (Levine & Eubanks, 1989), and involving parents in the governance of schools (Calfee, 1988). As Fred Newmann's research indicates (Chapter 6), these reforms are limited in their capacity to develop thinking. Although schools may need to be decentralized, empower teachers, and involve parents, these reforms must not end with massive reorganizations for educators without real transformations for students. It is critical to connect reforms for restructuring social and political organizations of schools with efforts to promote students' thinking.

## FUNDAMENTAL RESTRUCTURING IN SCHOOLS

### National Networks

A hopeful note on the restructuring horizon is the number of national networks whose purpose is to improve instruction and/or to accelerate learning, including some for students at risk. National networks in this category include: National Urban Alliance (see Cooper, 1989b), Sizer's Coalition of Essential Schools (Chion-Kenney, 1984; Sizer, 1989, 1990) Network for Educational Renewal (Goodlad, undated), Levin's Network for Accelerated Schools (Levin, 1986), the National Education Association's Mastery in Learning Network (McClure & Obermeyer, 1987), and the American Federation of Teachers School Project (e.g., Goldberg, 1988, 1989; Pearlman, 1988).

In addition, there are some elegant designs for tomorrow's schools in the making. Reigeluth (1988), for example, sees what he calls "third wave educational systems" characterized by such concepts as the teacher as guide, developmental levels instead of grade levels, parental choice of teachers, and clusters of teachers working in learning labs. In Chapter 8, Robert Calfee discussed more concepts of such inquiring schools that focus upon critical literacy. Other examples include the new professional development schools for teachers (e.g., Holmes Group, 1986; Schlechty, Ingwerson, & Brooks, 1988); IBM's Buddy System implemented in Indiana; Apple's Classrooms of the future (Engel, 1990); and designs such as the Corporate Community Schools of America which provide greatly improved support services for students and their families (Graham, 1990; Mootry, 1989).

These networks are expanding and becoming a critical resource in restructuring schools to promote thinking. Their focus includes: skills instruction that is limited largely to universal goals or essential learnings (Cooper, 1989a, 1989b; Sizer, 1989, 1990); students become workers (Reigeluth, 1988; Sizer, 1989); work at school is done for real audiences and real uses in the business world and community (Reigeluth, 1988); performance-based assessments are used to measure thinking and learning successes (Reigeluth, 1988; Sizer, 1989; Wiggins, 1989); university/school partnerships and collaborations (Goodlad, 1984); parent involvement (e.g., Henderson, 1987); and technology to solve problems and communicate with others (Goldberg, 1988, 1989; Reigeluth, 1988; Rhodes, 1988).

## Individual Schools

Although there are also numerous examples of individual schools whose reform efforts focus on thinking development, we cite two examples here. At the King/Drew Medical Magnet School in Los Angeles, students work one day a week at a nearby hospital where they can choose from 87 work stations. At each station they assist hospital workers in all tasks for that station. For example, if the station is in the X-ray department, students help make and read X-rays. In other classes students integrate and apply what they have learned. Students at this all-Black school have won numerous awards for science and writing, and the principal is very proud that many now attend Stanford University. Preschoolers in the Perry Preschool project in Ypsilanti, Michigan, begin their days deciding what they would like to accomplish during the day. They monitor how well they implement or modify their plans, and assess their learning at the end of the day (Prawat, 1990).

## CLASSROOM INSTRUCTION

In this section we describe critical characteristics of materials and classroom instruction, called *Breakthroughs,* that we have developed over the past 2 years (Jones & Tinzmann, 1990). We begin by defining the characteristics of thinking development applied in our materials. We give comments from 10 hours of videotaping and videotaped interviews with two teachers in Wisconsin whom we trained to use the materials. Both are 4th grade teachers, one in a suburban setting and one in an inner city setting. At the end of this section we report results of three independent evaluations (Magliocca, Amidon, & Tyree, 1989, in progress; Stevens, in progress) in four different settings across the country (Michigan, Ohio, New Jersey, and California).

Initial interviews with the teachers and observations of their classrooms indicated the following. The inner city teacher used traditional instructional methods almost exclusively. Questioning was in her hands; she imparted information to her students but seldom modeled thinking strategies or taught students to engage in metacognition. She had not taught her students to use graphic organizers. Her students did not work in collaborative groups, nor had they engaged in student-centered whole class discussions. The other teacher had modeled thinking prior to using *Breakthroughs* but had not directly taught thinking strategies or meta-cognitive thinking to her students. She had never taught graphic organizers. Her students had worked in cooperative learning groups since the beginning of the school year, but had had no experience in student-controlled whole class discussions.

*Breakthroughs* is based on *Dimensions of Thinking* (Marzano, Brandt, Hughes, Jones, Presseisen, Rankin, & Subor, 1988). In this framework, thinking processes are goal directed and complex and typically involve numerous skills. They include problem solving, decision making, concept formation, composing, and so on. Skills are organized into eight categories: (1) Focusing (e.g., setting goals, defining problems); (2) information gathering (e.g., observing); (3) remembering; (4) organizing (e.g., comparing, classifying); (5) analyzing (e.g., identifying relationships and patterns); (6) generating (e.g., inferring, predicting); (7) integrating (e.g., summarizing); and (8) evaluating (e.g., verifying). A major premise of this system is that thinking is not a hierarchy of skills. That is, students do not learn a set of "basic skills" before they move to "higher levels." Instead, skills are conceptualized as a pool or repertoire in that students draw upon particular skills and strategies as they engage in specific cognitive processes. Furthermore, content and one's purposes or goals determine which skills and processes are appropriate to use in a particular learning task.

When we developed the materials, we identified the processes and skills that would seem most appropriate for the issues and concepts of a unit. For example, problem solving is a major cognitive process in the units dealing with the garbage problem. We labeled the lesson activities with the skill or process we believed was primarily involved. An example is shown in Fig. 10.1. Thus, the activity labels and the experience of doing the activities provide a context in which students begin to think about skills they use.

The two major purposes of these materials are to help students accomplish the high level thinking skills they need both in school and in the future and to provide flexible models of instruction that addresses key problems in society. This series of 36 content-area units for grades 1–8 can be used by teachers across different content areas. In order to accomplish these purposes, we drew upon research in numerous areas: (1) problem-situated learning, (2) cooperative and collaborative learning, (3) considerate text and text structures, (4) graphic organizers, (5) thinking skills, (6) misconceptions, (7) authentic assessment, and (8) strategic teaching. Furthermore, we built the materials to be consistent with and to draw upon new curriculum guidelines and research-based principles in instruction, such as depth rather than breadth, scaffolding, and thematic curricula (e.g.,

## Activity A: Inferring, Summarizing, and Comparing

### What Events Can Affect the Aging of a Lake?

Directions: Think about (infer) natural or human events that might slow down, speed up or neither slow down nor speed up the aging of a lake. Write the events on the matrix in the column where you think each belongs. Then answer the question below.

### Lake Aging Comparison Matrix

| Events | Slow Down | Speed Up | Neither Slow Down nor Speed Up |
|---|---|---|---|
| Natural Events | | | |
| Human Events | | | |

Do you think that natural events or human events have more effect on the aging of a lake? Give a reason for your answer. _____

FIG. 10.1. Example of a Graphic Organizer: Comparison Matrix Graphic Organizer from the *Breakthroughs* unit "Are We Killing Our Lakes?" From Jones and Tinzmann (1990). Used with permission of the publisher, Zaner-Bloser, Inc., Columbus, Ohio.

connecting science, technology, and society). From this rich data base, we organized the materials around the following six components: problem-situated learning, phases of learning, recursivity, graphic organizers, metacognition, and collaborative learning, each of which is described below with its respective research base.

*Problem-Situated Learning.*    Consistent with findings from research, we believe that real world problems provide authentic content for thinking (Bransford et al., 1986; the Cognition and Technology Group at Vanderbilt, 1990). Real world problems, for example, may not have good solutions or they may lend themselves to more than one solution, thus, they are worth thinking about (Lipman, 1984, 1989). They also typically involve more than one content area, reflecting the interdisciplinary nature of learning in the real world. Furthermore, real world problems require judgment and thought, organizing, and collaboration. Because real world problems draw on academic knowledge, students are more likely to see connections between what they learn in school and these interesting, difficult problems that are important not only in school but also in the real world. In addition, couching academic knowledge in the real world makes academic content more memorable than when students associate academics with school but with nothing else in their lives (Minstrell, 1989; Resnick, 1987). Finally, because students' interest level in such problems is high, students become more actively engaged in their own learning.

There is no shortage of real world problems for students to tackle. Some examples in *Breakthroughs* are garbage, space debris, endangered species, world economy, destruction of ecological systems, air and water pollution, sources of energy, heart disease, and anabolic steroids. To elaborate, three units are about the growing problem of garbage in the world, each suitable for different age children. The 1st–2nd grade unit treats the garbage problem as a phenomenon of the young child's world. First and 2nd graders find garbage in their own classroom, on their playground, in neighborhood parks, and in their homes. The text discusses solutions that emphasize cooperation and rule setting, but, through discussion and their individual understandings of the problem, the children are invited to provide their own rationales for both cooperation and rule setting. (In fact, children may conclude that rules and cooperation are *not* necessary. Engaging children in true thinking does not preclude their disagreeing with their teacher, other students, or the "social norm.")

The garbage unit for 3rd and 4th graders discusses landfills, incinerators, recycling, and recycling experiments such as "glassphalt," as well as categories of waste and devices for separating types of garbage. The problem solving students engage in emphasizes not only human cooperation, but also proven and creative ways to dispose of or recycle garbage safely. Students are invited to add their own ideas about solving the problem to the ideas in the text or disagree with ideas in the text, provided they have reasoned through their conclusions. The grade 6–7 unit extends these concepts; and students also learn about biodegradable and nonbiodegradable waste, toxic waste, and wastes that harm the ozone layer. They grapple with problems such as where to put landfills and incinerators that will cause the least harm and be acceptable to local residents, motivating people to recycle, and devising new, untried ways to solve the garbage problem.

Does problem-situated learning, as applied in these materials, accomplish what we intended it to accomplish? Here are several comments from the Wisconsin teachers:

*Teacher 1:* (talking about the unit "Are We Killing Our Lakes?") The kids brought in articles from the paper almost every day. They found *something* on the area that we were talking about. So it turned out that the problems that our country is facing right now were really covered. . . . The content was really up to date and of high interest level to them.

And I know my boys and girls do not go home at night and read a newspaper or necessarily watch news on TV. So I don't think they really had any idea of the problem that our country is facing, both with lakes dying and the pollution problem itself and how do we get rid of pollution. Their eyes were really opened, and I know now they're thinking much more deeply about it than they ever had.

*Teacher 2:* (talking about the unit "Where Does Garbage Go?") . . . we also have a bill going through our senate that's dealing with recycling. . . . And so I think that the garbage unit is useful . . . anywhere.

*Phases of Learning.*   The structure of the units, and the lessons within each unit, reflect a cycle of teaching and learning to build attributes of deliberate thinking (Costa, 1985; Flower & Hayes, 1981; Jones, Palincsar, Ogle, & Carr, 1987). Specifically, deliberate learning seems to occur in three phases: before, during, and after learning. *Before students engage in learning tasks,* they focus, set goals and purposes, think about what they already know about the topic, preview materials, ask questions, and make predictions. The phases described here are based on Jones et al., (1987) and are supported by other research as appropriate.

Accordingly, in our materials, the first activity is called Focusing, which is often neglected in schools (Anderson et al., 1985; Durkin, 1983). Yet, if students are to make meaningful connections between new content and their prior knowledge, it seems worthwhile for students to spend more time on this phase. Comments from the Wisconsin teachers illustrate both the problem and the relative ease with which teachers can incorporate this phase into their instruction:

*Teacher 2:* This area to me is one of my favorites—the focusing . . . Most of our books and most of our curriculums don't have focusing and you just jump right in, "OK, folks, today we're going to do question marks." And they don't know *what* you're talking about. They don't have *any* background knowledge. They don't know *where* they're supposed to be going or how they're supposed to be thinking.

[on goal setting] I think we expect the children to just do whatever we tell them. "Today we're going to do math and that's it. And then we're going to do English and that's it." And we never give them a chance to say, "Well, what do *I* want to learn? What do I expect to get out of this?" And I think that this goal setting section allows the kids to . . . have their say. "I'd like to learn more about thinking." Or, "I'd like to learn more about the age of a lake or how a lake ages." And I think that's really important that the child has a say in . . . determining their learning.

I started doing [predicting and previewing] in reading, too. . . . It used to be where [I would say], "Don't look ahead!" And now [I say] "Go ahead, look at the pictures. Try and tell me what the story is about." . . . I think that's an important *new* part of the curriculum that we're not used to . . . but it was very easy to adjust to.

*In the during learning phase,* students are primarily engaged in assimilating the content at hand. We call the second phase in our materials Finding Out. Students read, discuss, and engage in activities that help them organize and think about information they read and information from their own prior knowledge. In addition, each lesson—both the content and activities—builds on previous lessons so that learning and instruction need not be fragmented. In fact, the cohesion among lessons permits in depth thinking and learning, something often missing from traditional curricula (Anderson et al., 1985; The Cognition and Technology Group at Vanderbilt, 1990; Hamm & Adams, 1989). When students have the opportunity to explore issues in depth, they also are more likely to engage in the kind of thinking they need now and in the future, as illustrated in the following comment from Teacher 2:

*Teacher 2:*  You find in normal curriculum . . . where you read a certain amount of material and then you do a worksheet . . . and the children never really . . . understand what it is they're learning. They're just going for the content. It's sort of a chew it up and spit it out kind of mentality that our curriculums generally profess. And I think that we need to get away from that. And *Breakthroughs* does that successfully, I think, because they allow the kids the *time* that it takes to internalize it and then be able to discuss, get other people's ideas, and in turn they can then put down on paper how they were *thinking* as well as the content. . . .

The newness of such an in depth approach was not always easy to adjust to, however, as this comment from Teacher 1 shows:

*Teacher 1:*  . . . it was very time consuming . . . any time you have a group discussion and then you're going back to your predictions that you set and your goals you set, and then you're going forward, . . . and you have graphic organizers to fill out and your conclusions to draw . . . it would usually end up to 45 [minutes].

*In the after learning phase,* learners summarize, review, reflect on what they have learned, ask new questions, and apply what they have learned to new situations (Jones et al., 1987). Like the before learning phase, we often spend too little time helping students in this phase.

An important after learning activity in *Breakthroughs* is the Application lesson. In this lesson, students apply what they learned in the body of a unit to a new, but related, issue. For example, in the unit "Dolphins—Our Newest Allies?", among other things, students think about ways humans have "used" dolphins—for entertainment, as models for torpedoes and submarines, and as underwater patrols in potentially dangerous naval operations. The applying lesson for this unit raises the issue of whether and/or when people should use other mammals for such endeavors as space and medical research, cosmetic testing, and so on. Students apply both the concepts they learned and the decision-making processes they engaged in as they dealt with the dolphin issues to these new issues.

Applying can serve several purposes. First, it reflects what effective learners often do in this phase. Second, it creates a potential transfer situation. Third, it can serve as an authentic assessment. Teachers—and the students themselves—can evaluate how students apply ideas to a new problem or issue. Such assessment does not intrude into the instructional process because it is also a learning experience (Gardner & Hatch, 1989; Valencia, 1990; Wiggins, 1989). Finally, it can help students draw some generalizations they might not envision if they deal with only one issue. Teacher 2 seems to have found this with her students in the first *Breakthroughs* unit she taught:

> *Teacher 2:* When I was doing our Fossil Fuels unit, my kids had a lot of trouble . . . When we finally got to the application part, I found them putting things together that I didn't think they understood. So I was happy to see them bringing the information out that I thought they didn't get and using it in the application which dealt not with fossil fuels [the content for the unit], but . . . with how many people are on the earth and do we have enough space. And they *used* the fossil fuel information to deal with the application.

*Recursivity.* When students are engaged in authentic thinking and learning, they often stop to reflect on what they have learned or think about what they will learn, often going through the skills in all three phases of learning. We call this stop–start phenomenon recursivity. For example, learners pause to reflect on new information—making analogies to familiar information, comparing new information to one's prior knowledge, resolving conflicts between new ideas and old beliefs, etc. Writing typically involves stopping and starting again such as when writers return to the planning stage after they have completed a piece based on a plan which they conclude is no longer useful for their purposes or audience. Looking ahead involves making new predictions, setting new goals, changing learning strategies, etc. The opportunity to stop for reflection and thinking ahead seems critical if students are to engage in higher level thinking. However, students do not always have this opportunity. For example, in writing tasks, students are often exhorted to develop a complete outline of a paper before they write and are led to believe that they must not deviate from that outline.

Our materials encourage recursive processing in a number of ways. For example, students activate their prior knowledge before a unit and before each lesson through brainstorming and other activities. Then, after they read and/or engage in activities, they have a chance to add to, or change, that prior knowledge. Throughout a unit, they return to their predictions and goals made in the Focusing lesson and, if they wish, change, or add to, them. The two teachers perceived that these recursive elements were effective with their students. They said:

> *Teacher 1:*  They're used to putting something down on paper, getting a grade, and that's it. With *Breakthroughs* they can put it down, make their prediction, and then later on in the discussion say, "Oh! Well, maybe I'm going to change this now or we can add this to it."

> *Teacher 2:*  [in response to Teacher 1] Yes. Usually in real life we get to change what we've done. And I think *Breakthroughs* follows through with that.

Two critical activities in every unit are also intended to capture recursivity. First, students turn to the unit graphic organizer in each lesson to add any information they have learned in a particular lesson plus any of their own ideas that seem appropriate. This activity encourages summarizing skills and representing information differently from the text.

The second recursive activity is metacognition. After each lesson, students identify the thinking strategies they used in that lesson, when they used the strategies and why they are helpful.

*Graphic Organizers.*    For decades, students have been taught linear outlining as the principal representation and organization of information in a chapter. This made sense because it was assumed that reading, writing, and perhaps even thinking, proceeded in a sequential, linear fashion. Because this assumption is being challenged, graphic organizers are being examined as valuable, nonlinear ways of representing information in matrices, cycles, and sequences. Such graphic organizers better reflect the structure of information, making the relationships among the ideas and concepts clearer, thus making information more meaningful and memorable (Jones, Pierce, & Hunter, 1988–1989; Kiewra, DuBois, Christian, & McShane, 1988; Mayer, 1984). In addition, graphic organizers tend to make students more aware of text structure (Mayer, 1989), and, learning seems to be positively affected (Goetz, 1984; Moore & Readance, 1984). Teacher-constructed organizers seem to work less well than when students construct their own or complete partially constructed organizers (Alvermann, 1988; Armbruster, Anderson, & Mayer, 1990; Barron & Stone, 1974; Berkowitz, 1986; Dewitz, Carr, & Patberg, 1987; Moore & Readance, 1984; Risch & Kiewra, 1989). Moreover, teacher modeling (Holley & Dansereau, 1984) and learning to construct organizers in cooperative groups (rather than independently) (Armbruster et al., 1990; Darch, Carnine, & Kameenui, 1986) help students select graphic organizers unprompted.

Graphic representations are visual illustrations of verbal statements. Frames are sets of questions or categories that are fundamental to understanding a given topic. Here are shown nine "generic" graphic forms with their corresponding frames. Also given are examples of topics that could be represented by each graphic form. These graphics show at a glance the key parts of the whole and their relations, helping the learner to comprehend text and solve problems.

**Spider Map**

Used to describe a central idea: a thing (a geographic region), process (meiosis), concept (altruism), or proposition with support (experimental drugs should be available to AIDS victims). Key frame questions: What is the central idea? What are its attributes? What are its functions?

**Continuum/Scale**

Low                                                          High

Used for time lines showing historical events or ages (grade levels in school), degrees of something (weight), shades of meaning (Likert scales), or ratings scales (achievement in school). Key frame questions: What is being scaled? What are the end points?

**Compare/Contrast Matrix**

|  | Name 1 | Name 2 |
|---|---|---|
| Attribute 1 |  |  |
| Attribute 2 |  |  |
| Attribute 3 |  |  |

Used to show similarities and differences between two things (people, places, events, ideas, etc.). Key frame questions: What things are being compared? How are they similar? How are they different?

**Series of Events Chain**

Used to describe the stages of something (the life cycle of a primate); the steps in a linear procedure (how to neutralize an acid); a sequence of events (how feudalism led to the formation of nation states); or the goals, actions, and outcomes of a historical figure or character in a novel (the rise and fall of Napoleon). Key frame questions: What is the object, procedure, or initiating event? What are the stages or steps? How do they lead to one another? What is the final outcome?

**Problem/Solution Outline**

Used to represent a problem, attempted solutions, and results (the national debt). Key frame questions: What was the problem? Who had the problem? Why was it a problem? What attempts were made to solve the problem? Did those attempts succeed?

FIG. 10.2.

Graphic organizers have been included in a number of study strategies developed by researchers and educators:

1. Dansereau's (Dansereau et al., 1979) MURDER—Mood, Understand, Recall, Digest, Expand, and Review with networking as part of the "recall" step.

2. Vaughan's (1984) ConStruct strategy for students who have limited knowl-

**Network Tree**

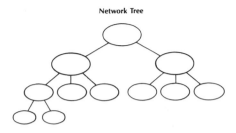

Used to show causal information (causes of poverty), a hierarchy (types of insects), or branching procedures (the circulatory system). Key frame questions: What is the superordinate category? What are the subordinate categories? How are they related? How many levels are there?

**Fishbone Map**

Used to show the causal interaction of a complex event (an election, a nuclear explosion) or complex phenomenon (juvenile delinquency, learning disabilities). Key frame questions: What are the factors that cause X? How do they interrelate? Are the factors that cause X the same as those that cause X to persist?

**Human Interaction Outline**

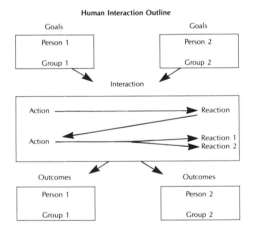

Used to show the nature of an interaction between persons or groups (European settlers and American Indians). Key frame questions: Who are the persons or groups? What were their goals? Did they conflict or cooperate? What was the outcome for each person or group?

**Cycle**

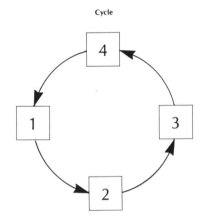

Used to show how a series of events interact to produce a set of results again and again (weather phenomena, cycles of achievement and failure, the life cycle). Key frame questions: What are the critical events in the cycle? How are they related? In what ways are they self-reinforcing?

FIG. 10.2. Generic Graphic Forms with Corresponding Text Frames. From Jones, Pierce, and Hunter (1988–1989). Used with permission of the North Central Regional Educational Laboratory, Oak Brook, Illinois.

edge about a topic. In this strategy, readers construct and use graphic organizers throughout the reading act. They list main concepts in their organizers from an initial survey of the text, add important information and then details, and finally use the organizers for study.

3. Jones's (1986) SPaRCS in which students survey the text and predict which

graphic organizer would be suitable for it, read, construct a graphic organizer, and summarize the information in the organizer.

4. DuBois and Kiewra's (1989) strategy that includes using matrices, hierarchies, and sequence representations.

5. Black and Black's (1990) Organizing Thinking enables teachers and students to use graphic organizers to attain content objectives. For example, students might be asked in a social studies text to write about the contributions of various leaders during the Civil War (e.g., Abraham Lincoln and Frederick Douglass).

By using a comparing and contrasting graphic organizer and with teacher guidance, students can note how the two men were alike and different, write a summary statement or paragraph about the similarities and differences between the two men, select important information that addresses the content objective, and create a general statement about their contributions.

Graphic organizers are a prominent part of our materials. We used the framework shown in Fig. 10.2 to develop these organizers.

The most distinctive use of graphic organizers, however, is that of the unit graphics. These are designed to reflect the primary thinking process in the unit. For example, the garbage units have problem-solution frames in which students organize information about the garbage problem. The unit graphic in "Are We Killing Our Lakes?" is a fishbone map that shows human and natural causes for the aging and eventual death of a lake, as shown in Fig. 10.3.

As discussed briefly before, unit graphics are effective devices for students to record their prior knowledge before they begin a unit, take notes as they read, and to summarize information at the end of a unit. They also permit students to add knowledge from other sources and their own prior knowledge easily. Sample comments from the Wisconsin teachers show that teachers find graphic organizers easy to teach, and incorporate them into other content areas.

Teacher 2: [commenting on the Lake Fishbone Map; see Fig. 10.3] I was so proud of them being able to understand that the two areas point to one another. The natural causes are pointing and the human causes are pointing to one particular effect, . . . death of a lake in this case. . . . This is a really useful way of organizing the information—especially since it's complicated information. This is not something that you can just easily see in a list.

[commenting on the Garbage Problem-Solution Frame; see Fig. 10.3] And the kids were able to recall that information that they couldn't have recalled before because *before* it was just lots of information. *Now* it became a series of steps and they could see visually what was happening—the first line, the second line—you could almost recall the whole organizer in your head—much easier than trying to recall 15 pages of text.

# Unit Graphic:  Identifying, Elaborating, and Summarizing

**Problem–Solution Frame**

Problem
Box

What?

Why?

Solutions                    Results

Solution
Boxes

Solution 1

Solution 2

Solution 3

End Result
Box

# Unit Graphic:  Identifying Relationships and Patterns and Classifying

**Lake Fishbone Map**

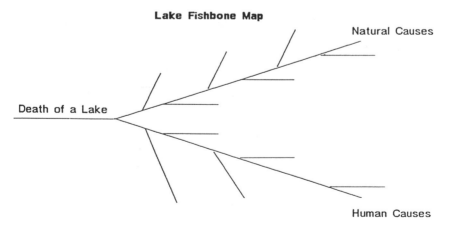

Natural Causes

Death of a Lake

Human Causes

FIG. 10.3.  Examples of Graphic Organizers: Problem-Solution Frame from the *Breakthroughs* unit "Where Does the Garbage Go?" and Causal Fishbone Map from the *Breakthroughs* unit "Are We Killing Our Lakes?" From Jones and Tinzmann (1990). Used with permission of the publisher, Zaner-Bloser, Inc., Columbus, Ohio.

*Teacher 1:* And I found it carries over to other areas. I tried it in a reading lesson. It was a story that was very difficult to understand, and so I gave them a little graphic organizer to take home when they read the story. And I was amazed at how well they could apply that in a different situation.

*Metacognition.*    After each lesson, students do a metacognitive activity. The activity has two parts. First, students identify, and talk about, at least one cognitive skill or process they used during the lesson (they may also discuss skills used in earlier lessons). They write the name of the skill on their thinking strategies concept map, shown in Fig. 10.4 below. The concept map provides a spatial representation of skills that facilitates students' understanding of where the skill they are using fits in the skill categories.

Next, students explain (orally or in writing) when they used the skill or process and why it is helpful. We stress that our intention is *not* to have students

## Thinking Strategies Concept Map

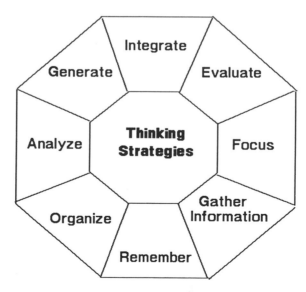

Directions: After each lesson, you and your classmates will work with your teacher to to complete this activity. Together you can decide which thinking strategies you used in that lesson.

FIG. 10.4. Thinking Strategies Concept Map from *Breakthroughs* units. From Jones and Tinzmann (1990). Used with permission of the publisher, Zaner-Bloser, Inc., Columbus, Ohio.

merely write the labels of activities, but to provide a model. The goal is for each student to think about the skills and processes used, regardless of what an activity is called. Indeed, some 4th graders we observed were able to accomplish this.

Teachers are encouraged to model metacognitive thinking, especially for students just beginning to use *Breakthroughs*. The teacher notes provide examples of modeling. Finally, students share their ideas with other students both in small groups and with the whole class. Such sharing accomplishes several things. First, students can learn to articulate their thoughts better if they must explain them to others. Second, students enrich their understanding when they listen to the thinking strategies their peers use.

Note that metacognitive activity does not cover the whole range of possible metacognitive processes. The materials do not, for instance, teach students *how* to use each strategy. For example, students are not taught steps involved in comparing and analyzing; nor are they explicitly taught comprehension monitoring or what to do if they do not understand something. Although we have attempted to provide a context which is highly conducive to students' learning such processes, we know from numerous research studies that many children need more than this. In future work, we intend to address these concerns.

A final issue regarding metacognition is students' ability to understand the complex terms we use—elaborating, establishing criteria, identifying attributes and components, etc. Although these terms are difficult, teachers who have used the materials note that young children can learn such "big, grownup" words (e.g., Many preschoolers use complex dinosaur names with facility and understanding). In any case, when children confront problems and issues that they can understand and that are relevant to them, they seem to have some understanding, for example, of the problem-solving process. Yet, teachers also inform us that when they first introduced metacognition to the students, they needed to spend time in order to explain terms. The following teacher comments illustrate this:

*Teacher 2:*  I think the terminology was very difficult for them to get used to . . . so we had to spend a lot of time preparing and going over what the terms were.

*Teacher 1:*  I would agree with that. In fact, I think it would take two or three *Breakthroughs [units]* to get them actually to where they could . . . think [about] those terms.

In spite of these concerns, these teachers recognized the value of helping students think about their own thinking, as the following comments show:

*Teacher 1:*  It [metacognitive activity] was good because I think the kids had never *thought* those things before. They had never thought to themselves, "How do I think?"

*Teacher 2:*  I think the What, When, Why, and modeling What, When, and Why
you did it is very effective. I can't suppose that I'm going to know
what my kids are going to be doing when they turn 35. But the least I
can give them are strategies to be able to think through problems. And
I truly believe that this is a way that we can help them to learn about
how they're thinking. . . .

*Teacher 2:*  I have used it in other subjects already, . . . in math and in reading. I
really appreciated having a way to introduce thinking skills because
that's . . . what I believe . . . we should be teaching [in] school.

*Collaboration.*    Research on collaboration between teachers and students,
and especially students with each other, has flourished in recent years (Bernagozzi, 1988; Evangelou, 1989; Forman & Cazden, 1986; Greenberg, 1989; Johnson & Johnson, 1989; Newmann & Thompson, 1987; Palincsar & Brown, 1989b; Slavin, 1987). One of the most significant findings is that, compared to competitive and individualized classroom structures, small group work facilitates not only students' learning, but also their motivation, self-concepts, and social skills when working with diverse groups. A major thrust of this research is in cooperative learning (Johnson & Johnson, 1989; Slavin, 1987). However, collaborative groups (less structured than cooperative groups) and think-pair-share structures are also effective (Forman & Cazden, 1985; Johnson & Johnson, 1989; Palinscar & Brown, 1989b; Slavin, 1987). In cooperative learning groups, students work "together to accomplish shared goals" (Johnson & Johnson, 1989, p. 2). Simply putting students in groups and expecting them to work together is not enough, of course. Students must see themselves as positively interdependent so that they take a personal responsibility for achieving group goals (Johnson & Johnson, 1989). Also, the interaction within groups must have certain qualities—helping, sharing resources, giving constructive feedback, challenging others' reasoning and ideas without engaging in personal criticism, keeping an open mind, promoting safety so that all members feel free to share their thoughts, etc. (Johnson & Johnson, 1989). Finally, groups need time to reflect on and evaluate the quality of their interactions.

Slavin (1987) has developed specific techniques for cooperative learning. Most of these emphasize both group and individual goals as well as differentiated roles within the group. For example, in Slavin's jigsaw, each group member is given a critical part of a whole task or project without which the group cannot succeed. Thus, no member can sit back and rely on the others to do his or her work.

Slavin, the Johnsons, and others stress that groups should be heterogeneous. Grouping according to supposed ability, achievement, interests, or any other characteristic is strongly discouraged. Combining the perspectives, experiences, and backgrounds of many different students in one group is important for enriching learning.

In addition to collaborating with each other, students can collaborate with their teachers. Thus, collaboration means shifting roles for both students and teachers. Students take more responsibility for their own learning and become more actively engaged. Teachers shift from the traditional role of dispenser of knowledge to mediator, facilitator, and coach (Jones, 1987; Moll & Greenberg, 1990; Palincsar & Brown, 1989a, 1989b; Tinzmann et al., 1990b).

Whole-group discussion is another way students and teachers collaborate. It contrasts sharply with recitation, in which a teacher asks a question to which he or she usually has an answer, one student answers, the teacher asks another question, another student answers, and so on. Thus, although there may be thirty children in the classroom, talking is between only two people at a time and entirely directed by the teacher. In whole-group discussion, students talk with each other, raise genuine questions, and respond to each other. The teacher may participate, but as an equal. Whole-group discussion permits children—and teachers—to ask genuine questions and to explore ideas in depth.

*Breakthroughs* encourages both small group work and whole-group discussion. In small groups, students share prior knowledge and their predictions and goals before they begin a unit; during learning, they work together on activities. They construct unit graphic organizers, share their metacognitive thinking, and may elect to complete the application lesson together. In addition, the teacher notes contain numerous suggestions for activities and projects that lend themselves to group work in other curricular areas.

The following teacher comments illustrate the effectiveness of collaboration from the point of view of the two teachers. They are especially enlightening because Teacher 1 had seldom asked her students to work in groups and had never tried whole-group discussion. Teacher 2 had not tried whole group discussion either, but her students had worked in collaborative groups from the beginning of the school year. First, sample comments about whole-group discussion . . .

*Teacher 2:* Did you find that your kids were afraid to have discussion with each other? I felt like my students were really hesitant to talk to one another without raising their hands.

*Teacher 1:* Yes. It took a lot of work with them to do it. They were afraid more than anything else. They'd never done it. And it was good! I was amazed! I didn't think they could do it. . . . I think that that was probably *the* major improvement over the other curriculum areas or the other basal texts that we have had—was the discussions that it [*Breakthroughs*] stimulated. I've *never ever* before had a group of kids that could discuss as well as they did when they got started on these with the guidelines that *Breakthroughs* set for them.

. . . and small group work:

*Teacher 2:*  I . . . felt that being in the collaborative groups was really a necessary part of this *Breakthroughs* because . . . working in a way that the kids were not facing each other would not suit this type of learning. They really needed to be in a group where they could face each other, talk about it, share their ideas.

. . . now they had to tell the other children what they thought and had to answer the questions out loud with each other as a group, and they had to work together. And I think that part of the dynamics of the group was one of the benefits that came out of this *Breakthroughs*.

*Teacher 1:*  I found that some of the children who are normally intimidated by a worksheet . . . started to shine in this . . . I had a young boy and a girl who normally say very little because they're afraid of making a mistake all of a sudden just came forth [sic] with really good ideas. . . . They didn't feel that they were going to be insulted or that this answer was going to be wrong.

In summary, this section has illustrated one application of instructional and curricular approaches urged by researchers, professional organizations, and forward-looking educators that provide a context in which high level thinking is most likely to occur. The content is worth thinking about because it relates to authentic world issues. The structure of the materials reflects phases of learning and recursivity in which effective thinkers engage. Graphic organizers provide flexible ways to represent information. The metacognitive activity enables students to think explicitly about thinking skills and processes. Finally, collaborative learning and thinking is valued and encouraged. An important question remains, however. Does *Breakthroughs* help students? We address that question next.

## Evaluation of Breakthroughs

Two types of evaluation studies have been, and are currently being conducted. Both types were conducted by independent evaluators. One evaluated students' critical thinking skills (cognitive component) and their attitudes toward problem solving (affective component).

*Students Studies.*  The first study (Magliocca, Amidon, Arnold, & Miller, 1991; Magliocca, Amidon, & Tyree, 1989) was conducted in an exurban school district in Ohio. Four 5th-grade teachers in the district who volunteered to participate were randomly assigned to either the experimental—those who received inservice training and the *Breakthroughs* unit "Where Does the Garbage Go?"— or enhanced control condition—who did not receive training and used specially developed materials developed in the district on the same topic as the *Breakthroughs* unit. Teachers spent approximately 45 minutes per day teaching the materials over a 2-week period and kept a journal of their comments. Students were pre- and posttested for cognitive gains with the *Cornell Critical Thinking Text,* Level X (Ennis, Millman, & Tomko, 1985) and for affective change with the *Attitude Toward Problem Solving* (Randal, Lester, & O'Daffer, 1987). The *Cornell* test was selected because of its suitability for detecting differences in critical thinking ability between groups due to different instructional approaches (Ennis et al., 1985). In addition, using a test that is not based on the *Breakthroughs* materials avoids using an evaluation measure that directly assesses the skills taught by the materials being evaluated (Nickerson, Perkins, & Smith, 1985).

Mean scores for the Cornell test are given in Table 10.1. Since distributions of scores (right minus one-half wrong) in the experimental and control groups did not reflect a normal distribution, the Wilcoxson Signed Rank Test was used to determine differences between groups. Students using *Breakthroughs* showed significant gains on three of the four subtests while no significant gains were evident for the enhanced control students. These results indicate that the experimental students were able to transfer the skills they learned in *Breakthroughs* to the problems and questions posed in the *Cornell* test.

Similar, though less dramatic, differential gain was made on some of the constructs of the attitude measure. In particular, *Breakthroughs* students showed a trend toward thinking of themselves as effective problem solvers. Qualitative analyses of teachers' journal entries have not yet been completed.

*Teacher Study.*    The second type of evaluation of *Breakthroughs* focuses on teachers' beliefs about teaching and learning, how these beliefs influence classroom practices within particular contexts, and teachers' perception and practice

TABLE 10.1
Changes in Cornell Critical Thinking Test
Subtest Scores by Groups

| Variable | | pretest | | | Postest | |
|---|---|---|---|---|---|---|
| | n | Mean | sd | n | Mean | sd |
| Control | | | | | | |
| JFACT | 59 | 9.76 | 5.31 | 60 | 9.23 | 5.15 |
| JCRED | 59 | 4.69 | 4.22 | 60 | 4.30 | 4.42 |
| DECID | 59 | 5.59 | 4.52 | 60 | 6.40 | 4.95 |
| JASSM | 59 | 0.59 | 3.01 | 60 | 0.75 | 2.97 |
| Experimental | | | | | | |
| JFACT | 51 | 9.41 | 6.58 | 50 | 10.88 | 4.76 |
| JCRED | 51 | 5.18 | 5.03 | 50 | 6.60 | 4.39 |
| DECID | 51 | 4.41 | 5.76 | 50 | 6.00 | 4.74 |
| JASSM | 51 | 0.31 | 3.02 | 50 | 0.74 | 2.81 |

JFACT = Judging Whether a Fact Supports a Hypothesis
JCRED = Judging the Credibility of Observation Reports
DECID = Deciding What Follows
JASSM = Judging What is Assumed in an Argument

of constructivist-based ideas about reading presented in a series of staff development programs. *Breakthroughs* units were an integral part of the staff development efforts.

The training goal was to provide some method to address needs of large numbers of teachers in rural and urban schools where sustained staff development was unlikely. The materials were developed in part to provide a model of good instruction, therefore, we reasoned that an introductory inservice plus teacher interaction with the materials would be sufficient training since the components and text were well-explained, including some modeling. One purpose of the training was to ascertain which of the six components—problem-situated learning, phases of learning, recursivity, graphic organizers, metacognition, and collaboration—would require additional staff development.

We conducted preliminary research with four teachers, two urban and two from a small city in a rural area, who had been identified by their principals as outstanding teachers. Video taped interviews and classroom demonstrations of these teachers revealed the following. First, although none of the teachers had used the components prior to using *Breakthroughs,* all of them were clearly able to describe and comment upon the elements with a level of fluency expected of a skilled novice. Second, most of the teachers were able to implement most of the components with some skill. However, the two inner city teachers did not implement the collaborative strategies well.

Reasons for this were that (1) there were strong norms supporting traditional grouping, and (2) the teachers themselves never collaborated. Therefore, we selected four inner city teachers for an eight-week training program with Dannelle Stevens as the staff developer. Preliminary interviews and survey data showed that the teachers were overtly hostile to collaborative strategies, but they liked the other components, and so decided to implement the program and training. This began with jigsaw (Slavin) and other exercises developed by Cohen. Following these, Stevens introduced the materials, modeling each of the components with students from the teachers' classes as well as observations of the teachers using the program with feedback on their implementation. The results were that all four teachers did incorporate the components into their conversations and beliefs about good instruction in varying degrees, but only one of the teachers really implemented the collaborative learning strategies well, though the other three continued to use the materials and grouping strategies through the remainder of the year even though they were not required to do so. During the summer of 1990, these four teachers became staff developers themselves for other teachers in their district in the use of the constructivist model using the *Breakthroughs* materials.

## Future Directions

We believe that *Breakthroughs* is one useful and flexible approach for teaching thinking in content area instruction. Early evidence indicates that students benefit from the components in this instructional approach. In addition to the studies described above, we believe that in depth case studies would be informative. In particular, examining changes in both student and teacher behaviors, attitudes, and skills and how these interact would be valuable. It is especially important to conduct such studies with at-risk students, the group who suffer most from lack of appropriate curriculum for higher level thinking.

In addition, the materials themselves can be enhanced. Especially critical in this regard is to provide more instruction on *how* to use various thinking skills (Swartz, personal communication, July 9, 1990). For instance, are there steps or strategies for thinking that compares and contrasts? A second improvement would be to include more instruction that helps students improve in skills such as evaluating ideas for solving problems and judging the appropriateness of predictions. Finally, instruction in how to use graphic organizers can be enhanced so that students clearly see connections between various organizers and text structures. Such added instruction needs to assist students to learn to construct their own organizers.

We also believe that the characteristics in *Breakthroughs* can be applied in other content areas. An obvious application is in content area texts and in reading and math materials. The model could also be used effectively, we think, in teacher education, both preservice and inservice. Providing such professional development materials, whatever model is used, might better prepare new teachers and help experienced teachers understand through experience how thinking can be developed in our schools in the 21st century.

## REFERENCES

Allington, R. (1991). How policy and regulations influence instruction for students at risk. In L. Idol & B. F. Jones (Eds.), *Educational values and cognitive instruction: Implications for reform* (pp. 273–296). Hillsdale, NJ: Lawrence Erlbaum Associates.

Alvermann, D. E. (1988). Effects of spontaneous and induced lookbacks on self-perceived high- and low-ability comprehenders, *Journal of Educational Research, 81,* 325–331.

Anderson, R. C., Hiebert, E. H., Scott, J. A., & Wilkinson, I. A. G. (1985). *Becoming a nation of readers: The report of the commission on reading.* Urbana, Il: University of Illinois, Center for the Study on Reading.

Armbruster, B. B., Anderson, T. H., & Meyer, J. L. (1990, May). *Improving content area reading using instructional graphics.* Unpublished manuscript.

Banks, J. A. (1988). Education, citizenship, and cultural options. *Education and Society, 1*(1), 19–22.

Barron, R. F., & Stone, V. F. (1974). Effect of students-constructed graphic post organizers upon learning vocabulary relationships. In P. L. Nacke (Ed.), *Interaction: Research and practice for college-adult reading* (pp. 172–175). Twenty-third Yearbook of the National Reading Conference, Clemson, SC.

Benjamin, S. (1989). An ideascape for education: What futurists recommend. *Educational Leadership, 47*(1), 8–14.

Berkowitz, S. J. (1986). Effects of instruction in text organization on sixth-grade students' memory for expository reading. *Reading Research Quarterly, XXI,* 161–178.

Berliner, D. C. (1984). The half-full glass. A review of research in teaching. In P. L. Hosford (Ed.),

*Using what we know about teaching* (pp. 51–77). Alexandria, VA: Association for Supervision & Curriculum Development.

Berliner, D. C. (1986). In pursuit of the expert pedagogue. *Educational Researcher, 15,* 5–14.

Berman, P., & McLaughlin, M. W. (1978). *Federal programs supporting educational change. Vol. VIII: Implementing and sustaining innovations.* Santa Monica, CA: Rand Corporation.

Bernagozzi, T. (1988). The new cooperative learning and one teacher's approach. *Learning, 16*(6), 38–43.

Berryman, S. (1988, October). *The educational challenge of the American economy.* Briefing paper prepared for a forum of the National Education Association, Washington, DC.

Black, H., & Black, S. (1990). *Book II: Organizing thinking.* Pacific Grove, CA: Midwest Publications.

Borko, H., & Shavelson, R. J. (1990). Teacher decision making. In B. F. Jones & L. Idol (Eds.), *Dimensions of thinking and cognitive instruction* (pp. 311–346). Hillsdale, NJ: Lawrence Erlbaum Associates.

Borkowski, J. G., Carr, M., Rellinger, E., & Pressley, M. (1990). Self-regulated cognition: Interdependence of metacognition, attributions, and self-esteem. In B. F. Jones & L. Idol (Eds.), *Dimensions of thinking and cognitive instruction* (pp. 53–92). Hillsdale, NJ: Lawrence Erlbaum Associates.

Bransford, J. D., Sherwood, R., Vye, N., & Rieser, J. (1986). Teaching thinking and problem solving. *American Psychologist, 41,* 1078–1089.

Brown, A. L. (1986). *Teaching students to think as they read: Implications for curriculum reform* (Reading Education Rep. No. 58). Urbana, IL: University of Illinois, The Center for the Study of Reading.

Brown, J. S., Collins, A., & Duguid, P. (1989). Debating the situation. *Educational Researcher, 18*(4), 10–12, 62.

Brown, A. L., Palincsar, A. S., & Purcell, L. (1986). Poor readers: Teach, don't label. In U. Neisser (Ed.), *The academic performance of minority children: New perspectives* (pp. 105–143). Hillsdale, NJ: Lawrence Erlbaum Associates.

Calfee, R. (1988). *Schools for the year 2000: A proposal and planning document for fundamental change in American schools.* Unpublished manuscript.

Carpenter, T. P. (1985). Learning to add and subtract: An exercise in problem solving. In E. A. Silver, (Ed.), *Teaching and learning mathematical problem solving* (pp. 17–40). Hillsdale, NJ: Lawrence Erlbaum Associates.

Catterall, J. S. (1988, May). *Tomorrow's workforce: Overcredentialized and under-prepared?* Paper prepared for the conference: Can California Be Competitive and Caring?, Institute of Industrial Relations, University of California, Los Angeles.

Chion-Kenney, L. (1984, Winter). A report from the field. The coalition of essential schools. *American Educator,* 18–27, 47–48.

Clark, C. M., & Peterson, P. L. (1986). Teachers' thought processes. In M. C. Wittrock (Ed.), *Handbook of research on teaching* (pp. 235–296). New York: Macmillan.

The Cognition Group at Vanderbilt. (1990). Anchored instruction and its relationship to situated cognition. *Educational Researcher, 19*(6), 2–10.

Collins, A., Brown, J. S., & Newman, S. (1989). Cognitive apprenticeship: Teaching students the craft of reading, writing, and mathematics. In L. B. Resnick (Ed.), *Knowing, learning, and instruction: Essays in honor of Robert Glaser.* Hillsdale, NJ: Lawrence Erlbaum Associates.

Cooper, E. J. (1989a). Toward a new mainstream of instruction for American schools. *Journal of Negro Education, 58,* 102–116.

Cooper, E. J. (1989b). Addressing urban school reform: Issues and alliances. *Journal of Negro Education, 58,* 315–331.

Costa, A. L. (1985). Toward a model of human intellectual functioning. In A. L. Costa (Ed.),

*Developing minds: A resource book for teaching thinking* (pp. 62–65). Alexandria, VA: Association for Supervision and Curriculum Development.

Council of Chief State School Officers. (1987a, November). *Assuring educational success for students at risk.* Washington, DC: A policy statement from the Council of Chief State School Officers.

Council of Chief State School Officers. (1987b). *Children at risk: The work of the States.* Washington, DC: A report from the Council of Chief State School Officers.

Crandall, D. P., Loucks, S. F., Baucher, J. E., Schmidt, W. B., Eiseman, J. W., Cox, P. L., Miles, M. B., Huberman, A. M., Taylor, B. L., Goldberg, J. A., Shive, G., Thompson, C. L., & Taylor, J. A. (1982). *People, policies, and practices: Examining the chain of school improvement.* Andover, MA: The Network, Inc.

Dansereau, D. F., Collins, K. W., McDonald, B. A., Holley, C. D., Garland, J., Diekhoff, G., & Evans, S. H. (1979). Development and evaluation of a learning strategy training program. *Journal of Educational Psychology, 71,* 64–73.

Darch, C. B., Carnine, D. W., & Kameenui, E. J. (1986). The role of graphic organizers and social structure in content area instruction. *Journal of Reading Behavior, 28,* 275–295.

Darling-Hammond, L. (1988). The future of teaching. *Educational Leadership, 46*(3), 4–10.

Denton, W. H. (1989). The next educational reform: Family support systems. *Community Education Journal, XVI*(2), 6–10.

Derry, S. J. (1990). Learning strategies for acquiring useful knowledge. In B. F. Jones & L. Idol (Eds.), *Dimensions of thinking and cognitive instruction* (pp. 347–379). Hillsdale, NJ: Lawrence Erlbaum Associates.

Derry, S. J., & Murphy, D. A. (1986). Designing systems that train learning ability: From theory to practice. *Review of Educational Research, 56,* 1–39.

Dewitz, P., Carr, E. M., & Patberg, J. P. (1987). Effects of inference training on comprehension and comprehension monitoring. *Reading Research Quarterly, XXII,* 99–121.

Dossey, J. A., Mullis, I. V. S., Lindquist, M. S., & Chambers, D. (1988, June). *The mathematics report card. Are we measuring up? Trends and achievement based on the 1986 national assessment* (Report No. 17-M-01). Princeton, NJ: Educational Testing Service.

DuBois, N. F., & Kiewra, K. A. (1989, October 20). *Selected issues in note taking research.* Paper presented at the Midwestern Educational Research Association, Chicago.

Duffy, G. G., Roehler, L. R., & Rackliffe, G. (1986). The relationship between explicit verbal explanations during reading skills instruction and student awareness and achievement: A study of reading teacher effects. *Reading Research Quarterly, XXI,* 237–252.

Durkin, D. (1983). *Is there a match between what elementary teachers do and what basal reader manuals recommend* (Reading Ed. Rep. No. 44). Urbana, IL: University of Illinois, Center for the Study of Reading.

Dyasi, H. (1989). *Report of the science inquiry program (Saturday Academy) for District Five at City College.* New York: City College of the University of New York, City College Workshop Center.

*Education Daily.* (1988, June). *Hawkins/Stafford ESSIA Title I—Elementary and secondary education act (ESEA) amendments.* Special Supplement.

Engel, M. (1990). From B.C. to PC. In *Noteworthy,* Annual Report from the Mid-continent Regional Educational Laboratory, (17–19). Aurora, CO: Mid-continent Regional Educational Laboratory.

Ennis, R., Millman, J., & Tomko, T. (1985). *Cornell Critical Thinking Test.* Pacific Grove, CA: Midwest Publications.

Evangelou, D. (1989). Mixed-age groups in early childhood education. *ERIC Digest* (EDO-PS-89-4). From ERIC Clearinghouse on EECE.

Feuerstein, R., Rand, Y., Hoffman, M. B., Epozi, M., & Kaiwel, S. (1991). Intervention programs for the retarded performer: Goals, means, and expected outcomes. In B. F. Jones & L. Idol

(Eds.), *Dimensions of thinking and cognitive instruction* (pp. 139–178). Hillsdale, NJ: Lawrence Erlbaum Associates.

Figueroa, R., & Amato, C. (1989). *Issues in special education*. Santa Barbara: University of California Linguistics Minority Research Project. No. 1 in the Research and Policy Series.

Flower, L., & Hayes, J. R. (1981). The pregnant pause: An enquiry into the nature of planning. *Research in the Teaching of English, 15,* 229–244.

Forman, E. A., & Cazden, C. B. (1985). Exploring Vygotskian perspectives in education: The cognitive value of peer interaction. In J. V. Wertsch (Ed.), *Culture, communication, and cognition: Vygotskian perspectives* (pp. 323–347). New York: Cambridge University Press.

Gardner, H. (1987). Developing the spectrum of human intelligences. *Harvard Educational Review, 57,* 187–193.

Gardner, H., & Hatch, T. (1989). Multiple intelligences go to school. *Educational Researcher, 18* (8), 4–10.

Goetz, E. T. (1984). The role of spatial strategies in processing and remembering text: A cognitive-information-processing analysis. In C. D. Holley & D. F. Dansereau (Eds.), *Spatial learning strategies: Techniques, applications, and related issues* (pp. 47–77). Orlando, FL: Academic Press.

Goldberg, B. (1988). Restructuring and technology: Part one. *Radius, 1*(3), 1–9. Washington, DC: The American Federation of Teachers Center for Restructuring.

Goldberg, B. (1989). Restructuring and technology: Part two. *Radius,* 1(4). Washington, DC: The American Federation of Teachers Center for Restructuring.

Goodlad, J. (1984). *A place called school: Prospects for the future.* New York: McGraw-Hill.

Goodlad, J. I. (undated). *The National Network for Educational Renewal.* Seattle, WA: Center for Educational Renewal, Institute for Policy Studies in Education, University of Washington.

Goodlad, J. I., & Keating, P. (Eds.). (1990). *Access to knowledge; An agenda for our nation's schools.* New York: The College Entrance Examination Board.

Graham, E. (1990, February 9). Bottom-line education: A business-run school in Chicago seeks to improve learning without a big rise in costs. *The Wall Street Journal,* pp. R22–R25.

Greenberg, J. B. (1989, April). Funds of knowledge: Historical constitution, social distribution, and transmission. In *Collaborative Research: Combining Community and School Resources to Improve the Education of Hispanics in Tucson.* Session conducted at the annual meeting of the Society for Applied Anthropology, Annual Meetings, Santa Fe, NM.

Hamm, M., & Adams, D. (1989). An analysis of global problem issues in sixth- and seventh-grade textbooks. *Journal of Research in Science Teaching, 26,* 445–452.

Heath, S. B. (1982). Protean shapes in literacy events: Ever-shifting oral and literate traditions. In D. Tannen (Ed.), *Spoken and written language: Exploring orality and literacy* (pp. 91–117). Norwood, NJ: Ablex.

Henderson, A. (1987). *The evidence continues to grow: Parent involvement improves student achievement.* Columbia, MD: National Committee for citizens in Education.

Hodgkinson, H. (1988, February). The right schools for the right kids. *Educational Leadership, 45* (9), 10–14.

Holley, C. D., & Dansereau, D. F. (1984). Networking: The technique and the empirical evidence. In C. D. Holley & D. F. Dansereau (Eds.), *Spatial Learning Strategies: Techniques, applications, and related issues* (pp. 81–108). Orlando, FL: Academic Press.

Holmes Group. (1986). *Tomorrow's teachers: A report of the Holmes Group.* East Lansing, MI: Michigan State University, College of Education.

Hull, G. A. (1989). Research on writing: Building a cognitive and social understanding of composing. In L. B. Resnick & L. E. Klopfer (Eds.), *Toward the thinking curriculum: Current cognitive research* (pp. 104–128). Alexandria, VA: Association for Supervision and Curriculum Development.

James, B. H. (1989). *Parent-community involvement: Collaboration by another name* (Annual Report on Urban Education). Charleston, WV: Appalachia Educational Laboratory, Regional Liaison Center.

Jenkins, J., Pious, C. G., & Jewell, M. (1990). Special education and the regular education initiative: Basic assumptions. *Exceptional Children, 56*, 479–491.

Jensen, A. R. (1969). How much can we boost IQ and scholastic achievement? *Harvard Education Review, 39*, 1–123.

Johnson, D. W., & Johnson, R. T. (1989). *Cooperation and competition: Theory and research.* Edina, MN: Interaction Book Company.

Johnston, W. B., & Packer, A. H. (1987). *Workforce 2000: Work and workers for the 21st century.* Indianapolis: Hudson Institute.

Jones, B. F. (1986). SPaRCS Procedure. In *Teaching reading as thinking. Teleconference resource guide* (pp. 32–41). Elmhurst, IL: The North Central Regional Educational Laboratory.

Jones, B. F. (1990). The importance of restructuring to promote learning. In D. S. Ogle, W. T. Pink, & B. F. Jones, (Eds.), *Restructuring to promote learning in America's schools: Selected readings, Vol. I* (pp. 13–33). Columbus, OH: Zaner Bloser.

Jones, B. F., & Fennimore, T. (1990). *Restructuring to promote learning in America's schools* (Guidebook 1). Elmhurst, IL: North Central Regional Educational Laboratory.

Jones, B. F., Palincsar, A. S., Ogle, D. S., & Carr, E. G. (1987). *Strategic teaching and learning: Cognitive instruction in the content areas.* Alexandria, VA: Association for Supervision & Curriculum Development.

Jones, B. F., Pierce, J., & Hunter, B. (1988–89). Teaching students to construct graphic organizers. *Educational Leadership, 46*(4), 20–25.

Jones, B. F., & Tinzmann, M. B. (1990). *Breakthroughs: Strategies for thinking* (Grades 1–8). Columbus, OH: Zaner-Bloser.

Kiewra, K. A., DuBois, N. S., Christian, D., & McShane, A. (1988). Providing study notes: Comparison of three types of notes for review. *Journal of Educational Psychology, 80*, 595–597.

Kirsch, I. S., & Jungeblut, A. (1986). *Literacy: Profiles of America's Young Adults.* (Report No. 16-PL-02). Princeton, NJ: National Assessment of Educational Progress, Educational Testing Service.

Lanier, J. E., & Featherstone, J. (1988). A new commitment to teacher education. *Educational Leadership, 46*(3), 18–22.

Leinhardt, G. (1986). Expertise in mathematics teaching. *Educational Leadership, 43*(7), 28–33.

Levin, H. M. (1986). *Educational reform for disadvantaged students: An emerging crisis.* Washington, DC: National Education Association.

Levine, D. U., & Eubanks, E. E. (1989, July). *Site-based management: Engine for reform or pipedream? Problems, pitfalls, and prerequisites for success in site-based management.* Unpublished manuscript.

Levine, D. U., & Havighurst, R. J. (1989). School reform and effectiveness. *Society and education* (pp. 493–557). Boston: Allyn and Bacon.

Lipman, M. (1984). The cultivation of reasoning through philosophy. *Educational Leadership, 42* (1), 51–56.

Lipman, M. (1988). Critical thinking—what can it be? *Educational Leadership, 46*(1), 38–43.

Lytle, J. H. (1988, December). Revised Chapter 1 opens options for schoolwide plans. *Education Week,* 32.

Magliocca, L., Amidon, S. R., & Tyree, R. L. (1989, unpublished paper). *Teaching thinking through content: The* Breakthroughs *model.* The Ohio State University.

Magliocca, L., Amidon, S. R., Arnold, K. D., & Miller, S. (1991, April). *The effectiveness of teaching critical thinking through context: An application of the Dimensions of Thinking Framework.* Paper presented at the Annual Meeting of the American Educational Research Association, Chicago.

Magliocca, L. Amidon, S. R., & Tyree, R. L. (in progress). *Teaching thinking through content: The* Breakthroughs *model.* The Ohio State University.

Marzano, R. J., Brandt, R. S., Hughes, C. S., Jones, B. F., Presseisen, B. Z., Rankin, S. C., &

Suhor, C. (1988). *Dimensions of thinking: A framework for curriculum and instruction.* Alexandria, VA: Association for Supervision & Curriculum Development.

Mayer, R. E. (1984). Aids to text comprehension. *Educational Psychologist, 19,* 30–42.

Mayer, R. E. (1989). Models for understanding. *Review of Educational Research, 59,* 43–64.

McClure, R. M., & Obermeyer, G. (1987). *Visions of school renewal.* Washington, DC: National Education Association.

McKnight, C. C., Crosswhite, F. J., Dossey, J. A., Swafford, J. O., Travers, K. J., & Cooney, T. J. (1987). *The underachieving curriculum: Assessing U.S. school mathematics from an international perspective.* Champaign, IL: Stipes Publishing Company.

Michigan Reading Association and Michigan Department of Education. (1985). *What research says to the classroom teacher about reading.* Lansing, MI: Communications/MEAP Ad Hoc Committee and the Michigan Reading Association.

Mid-continental Regional Educational Laboratory. (1989). *What's noteworthy on rural schools and development.* Aurora, CO: Author.

Minstrell, J. A. (1989). Teaching science for understanding. In L. B. Resnick & L. E. Klopfer (Eds.), *Toward the thinking curriculum: Current cognitive research* (pp. 129–149). Alexandria, VA: Association for Supervision & Curriculum Development.

Moll, L. C., & Greenberg, J. B. (1990). Creating zones of possibilities: Combining social contexts for instruction. In L. C. Moll (Ed.), *Vygotsky and education* (pp. 319–348). Cambridge, England: Cambridge University Press.

Moore, D. W., & Readance, J. E. (1984). A quantitative and qualitative review of graphic organizer research. *Journal of Educational Research, 78*(1), 11–17.

Mootry, P. (1989). *School as hub in a network of social services.* Chicago: Corporate Community Schools of America.

National Assessment of Educational Progress. (1983). *Science assessment and research project, images of science: Summary of results from the 1981–82 national assessment in science* (Rep. No. 08-5-00). U.S. Department of Education: Center for Statistics.

National Assessment of Educational Progress. (1985). *The reading report card: Progress toward excellence in our schools* (Rep. No. 15-R-01). U.S. Department of Education: Center for Statistics.

National Assessment of Educational Progress. (1986). *The writing report card: Writing achievement in American schools, 1984* (Rep. No. 15-W-02). U.S. Department of Education: Center for Statistics.

National Commission on Social Studies in the Schools. (1989, November). *Charting a course: Social studies for the 21st century: A report of the curriculum task force of the National Commission on Social Studies in the Schools.* Washington, DC: Author.

National Council of Teachers of Mathematics. (1989). *Curriculum and evaluation standards for school mathematics.* Reston, VA: Author.

National Governors' Association Center for Policy Research and Analysis. (1986, August). *Time for results: The governors' 1991 report on education.* Washington, DC: Author.

Newmann, F. M., & Thompson, J. A. (1987). *Effects of cooperative learning on achievement in secondary schools: A summary of research.* Madison, WI: University of Wisconsin-Madison, National Center on Effective Secondary Schools.

Nickerson, R. S., Perkins, D. N., & Smith, E. E. (Eds.). (1985). *The teaching of thinking.* Hillsdale, NJ: Lawrence Erlbaum Associates.

O'Neil, J. (1988, September). How "special" should the special education curriculum be? *ASCD Curriculum Update,* 123–130.

Palincsar, A. S., & Brown, A. L. (1984). Reciprocal teaching of comprehension-fostering and comprehension-monitoring activities. *Cognition and Instruction, 1*(2), 117–175.

Palincsar, A. S., & Brown, A. L. (1989a). Instruction for self-regulated reading. In L. B. Resnick & L. E. Klopfer (Eds.), *Toward the thinking curriculum: Current cognitive research* (pp. 19–39). Alexandria, VA: Association for Supervision and Curriculum Development.

Palincsar, A. S., & Brown, A. L. (1989b). Classroom dialogues to promote self-regulated comprehension. In J. Brophy (Ed.), *Teaching for understanding and self-regulated learning* (Vol. 1, pp. 35–71). Greenwich, CT: JAI Press.

Parnell, D. (1986). *The neglected majority*. p. 37. Washington, DC: Community College Press.

Pearlman, B. (1988). Restructuring and technology: Part two. *Radius, 1*(4), 1–14. Washington, DC: The American Federation of Teachers Center for Restructuring.

Perkins, D. N. (1986). *Knowledge as design*. Hillsdale, NJ: Lawrence Erlbaum Associates.

Pinnell, G. S., Lyons, C., Young, P., & Deford, D. (1987). *The Reading Recovery Project in Columbus, Ohio: Volume VI Year 2 1986–87* (Technical Report). Columbus, OH: The Ohio State University.

Prawat, R. (1990). *Changing school by changing teachers' beliefs about teaching and learning* (Research Report No. ESC19). East Lansing, MI: Michigan State University, Institute for Research on Teaching.

Randal, C., Lester, F., & O'Daffer, P. (1987). *How to evaluate progress in problem solving*. Reston, VA: National Council of Teachers of Mathematics.

Reigeluth, C. M. (1988). The search for meaningful reform: A third-wave educational system. *Journal of Instructional Development, 10*(4), 3–14.

Resnick, L. B.(1984). Cognitive science as educational research: Why we need it now. In *Improving education: Perspectives on educational research* (pp. 36–41). Pittsburgh: University of Pittsburgh, Learning Research and Development Center.

Resnick, L. B. (1987, December). Learning in school and out. *Educational Researcher, 16*(6), 13–20.

Resnick, L. B., & Klopfer, L. E. (Eds.). (1989). *Toward the thinking curriculum: Current cognitive research*. Alexandria, VA: Association for Supervision and Curriculum Development.

Rhodes, L. (1988). We have met the system—and it is us! *Phi Delta Kappan, 70,* 28–30.

Risch, N., & Kiewra, K. A. (1989, October 20). *Content and form variations in note taking: Effects among junior-high students*. Paper presented at the Midwestern Educational Research Association: Chicago.

Romberg, T. (1990). Principles for an elementary mathematics program for the 1990s. Paper prepared for the California Invitation Symposium on Elementary Mathematics Education (rev. ed.). In D. S. Ogle, W. T. Pink, & B. F. Jones (Eds.), *Restructuring to promote learning in America's schools: Selected readings, Vol. I* (149–168). Columbus, OH: Zaner Bloser.

Roth, K. J. (1990). Developing meaningful conceptual understanding in science. In B. F. Jones & L. Idol (Eds.) *Dimensions of thinking and cognitive instruction* (pp. 139–175). Hillsdale, NJ: Lawrence Erlbaum Associates.

Schlechty, P. C., Ingwerson, D. W., Brooks, T. I. (1988). Inventing professional development schools. *Educational Leadership, 46*(3), 28–31.

Schlesinger, A. M., Jr. (1986, July 27). "The Challenge of Change," *The New York Times Magazine,* pp. 20–21.

Schon, D. A. (1987). *Educating the reflective practitioner*. San Francisco: Jossey-Bass.

Schwartz, P., & Ogilvy, J. (1979). *The emergent paradigm: Changing patterns of thought and belief*. Menlo Park, CA: Values and Lifestyles Program.

Shavelson, R. (1983). Review of research on teachers' pedagogical judgments, plans, and decisions. *Elementary School Journal, 83,* 392–413.

Shulman, L. S. (1987a, August). Teaching alone, learning together: Needed agencies for the new reforms. Paper prepared for the conference on *Restructuring Schooling for Quality Education,* Trinity University, San Antonio, TX.

Shulman, L. S. (1987b). Knowledge and teaching: Foundations of the new reform. *Harvard Educational Review, 57*(1), 1–22.

Sinclair, R. L., & Ghory, W. J. (1987). *Reaching marginal students*. Berkeley, CA: McCutchan Publishing Corporation.

Sizer, T. R. (1989). Diverse practice, shared ideas: The essential school. In H. J. Walberg & J. J.

Lane (Eds.), *Organizing for learning: Toward the 21st century* (pp. 1–8). Reston, VA: National Association of Secondary School Principals.

Sizer, T. R. (1990, February 26). Lessons from the trenches. *U.S. News & World Report*, pp. 50–55.

Slavin, R. E. (1987). Cooperative learning and the cooperative school. *Educational Leadership, 45* (3), 7–13.

Stevens, D. (research in progress). *Specifying teacher thinking: The relationship among teachers' theories about learning, their perceptions of their context, and their response and practice of constructivist-based ideas in reading* (working title).

Tinzmann, M. B., Friedman, L. B., Jewell-Kelly, S., Mootry, P., Nachtigal, P., & Fine, C. (1990a). *Restructuring to promote learning in America's schools* (Guidebook 5). Elmhurst, IL: The North Central Regional Educational Laboratory.

Tinzmann, M. B., Jones, B. F., Fennimore, T. F., Bakker, J., Fine, C., & Pierce, J. (1990b). *Restructuring to promote learning in America's schools* (Guidebook 3). Elmhurst, IL: The North Central Regional Educational Laboratory.

Tucker, M. S. (1988). Peter Drucker, knowledge work, and the structure of schools. *Educational Leadership, 45*(5), 44–66.

Tyler, G. (1990). *Educating in a democracy*. In *Noteworthy*, Annual Report from the Mid-continent Regional Education Laboratory (17–19). Aurora, CO: Mid-continental Regional Educational Laboratory.

United States Department of Education. (1988). Request for Proposal No. 88–050, "Chapter I— Technical Assistance Centers."

Usiskin, Z. (1985). We need another revolution in school mathematics. In *Secondary school mathematics* (pp. 1–21). Reston, VA: National Council of Teachers of Mathematics.

Valencia, S. (1990). A portfolio approach to classroom reading assessment. The why, whats, and hows. *The Reading Teacher, 43*, 338–342.

Vaughn, J. L. (1984). Concept structuring: The technical and empirical evidence. In C. D. Holley & D. F. Dansereau (Eds.), *Spatial learning strategies: Techniques, applications, and related issues* (pp. 127–146). Orlando, FL: Academic Press.

Weber, L., & Dyasi, H. (1985). Language development and observation of the local environment: First steps in providing primary-school science education for non-dominant groups. *Prospects. XV*(4), 565–576.

Wehlage, G. G., & Rutter, R. A. (1987). Dropping out: How much do schools contribute to the problem: In G. Natriello (Ed.), *School dropouts: Patterns and policies* (pp. 70–88). New York: Teachers College Press.

Weiner, S. (1989, September 18). We decided to show how things can work. *Forbes*, pp. 180–181, 184, 188.

Weinstein, C. E., Goetz, E., & Alexander, P. (1988). *Learning and study strategies: Issues in assessment, instruction, and evaluation*. New York: Academic Press.

White, M. A. (1987). Information and imagery education. In M. A. White (Ed.), *What curriculum for an information age?* (pp. 41–60). Hillsdale, NJ: Lawrence Erlbaum Associates.

Wiggins, G. (1989). A true test: Toward more authentic and equitable assessment. *Phi Delta Kappan, 70*, 703–714.

Wisconsin Department of Public Instruction. (1986). *A guide to curriculum planning in reading* (D. Cook, Ed.). Madison, WI: Author.

Wisconsin Department of Public Instruction. (1989). *Strategic learning in the content areas* (D. Cook, Ed.). Madison, WI: Author.

Wolf, D. P. (1989). Portfolio assessment: Sampling student work. *Educational Leadership, 46*(7), 35–39.

Yager, R. E. (1989). New goals for students. *Education and Urban Society, 22*(1), 9–21.

Zuboff, S. (1988). *In the age of the smart machine: The future of work and power*. New York: Basic Books.

# Introduction to Chapter 11

*Kenneth Wolf, Research Associate, Far West Laboratory for Educational Research and Development, and Research Assistant Stanford's Teacher Assessment Project, Stanford University.*

Of the many educational reforms sweeping the nation, assessment reform may be the most critical. As Paris, Lawton, and Turner point out, the diverse and innovative efforts currently underway to enhance students' thinking and learning may all fail for the same reason: they do not improve students' scores on standardized tests.

Standardized testing has come to assume enormous power in our educational system, power enough to derail needed reforms and demoralize teachers and students. In this chapter, the authors add their voices to those who decry the destructive influences that standardized tests exert at all levels of the educational system, but what is especially compelling about their indictment is that they take *a student's-eye view* and survey the damage from the perspective of those taking the tests and in whose supposed interest these tests are carried out. Based upon their multi-state survey of student attitudes, the authors found that the competitive and comparative nature of standardized tests increase student anxiety, decrease motivation, and diminish self-esteem. Standardized testing may meet the needs of many stakeholders in the educational system, but students are clearly not among them.

It is time to reorder our priorities. The primary goal of assessment should be to foster students' intellectual and emotional growth. Other purposes for assessment, such as public accountability, while legitimate, should not be allowed to subvert this goal. Assessment should begin with the child, and it should help students, parents, and teachers learn what students *can* do and provide them with infor-

221

mative feedback for improving student performance. Moreover, assessments of student achievement must be broad and deep enough to capture the diversity of children's experiences and backgrounds as well as the different rates and routes in children's development.

One assessment alternative gaining popularity at the national state, district, and classroom level is the use of portfolios to assess student progress. A portfolio approach to assessment allows students and teachers to gather multiple measures of progress as students are engaged in a variety of authentic learning activities. These collections of student work samples and teacher records can provide evidence of a student's accomplishments, as well as the thinking behind these products and performances. In addition, portfolios can be customized to reflect the distinctive strengths and needs of individual students and programs. However, while portfolios hold great promise for student evaluation, many complex issues remain to be resolved. What kinds of information go into a portfolio? How much? How is a portfolio evaluated? By whom? Without careful consideration of these and other questions of content and purpose, portfolios can easily turn into unwieldy scrapbooks which do little to promote student thinking and learning.

The movement towards more authentic, performance-based assessment has not only begun to change the landscape in student assessment but in teacher assessment as well. Stanford's Teacher Assessment Project, for example, recently completed a multi-year exploration of alternative approaches for assessing teachers. This research endeavor is intended to guide the National Board for Professional Teaching Standards in its attempt to create a voluntary program for the national certification of accomplished teachers. As teachers document their professional competence by including samples of their students' work in their teaching portfolios—in some cases, they will use the very same samples that students presented in their portfolios. Teachers and students, however, might draw on the same work for different purposes. The writing samples that students submit to portray their increasing sophistication as writers might be used by teachers to illustrate the various ways that they create authentic writing opportunities in their classrooms.

Paris, Lawton, and Turner end their chapter with a radical recommendation: Declare a 3-year moratorium on standardized testing so that we can devote our resources and attention to exploring other forms of student assessment. Placing the standardized testing movement on hold, a daunting task in itself, however, is a limited solution at best. Replacing standardized tests with more productive forms of assessment is the major challenge. In this chapter, the authors made a number of valuable recommendations for reforming achievement testing. Thoughtful implementation of these recommendations and careful research on the advantages and limitations of new forms of assessment are crucial. Otherwise, in our headlong rush to embrace alternative forms of assessment, we may trample our own good intentions.

# 11

# Reforming Achievement Testing to Promote Students' Learning

Scott G. Paris
Theresa A. Lawton
Julianne C. Turner
*University of Michigan*

America is awash in a tide of educational reform movements. The impetus for changes and the specific targets of reform vary tremendously among schools across the country but one overarching goal is to improve the quality of students' thinking—to promote a critical, thoughtful orientation to academic subjects that students generalize to situations beyond school. Ironically, these innovative reforms may fail for the same basic reason; they may show no significant gains in the standardized achievement test scores of students. The tragic misuse of standardized achievement tests as evaluation instruments for diverse educational reforms may thwart improvements, stifle the creativity of teachers, and deprive students of important opportunities to develop their talents.

We believe that assessment of student progress is essential but that it must be improved substantially if it is to reinforce broad changes in curriculum, instruction, and leadership. Standardized achievement testing, in particular, because it is a pervasive, repetitive, high-stakes form of assessment, needs to be considered from the students' point of view in order to understand how testing influences students' thinking strategies and motivational goals. Research suggests that traditional assessment practices exaggerate the differences among students, inappropriately identify students as *winners* and *losers,* and produce cumulative negative orientations to schooling among many students (Covington, 1983; Nicholls, 1989). It is also important to examine how achievement testing influences other "assessment consumers" including teachers, parents, and administrators because their beliefs and practices regarding achievement tests directly affect students.

Our main purpose here is to offer suggestions for evaluating and reformulating assessment practices in schools so that they foster students' thinking. This chapter has three sections. In the first section, we describe research on students' views of achievement testing that reveal how standardized tests engender maladaptive attitudes and strategies. Next, we argue that traditional achievement testing can distort educational curricula and instructional practices designed to improve the quality of students' thinking. In the final section, we describe how educators can evaluate and revise assessment practices within their districts.

## STUDENTS' VIEWS OF STANDARDIZED ACHIEVEMENT TESTS

Among the many things that students learn in school, perhaps the most distressing is reflected in the question, "Is this going to be on the test?". Because students learn to study information that will be tested and ignore other information, testing defines their focus of attention and learning. Assessment is woven into the fabric of schooling from readiness tests for kindergarten to competency examinations for graduation. Every year students take more tests in more subjects. They learn that some tests are more important than others and that test scores are used to identify successful students. Tests become ever more daunting challenges, especially for unsuccessful students, who learn directly the consequences of high-stakes testing. As Sir Richard Livingston said, "Examinations are harmless when the examinee is indifferent to their result, but as soon as they matter, they begin to distort his attitude to education and to control its purpose."

It is important to measure students' views of standardized tests because children's perceptions of school and the classroom climate have profound influences on their achievement and motivation (Stipek & MacIver, 1989; Weinstein, 1983). For example, children learn in elementary grades how group membership signifies ability, which students teachers expect to be successful, and whether their parents share the same values as teachers. As students become socialized into the practices of public evaluation in school, grades and standardized test scores influence how students regard themselves and their peers. We want to advocate the students' position in achievement testing by considering the impact of current practices on students' perceptions of competence and schooling, strategies for taking tests, and motivation and affect. Our research indicates that these characteristics of students change dramatically during the course of schooling and not always in positive ways.

### The Development of Disillusionment

Students' perceptions of school parallel the development of students' perceptions of competence. In 1st grade, children evaluate their ability according to teacher praise and rewards, but by 5th grade, children learn that academic competence is signaled by comparative academic performance, notably grades and test scores

(Stipek & MacIver, 1989). At the same time, students are developing more differentiated self-concepts and clearer understandings of the factors that control their own success and failure in the classroom (Connell, 1985; Harter, 1985). The development of self-perceptions related to achievement reaffirms the impact of tests noted by George Madaus (1988), namely, ". . . if students, teachers, or administrators believe that the results of an examination are important, it matters very little whether this is really true or false—the effect is produced by what individuals perceive to be the case" (p. 88).

How do students view standardized achievement tests and how do those perceptions change with increasing age and experience? To investigate this question, we designed several surveys of students' attitudes and test-taking strategies. Teachers in Michigan, California, Arizona, and Florida gave the surveys to almost 1000 students in their classes, grades 2–11 (Paris, Turner, & Lawton, 1990). The first survey included 40 items that were read aloud to students who indicated on a 5-point scale whether they agreed or disagreed with each statement (1 = strongly agree; 5 = strongly disagree). We found significant age differences on 12 items that appeared to reflect some general developmental changes in students' perceptions of standardized tests.

The first trend is the *growing suspicion about the validity of test scores*. Older students disagreed with the following three items significantly more than younger students: "Test scores show how intelligent you are"; "My test scores show that I am a good student"; and "Test scores help to identify which teachers do the best job." By high-school, many students believe that intelligent students do not always get good test scores and that test scores do not necessarily reflect the qualities of a good student. It is also interesting to note that students become increasingly skeptical about test scores as an indicator of teacher effectiveness.

The second trend is the *realization among older students that they are not well informed about the purposes and uses of achievement tests*. They indicated higher disagreement than younger students with the following items: "The teacher explains to the class why we take tests" and "The school provides useful information to my family about standardized test scores." Young children place their trust in the teacher and accept the face validity of testing: they also assume that good information is provided to the family. This may indicate a naive presumption of the positive value of the test among young students and increasing skepticism among older students.

The third trend reflects the *increasing apprehension that test scores may become the basis for comparative social judgments*. Older students were significantly more likely to agree with the following statements: "I'm afraid that people will think I'm stupid if I get a low score on a test" and "Most students know each other's test score." With the advent of increasing social comparison based on a tangible achievement such as grades and test results, students become competitive and anxious about their relative performance. They often feel that test scores become common knowledge and are worried about the perceptions of others. Although most students may worry that their low scores will be viewed with contempt, some students may be embarrassed by their successes and try to conceal high test scores.

The fourth general trend is that *older students report decreasing motivation to excel on standardized tests*. They were less likely than younger students to agree with the following statements: "I gave my best effort on the test we took"; "Most students try to do their best on tests"; and "I want to do well on the test because my teacher really cares how well I do." There are several reasons why students may not try to do their best on the achievement tests. First, they might think that the test results have no impact on their grades or, second, they may believe that teachers and parents do not really care how individual students score on these tests. Third, decreasing motivation may reflect a self-preservation of their own esteem so that students who do not excel on the tests can always claim a lack of effort as an excuse (Covington, 1983). Fourth, students may feel that the tests serve political purposes for the district and express their hostility with a lack of effort or even deliberate sabotage of the tests. The cumulative decline in motivation may be due to depersonalization of the tests and minimalization of the importance of success with increasing age of the test taker. Whatever the reason, lowered motivation threatens the validity of the test scores.

The fifth trend that we observed was the *surprising admission among older students that they felt less prepared to take the tests*. In particular, they were more likely to disagree with the following statement: "I have good strategies for taking tests." We expected the frequency of good test-taking strategies to increase with age and experience, but, in contrast, older students felt that they had fewer appropriate strategies to employ on these tests. Perhaps they were more aware than younger students of the need to apply test-taking strategies or perhaps they felt more anxiety about their own abilities to use these strategies. Whatever the source of their lack of confidence, it is surprising that high school students reported a lack of good test-taking strategies.

Of course, not all students view tests negatively nor do they undermine their own test performance. We hypothesized that high achievers and low achievers might have vastly different perceptions and approaches to standardized achievement tests. Therefore, we conducted another survey of 250 students in grades 4, 7, and 10 about the new Michigan Educational Assessment Program (MEAP) Reading Test, a state-mandated, criterion-referenced achievement test. Students were asked to rate their agreement or disagreement with a series of items. On the positive side, most students reported that they tried hard, they thought they did well, they thought the test was not difficult or confusing, and they felt there was little cheating. On the negative side, older students, and 10th graders in particular, cared less about how well they did on the test, thought that parents and teachers did not care about their test scores, felt less prepared to take the tests, received less explanation and encouragement from teachers, were more bored as they read the passages so they often did not read the entire passage, thought it was "OK" to let their friends see their answers, were less likely to go back and check their answers, and were more likely to fill in the bubbles without thinking. These findings confirmed the results of our earlier surveys.

Next, we divided the sample into high and low achievers to determine if students with different histories of success on the California Achievement Test had different views about standardized tests. High achievers were more likely than the low achievers to report that they did well on the reading test, the test was easy, the test was not confusing, and they often reread parts of the passage. They reported less often that they just responded without thinking and less often that they got bored and did not finish reading the passage. Thus, persistence, appropriate test-taking strategies, and positive self-perceptions distinguished the high from the low achievers.

We believe these data reflect a growing split between high and low achieving students in their perceptions of the usefulness of standardized achievement tests, their recruitment of legitimate goals and strategies, and their motivation to excel. It appears that the results of standardized achievement tests become increasingly less valid for low achievers, exactly the group who are most *at-risk* for educational problems and who most need diagnostic testing. Their scores may be contaminated by inappropriate motivation and learning strategies in ways that further debilitate their performance and affirm a self-fulfilling prophecy. Apparently, in their efforts to decrease personal anxiety and increase the protection of their own self-esteem, they relinquish effort and appropriate strategies on standardized achievement tests. The ironic consequence is that the scores become high-stakes discriminatory markers of their lack of success. This debilitating pattern of motivation and learning increases developmentally and undercuts the essence of education. What price must students pay to preserve their sense of self-worth in school?

## The Development of Test-wiseness

A typical student in an American elementary school is given both a norm-referenced standardized achievement test (e.g., Stanford Achievement Test, California Achievement Test, Iowa Test of Basic Skills) and a state-mandated, criterion-referenced achievement test in reading and mathematics every year beginning by 3rd grade. Some districts add their own tests, many states test more subjects than just reading and mathematics, and teachers, of course, administer their own periodic tests. Some schools provide test coaching, but even without any special instruction, children have many opportunities to develop their attitudes and strategies regarding tests.

Despite the prevalence of testing, there is surprisingly little information on the development of test-wiseness. In an initial attempt to determine if students acquire and use good test-taking strategies, we designed a 20-item survey that described appropriate and inappropriate tactics that students might use while taking a standardized test. Ten of the strategies presented positive tactics. For example, one positive item read "Jim always answers the questions he knows first, and then goes back to the ones he wasn't sure of. Is this like you?". The other 10 items were considered negative strategies. For example, "Sometimes Chris finishes a test early. He thinks it is boring to go back and check his answers so he puts his pencil down and does something else. Is this like you?". Students indicated on a 4-point scale how much the hypothetical characters' behavior was like their own (1 = A lot like me, 4 = Not at all like me). The survey was given to nearly 1000 students from grades 2–11 in order to examine developmental changes in students' understanding about test-taking strategies. We anticipated a progressive increase with age in the use of positive strategies for taking tests and a progressive decrease among older students in the use of negative strategies.

Our hypotheses were not confirmed. Students from all grades reported modest agreement about using the positive strategies described in the scenarios. We were surprised, however, that the level of endorsement of the positive strategies was not very strong at any grade level and there was no indication of stronger agreement with increasing age and experience. Thus, the youngest students were not naive about the benefits of positive strategies nor did the oldest students report that they used them frequently. Strategies such as checking ones' answers, maintaining attention, monitoring the testing time, and moving away from a student who is distracting are regarded as useful tactics by all students. In contrast, we were alarmed to note a significant developmental change in the appraisals of negative strategies. Older students, compared to younger students, reported that the negative scenarios were *more* like them. For example, older students agreed more that they often "get tired and start to fill in bubbles without reading the questions" or they "just guess on questions that are confusing." Older students were more likely to cheat, to become nervous, to have difficulty concentrating, to guess, and to look for answers that matched the questions without reading the passage. All of these strategies are detrimental to higher order thinking and intrinsic motivation.

The developmental implications of the surveys are disturbing. Instead of increasing motivation and test-wiseness with age, older students apparently feel greater resentment, cynicism, and mistrust of standardized achievement tests. We should temper that sweeping indictment with the observation that many students reported that they try to do well on tests, believe that it is important to do well on standardized achievement tests, and feel satisfied with their scores. However, there is a growing disillusionment with increasing experience that is manifested in inappropriate test-taking strategies. These consequences can be immediate and localized, but for some students, they can lead to long-term disenfranchisement. Older students apparently are more likely to minimize effort and respond randomly to standardized tests than younger students. They may sabotage the tests or use mindless strategies such as drawing patterns of answers (e.g., Christmas tree designs, alternating letters, etc.). Their anger may be manifested more generally if the cumulative reports of low ability causes them to discredit teachers, tests, and schools. Hostility and withdrawn participation are the last resorts for many students to escape the frustrations of testing. These outcomes are diametrically opposed to reforms aimed at promoting students' higher order thinking and commitment to education.

Do students learn to take tests more effectively with increasing age and experience? The general answer appears to be "No" except for the successful, high-scoring students who adhere to useful strategies and eschew negative tactics. Even 7–8 year-olds can discriminate useful from harmful test-taking strategies. With increasing age, there is little appreciable change in students' reported use of the beneficial strategies, but, paradoxically, a large increase in the reported use of inappropriate strategies. One might conclude that standardized testing undermines the learning, thinking, and motivation of many students and that these effects become more pronounced with age. In order to understand these developmental trends, it might be helpful to distinguish two senses of test-wiseness.

In the first sense, test-wiseness reflects positive expectations for success, a clear understanding of task demands for self-monitoring, and judicious use of appropriate strategies. This type of test-wiseness enhances test-taking performance and is useful for students on similar tests that they will confront in education and beyond school. There is nothing wrong with students learning how to take time-constrained, group-administered, multiple-choice tests. This kind of knowledge and motivation may be encouraged through instruction and coaching as well as through successful test-taking experiences. However, the second sense, which we call "test-savviness," is maladaptive because what students learn are shortcuts for completing tests with minimal effort and thoughtfulness. They learn to answer questions without reading passages, to avoid time-consuming answer checking, to guess randomly if they are confused, and to discount the results of the test. This kind of test savvy is not limited to low-achieving students, although the effects may be more pronounced for them if they do not have knowledge of the first sense to muster when needed. The danger of students who become test-savvy but not test-wise is that they may generalize counterproductive motivation and behavior to other aspects of schooling.

## Debilitating Effects of Test Anxiety

Student apprehension about standardized achievement tests affects a substantial proportion of students. For example, Karmos and Karmos (1984) measured the attitudes of 360 students in grades 6–9 and correlated the data with scores on the Stanford Achievement Test. Their survey revealed positive attitudes in general, but an alarming proportion of student dissatisfaction and worry. Among other things, Karmos and Karmos (1984) found that: 47% of students thought taking achievement tests was a waste of time, 30% thought more about getting the achievement test over with than doing well, 36% thought achievement tests are dumb, 22% believed there was no good reason to try to do well on achievement tests, and 21% did not try very hard on achievement tests. As might be expected, high achievers, compared to low achievers, believed that standardized tests are more important and they invested more effort in doing well.

These results are consistent with some of the findings of Kellaghan, Madaus, and Airasian (1982) who found a substantial number of disaffected students in 6th grade, even in Ireland where standardized testing in elementary grades is uncommon. When asked about norm-referenced tests, 16% reported they did not enjoy sitting for the test, 29% did not care whether they sat for them, 11% disliked them, 21% felt afraid, 19% did not feel confident, 29% felt nervous, 16% felt bored, and 15% did not find them an interesting challenge. The results of these various surveys indicate that, by adolescence, a great many students feel threatened, worried, or bored by standardized achievement tests. These feelings can stimulate inappropriate preparation and test-taking behavior among students.

Anxiety compounds the problems of unsuccessful students. First, they may have poor study habits and difficulty organizing material presented in class so their mastery of the material is incomplete. Second, evaluations on poorly learned material demonstrate poor achievement and further reinforce their low self-perceptions of ability. Because low achieving students are not learning in school, anxiety may increase with failure experiences over the years (Benjamin, McKeachie, & Lin, 1987). However, it is not just low-achieving students who experience test anxiety; students of all achievement levels suffer from preoccupation about doing poorly on tests. Bright students may perceive unrealistic parental, peer, or self-imposed expectations to excel in all academic areas, and thus feel heightened anxiety in testing situations (Wigfield & Eccles, 1989). Although these students may have learned the material, they become unable to demonstrate mastery because they cannot cope with the pressures of evaluation and the potential negative attributions about their own ability that they fear will follow.

The effects of ability perceptions on children's motivation and their reactions to evaluative situations are related to increases in anxiety. Children who have more failure experiences will determine that they are less able than their peers and will have more cause to worry about their performance on a test than those who are confident that they will compare favorably. When children attribute their failures in school to low ability, they may feel shame, humiliation, and anxiety in evaluative situations (Weiner, 1986). Additionally, such children may develop elaborate strategies to avoid tests so that they can buffer their self-esteem against certain decline (Covington, 1983). These coping tactics are mirrored in the developmental trends that we observed in our surveys, for example, increasing distrust and apprehension, feigned effort, and counterproductive strategies.

School practices promote anxiety in some children by reinforcing negative ability perceptions. As children progress through school, public evaluations of ability and normative comparisons become more common. Emphasis on letter grades and tests can encourage a focus on ability perceptions, competition, social comparison, and negative self-evaluations (Hill & Wigfield, 1984). Use of grades and standardized test scores to provide recognition for students (e.g., honor roll, gifted classes), leads students to focus on the "currency value" of achievement rather than on its intrinsic value. In addition, such narrow definitions of academic success further separate the "haves" from the "have nots."

Because tests are introduced as measures of ability, they establish competitive situations among students. Highly anxious students are the first to drop out of competition because their responses to evaluative situations place them at a disadvantage. Diener and Dweck (1978) observed that repeated failure on tasks caused helpless children to withdraw from challenges, to decrease strategy use, and to forego expectancy for success. Anxious children focused more on themselves and were often consumed with negative thoughts about their personal inadequacies, deficient intelligence, poor memory, or inept problem-solving abilities. Thus, immobilized learning due to test anxiety has far reaching consequences.

## DISTORTING THE NEW EDUCATIONAL AGENDA

The effects of achievement testing become cumulative and debilitating for many students by the time they reach secondary schools. There are many consequences that undermine education but, in this section, we describe three ways that traditional achievement tests can inhibit effective learning and teaching in the classroom.

### Traditional Tests Encourage Low-level Thinking

The most frequently used achievement tests, such as the California Achievement Test, the Comprehensive Test of Basic Skills, and the Iowa Test of Basic Skills, reveal similar formats and psychometric principles. Testing is usually done in a few days with several timed testing periods; each subtest, (e.g., mathematics, reading, etc.), includes a small set of objective items; teachers administer the tests with standardized instructions; and students work silently and independently. These conditions prohibit many of the thinking strategies that teachers impart to students and that research has shown to be effective. For example, many students learn better when they work with a partner or small group in collaborative problem solving (Palinscar & Brown, 1984; Slavin, 1980). Many innovative approaches to critical thinking teach children to become aware of their own thinking, to reflect on how, when, and why to use various strategies, so that they can use the tactics selectively (Paris & Winograd, 1990). They are taught to use strategies such as rereading, checking answers, using dictionaries, seeking help, and so on that are often prevented within achievement testing situations.

Furthermore, the tests are biased to the assessment of discrete skills rather than richer, higher level thinking skills such as reasoning, decision making, critical thinking, writing in response to reading, or hypothesis generation. Resnick and Resnick (1990) contend that measurement of basic skills assumes the *decomposability* of cognition. This reductionistic, hierarchical model of learning contradicts current views of thinking and schooling. They also criticize traditional testing as *decontextualized* because the tests lack authentic purposes and assume that skills are stable regardless of when or why they are used. Resnick and Resnick (1990) conclude,

> In summary, the standardized tests fare badly when judged against the criterion of assessing and promoting a thinking curriculum. They embody a definition of knowledge and skill as a collection of bits of information, and they demand fast, nonreflective replies. The tests and the classroom practices that might be used to prepare for them suggest to students a view of knowledge counter to what the thinking curriculum seeks to cultivate. . . . (p. 73)

## Students' Misdirected Motivation

Many new curricula, instructional arrangements, and learning materials are designed to promote students' motivation and mastery learning. Authentic tasks that are challenging, yet stimulating, have begun to replace workbook exercises, seatwork, and unnecessary drills with an overarching purpose of fostering students' genuine effort. Research has shown convincingly that learning and thinking are better when students are involved in the task because they find it interesting and challenging rather than when they are working for external rewards or merely to complete the job (Nicholls, 1989). Unfortunately, most standardized tests are not intrinsically motivating; they promote competition and social comparison with an exclusive focus on outcome measures of achievement. These performance goals lead to anxiety among some students and reluctance to participate or try hard among others because they worry that the test results will indicate that they have low ability. Because tests pose recurring threats to students' self-worth, they undermine legitimate effort and persistence and prohibit personal satisfaction for many students (Covington, 1983).

## Misaligned Curricula and Instruction

A third way in which standardized achievement tests influence classroom practices is through the curriculum objectives they help to establish. Educators have long known that "testing drives the curriculum" and many have even advocated "measurement-driven instruction" as a virtue of tests for realigning curriculum goals (Airasian, 1988). But the innovative approaches to the "new thinking curriculum" are not always compatible with traditional achievement tests

(Shepard, 1989). Teachers are forced to choose whether to prepare their students for the goals of the curriculum or the criteria provided by the test.

Many teachers subvert or compromise their own values in order to teach students the discrete, and sometimes esoteric, skills measured by tests. Students may learn how to narrow their choices on multiple-choice items, how to monitor time, when to skip difficult items, and the value of checking one's answers. Regardless of the effects of such coaching, training in test-wiseness takes time and depends on teachers' knowledge about test-taking tactics and their beliefs in the value of test-wiseness. Of course, there are also commercial interests involved in coaching students how to take tests. The proliferation of materials, often by the same publishers who produce the tests, and expensive test preparation courses are further indications of how testing subjugates learning and instruction. All these sources of test-wiseness training confound interpretations of test scores because they contribute extraneous variance to students' scores. They also widen the gulf between high and low achievers if coaching is not uniformly available to low achievers. Educators with good intentions can direct their efforts to raise students' test scores by increasing their test-wiseness, but inadvertently they might divert attention and time from the main curriculum and only teach their students test-savviness. The result is misalignment among the curriculum, instruction, and assessment that frustrates students and teachers and reduces the validity of the test scores.

The extent of distortion in the educational agenda is clearly revealed in a survey of more than 2400 teachers and administrators in Arizona (Nolen, Haladyna, & Haas, 1990). They found abundant evidence that teachers orient their curriculum and instruction specifically to the format and content of standardized achievement tests. For example, two thirds of elementary teachers reported that they usually teach or review topics covered on the test prior to test week. Nearly half the teachers reported using commercial test preparation packages that teach specific skills measured on standardized tests. Almost two thirds reported that they were encouraged by administrators to raise test scores by using the format of the standardized test for their classroom tests and activities. Many teachers reported that they taught the specific vocabulary used in tests and had students take practice tests from the previous year. An alarming 10% reported teaching students the actual items from the current test.

Although educational policymakers deny that achievement test scores should be used in isolation or be given too much credit, they become the *sine qua non* of educational effectiveness when the scores are the only comparative measures of achievement available, when those data are reported in the local newspapers, and when they are used as public benchmarks for success. Madaus (1985) said,

Frankly, I am alarmed that policymakers, when they mandate tests for decisions about graduation, promotion, or merit pay increments, are attempting to legislate testing as *the* engine or primary motivating power in the educational process. My concerns are rooted in history, which provides many examples of the results of such a policy: The exam becomes the master and not the servant of the educational process; it invariably leads to cramming; it narrows the curriculum, it concentrates attention on the skills most amenable to testing, and today this means skills amenable to the multiple choice format; it constrains the creativity and spontaneity of teachers and students; and finally, it demeans the professional judgment of teachers. (p. 6)

## The High Costs of Standardized Testing

What can we conclude about the impact of standardized achievement tests on students? First, there is increasing skepticism among older students about the validity of the tests and the use of the results. Second, there is increasing anxiety about social comparisons based on test scores. Third, older students show increasing dissatisfaction with their test preparation, strategies, and feedback. Fourth, older students report less effort and motivation to do their best. Fifth, older students report using more counterproductive strategies that are shortcuts to task completion rather than strategies designed for thoughtfulness and mastery. Sixth, low-achieving students may suffer the most distress and be forced to abandon legitimate efforts to succeed in the high-stakes measures of their academic achievement. Seventh, traditional tests misdirect students' learning toward discrete skills and test-savviness. Finally, standardized tests narrow the classroom curriculum and undercut teachers' judgments.

We interpret these findings in the context of children's developing theories about themselves and education (Paris & Byrnes, 1989). That is, students form concepts about themselves as learners, about the goals of school tasks, about the roles of teachers, and about the value of resources at their disposal as they try to make sense of their own activities in school. Tangible evidence of the degree of success in school is provided in many forms to students from reading groups, tracking, grades, tests, and teachers' comments. There are multiple sources of information to fuel students' perceptions of their own successes and failures in school. We believe that standardized achievement tests provide negative cues for many students because they signal unsuccessful performance compared to other students, their past record of success, or their parents' expectations. Traditional achievement tests can exaggerate differences among students and create winners and losers according to debatable criteria. Thus, the tests subvert students' thinking and learning, overdetermine educational opportunities, and undermine innovative educational reforms.

## THE CHALLENGE OF ASSESSMENT REFORM

If standardized achievement tests so clearly threaten the success of educational reform in America, why are they so difficult to change? Part of the problem is that these tests are imposed by political agencies with different goals than the teachers and parents who want to measure individual student progress and remedy individual needs. Politicians, superintendents, and even real estate agents have substantial interests in collecting simple measures of how well schools are doing their job of educating students. Simply stated, the public (i.e., schoolboards, parents, and politicians) wants quantifiable measures of effectiveness to hold educators *accountable* for students' achievement.

## Blind Faith in Achievement Testing

Although public support for testing is strong today, its popularity has vacillated. In the early 1970s there was public discontent about the potential discriminatory consequences of educational testing so the National Education Association proposed a moratorium on standardized testing. But in 1985, George Madaus, in his presidential address to the National Council of Measurement in Education, noted that "testing is the darling of policymakers across the country" (p. 5). Madaus noted several reasons for the shift in momentum in favor of standardized achievement tests. First, policymakers had increasing needs for objective measures of educational accountability and standardized achievement test scores provided a convenient barometer. Second, the public, had little respect for teachers' judgments and wanted more than their subjective opinions about students' progress. The public also considered test scores to serve as external evaluations of teachers' performance. Third, educational testing in America has become a multi-billion dollar business in the 1990s and is lobbied by those with commercial interests at stake. Greater use of standardized testing is therefore advocated by educational administrators, elected politicians, the general public, and the commercial testing industry, all powerful decision makers in educational policies.

We hope that recent criticisms of standardized testing stimulate a public re-examination of testing practices, but that may be unlikely. The public is unaware of the problems with tests and blithely makes inferences based on the assumptions of the validity of the tests. The irony of this blind faith is that parents and schoolboards want to know that their students are achieving well, but they do not examine or understand assessment practices in their own districts.

Even the recent disclosure that most students in most states score above average on commercial tests has not dissuaded the public cry for accountability (Cannell, 1988). Several studies confirm that virtually all districts in all states score above average on the most frequently used achievement tests. For example, Cannell (1988) conducted a detailed examination in Michigan (as an average representative of other states) and found that more than 90% of the 525 Michigan school districts tested above the national average on standardized tests. The inflated test scores commonly reported to the public have been called the "Lake Wobegone effect" because all the children appear above average. Whether the test scores are fraudulent or simply misleading may not be the most alarming aspect of this report. In our opinion, it is most distressing that parents remain uninformed and unaffected by this revelation. Their trust in standardized achievement tests and statistical comparisons reported in local newspapers, even when they do not understand the tests and results, fuels the public demand for continued testing.

Evans, Barber, Gadsden, Paris, and Park (1989) conducted a survey of more than 100 parents in Michigan about their understanding of the Michigan Educational Assessment Program (MEAP). Parents' knowledge about the test was assessed with questions derived from the MEAP manuals that schools are encouraged to present at parent-teacher sessions. The survey revealed only modest understanding of what the MEAP measures, who takes the test, and how the results are used. Most of the parents did not understand how the test measured children's mastery of basic skills, nor did they understand the scoring report. Most parents mistakenly interpreted the criterion-referenced test scores as normative percentiles. In other words, most parents interpreted a score of 85% as indicating a performance level in the 85th percentile compared to the students' peers. But nearly all students in Michigan pass the test and meet at least 85% of the objectives so a student who passes 85% of the objectives may be among the poorest readers in the state. It is this gross misinterpretation of test scores that perhaps is responsible for the parents' overwhelming support for the MEAP and faith in its ability to measure educational progress.

The problem cannot be solved simply by providing information to parents. Michigan educators devote considerable time and energy to informing the public about the MEAP test but, despite these efforts and the good intentions of teachers and administrators, it is clear that a large proportion of parents in the state do not understand the test scores that are published in their newspapers. Yet these indices are used to allocate funds, reward districts, and certify continued achievement of pupils. We wonder if this trust would be shaken if parents knew about the variability across the state in test preparation and administration or if they knew how to interpret the scores. Michigan parents are not alone in their quandary. It is clear that you can fool most of the public most of the time with standardized test scores. The tragedy is that public willingness to be duped may lead to the failure of many worthwhile educational reforms.

## TAKING CONTROL OF ASSESSMENT IN SCHOOLS

Traditional tests are diametrically opposed to many of the innovations and the new cognitive and motivational agenda in schools. If the tests are used as benchmarks of success for these educational reforms, they are doomed from the start because they are misaligned and misrepresentative of the types of educational changes that are encouraged. It is time for reforms in educational assessment to augment progressive changes in curricula, instruction, technology, and materials.

## Policies Established by Districts

Most school districts feel pressured by politicians and the public to produce summative measures of students' achievement. They need statistical and comparative data that document the progress of students and teachers. How can they combat the deleterious affects of testing and still produce these measures? We offer the following suggestions for policymakers who desire to improve their forms of assessment.

1. The curriculum, instructional practices, and assessment procedures must be aligned and consistent within a district. The educational objectives stated in the curriculum and reflected in the materials must be measured in the assessment instruments. Standardized tests that do not reflect the curriculum objectives and materials used in the schools should not be administered. Districts can devise their own tests or select from a wide range of commercial products. Variability in the teaching, textbooks, curriculum, and assessment procedures will all lead to increased variability in test scores. Thus, it is important to report, for every classroom, how these practices are aligned and assessed.

2. Districts must use multiple measures of student progress. We support the development of portfolio and performance assessments that use students' work samples, projects, self-reports, teacher checklists, and other forms of data as indicators of their learning, thinking, and achievement. Test scores may be included in portfolios but we caution that a standardized test score, even when it is one assessment among many, will often overshadow other measures.

3. Districts should not administer standardized achievement tests to all students. Although districts need to provide benchmarks of accountability, there is no reason that all students should be tested and that test scores should be compared among students, classes, and schools. Districts can randomly sample 20–30% of the students in their districts to report average achievement levels. This practice would save a considerable amount of money spent on test administration and scoring, but more importantly, it would attenuate competition based on test scores. Teachers and principals would not feel threatened by reports of their scores because the scores do not reflect the total performance within a classroom or building. This would reduce the "stakes of the game" and the dubious testing practices that have been elicited by traditional comparisons.

4. Districts should use assessment results to increase the quality of students' thinking and learning. Too often the results of tests are used to make invidious comparisons and conclusions about students, teachers, and school districts. Most of the time, test scores are reported in the newspapers and filed in school records but provide little educational benefit to students, teachers, or parents. Indeed, it is ironic that many test results from spring testing are received by schools in the summer and serve no purpose for students or teachers whatsoever. We believe that if assessment is worth the time and energy invested by teacher and students,

then the results ought to benefit them directly. Results need to be provided in a timely fashion; the data need to be informative not threatening; the scores need to be comprehensible to parents; and the prescriptions for learning need to be evident. If they are not, then the test is worthless for helping students, regardless of the psychometric or political value of the test.

5. Districts should devise "meta-assessment" procedures to evaluate consumer knowledge and satisfaction. Every school district can do a better job of surveying the satisfaction of students, teachers, and parents with current assessment procedures. Most testing personnel in school districts do not assess students' perceptions of the tests, teachers' preparation activities, or parents' understanding about the tests given to their children. We believe that districts can design surveys that can be given randomly to small samples across a district on an annual basis so that better information about academic assessments can be provided to the consumers of test information. Collaboration for reform mirrors an emphasis on collaboration for learning that is the cornerstone of contemporary reform movements. Accountability is a two-way street; school districts must be accountable to students, teachers, and parents to show that assessment practices serve their needs. This also implies that students, teachers, and parents will become involved in the decision making about assessment practices. They need to select and design tests used to measure educational success. They need to understand assessment practices and participate in interpretation of the scores so that each assessment is interpreted according to the developmental history of the individual student.

## Practices Established by Principals and Teachers

Teachers and principals can also take control of assessment at a more local level. It is necessary for assessment practices to be generated "internally" instead of being externally imposed by schoolboards and legislatures. Site-based management and local decision making are current platforms for many other educational reforms, why not assessment? If teachers and principals are to emerge as educational leaders, they must exercise decision making in assessment as well as instruction and curriculum. This responsibility will empower teachers to create better forms of educational assessment. We make the following suggestions for teachers and principals to consider.

1. Create portfolio assessments that reflect the unique talents of your students and your curriculum. Every school building has distinctive strengths and weaknesses. They are not always measured by a uniform test. A portfolio assessment approach can be used to create measures of students and programs that are unique to a school. For example, if health education or bilingualism or cooperation or

minority history or study skills is the focus of instruction during the year, then teachers and principals can design specific assessments of students' learning in each domain. These data may include audiotapes, videotapes, projects, papers, and other evidence of the quality of students' thinking on real tasks that are core features of their daily curriculum (Valencia, 1990).

2. Teachers should measure the growth of cognitive processes in addition to outcomes. We believe that every teacher emphasizes particular thinking skills that may not be measured by a standardized test. Teachers should be allowed to demonstrate their students' learning and the effectiveness of their own instruction by designing assessments of students' abilities to think critically and creatively. These will almost certainly vary across content areas and so teachers of mathematics, science, history, and language arts may all design different measures of thinking and problem solving. The creation of these tests will provide diagnostic information to teachers about the quality of thinking that their students exhibit.

3. Teachers and administrators should create noncognitive measures of achievement. Testing often measures cumulative knowledge and a variety of problem solving skills but there is no reason that the focus must be exclusively cognitive. Teachers should be encouraged to design assessments of social development including cooperation, collaboration, sharing, and the abilities to give and receive help. They should also collect data on students' motivation including their goals, effort, attributions, self-perceptions, and affect. Although students may not all achieve above average scores on a fair norm-referenced test, teachers want to encourage all students to try hard, to increase their self-esteem, and to respect others. If these are valuable educational objectives, they should be measured and the results should be shared with students and parents.

4. Teachers should encourage a developmental model of progress rather than a comparative model of achievement. Many of the negative effects of testing are due to the comparisons that test scores invite among students. Even high-achieving students may feel frustrated and embarrassed because their scores are below other students' scores. American education has unduly emphasized self-worth as a function of competition and comparison at the expense of many students' self-esteem and investment in school (Nicholls, 1989). We suggest that teachers hold regular conferences with students and parents to discuss the various indicators of educational progress and to chart that progress longitudinally. Diagnostic and formative assessments should lead to instructional prescriptions which, in turn, should lead to developmental progress. Successful teachers will improve the learning and motivation of all students but may not alter the relative ranking of students within a class. Comparative measures discount individual progress by focusing on relative ranking instead of individual accomplishments. A developmental model of assessment is more consistent with the developmental models of learning and thinking that teachers seek to establish in school.

## CONCLUSIONS

We think the problems of standardized achievement testing are large and ominous. They threaten to undermine innovative educational reforms, the legitimate efforts of teachers and administrators to improve the quality of schools, and students' motivational orientations to education. Educational assessment must be changed to serve students, teachers, and parents rather than political purposes. The public's mistrust of teachers' professional judgment must be allayed by better assessments. Teachers' frustration and hopelessness in the face of externally imposed high-stakes testing must be abolished. Students developing discontent and disillusionment with educational assessment must be rectified. These serious problems require serious attention—immediately. Piecemeal changes have not worked in the past and cannot keep pace with important educational reforms.

Our final recommendation is perhaps the most radical but potentially the most useful. We believe that districts and states should seize control of educational assessment and declare a moratorium on standardized achievement testing. They should stop all criterion-referenced and norm-referenced testing for a period of 3 years during which time each state and district can reconsider their policies and practices. The savings in money, morale, and instructional time would be enormous and allow greater resources to be devoted to other innovations and reforms. The key, of course, is not to abandon testing altogether but to create new solutions to long-standing problems. Districts cannot retain inadequate assessments just because they are the only data available; this is a propitious time for fresh approaches. In 3 years, local committees should be able to evaluate and establish sensible alternative assessment programs. Even if current assessment practices are changed only a little, the involvement of parents and teachers and the confirmation of the positive aspects of a district's policies are useful outcomes. We urge every parent and every school board to consider a moratorium and to initiate a review of assessment practices in order to enhance the quality of thinking in education for all students.

## REFERENCES

Airasian, P. W. (1988). Measurement driven instruction: A closer look. *Educational Measurement: Issues and Practice, 7,* 6–11.

Benjamin, M., McKeachie, W. J., & Lin, Y-G. (1987). Two types of test anxious students: Support for an information-processing model. *Journal of Educational Psychology, 59,* 128–132.

Cannell, J. J. (1988). Nationally normed elementary achievement testing in America's public schools: How all 50 states are above the national average. *Educational Measurement: Issues and Practice, 7,* 5–15.

Connell, J. P. (1985). A new multidimensional model of children's perception of control. *Child Development, 56,* 1018–1041.

Covington, M. V. (1983). Motivated cognition. In S. Paris, G. Olson, H. Stevenson (Eds.), *Learning and motivation in the classroom* (pp. 139–164). Hillsdale, NJ: Lawrence Erlbaum Associates.

Diener, C. I., & Dweck, C. S. (1978). An analysis of learned helplessness: Continuous changes in performance, strategy, and achievement cognitions following failure. *Journal of Personality and Social Psychology, 36,* 451–462.

Evans, M., Barber, B., Gadsden, V., Paris, S., & Park, S. (1989). *What knowledge do parents have about educational achievement tests?* Paper presented at the Society for Research in Child Development, Kansas City, MO.

Harter, S. (1985). Competence as a dimension of self-evaluation: Toward a comprehensive model of self-worth. In R. L. Leahy (Ed.), *The development of the self.* New York: Academic Press.

Hill, K. T., & Wigfield, A. (1984). Test anxiety: A major educational problem and what can be done about it. *Elementary School Journal, 85,* 105–126.

Karmos, A. H., & Karmos, J. S. (1984). Attitudes toward standardized achievement tests and their relation to achievement test performance. *Measurement and Evaluation in Counseling and Development,* July, 56–66.

Kellaghan, T., Madaus, G. F., & Airasian, P. M. (1982). *The effects of standardized testing.* Boston: Kluwer-Nijhoff Publishing.

Madaus, G. F. (1985). Public policy and the testing profession-You've never had it so good? *Educational Measurement: Issues and Practice, 4,* 5–10.

Madaus, G. F. (1988). The influence of testing on the curriculum. In *Critical issues in curriculum,* in Eighty-seventh Yearbook of the National Society for the Study of Education.

Nicholls, J. G. (1989). *The competitive ethos and democratic education.* Cambridge, MA: Harvard University Press.

Nolen, S. B., Haladyna, T. M., & Haas, N. S. (1990). *A survey of actual and perceived uses, test preparation activities, and effects of standardized achievement tests.* Paper presented at annual meeting of Amer. Ed. Res. Association, Boston.

Palinscar, A. S., & Brown, A. L. (1984). Reciprocal teaching of comprehension-fostering and comprehension-monitoring activities. *Cognition and Instruction, 1,* 117–175.

Paris, S. G., & Byrnes, J. P. (1989). The constructivist approach to self-regulation and learning in the classroom. In B. Zimmerman & D. Schunk (Eds.), *Self-regulated learning and academic achievement: Theory, research, and practice* (pp. 169–200). New York: Springer-Verlag.

Paris, S. G., & Winograd, P. (1990). How metacognition can promote academic learning and instruction. In B. F. Jones & L. Idol (Eds.), *Dimensions of thinking and cognitive instruction* (pp. 15–51). Hillsdale, NJ: Lawrence Erlbaum Associates.

Paris, S. G., Turner, J. C., & Lawton, T. A. (1990). *Students' views of standardized achievement tests.* Paper presented at the American Educational Research Association, Boston, 1990.

Resnick, L. B., & Resnick, D. P. (1990). Tests as standards of achievement in school. In *The uses of standardized tests in American education* (pp. 63–80). Princeton, NJ: Educational Testing Service.

Shepard, L. A. (1989). Why we need better assessments. *Educational Leadership, 46,* 4–9.

Slavin, R. (1980). Cooperative learning. *Review of Educational Research, 50,* 315–342.

Stipek, D., & MacIver, D. (1989). Developmental changes in children's assessment of intellectual competence. *Child Development, 60,* 521–538.

Valencia, S. (1990). A portfolio approach to classroom reading assessment. *Reading Teacher, 43,* 338–340.

Weinstein, R. S. (1983). Student perceptions of schooling. *Elementary School Journal, 83,* 287–312.

Weiner, B. (1986). *An attributional theory of motivation and emotion.* New York: Springer-Verlag.

Wigfield, A., & Eccles, J. S. (1989). Test anxiety in elementary and secondary school students. *Educational Psychologist, 24,* 159–183.

# Introduction to Chapter 12

*Senator William E. Brock, member of President Bush's Advisory Committee on Education, former Secretary of Labor, and author of Workforce 2000.*

It is fun to become the best, and tempting to rest on your laurels for a bit when you do. Well, the United States is still the world's most productive economy, but our new workers are coming out of schools with and education that ranks from 14th to 20th in the world. This is not just for science and mathematics. A new Times Mirror study has found that today's young Americans, aged 18–30, know less and *care* less about news and public affairs than any other generation of Americans in the past 50 years. Unless we change— radically and quickly—there is simply no prospect of our remaining on the top 10 years from now.

We have been resting on our laurels. Real average weekly wages in the United States have fallen by 12% since 1969. We, inadvertently, even unknowingly, are trying to compete in the new global economy on the basis of lower wages, rather than higher skills. This must not continue.

No one has a greater stake in our schools than United States business. No partnerships could be productive, properly structured, for all parties than one encompassing our enterprise system and our education community. Initiating, nurturing, focusing, and sustaining such a new All American Team may prove our most challenging and rewarding task.

# 12 Business Partnerships to Build a Thinking Populist

Jim Duffy
*Former President of Communications Capital Cities/ABC Inc.*

## INTRODUCTION

The year 2000 for decades has symbolized a technologically advanced civilization and served as the time frame for science fiction novels and fantasy movies (e.g., *2001: A Space Odyssey*). Now the dawn of the 21st century is only short years away and the turning of the millennium is no longer a hazy shorthand for a life filled with technowizardry or fodder for psychics. It is a reality fast approaching and we need to understand it. Within this chapter, we will explore statistics and projections. We highlight creative ways business and education partnerships are creating an America not on the decline, but in fact vibrant, technologically supreme—the leader in international trade, science, and culture. We will examine how the 1990s will be a time of difficult adjustments. With early seedings and optimism as indicators, the 21st century may become the first in history when education and the application of knowledge become the fulcrums for all advancements and activities in life.

If you bear with me, I would like to begin by relating a series of present and existing conditions in the relationship between business and education. Although the series may appear to be random, it is not. Positive and negative statistics and forecasts are intertwined, purposefully, so as to demonstrate the way they coexist in our world. As you read, I challenge you to project as to the types of business and educational partnerships that are already formed, based on these conditions in our world.[1]

---

[1]Data reported has been obtained from statistics created by Department of Labor, Department of Education, and Marvin Cetron and Owen Davies, in their book *American Renaissance: Our Life at the Turn of the 21st Century.*

Today and in the 21st century we find that:

1. State and federal governments, at *The Governors' Conference,* decree that by the year 2000, 90% of all students will graduate; all students will start school ready to learn; all adults will be literate; and society in the United States will be conducive to learning and drug-free.

2. About half of all service workers (44% of the labor force by year 2000) will be involved in collecting, analyzing, synthesizing, structuring, storing, or retrieving information as a basis of knowledge.

3. In 1990, one in four of America's 19–23-year-olds is a high school drop-out, and 13% (or approximately 30 million) of the United States workforce is illiterate.

4. By 2000, expert systems will issue reports and recommend actions on data gathered electronically without human intervention.

5. By 2001, artificial intelligence will be in almost universal use among companies and government agencies to help assimilate data and solve problems beyond the computer's range. Artificial Intelligence's uses will include robotics, vision and speech recognition, health and human services, business administration, and airline pilot assistance.

6. By 2001, the quality of products and services will be increasingly emphasized, and time intervals (i.e., time from invention, innovation, imitation) will steadily decrease, making it necessary to market successful products quickly.

7. All the technological knowledge with which we work today will represent only 1% of the knowledge that will be available in 2050.

8. By 2001, new network architecture, operating synergistically with intelligence in terminal systems, will form the foundation on which an infinite variety of telecommunication services will be built.

9. Half-life of engineers knowledge today is 5 years; in 2001 90% of what they know will be on the computer.

10. Presently, 4% of the labor force is in job retraining programs. By 2000, schools will train both children and adults around the clock; the academic day will be lengthened to 7 hours for children, and adults will be working a 32-hour workweek and will be preparing for their next job in the remaining hours.

11. By 2001, businesses will have to provide continuous training to their workers to keep up with the greater demands of their jobs. The investment corporations will make in employee education and retraining, which is now $80 billion a year, will double by 2001.

12. Most new jobs are presently generated by small businesses which cannot afford to pay for workforce training. Presently, one-half of all funding for formal training in the United States comes from 200–300 large companies in business and industry. By 2000, 85% of the labor force will be working for firms employing fewer than 200 people.

13. By the 21st century, unconventional learning techniques, such as sleep learning, mental practice, and computer-supported approaches, will improve learning techniques, increase the amount possible to learn, and reduce the amount of time it takes to learn to one-sixth of the learning time.

14. While in 1985, only 49% of all families were two-income earners, but by 2000, 75% of all families will be two-income earners.

15. The decline in the birthrate means a smaller number of young people entering the job market in 1990–2000. The number of career changes will significantly increase in the twenty-first century, with career changes occurring every 10 years on the average.

16. By 2000, institutions of higher education, businesses, and the military will all vie for youth (ages 16 to 24 years-of-age) as this group shrinks from 30% of the labor force in 1985 to 16% in the year 2000.

17. As shown in Table 12.1, presently the 13 year-olds in the United States rank *last* in mathematical proficiency among all the industrialized nations in the world.

18. By 2000, 39% of the products will be created by multinational corporations. These corporations will value their employees' higher order thinking skills of knowing the consequences, expenses, and likelihood of irreversibility before decisions are made and being able to anticipate problems which could develop.

Because our society in the next century will become even more rapidly changing and unpredictable than in years past, businesses, more than ever before, need

TABLE 12.1
Average Mathematical Proficiency Data of 13-Year-Old Citizens in the Industrialized Nations of the World

| Nation | Level |
| --- | --- |
| Korea | 567.8 |
| Quebec (French) | 543.0 |
| British Colombia | 539.8 |
| Quebec (English) | 535.8 |
| New Brunswick (English) | 529.0 |
| Ontario (English) | 516.1 |
| New Brunswick (French) | 514.2 |
| Spain | 511.7 |
| United Kingdom | 509.9 |
| Ireland | 504.9 |
| Ontario (French) | 481.5 |
| United States | 473.9 |

Data are from A World of Differences. An International Assessment of Mathematics and Science (Washington Educational Testing Service. January, 1989. The level represents an indexed scale of proficiency in performing mathematical computations.

their workforce to have more generalized thinking strength; strength that will not become obsolete as new specialties and technologies develop. Furthermore, because our world is becoming so intricately related, we can no longer deny any person or country, viewed as less advantaged, to go without instructional practices that strengthen thinking.

In essence, the 21st century will usher in a new era in educational philosophies and perspectives, in my opinion. Prior to the informational age in which we now live, the philosophy of education, from a business perspective, was "you teach students all they need to know basically; We'll apprentice them and teach them all they need to know to earn money in a specific way." With the advent of our high technology, information generating society, the philosophy of education has shifted to "Schools teach the basics; human resource development offices will continuously update all workforce members about changes in business." By the 21st century, I project that a new philosophy will begin to emerge. That philosophy will be that schools will become the lifelong stations for learning, with businesses giving schools new needs to meet, while schools function to create new ideas and technologies to advance business.

## BUSINESS PARTNERSHIPS

Leaving the above statistics in place, let's analyze the ways that present business and educational institutions are working together. Presently, there are four types of partnerships being built.

*Create New Ways for Schools to Impact the Thinking in American Business Before Students Leave School.* In a few cities, students, teachers, and business leaders are working together to complete projects. These teams are most easily characterized as "reverse apprenticeships" because they do not follow traditional mentorship formats. As we are all aware, in the 1800s schools taught community mores, religious doctrine, reading, writing, and arithmetic. Students were then dismissed and groomed through apprenticeships, in which they were shown how to think through modeling by productive tradesmen. In the early 1900s these systems began to falter as child labor laws prohibited apprenticeships before adolescence and those that endured became increasingly technological, centering more upon the correct use of tools rather than the correct use of the mind.

Today, through reverse apprenticeships, students could take the most advanced thinking methods to businesses; and in a wide variety of ways businesses bring problems to students, asking students to help solve them. In addition, through these reverse apprenticeships, communities receive a double benefit. Many community and business problems are solved, and students who participate in these solutions not only enhance and improve their community but also will more likely preserve it in the future. We can begin to develop more of the following reverse apprenticeships in our schools.

• Businesses network with schools through technological connections. Such connections allow students to develop a sense of the value and cost of information and enable industries to interact with the newest strategies of advanced thinking. One such connection is being established between a university, the supercollider project in Texas, and high school students. Through computer connections, students apply thinking methods that they learn in school to the new data created at the supercollider site. As new information is instantly transmitted, scientists, teachers, and students can work together to advance thinking skills, expand the data's application possibilities, design new ways of thinking about the information, and build innovative ways of disseminating new findings to other schools. Mr. Primus Moatry, Project Director of Corporate/Community Schools of America is doing a lot of work in this area.

• In South Dakota, through a course for high school freshmen and sophomores entitled "Research and Development," students are involved in completing research for business/civic leaders. In one such project, juniors and seniors contacted every member of the community in a house-to-house survey which resulted in increased community involvement in problems as well as heightened community spirit.

• Students are "hired" by businesses to train personnel in such thinking strategies as using a "line list" to connect prior knowledge to present problems translating by relating to the opposite of a point of view, and inducing limited coverage. Students study both sides of an issue before they enter the work force fulltime. Doing so enhances the likelihood that they will use broader perspectives when making decisions on-the-job, an important ability when company biases and employee loyalty are likely to impact a decision. For other examples, you may wish to contact Starla Jewell Kelly, Executive Director of National Community Education Association.

• Many media companies are contracting with high school journalism classes to find subjects for news coverage. Such reverse apprenticeships have culminated with students writing a newspaper column or producing a weekly half-hour television/radio broadcast to describe different problem solving and thinking processes that they have learned.

*Simultaneously Train Teachers, Students, and Community Leaders to use Similar Thinking Strategies.*   These training sessions occur in three basic ways. First, human resource training directors from businesses are being invited to school district inserviced training sessions where new thinking development approaches are introduced. Following the training, partnerships are built between the school and community to network resources and implement these newly acquired thinking strategies cooperatively.

A second method is illustrated in the work being done by the Center For Creative Leadership of the University of North Carolina. In this method, the community identifies a major problem and a consultant leads students, educators, and community members to think about the problem in new ways with all people in the community contribute resources to solve it. This past summer, this approach was utilized in a rural town in Minnesota to attract new residents. By the end of summer, a new company had relocated, and students were volunteering to construct new housing units.

A third method is to train business leaders, teachers, preservice teachers and students to use the same methods of thinking. Such work is being done by Laurence Martell at the Center for the Study of Learning and Retention, where the Integrative Learning Model is being taught to employees at Kodak Mutual of New York, Guggenheim Elementary School, Bell Atlantic Corporation, Shell Petroleum, and other schools and institutions (Martell, 1989). In addition to the growth in students' thinking ability, joint training programs enable businesses to hire new employees that are experienced in the thinking processes they use.

*Businesses Assist in Preparing Students to Think Before Graduation by Creating Educational Divisions Within Their Companies.* For example, in addition to grants given to individual schools, IBM created the Educational Systems Division. In 1985, the IBM Educational Systems Division began hosting "think tanks" with the purpose of aiding the education system to make significant innovative change. In this way, inventive thinking can advance American citizenry so that future investments for retraining are significantly reduced for all American businesses. One innovation to evolve from these meetings is the creation of information management systems that link classrooms, principals, superintendents, and state departments of education and labor in order to coordinate testing, grading, diagnostics, and a variety of literacy, mathematics, science, and special creative thinking developmental programs for all ages of our population.

*Partnerships that Serve the Pivotal Role of Approaching and Solving the Complex and Disturbing Social Problems of our Country, Especially Those Related to Education.* Having worked in media for all of my life, I feel very strongly about the partnering and pivotal role that media can play in approaching the complex and disturbing social problems of our country. Media is now highlighting the need for national service organizations to take initiatives in every community to aid thinking development for children and adults.

In conjunction, there is a rising acceptance of the value of mentoring, tutoring, of giving, and of working together. People from business, education, and community agencies are working together, overriding outdated and counterproductive turf issues. Media performs, and must play, a *vital* role in building more of these partnerships. Newspapers and magazines, with depth and detail, are providing the localism and continuity to educational innovations, among which success stories of people inventing and using creative thinking are growing exceedingly popular and important.

# A CASE STUDY

Broadcasting is also a powerful messenger to every community in the world. Furthermore, it is one of the few links to many of our youth who have become disconnected from families, schools, and society. With this link as a partner and facilitator in thinking development, broadcasting can unify and call to action many who can correct the crippling problems that affect our youth, workforce and the quality of all our lives, now and in the future.

For example, one of my major responsibilities is to serve as the National Spokesperson for *Project Literacy U.S.—Plus* for Capital Cities/ABC, along with PBS, our affiliated stations, radio networks, National Public Radio, and 150 business and educational associations, have made maximum use of one of the most powerful facets of the broadcast industry to respond to the illiteracy crisis in America. That is, the coordination of both the national and local communication dimensions of the system over an extended period of time.

Broadcasting has always been at its best in responding to crisis; be it in major news coverage or the telling of historic events. We are entering a new era of need in our country, one that demands the participation and prominence by all of us, and particularly by broadcasters, as never before. America is approaching a human resource crisis that threatens our economy, our communities, and our quality of life. Unless all sectors of our society work together to better all people's problem solving skills, as a nation we will be ill-prepared to face the twenty-first century.

Throughout our experience with *Project Literacy U.S.—PLUS,* we have seen this partnering system work, dramatically and emphatically. With continued visibility in our programming, working with PLUS task forces across the country, we have seen the problem of illiteracy come from ground zero—America's tragic hidden problem—to a place on the national agenda. We have witnessed hundreds of thousands of Americans breaking through the cycle of frustration and shame by coming forward to learn to read and write. Most important of all, by working together, we have helped to remove a humiliating stigma and made it possible for people to improve their lives. And yet we have only just begun.

We are now expanding our arena to include "Youth in Crisis" and "Workplace Literacy" where we will begin to teach basic literacy and thinking skills to youth and adults.

Certainly, PLUS does not stand alone as the only broadcasting partnership with business and education. There are many others which deal effectively with issues related to quality thinking development. The National Alliance of Business, for example, in cooperation with the National Association of Broadcasters, has a very successful campaign called "Work Works" with rock musicians carrying the message to at-risk youth about the importance of job skills and working; to date over 27,000 young people have signed up for training programs. The Partnership for a Drug-Free America campaign is another illustration, and there are many highly successful local broadcasting campaigns. We *must* do more, and the time for action is *now*.

## MOVING AHEAD WITH RESOLUTION

In closing, I would like to suggest how we can move ahead into the 21st century with resolution that we will leave our great country stronger than when we came and richer and more promising for those yet to come.

First, businesses must help to develop emerging initiatives which will not merely reform but rather *restructure* the nation's educational system in bold new ways. Ways that will be the testing ground for newest types of thinking development.

Second, businesses must work with education to minimize the dropout rate. There are two major things to consider about the present drop out rate in our country. First, we tell our youth that education is one of the most important things in their lives. However, at the same time, we say: You have to be 18 before you are wise enough to vote, to make the complicated decisions concerning selection of people to represent you. You must be 18 to risk losing your life in war. You must be (in most states) 21 before you can make the difficult decision to use alcohol. Yet, in most states, we say that you only need to be 16 before you can make the *tiny* decision that will impact the rest of your life—whether or not to stay in school.

The reasons students drop out of school goes beyond legality. The process of learning and thinking is clearly not connecting for them. Students do not "drop out of school," they drop out of teachers' classrooms. We must assist individual educators to address that issue. Studies show that one of the prevailing reasons students drop out of school is that they feel no one cares. By permitting them to drop out proves to them that this belief is true.

Third, educators, community agencies, and businesses must work together to identify the really deep-seated problems in education today. Each must seek the others assistance for solutions. In the past, media, for example, was the only contact to share successes. The community, through the media, has the capacity to provide recognition, understanding, and support to the problems of thinking development in our country. We should work to bring media leaders, in every community, in at the beginning stage of planning for educational initiatives for all ages of the community. As a true partner, these leaders will not only report and serve as public relation experts, but they can assist to see that the kinds of coverage the innovation receives are those that will be most beneficial and successful.

Last, business partnerships can play a major role in providing many tools to expand thinking. For example, most institutions in America have not yet embraced technology. In this age of technology, how many teachers have computers to assist in grading, and in doing evaluations, reports, or course preparation? How many use VCR's or videodisc's or telecommunication as tie-ins to major and historic television events to get the excitement of the visual to the brain. If education was allowed access to only the technology we now have, the productivity and development of thinking of our youth would explode immediately.

As John Pepper, the President of Proctor and Gamble says, "We're in a war, but it's a winnable war. It's winnable because of the innate talents and capabilities of our youth. If we set the right example, if we provide discipline and support, if we challenge them, our young people from even the most impoverished backgrounds can compete with anyone in the world" (Pepper, 1990).

It is important to me that I close with an important change I see emerging in America. In my travels around the country, talking to teachers, business people, government leaders, and just plain folks, a picture is starting to come together. America will be a better, more vibrant, fresher community of people in the 21st century, and this community of people will have the whole processes of learning, and thinking, right in the center of it.

## REFERENCES

Martell, L. (1989). *Executive summary: Integrative learning*. Syracuse, NY: Center for the Study of Learning and Retention.

Pepper, J. (1990). *Keynote Address to the Business Roundtable*, April, New York City.

# Introduction to
# Chapter 13

*Dee Dickinson, President/Founder,*
*New Horizons for Learning*

Two of the most important characteristics of our time are the growing diversity of our population and the escalation of change and new information. Collaboration among the diverse individuals in every setting has now become essential. Integration of new and old ideas in rapidly changing contexts also has become essential. Every social institution is dealing with these challenges, and must find ways to survive and thrive in these rapidly changing times—most especially educational systems that have the critical responsibility of preparing students for a new kind of world. How can schools alone do what is being expected and needed for all their students? Education must surely now become a collaborative effort.

The subsequent chapter by Larry Decker describes the importance of learning centers which: accommodate a growing diversity of students, are responsive to the characteristics and needs of their community, and draw upon the unique strengths of their staff.

There are increasing numbers of such centers throughout the United States today. For example, in Poland, Ohio, a 103-year-old elementary school building that was about to be closed was turned into a Continuing Education Center, which now offers lifelong learning opportunities for all ages from preschool to senior citizens. It is operated by the public schools but open to the community nearly around the clock.

An extension of the community learning center concept is found in the Fidalgo Elementary School in Anacortes, a small town on the Northern coast of Washington state. Fidalgo has a sister school in Japan, with an exchange program for the teachers and students. The children at Fidalgo are all learning to speak Japanese, and since many members of the community have fishing-trade relationships with Japan, they are also studying Japanese at the school along with the students. This community learning center offers a latch-key program before and after school, adult education classes, and collaborates with businesses, the local community college, and Western Washington University—where the teachers are earning credit leading to a Master's Degree for all the new skills they are learning. The students are thriving and achieving at high levels!

The following chapter presents clearly the need for such learning centers, the educational philosophy upon which they are built, and the characteristics of these exciting, intergenerational places for learning which are now at the heart of many communities.

# 13 Thinking and Acting from a Broad Perspective: Community Education

Larry E. Decker
*University of Virginia*

In the context of the wide diversity in factors influencing learning, many of today's educational reports and reform initiatives are so narrowly focused that they seem to be a result of "tunnel vision." Across all types of educational institutions, one seldom finds the generalist who advocates the integration of diverse areas of specialization in order to enhance learning. Even the new National Education Goals, which the Governors and the President are using to set the stage for thinking and allocating resources in the 21st century, are narrowly focused in some areas.

This narrowness of perspective is the result of two primary causes. The first is the increased emphasis being placed on discrete bodies of knowledge, commonly referred to as "disciplines" or "areas of specialization," and the tendency of individuals to promote and protect their particular interests or turf. For example, one of the new National Education Goals (1990) sets forth mathematics and science as our top academic priorities. (Science and Mathematics—By the year 2000, U.S. students will be first in the world in science and mathematics achievement).

This appraisal is not meant to say that the disciplines of mathematics and science are not important in building a knowledge base for the economic and educational development of advanced societies. Rather, it is meant to point out that the selection of goals is a matter of perspective. For example, the goals of "Readiness for School" (By the year 2000, all children in America will start school ready to learn.) and "Adult Literacy and Lifelong Learning" (By the year 2000, every adult American will be literate and will possess the knowledge and skills necessary to compete in a global economy and exercise the rights and responsibilities of citizenship.) engender a much broader viewpoint in thinking

257

about how we develop learning opportunities and allocate resources for all age groups than the "Science and Mathematics" goal.

A second cause of narrowness of perspective is similar to the first. In thinking about education, we tend to single out a particular age group, e.g., early childhood, elementary, middle, high school, or adult populations. We have promoted learning as a series of steps, not as a continuum, and have grouped students primarily by age and sometimes by academic ability, which is assessed by performance on a standardized test. This tendency to stratify particular age groups and assess performance at predetermined levels is also present in the National Education Goals of "High School Completion" (By the year 2000, the high school graduation rate will increase to at least 90%.) and "Student Achievement and Citizenship" (By the year 2000, American students will leave grades 4, 8, and 12 having demonstrated competency in challenging subject matter including English, mathematics, science, history, and geography. . . .)

Steve Parson (1990) succinctly sums up our test-oriented society in his observation that:

> Learning to learn is not often high on the list of priorities in our schools. The focus is on certain quantities of subject matter that must be consumed by the learners, especially those subject areas that will later appear in national examinations that are used to measure the quality of the schools.

The purpose of this chapter is to describe how community schools can become the nucleus from which all citizens expand their thinking to enhance the quality of their lives.

## THINKING DEVELOPMENT FROM A BROAD PERSPECTIVE

For a number of years, Harold Hodgkinson, a leading demographic researcher, has been encouraging educational leaders and policy makers to think more broadly. In *All One System* (Hodgkinson, 1985), he asserts that:

> Almost everyone who works in education perceives it as a set of discrete institutions working in isolation from each other. These institutions restrict the age range of their students: nursery schools, day-care centers, kindergartens, elementary schools, junior high schools, senior high schools, two-year colleges, four-year undergraduate colleges, universities with graduate programs, and post graduate institutions. People working in each of the above institutions have virtually no connection with all the others and little awareness òf educational activity provided by the total. Because of this, the school is defined as the unit, not THE PEOPLE WHO MOVE THROUGH IT. (p. 1)

In his most recent publication, *The Same Client,* Hodgkinson (1989) continues his argument, urging educators to integrate the demographic profiles for education, health care, transportation, housing, and corrections and appeals for students at all levels. He asks educators:

> . . . to begin to become familiar with other service providers at their level, as *they are serving the same children and families as clients.* It is painfully clear that a hungry, sick or homeless child is by definition a poor learner, yet schools usually have no linkage to health or housing organizations outside those run by the schools themselves. There are . . . interlocking effects of deprivation. (p. 1)

The Committee for Economic Development in its report *Children in Need* (1987) also calls for thinking broadly from an economic perspective and urges business leaders, educators, and policy makers to "invest in the future" and to:

> . . . look beyond the traditional classroom boundaries and provide early and sustained intervention in the lives of [educationally disadvantaged] children . . . [and develop] new partnerships among families, schools, businesses, and community organizations that can bolster the health, education, and well-being of the whole child, beginning with the formative years. (p. ix)

As the 1989 Metropolitan Life Survey of the American Teacher (*The American Teacher Survey, 1989*) demonstrates, teachers acknowledge a relationship between the conditions in students' communities and the problems that students currently face. A majority of the teachers surveyed believed that schools should be an access and referral point for social services. Furthermore, 84% of the teachers felt that providing "integrated, collaborative health, education and social services in school will be the key to helping" at-risk students. Almost all teachers (90%) agreed that "schools should mobilize these resources so that they can refer their students to them, but [schools] should not be expected to provide for all social/human needs."

Lauro Cavazos, former Secretary of Education, in an *USA Today* article (September 7, 1990), underscores the importance of parental involvement in the learning process. He stresses that parents hold the key to learning, pointing out that "studies have shown that the best single predictor of academic achievement is the level of parental involvement in a child's education."

## RESTRUCTURING EDUCATION

Pluralism and the rapid change of the global society have created numerous new thinking and learning needs or concerns. These concerns and the educational reform rhetoric have focused on a broad range of topics, ranging from what has been to what could be or should be the ways in which public education serves our democratic society. Most studies have recommended higher academic standards, stricter discipline, an emphasis on basics in school curricula, and incentives to improve teaching. However, many studies are silent about the development of values which might enhance social equality and foster healthy, productive citizens willing and able to participate in the civic affairs of their communities and their nation in thought-filled ways. Although the last part of the National Education Goal on "Student Achievement and Citizenship" (By the year 2000, . . . every school in America will ensure that all students learn to use their minds well, so they may be prepared for responsible citizenship, further learning, and productive employment in our modern society.) briefly discusses this point, the proposed interagency efforts and administration activities, programs, and initiatives which support this National Education Goal focus primarily on such achievement on students aged 5–18 and not on citizens outside that age range.

It is the "how to" restructure that seems to be the barrier. For the most part, the reports and publications contain generalities and lack specific suggestions for a restructuring process. For example, in the publication on the National Education Goals (July 29, 1990), President Bush's letter to the Governors states:

> . . . achieving the national education goals will require fundamental changes in the way we educate our citizens, in our attitudes toward teaching and learning, and in our very culture. . . . [but] our restructured education system must reflect the values and traditions which have served American well for over two centuries. Education in America will always be about opening doors of opportunity for the individual.

The question of how to change still remains to be answered. In formulating the plans for learning and education today as well as in the 21st century, Larry Lezotte, in a presentation at the 1990 American Association of School Administrators Convention, seems to sum up the challenge accurately when he asked, "How do we find a way to perfect the human democratic democracy?"

## CHANGE: THE BLENDING OF COMMON SENSE AND DEMOCRATIC VALUES

One of the foremost futurists, Herman Kahn (Kahn & Wiener, 1967), provides a useful perspective for looking to the future. He believes that the future will look very much like today and that the more individuals know about the world today, the better they will be prepared for the future. Thus, in order to prepare for the future, educators must take into consideration a broader role for a comprehensive educational system serving the same clients. (*The Year 2000,* 1967)

In the past, people have looked to education to solve the problems of society. Education has been expected to form character, develop good citizens, keep family mores strong, advocate high morals, cure social vice and disease, and prepare individuals for the world of work. However, as many Americans have become dissatisfied with political and social institutions in general, they also have lost their faith in education. Unlike the early part of this century, many people now perceive school systems and schools as remote, bureaucratic institutions unresponsive to society's changing needs.

If education is to reclaim its prominent place in America, a new direction must be found that revitalizes and expands learning opportunities. However, designing a curriculum that resolves the educational and social issues is complicated by the limitation we face, both in terms of local resources and the number of qualified personnel. In addition, effective responses require cooperation among the schools themselves and between the schools and the communities they serve. A logical solution which incorporates our democratic values is the creation of a learning community where home, school, and community work together to expand learning opportunities and address the issues confronting education and a thinking society (Decker & Decker, 1987).

Although Americans have traditionally placed a high value on education, the concept of a total learning environment has not been widely promoted to the general public. Yet a "learning society," as Gross describes in Chapter 7, is one of the most long-standing ideas in education. Our Founding Fathers articulated it in the 1787 Northwest Ordinance and many state constitutions incorporated the intent of this early statute, declaring that not only "schools" but the "means of education shall forever be encouraged." In *A Nation at Risk,* the National Commission on Excellence in Education (1983) also proposed the creation of a learning community as the direction for educational reform. It asserted that reforming our educational institutions could be achieved without compromising our tradition commitment to the equitable treatment of diverse school populations, recommending that:

> . . . education reform should focus on the goal of creating a Learning Society. At the heart of such a society is the commitment to a set of values and to a system of education that affords all members the opportunity to stretch their minds to full capacity, from early childhood through adulthood, learning more as the world changes.

As Calfee noted in Chapter 9, in 1899 John Dewey's *School and Society* became the first book to stress that in addition to educating the child, schools have a social responsibility. Dewey promoted the idea that each school should be an embryo of community life in which education was perceived as:

• A continuous, lifelong process.

- Largely social in nature in that the individual interacts with the environment of the community.
- Broader than schooling, encompassing both the formal and informal aspects of experience.

Dewey believed that the democratic process should be integral to the educational process, that members should participate in decisions which affect their lives. In his view of education, professional educators have the responsibility to help individuals plan for themselves as much as possible, choosing from all the diverse learning environments of the community. Fulfilling this responsibility necessitates a coordinating function for the professional in which the educator works in a community towards the goal of improving the community itself, as well as improving the quality of the individual's educative experience within that community.

Although proposed almost 100 years ago, this perception of education is very much in evidence today. In John Goodlad's view, "education is part of the fabric, interweaving with politics, religion, economics and family life. Education is no more confined exclusively to schools than is religion confined to churches, mosques, synagogues . . ." (*A Place Called School,* 1984, p. 349).

Mario Fantini suggests that the challenge to public education is to break down the boundaries of the schoolhouse and move out into the larger community for educational services ("Changing Concepts of Education," 1983). Harry Silberman agrees, adding that:

> The separation of youth from adults is a product of the decline of the family and the separation of school and work. It is becoming increasingly apparent that the educational development of youth cannot succeed solely through the efforts of the schools. Learning must be enhanced through exposure of young people to a variety of opportunities to test themselves in the community and the workplace alongside supportive adults (*Education and Work,* 1982).

## COMMUNITY EDUCATION—A RESTRUCTURING PROCESS

The restructuring of schools and education is underway in many communities. Community education is one restructuring process that is being used. Community education is not new, but it is a process that increasingly is being implemented. The publication, *Community Education Across America* (Decker & Romney, 1990), contains state-by-state descriptions of the status of community education and of exemplary projects underway in local communities which address a variety of community needs and problems. This national research report documents the fact that implementation of the community education process has resulted in increased academic achievement, improved school climate, and more effective communities.

In the foreword to *Community Education: Building Learning Communities* (1990), David Mathews, President of the Charles F. Kettering Foundation, enumerates the factors that appear to make some communities more effective in solving their problems than others. Effective communities are different in at least 5 ways. An effective community:

1. Is a community that educates itself as a *whole,* in all of its subdivision and groups, about the *whole* of its interests.

2. Seems to have a different kind of public information available—it has more than just facts; it knows what the facts mean in the lives of the diverse people who make up the community and assists people to think and use those facts effectively.

3. Talks through issues to generate shared knowledge.

4. Appears to have a different way of understanding opinions and knows the difference between mass opinion and "public judgments."

5. Seems to be different in the way it thinks about public leadership and makes a distinction between government officials and public leaders.

Community education stresses broad-based community involvement in meeting community needs using community resources. The focus on involvement is based on a well-known trait of human nature—people usually develop commitment to causes, organizations, and activities for which they have had some responsibility.

The community education process has 4 major components:

1. Provision of diverse educational services to met the varied learning needs of community residents of all ages;

2. Development of interagency cooperation and public–private partnerships to reduce duplication of efforts and improve overall effectiveness of the delivery of human services;

3. Encouragement of community improvement efforts that make the community more attractive to both current and prospective residents and businesses; and

4. Involvement of citizens in community problem solving and decision making.

Communities using the community education process exhibit the following characteristics (Decker and Associates, 1990):

- Someone has an official leadership role in coordinating the various community and school efforts.

- Volunteers help deliver community services.
- Businesses work in partnership with schools to improve student learning as well as to expand economic development in ways described by Duffy in Chapter 12.
- Agencies and institutions cooperate to deliver improved services to the total community.
- Public school facilities are used by community members of all ages.
- Parents are involved in their children's learning and in school governance.
- Community resources, material and human, are used to enhance and enrich the schools' curriculum.
- Educational alternatives are available for students with special problems and special talents.
- Lifelong learning opportunities are available for learners of all ages, backgrounds, and needs.
- Large numbers of citizens are participating actively to help solve community problems.

## THE COMMUNITY SCHOOL

In the community education model, the school functions as a support center for the network of agencies and institutions committed to meeting community needs and expanding learning opportunities for all members of the community (see Fig. 13.1).

Using schools as community centers is a cost-effective, practical way to use one of a community's largest investments: its school buildings. Use of school facilities is desirable for many reasons;

- School buildings are located in most neighborhoods and are easy to reach.
- Schools are owned by the public and represent a large public investment.
- Schools have good facilities, resources, and professional staff.
- Traditional school hours leave plenty of time to schedule other uses.
- Schools are often a second home to children.
- Schools are focal points for many families, building group process skills and inspiring confidence and loyalty.

Parson (1990) contrasts the community school model to the traditional one, pointing out that:

Our system of schooling today resembles an industrial model of the early 1900s. The assembly line approach tends to consider the learners as raw material to be

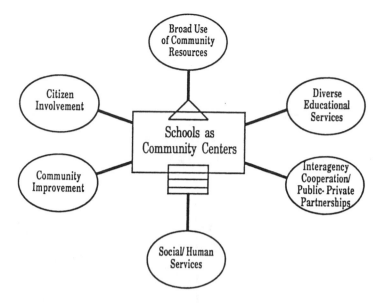

FIG. 13.1.   Components of the community school. Source: *Commu-nity Education: Building Learning Communities.*

transformed into a finished product (educated adults) by passing them through the 'factory' (the school). The factory is designed to provide the same basic program to all students, regardless of their needs, learning styles and abilities, using only the resources contained within the factory.

A community school reflects the fact that people's learning needs are both full-time and lifelong. In contrast to the traditional school, a community school serves all ages and functions 12 to 18 hours a day, 7 days a week, 12 months a year.

When a community education program is established, a community can tailor its component parts to local needs and local resources (see Fig. 13.2). Some of the most common components of community education programs are:

- Remedial and enrichment activities for children outside of school hours.
- Noncredit general interest and cultural enrichment classes and activities for adults.
- Recreation, craft, and sports activities for adults and children.
- Preschool and after-school child care programs.
- Career and technical education in partnership with employers in the community.
- Programs for senior citizens and other special populations.
- Intergenerational programs.
- Community service and volunteer programs for young people and adults.

# Community Education Is
# People Helping People

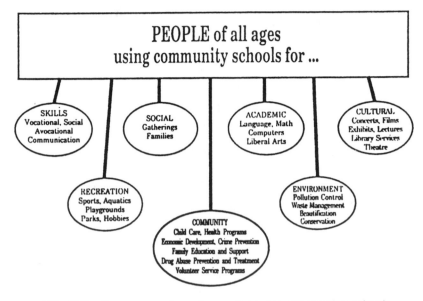

FIG. 13.2. Program and service options for community schools.
Source: *Community Education: Building Learning Communities.*

- Family support and education programs.
- Literacy programs.
- Adult education and vocational classes.
- Programs that address family and other interpersonal relationships.
- Health and human services programs.
- Community newsletters and other forms of communication.
- Programs that address specific community problems.

## THE CHALLENGE OF IMPLEMENTING THE
## COMMUNITY EDUCATION PROCESS

Implementing a broad-base community education program does not happen without planning nor does it happen overnight. It takes both leadership and a shift in thinking from the traditional to a broader perspective.

In terms of leadership, it requires an individual or group, who recognizes the opportunity to improve the community and is able to act as a catalyst in bringing together community agencies, organizations, businesses, and residents to talk about community problems and devise plans for solutions. The leadership must also find a way to overcome what has been characterized as the "terrible t's"—tradition, turf, and trust-level—which can negate community involvement initiatives.

The complexity of our ethnic, environmental, and educational experiences affect both our perceptions and attitudes. Although many people agree it is time to stop prescribing simple, one-strategy solutions which create adversarial relationships and instead to shift the emphasis from individual "do-it-alone" action, it is difficult to get them to agree on a course of action.

Traditionally, educational administrators and teachers have had little or no training in how to involve parents and community citizens in students' learning experiences. Neither are they trained in the use of community resources to enrich curriculum or experienced in community outreach efforts.

Many policy makers and officials are reluctant to share power or delegate responsibility in certain areas, often fearing that they may be perceived as weak leaders. Rather than perceiving the benefits of teamwork and community input and advice, they think that a loss of control will accompany shared decision making.

Administrators and officials also realize that to invite broad-based community participation in planning and decision making is likely to increase conflict initially until differing perspectives are understood and trust levels increase. They also know that encouraging collaborative use of community resources and coordination of service delivery is likely to raise expectations for the level of services provided.

If community education is to be successfully implemented, schools must have the autonomy and flexibility to respond to the diverse learning needs across the age spectrum of their particular community. The dependence of the school on its community in the teaching/learning process must be recognized. Efforts must be made to strengthen home-school-community linkages. Some power must be shifted from the central office to local schools. Teachers and community members must be involved in decisions and activities designed to improve the instruction for learners of all ages.

Finally, community education must be viewed as a process, not as a program. All four of its major components must continue to change as community conditions change. Over time, learning and human service needs change; cooperative ventures and partnership activities need to be modified or refocused; community improvement efforts need to be redirected; and new participatory problem-solving efforts must be initiated.

For long-term effectiveness, community thinking and action must continue to use a broad perspective with the goal of nurturing human growth in a learning community. Community education efforts must:

1. Analyze community needs accurately and synthesize the use of community resources in addressing them.

2. Secure and retain consensus in community decision-making and problem-solving initiatives;

3. Achieve and maintain effective two-way communication with all segments of the community; and

4. Emphasize the process, not the program, and encourage community understanding of the exercise of power as it relates to problem solving.

## REFERENCES

*American Teacher Survey.* (1989). New York: Metropolitan Life Insurance Company.

Cavazos, L. (1990). Parents hold the key to learning. In *USA Today*, September 7, 11a.

Decker, L., & Associates. (1990). *Community education: Building learning communities*, Alexandria, VA: National Community Education Association.

Decker, L., & Decker, V. (1987). Community education: Common sense and democratic values. In *National Civic Review*, 76(3), 208–16.

Decker, L., & Romney, V. (1990). *Community education across America*. Charlottesville: University of Virginia.

Fantini, M. (1989). Changing concepts of education: From school system to educational system. In D. Hager-Schoeny & L. Decker (Eds.), *Community, educational, and social impact perspectives* (pp. 25–46). Lanham, MD: University Press of America, Inc.

Goodlad, J. (1984). *A place called school: Prospects for the future*. New York: McGraw-Hill.

Hodgkinson, H. (1985). *All one system: Demographics of education—kindergarten through graduate school*. Washington, DC: Institute for Educational Leadership.

Hodgkinson, H. (1989). *The same client: The demographics of education and service delivery systems*. Washington, DC: Institute for Educational Leadership.

Kahn, H., & Wiener, A. (1967). *The year 2000: A framework for speculation on the next thirty-three years*. New York: Macmillan.

Lezotte, L. (1990). Presentation in "Leadership for the year 2010: A panel of experts." *American Association of School Administrators Video Cassette*. Arlington, VA: American Association of School Administrators.

Mathews, D. (1990). Effective communities are different. In L. Decker & Associates (Eds.), *Community education: Building learning communities* (pp. i–ii). Alexandria, VA: National Community Education Association.

*A Nation at Risk.* (1983). Washington, DC: National Commission on Excellence in Education.

*National Education Goals: A Report to the Nation's Governors.* (1990, July 29). Washington, DC: The White House.

Parson, S. (1990). Lifelong learning and the community school. In C. Poster & A. Kruger (Eds.), *Community education in the western world* (pp. 29–38). New York: Routledge, Chapman, and Hall.

Research and Policy Committee. (1987). *Children in need: Investment strategies for the educational disadvantaged*. Washington, DC: Committee for Economic Development.

Silberman, H. (Ed.). (1982). *Education and work: Eighty-first yearbook of the National Society for the Study of Education, Part II*. Chicago, IL: University of Chicago Press.

# Introduction to
# Chapter 14

*Wade F. Horn, Ph.D. Commissioner,*
*Administration for Children, Youth, and*
*Families Department of Health and Human*
*Services Washington, D.C.*

When President George Bush convened the nation's governors in Charlottesville, Virginia, for the first-ever "Education Summit," the need to ensure that all children enter
school "healthy and ready to learn" was embodied in the
first of a series of national education goals. Fortunately,
most children do enter school healthy and ready to learn due
to the support and nurturance of well-functioning families.
However, there are some children who, through poverty,
neglect, or abuse, are in need of preschool intervention
programs to ensure that they are not at a disadvantage relative to their peers when they enter the primary grades.

One program that has successfully intervened with disadvantaged children is Head Start. President Bush has demonstrated his commitment to this program during his first two
years in office by requesting the two largest single-year
budgetary increases in the history of the Head Start program. The nation's governors are also making good on their
commitment to compensatory preschool programs as evidenced by the fact that 34 states currently provide funding
for a preschool initiative, including twelve states which
make available funds directly to the Head Start program.
The challenge facing us now is to discover ways to coordinate Head Start with state-funded compensatory preschool
programs so that every disadvantaged child can be afforded
the opportunity to enroll in Head Start or a Head Start-like
program so that all our nation's children can enter school
healthy and ready to learn.

One way that children in poverty can be disadvantaged
relative to their more affluent peers is through less exposure
to computer technology. To be sure, even children in pover-

ty are exposed to a great many devices which contain microcomputer technology, such as computerized cash registers. But compared to their more affluent peers, they are certainly less likely to have early computer exposure in the home. Consequently, children in poverty are at a disadvantage when they enter school and must compete with their peers who come from homes where computers are a natural part of the landscape.

The following chapter by Linda A. Tsantis and David D. Keefe effectively demonstrates how multimedia computer technology can be integrated into the preschool classroom to enhance learning. Of particular importance is the authors' observations of how multimedia computer technology can be used to enhance, not diminish, interpersonal interaction between preschoolers and other children, teachers, and parents. Indeed, they cite evidence that when computer technology has been introduced into Head Start classrooms, not only the children but also their parents benefit from increased self-esteem, achievement motivation, and positive interactions.

Our world has been changed by the introduction of the computer. As Tsantis and Keefe have pointed out, computer technology has not just added to our experience, it has transformed it. Computers can be a valuable resource to help a child learn, as well as to empower families. The challenge is to ensure that all children can benefit from such exposure and not just those who come from affluent families. For that reason, those who administer compensatory preschool programs for the disadvantaged should engage themselves in a thorough reading of the following chapter to discover creative ideas for integrating multimedia technology into preschool classrooms in ways that will enhance the thinking development of young children.

# 14 Preschool Children . . . Masters of Change

Linda A. Tsantis
David D. Keefe
*IBM Educational Systems, Bethesda, MD*

Educators concerned with preschool children in these last days of the 20th century are dealing with the effects of more than 30 years of societal change, which has influenced the environment for thinking, the tools of thinking, and the nature of thinkers themselves. This chapter presents a perspective on how these changes affect thinking skill development for preschool children. Our perspective is that new psychological constructs are in place in our society. These constructs address different aspects of thinking ability, processes, and motivation to think. The effects of computers on the development of emergent thinking skills in young children are discussed, and multimedia technology is proposed as a tool for helping teachers mediate and enhance this development.

The goals for the chapter are to:

• describe a theoretical framework for juxtaposing three current psychological constructs to create optimal early experiences to develop thinking;

• share a perspective on the potential of multimedia technology as a vehicle for implementing this framework to help preschool children develop thinking skills, self-confidence, and love-of-learning;

• suggest methods by which parents and teachers can use multimedia technology as a tool for observing and enhancing the reasoning process and learning styles of young children.

• encourage the reader to contribute to the body of research on the effects of technology in preparing preschoolers for the world in which they will live.

*Change as a Way of Life for Preschoolers.* Technological and societal changes have become so rampant that traditional forecasting tools are often no longer relevant. It is far easier to state with confidence that technology, for example will continue to change dynamically between now and the early 21st century, than to predict what any specific change will be. In an era when the only factor which can be predicted with confidence is change itself, those who master change, thrive. To become *Masters of Change,* children must develop both a set of thinking tools to help them "learn how to change", and the attitude best described as a "love-of-learning and thinking" from their earliest years.

For the first time in history, technology must be present if optimal early experiences to develop thinking are to exist. Technology has become a part of the everyday environment for young children. Preschool children observe microcomputers throughout their homes, and in stores. These devices are not always labeled "computer," (i.e., supermarket checkout stations, microwave ovens, cars, and television sets), but they perform intelligent operations which children learn to associate with "computerness" and thinking at a very early age. In contrast, adults often find themselves challenged and intimidated by these new and complex machines. Young children, however, appear to accept these wonderful machines as just another part of their world (Wright, 1990c).

The preschooler of today is not like the 4-year-old of previous decades in other ways as well. An increasing number have already attended child care or nursery school. While many have traveled widely and enjoyed advantaged environments, others have experienced stress, trauma, and psychological neglect and/or poverty. Both collectively and individually, the experiential backgrounds of preschoolers are quite different from those of previous generations and more distinct from each other than ever before (Morrison, 1988). They appear to be thinking and processing information in different ways as well. As one example, Armstrong (1987) discovered that the sheer volume of information which enters preschooler's lives every day fosters learning styles based on quick, multisensory scanning strategies, rather than the linear, classifying, and categorizing methods their parents and teachers learned.

When the preschool children of today enter college in the 21st century, the most valuable commodity in their world will be information, and technology will be the currency for success. The children who will thrive in this world must have a broad range of thinking skills. As adults, these children will need the ability to think both creatively and critically; identify and solve complex problems; speak, write, and read fluently; understand how to access, organize, and communicate information; and develop interpersonal skills to work effectively in cooperative teams (Butzin, 1990). Helping children develop the thinking skills needed to successfully participate in an era of rapidly changing technology poses a challenge to all who are committed to young children.

# DEVELOPING MASTERS OF CHANGE

Three psychological constructs provide the theoretical framework of a model for developing Masters of Change. The first concerns new conceptualizations of intelligence shown in Fig. 14.1. The second mediates the learning experience (Vygotsky's Zone of Proximal Development) as described by Salinger in Chapter 16 and depicted in Fig. 14.2. The last construct has been researched by Csikszentmihalyi (1975, 1988). His research suggests that the "flow state" as shown in Fig. 14.3, is the optimum climate in which thinking and learning can occur.

*Multiple Intelligences.* Current research in the cognitive sciences reflects the belief that intelligence is not a monolithic quality, but has multiple components. Gardner's (1984) theory of multiple intelligences postulates that each child's abilities are unique, and may be described in terms of potential for achievement in seven areas of intellectual competence or intelligence (see Fig. 14.1). This theory is complemented by Robert Sternberg's (1988) analysis that distinguishes three qualitatively different types of intelligence: componential (assessed by traditional tests), contextual (capacity for creative insights), and experiential (the "street smarts" of intelligence).

*The Zone of Proximal Development (ZPD).* Vygotsky (1978) believed that problem solving could be facilitated through the intervention of the guide or mediator, who provided support to help learners solve problems which they would not otherwise be able to independantly solve. Bruner describes the need for the guide to first lure the learner into the "Zone" and then to provide *scaffolding* by segmenting and ritualizing the task to be performed, in order to provide a framework for supporting the learner through the process of discovery (Wood, Bruner, & Ross 1976). The ZPD construct (see Fig. 14.2) provides an approach to intervention to help children learn to think effectively:

- under the skilled guidance of an adult mentor, who provides appropriate scaffolding;
- working cooperatively with a peer;
- as an apprentice to a more experienced peer; and,
- while serving as the mentor or guide for another child.

*Flow State or Autotelic Experience.* For more than 2 decades, Csikszentmihalyi (1975) has been studying "flow state experience," or those times when people report feelings of sustained peak enjoyment, intense concentration, and deep involvement in a significant task. The relation of flow state to skill level and

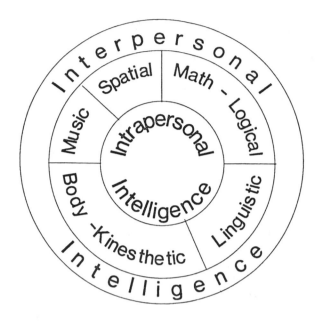

*Gardner's Theory of Intelligence: The Seven Intelligences*

| Intelligence | End-States | Core Components |
|---|---|---|
| Logical-mathematical | Scientist<br>Mathematician | Sensitivity to, and capacity to discern, logical or numerical patterns; ability to handle long chains of reasoning. |
| Linguistic | Poet<br>Journalist | Sensitivity to the sounds, rhythms, and meaning of words; sensitivity to the different functions of language. |
| Musical | Composer<br>Violinist | Abilities to produce and appreciate rhythm, pitch, and timbre; appreciation of the forms of musical expressiveness. |
| Spatial | Navigator<br>Sculptor | Capacities to perceive the visual-spatial world accurately and to perfor transformations on one's initial perceptions. |
| Bodily-kinesthetic | Dancer<br>Athlete | Abilities to control one's body movements and to handle objects skillfully. |
| Interpersonal | Therapist<br>Salesman | Capacities to discern and respond appropriately to the moods, temperaments, motivations, and desires of other people. |
| Intrapersonal | Person with detailed, accurate self-knowledge | Access to one's own feelings and the ability to discriminate among them and draw upon them to guide behavior; knowledge of one's own strengths, weaknesses, desires, and intelligences. |

FIG. 14.1.   Gardner's theory of intelligence: The seven intelligences. Adapted from Gardner and Hatch (1989). Copyright (1989) by the American Educational Research Association. Adapted by permission of the publisher.

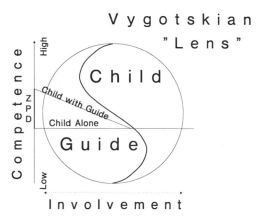

FIG. 14.2.   Vygotsky's zone of proximal development (ZPD).

challenge level is shown graphically by the chart in Fig. 14.3. To remain in flow as skills develop, one must increase the complexity of the activity or take on new challenges. Flow compels people to stretch themselves, to always take on another challenge, to improve on their abilities (Csikszentmihalyi & Csikszentmihalyi 1988).

Flow state has not been extensively studied with preschool children for good reason . . . most preschool children are in enough control of their own play environments to be self-regulated, and choose play activities which provide extensive opportunity for autotelic experience. As these children begin to enter more formal learning environments, flow state theory provides an opportunity for educators to structure programs which allow children to experience thinking

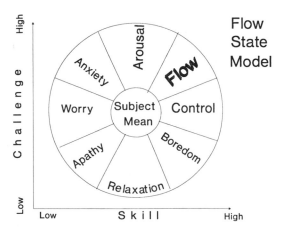

FIG. 14.3.   Csikszentmihalyi's flow state. Adapted from Massimini and Carli (1988).

and learning as autotelic activities. In such a pleasurable, though sometimes difficult or risky state, thinking and learning become their own rewards.

## TECHNOLOGY—THE AGENT OF DEVELOPING THINKING FOR PRESCHOOLERS

Contemporary cognitive scientists see the computer as an instrument to both stimulate and explore the various domains of young children's thinking. In the words of O. K. Tikhomirov, *"Just as the development of gasoline engines provided a tool for human physical activity, so the development of the computer provided a tool for human mental activity. . . Tools are not just added to human activity; they transform it."* (Greenfield, 1984, p. 153).

Papert (1980) proposed that computer environments can provide materials and subjects that help children develop and refine their thinking skills. Appropriate software programs enable the child to communicate ideas, concepts and relationships which might otherwise remain unexpressed. This ability is the "plus" factor that Papert defines as the possibility of representing abstract ideas and mathematical concepts in a more concrete, manipulable form. Papert coined the term "micro-worlds" to describe the problem solving environments which children experience during computer-based discovery. Microworlds are child-centered computer simulated environments having a small number of well-defined and unambiguous rules. In an ideal microworld, the child remains in control, acting on events to make events happen rather than reacting to predetermined questions and close-ended problems. Papert's expectations are confirmed by numerous research reports of the gains made by young children when they are allowed to experience discovery through their interactions with computers. (Clements 1985, 1987; Clements & Nastasi, 1981; Haugland & Shade, 1985, 1990; Wright 1985, 1990b; Wright, Shade, Thouvenelle, & Davidson, 1989). Extensive observation of children interacting with a variety of software programs has led to the identification of hierarchical stages through which children move as they develop their command of microworlds (Wright, 1985):

> *Discovery:*  growing awareness that what appears on the screen is what I created or decided
> *Involvement:*  motivation to achieve mastery of basic commands and sequences
> *Self-confidence:*  ability to execute a plan and to predict outcomes
> *Creativity:*  invention of solutions and design of challenges for others

We propose that such stages parallel and complement thinking skill development.

Lepper and Milojkovic (1986) describe three primary features which enable the computer to become a powerful tool to advance thinking development and that position it as an agent of change:

- the interactive nature of the computer (the ability to elicit, receive and interpret information from the learner)
- the intelligence of the computer (the ability to respond differentially based upon the information obtained)
- the multifunctionality of the computer (the ability to present information through both auditory and visual modes).

The computer has characteristics which may make it an ideal mediator or guide particularly with students who have special needs (Behrman, 1988). The computer:

a. is infinitely patient and permits learners to proceed at their own pace;
b. is easily individualized and tailored to the capability of the learner;
c. is totally non-judgemental;
d. encourages experimentation, trial and error, in a risk free environment.

Advances in multimedia computer technology are vastly expanding the range of functions to combine pictures, voice, music, animation, full-motion video and massive data storage in highly engaging interactive applications which provide multisensory appeal. As an example, video games create environments in which skill level and challenge level are well matched, providing flow state opportunities for their users. These games routinely permit the user to select a level of estimated skill; the game then adjusts the challenge level to match the selected skill level. As the player demonstrates proficiency, the game increases the challenge level, continually rewarding the player for proficiency while adding to the level of difficulty.

White (1987) observes that preschool children often operate as "two channel learners—one channel is what they learn at school and the other channel is what they learn from the entertainment industry." Her concern is that children will not be taught to figuratively read images as they will be taught to read text, and therefore will not know how to distinguish real information from information in which the quality is distorted for entertainment purposes. The solution to White's concern is to provide educational applications that are pedagogically sound, and as engaging and provocative as those found in the entertainment industry.

## GUIDED MICROWORLDS—INTEGRATING THE FRAMEWORK INTO INSTRUCTION

In education environments from corporate training to preschool, multimedia technology makes possible a new form of instructional design, *Guided Microworlds* (Pea, 1985), which combines Vygotsky's "Guide" with Papert's concept of microworlds. In a guided microworld, the child is encouraged to explore various activities within the constraints of the microworld parameters with mediation offered as needed by the guide.

Guided microworlds offer the excitement of "real experience" in a simulated environment while providing learners with "scaffolding," or instructional support for tasks which they could not otherwise independently solve. As the learner becomes increasingly proficient, scaffolding is gradually reduced until it totally "fades" as competencies are achieved and the learner gains independence (Pea & Soloway, 1987). (An analogous example of this type of scaffolding process is the task of helping a child learn to ride a bicycle.)

As an alternative to fading, Bruner (1985) describes ways that the guide can "raise the ante" to enable the child to deal with increasing task complexity. The guide supplies as much aid as the child needs at any give time, but raises the expectation level as a child becomes more proficient. This continual adjustment of challenge to developing skill is essential to achieving a flow state experience.

Teachers can use guided microworlds as *cognitive windows* (Solomon, 1983) to observe how children process information and exhibit their individual learning abilities. The computer program can also maintain a record of the decisions made by the child, to provide a "cognitive trace" to aid the teacher in monitoring the child's progress during successive experiences with a particular guided microworld. (Pea, 1985).

Guided microworld materials can draw on the child's dominant Multiple Intelligences (M.I.) abilities to help the child comprehend material targetted at a different M.I. category (i.e., teaching through the child's strength). Figure 14.4 shows a metaphorical view of this construct . . . from the child's viewpoint the guided microworld acts as a telescope, opening up new worlds of discovery in each of the M.I. categories. From the teacher's perspective the guided microworld serves as a cognitive window into the reasoning process of the child. The

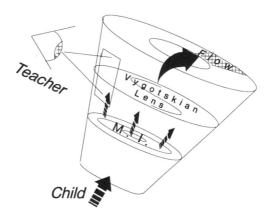

FIG. 14.4.  Guided microworld model.

ZPD scaffolding and mediation is the process controlling the microworld as "lens" . . . as the guide observes the learner gain proficiency, the scaffolding is adjusted to present a more challenging environment . . . a continual process which leads to autotelic discovery.

The multiple intelligences that children bring to a collaborative learning situation challenge the teacher/mediator to design an environment in which each child can offer a unique contribution. The integrated curriculum lesson that follows (Fein et al., 1988; Wright, 1985) embodies linguistic, spatial, logical-mathematical, and interpersonal intelligences.

> Heterogeneous groupings of four preschool children whose narrative ability ranges from low to expert are asked to create a "world" for a robot turtle. The turtle is connected to a microcomputer and directed by single key stroke Logo commands. A variety of materials are available to create the "world" from which each group fashions an original setting (forest, Ocean City—a popular resort, a town house, and a castle). In the forest group, one child focuses on creating a river with logs (corrugated cardboard) in it. Another child estimates distance and direction to navigate the river with Logo commands. A third begins to narrate the story of the turtle's adventure while a fourth is busy making trees. After enacting the adventure, the four children gather to tell their story to the recorder who uses a word processor with primary print. The recorder (and mediator) demonstrates how the words can be altered (i.e., edited) if the children change their mind.
>
> Only the mediator notices the subtle impact of the cooperative learning experience. The expert storyteller begins the tale. Several others join in . . . then the child who seldom writes or dictates a word picks up the gist of the expert's tale and the humor of his repetitive refrain and begins to expand in parallel style. His enthusiasm carries him off into the world of fantasy, no longer dependent upon the peer who was unknowingly scaffolding him. *"Once there was a robot called TJ. Now this is the story. He swam along and bumped into a log and then he flew into the sky. He came back and swam and bumped into a tree and then he flew into the way of a big bird. So he swam some more, looking for fish, until he bumped into. . . ."* At the end of the story one member of the group remained fascinated with the large letters and added all the individual words she knew.

Perhaps the most predictable part of designing a guided microworld for young children is that each child will forge his or her own unique trail, a path which will allow the observant teacher to look through this cognitive window into the mind of the child (Wright, 1990c).

*Parents and Guided Microworlds.*   The parent, as the young child's first and most important teacher, is an ideal mediator for guided microworld applications. Children are accustomed to answering questions asked by their parents, and most children react very comfortably to the parent as mediator. "LapWare" computer software is designed to be "controlled" by the child while sitting on the parent's lap (Lapware, 1986). The child and parent jointly make decisions, which lead to selections of text to be read by the parent. The parent mediates the shared experience to give the child a feeling of being in control. The story becomes a form of guided microworld which requires both parent and child to collaborate on the decisions needed to resolve the dilemmas posed by the program. This process contributes to the development of thinking skills while building a feeling of regard toward the learning experience. The child observes that the parent values this type of joint activity, and is encouraged by the parent's active interest in learning.

Parents have reacted very positively to the introduction of computers into their children's preschool programs. *"The computer will be just like the telephone. Everyone will have one—my kids gotta learn this, and so do I!"* These words from a mother in a Head Start program reflect the feelings shared by other parents whose children participated in a study to investigate the impact of integrating computers into the preschool curriculum (Tsantis, Wright, & Thouvenelle, 1989). Results from this study support previous research findings that early intervention programs involving both children and their parents can: influence lifelong learning patterns; significantly contribute to improvement of quality of life; and break the cycle of disadvantage (Comer, 1980; NASBE 1988; Schorr & Schorr, 1988; Swick & Robinson, 1990; Weikart, 1987).

Children in the Head Start study were eager to use the computer. They were proud to have as one of their learning tools a machine which they perceived as being important to adults. While teachers and aides approached the computer with some reserve, these energetic 3- and 4-year-olds saw the computer as an electronic toy box, filled with games, letters, words, paints, pictures, shapes, maps, and all sorts of materials from which they could construct their own worlds . . . microworlds. The children knew that they were the masters of the computer and it would follow their command. Through it, they would combine and recombine objects to create and recreate their microworlds. Best of all, the computer could speak. It could use its digitized human quality voice to speak words too difficult for the children to read. This speech could be in any language, and even in the children's own voices. Up to this point, the computer had held a fascination in the classroom that might be considered a "novelty effect." However, once the children began to have personalized programs with their own name and their own voice something almost magical happened.

Children began to demonstrate more robust language, describing, for example, how they had used a program about gardens to prepare the soil to help the plants grow. Children began to take particular pride in learning the new skills of selecting and running their favorite programs for friends and family and then providing their audience with a personalized printout of the activity. Parents who often had difficulty finding a comfortable way to join in their child's enthusiasm in other activities, now found themselves wanting to be involved to the point of having children become impatient for the parent to "get finished." Many children exhibited leadership skills and levels of confidence not realized in other learning centers. Even children whose energy and interest were often difficult to harness were reported to be far more motivated, compliant, and happy when working on the computer (Tsantis & Keefe, 1989). These findings support earlier research (Clements & Gullo, 1984; Shade & Watson, 1987; Wright, 1985) that the addition of the computer provided a powerful stimulus for thinking development as well as cooperative learning and socialization.

These collaborative activities allowed children to use their work to strengthen bonds with their parents. At the same time, parents began to view their child as being more capable. Seeing their child empowered made parents feel more confident about their child's abilities and more positive about themselves as competent parents. The following newspaper excerpt provides an illustration of other parents' reaction to this phenomenon:

> *Marietta W. was taken aback when her preschooler, Dion, started bubbling over with talk of counting petals, creating animals, combining colors—all the fun things he and his classmates were doing with their new computers. "He was so excited, and he seemed to know so much more. I just had to go down to the school and see for myself" . . . Over in the preschool classroom, Delmy H. seemed quite at home as she used the computer's mouse in a counting game. As the screen showed a colorful ladybug moving from petal to petal, the computer's voice counted each one in Spanish. She correctly told the computer how many there were, and it responded by making the ladybug dance. She giggled, twisting her dress in excitement. "My 4-year-old can't wait to come to school—and she wants to bring her brother and sister so they can see what she's doing," Juanita P. said. (Merl, 1990).*

## New Tools for Learning—Multimedia Technology in Guided Microworlds

Just as there are new approaches to understanding children's thinking, there are also new tools to better "reach the learner." Multimedia computer technology can extend and elaborate thinking and learning experiences through:

• photo-quality visual images or multicolored artwork (which can be made into dynamic presentations through techniques ranging from simple animation through full-motion video);

• voiced phrases, in synthesized text-to-speech or digitized natural human-quality voice (which can be presented in a variety of languages, or in the teachers, parent's, or child's own voice);

• music ranging from single instrument tunes through full orchestral arrangements featuring several instruments (which can be chosen by the child);

• kinesthetic input devices including keyboard, touch pad, joystick, mouse, touch screen (which permit use of the computers by children at various levels of motor skill development).

- expert system functions (which provide guided microworld scaffolding for the children, and powerful assessment assistance for the teacher);
- optical storage (which can provide instruction using complete video segments with alternative storyline options);
- printing of material produced by children (allowing children to share their creations with parents, siblings, and friends).

Applications built upon multimedia technology can provide children with unique educational experiences, not possible with any other media. The "hypermedia environment" (Shneiderman, 1990), allows a child to explore information on a topic which is presented either as text or in some other form (pictures, maps, symbols–music; math expressions). When the child selects a particular item, the computer offers a different perspective on that topic . . . which can be in another medium. An example is a screen that contains a series of letter symbols. As the child selects a letter ("C"), the computer responds with pictures of several animals (cow, cat, . . .) whose names begins with the selected letter, and the computer voice speaks the names of the animals. Select one animal's picture, and the computer responds with greater detail . . . a brief animation sequence of the animal in motion, the sound that is normally associated with the animal (moo, meow, . . .), the name of the animal in text. This provides the child with a technology-based medium for thinking, learning, and communicating which is inherently multisensory, and highly compatible with the way young children learn.

As expert systems find greater application in education environments, the computer will increasingly assume the role of a skilled scaffolding mentor, and will provide assistance to the teacher, or interact directly with the child.

*Guided Microworlds for the Masters of Change.*    Most examples of current research involving computers with preschool children are based on use of what might be considered to be relatively primitive computers (with limited memory, image, sound, and animation capability). This section presents examples of how multimedia technology might be used as the base for research into guided microworlds, to enable flow state experience in each of the multiple intelligence categories.

**Spatial Intelligence**—Computers today can provide particularly rich capabilities for appreciating or creating art. Photo-quality images using hundreds of discrete colors can be included in computer materials which can include pictures of great works of art, or children's classics. Children can play by editing colors to see the effect this has on a picture. Small pictures can be selected and placed on the screen (similar to selecting a rubber stamp and stamping the image across the paper). Children may create an object, then save the object for use in other pictures. Children can also draw either free-form with a variety of pencils or brushes, or by using shape generators for straight lines, boxes, circles, etc. Paint functions allow the child to color various objects on the screen. Again, the richness of function offered to the child depends on the child's developmental level and artistic ability.

Studies of individual differences or patterns of interest (Gardner & Wolf, 1979) suggest that children exhibit one of two broad approaches to experience:

a. the "patterner" demonstrates sensitivity to objective dimensions such as quantity, size, shape, and enjoys visual spatial tasks and construction of designs— this child is often found in the block corner;

b. the "dramatist" is responsive to personal and social dimensions and enjoys language-related activities such as story telling and sociodramatic play—this child is often found in the housekeeping corner.

An illustration of how the computer environment can be used as a cognitive window to observe thinking and learning processes is provided by the response of 4 and 5 year-olds to an open-ended computer construction program (Wright, 1990b). The program (Electronic Builder, 1988) allows the children to create images using geometric shapes of various sizes. Some children created pictures of trucks, buildings, or "fantastic caterpillars," using circles for wheels, and squares or triangles for bodies and roofs. The children then dictated their stories about what happened in their pictures. These children were the dramatists. Other children created designs by varying size, shape, and color attributes into symmetrical or repetitive patterns which conveyed their awareness of spatial order. These children were the patterners.

One of the patterners created an overlayed design by choosing a large white square within which she placed two overlapping colored triangles with opposite orientations. This placement left a third triangle showing in the portion of the square that was still visible. Knowing that there was no comparable triangle in the menu, she turned to a friend with an impish grin and issued her challenge: "Jonathan, make a white triangle like mine!" This child displayed a cognitive awareness of how she had created a new shape and a metacognitive awareness of the challenge her friend would face in solving her puzzle (Wright, 1990a).

Another child came to an understanding of the "white spaces" (an insight that required figure-ground and part–whole awareness) through an attempt to transfer to the computer screen a symmetrical design the child had previously created using a set of mosaic blocks. Again, the white "background" triangles that existed on the mosaic blocks did not exist in the menu of shapes. After several attempts at placing only triangles, the child exclaimed, "Wait! I know how to do it!" and proceeded to place white squares on the screen and then overlay the colored triangles on to the squares, leaving visible the desired triangular shapes. The ability to overlay an infinite number of objects in rapid succession offers the child a scaffold for experimentation not easily duplicated in the three dimensional world. Indeed, some 4-year-olds become more proficient than some adults at discerning which shapes are oriented in the direction they need to complete their image

**Logical–Mathematical Intelligence**—Multimedia technology is showing great promise for logical-mathematical applications with preschoolers. In 1990, the National Council of Teachers of Mathematics presented an award to a software program which complements a NCTM counting book "I Can Count the Petals of a Flower" (1989). The program uses voice, animation, and the digitized pictures of the flowers that are in the book. The child can use the book with a parent, and can then rehearse and practice with the computer.

Programs designed for use with elementary-aged children can be used as a guided microworld for preschool children with a teacher or parent providing scaffolding. For example, the parent and child can explore the time sections to Exploring Measurement Time and Money (IBM, 1988) and discuss the orderly sequence of awakening, brushing teeth, eating breakfast, leaving for school, without regard to specific clock times. The child can place coin combinations on the screen and hear, through digitized speech, the total sum of the set created. With the computer's help, children are less likely to build inaccurate conceptions, while concurrently, the software provides the "pat on the back" that encourages children to continue (Perl, 1990).

When children can answer a problem but do not understand how they solved it, it is possible to help them verbalize and reflect on their actions which will consolidate the new thought structures (Clements, 1985). This type of learning involves a child–adult partnership where the adult serves as guide or mediator, and provides scaffolding to encourage initiative and inquiry from the child to set the stage for discovery. Using computer technology to provide the adult with a cognitive window that makes children's thinking more accessible to discrete study is a highly compelling prospect.

**Linguistic Intelligence**—Research studies using computers with preschool children have shown that children use more language when working on the computer than in other areas of the preschool classroom (Bialo & Sivin, 1990; Clements & Nastasi, 1991). Additionally, the computer contributes to enhanced language development by exposing the child to many new concepts. Many preschool programs are introducing words from other languages (which are part of the cultural heritage of the children's families) in order to affirm cultural uniqueness, and encourage the children to discuss their family histories with parents and grandparents. Researchers in Canada, France, and Israel are developing educational software which uses digital voice to enable the child to request the story information spoken in one language, and then to ask that the language be changed and the information be respoken. This can be very useful in multicultural preschool programs (Labelle & Gelinas, 1989).

As preschool children approach readiness for school, some of them may show great interest in beginning reading. Word processors which combine voice with text (Listen to Learn, 1985) and pictures on the screen (Primary Editor Plus, 1988) are particularly helpful at this stage of development. Typically the child creates a picture on the screen and then is encouraged to tell the story. The parent or teacher serves as mediator to scaffold . . . entering text into the word processor to record the story, as it is told in the child's own words. The resultant document contains text and pictures which the child can have printed to share with family and friends (Zurn, 1987).

Hofmann (1986) suggests that 4-year-olds can use the computer as a language arts learning tool in order to confirm a hypothesis, to compare two opposing positions, or explore the effect of changing letters on pronunciation. One group of children discovered what they called "magic letters." If they asked the computer to speak a group of letters which did not contain a magic letter, the computer would speak back the names of the letters. If they inserted a magic letter, the computer spoke back . . . a word! The magic letters were A, E, I, O, and U.

**Musical Intelligence**—Teachers have long used the piano to introduce children to beginning instrumental music. One reason is the nature of the piano itself. No matter how the student presses a key, the piano will produce a "well-formed" note with a pleasant sound. The child can explore the effects of pressing other keys, holding the key down for a long time, etc. The preschool teacher uses the piano with the child as a form of guided microworld for musical notemaking. Many other instruments require children to develop a considerable amount of skill before well-formed notes can be produced. Drums, cymbals, and other percussive instruments produce well-formed notes, but have much more limited abilities to play recognizable songs. These limitations to the exploration of music have been removed by the music synthesizer feature on a computer. Now even preschool children can feel musically empowered.

Using a computer with a music synthesizer, a keyboard, and appropriate software, the child presses a key and hears a well-formed note with a pleasant sound which may mimic the piano, or any of more than 300 other instruments. From the very start, the child feels in control and is able to take pride in the results created at each stage of experimenting with either original musical play, or guided play within the context of a familiar tune.

Depending on the degree of ability shown by the child, an appropriate guided microworld environment provides just enough scaffolding to enable the child to enjoy the current activity, while leaving open new avenues of musical experience for discovery. For example, a child who shows little natural insight may be given a program that allows selection of one of several well-known animal shapes (weasel, lamb, pig, wolf, etc.). As the child points to and selects an animal (say the lamb) an appropriate theme is played (Mary had a Little Lamb). Options to enrich this microworld are extensive and extend across all of the intelligences.

**Intrapersonal Intelligence**—One of the most consistent observations of researchers studying young children involved in guided microworlds is the enthusiasm, excitement, and obvious self-esteem which these experiences build. Developmentally appropriate (Bredekamp, 1987) applications will give the child an immediate feeling of being in control, while the scaffolding protects the child from confusion or tedium which might otherwise be connected with each task.

Some of the strongest support for the preschool child's use of the computer emphasizes gains in the area of socio-emotional development which are then linked to cognitive development (Donohue, Bough, & Dickson, 1987). Review of the literature highlights the "empowerment" of the young child which occurs when using the computer. For example, it is proposed that as a child experiences increased proficiency in use of the computer, self-confidence, personal satisfaction, and general feelings of success also increase, resulting in the child's beginning to develop a sense of autonomy as a learner (Clements, 1985; Donohue et al., 1987; Shade & Watson, 1987).

Wright and Samaras (1986) linked preschool children's sense of mastery over the computer to their feelings of developing a positive self image. Preschool children who appeared reticent and shy during play activities in other areas of the classroom have become leaders during play activity involving the computer, based on the confidence they develop during guided microworld activities. Voice technology, particularly when the child's own voice is used, seems to play a large role in helping the child develop both a comfort level with the technology, and a feeling of ownership, even protectiveness towards the computer (Wright, 1990b).

**Interpersonal Intelligence**—Clements and Nastasi (1991) and Wright (1990a) have reported on the transformation observed with 4-year-olds involved in small group activities with the computer. Initially, the children witnessed the activity impatiently, each awaiting their turn. Gradually (and with the guidance and encouragement of the teacher), the children began to offer suggestions, and operate cooperatively as a team. One emerging area for research is the degree to which well-designed preschool applications will eliminate gender bias on computers, so that neither boys or girls develop the attitude that "girls can't do this as well as boys" or "girls don't like to work with computers" (Sanders & Stone 1986).

The teacher can adapt guided microworlds designed for use with a single child as mediator for a small group of children by attaching a large screen monitor or projection device to the computer. Each child participates and contributes to the solution of a problem or completion of a story. This helps the child develop interpersonal skills, as well as practice cooperative learning.

**Body-Kinesthetic Intelligence**—Computers are not usually thought of as having much applicability in developing body-kinesthetic thinking skills, particularly at the preschool level. However, multimedia technology does have some rather unique capabilities, particularly when it is used to mix live video imaging with computer generated or stored video imaging. For example, the computer can show the child a video sequence in which several children are exercising, tumbling, marching, etc. and invite the child to join in. A TV camera is connected to the computer and the image of the child is mixed into the picture in much the same manner as the image of the TV weatherperson is mixed into a composite picture with a weather map on the nightly news. The child can perform and observe his performance relative to the other images on the screen . . . the performance can be taped for later sharing with family and friends on a home VCR.

A variation of this theme called "MANDALA" (1988) is currently found in a number of childrens or technology museums. Mandala is capable of detecting "collisions" between the child's image, and other images in the background screen. This permits the computer program to modify the action as the child touches objects on the screen. A common application is to surround the child with a group of objects like bells, each having a different pitch, and to let the child play music by touching the bells. Also, the TV camera zoom lens permits using only a part of the child's body—a hand perhaps—which can enable a child with severe physical disabilities to participate in the application. The technology provides all users with equal capability, regardless of their size or shape, enabling smaller preschool children to share the experience equally with older, larger children.

The widespread introduction of computers into education has attracted the attention of education researchers, many of whom have become computer advocates. One of the most common themes of these adherents has been that the computer will make learning more intrinsically motivating (Brown, 1985; Lepper & Gurtner, 1989; Papert, 1980; Schank, 1984). Other educators hold strong reservations about the inclusion of technology into preschool education, and are calling for research to substantiate the value of technology with young learners.

## A "THEORY OF RELATIVITY" FOR EDUCATION? FUTURE RESEARCH AND INSTRUCTIONAL NEEDS

The challenge to education researchers today is highly analogous to that faced by physicists in the early-20th century. Physicists' belief systems at that time were being challenged by experimental evidence and new theories about the nature of the world. Isaac Newton's PRINCIPIA, published in 1687, represented the culmination of thousands of years of striving to comprehend the system of the world, the principles of force and of motion, and the physics of bodies moving in different media (Cohen, 1985). Newton's work, which had stood the test of two centuries of scientific study and practical application, no longer sufficed to explain the phenomena that were being observed during experimentation with electromagnetic energy. This experimentation gave glimpses of a more complex structure of the world, a structure which could no longer be fully explained in Newtonian terms. New theories (relativity, quantum physics), and experimental tools (electronics) enabled the research to progress as scientists began to look at molecular structures, followed by atomic structures, then further levels of sub-atomic structures. Einstein, one of the first *modern physicists* to contribute to a new understanding of the physical world, commented that Newton achieved "the greatest intellectual stride that it has been granted to any man to make." Newton continues to be revered for his contributions to the foundation of understanding of the world. However, Newton's laws are no longer sufficient to understand the phenomena of modern physics.

Piaget, Montessori, Dewey . . . the *Newtons of education theory* during this century, have provided models of learning upon which much contemporary educational research is built. New interpretations of intelligence and expanded theories of cognition may offer a more inclusive perspective than that provided by these earlier seminal thinkers. Change, with its resultant challenge to beliefs, has been the hallmark of the latter half of this century, and those who are concerned with preparing children for successful lives as adults must be attuned to this phenomenon. As Ornstein and Ehrlich (1989) have observed: ". . . the world has changed in critical ways to a greater extent since World War II than it changed between the birth of Christ and that war." Significant changes in the environment, the tools, and quite possibly the subjects for educational research are forcing paradigm shifts in traditional models of learning.

Are we reaching the limits of human capability to deal with such rapidly accelerating change? Not likely. Lepper and Gurtner (1989) remind us that the computer offers opportunities for learning, in Walker's (1983) felicitous phrase, "nearer the speed of thought." And we are not operating in competition with computers . . . these tools can extend and amplify our own capabilities. Leo Buscaglia (1986) states the prospects well:

The human mind is a miracle.
Once it accepts a new idea or learns a new fact,
it stretches forever and never goes back
to its original dimension. It is limitless.
No one has even guessed at its potential.
Still, so many of us spend a lifetime
marking boundaries and defining limits.
Young children in their innocence have not yet
learned their limitations and so joyfully
and instinctively stretch to learn,
and so should we all!

# DISCUSSION QUESTIONS FOR FUTURE RESEARCH

• Innovative applications of computers in education can provide teachers cognitive windows into the child's mental representations and processes.

What implications does this have on the design of programs for preschool children?

• Robert Sternberg's concept of the "Triarchic Theory of Intelligence" offers complementary dimensions to Gardner's Multiple Intelligences construct.

In what ways could Sternberg's concept be directly applied to the framework which has been presented in this chapter? Would this affect the structure of the guided microworld?

• Gardner describes seven potential multiple intelligences (M.I.).

What M.I. characteristics would you expect to be dominant in the child who will become a "master of change?"

• Psychologists and educators are seeking new forms of assessment which measure individual learning capabilities, progress, and motivation. It has been established that technology can affect all of these.

What role can/should technology play in the assessment process?

• The role of motivation in learning, and factors which produce environments conducive for learning and achievement versus those which lead to boredom or anxiety, have been studied with older children and adults, but not with preschool children.

What are some of the special considerations for research into motivation and autotelic experience with preschool children?

• Over-stimulating image and sound intensive home environments may have measurable effects on the ways young children learn and think. Scientists have long noted that the act of observing certain phenomina influences the phenomena itself (Heisenberg's Uncertainty Principle).

How can research be designed to study how these conditions affect young children's thinking without causing change due to the research itself (e.g., Hawthorne effect) confounding the study data?

• Interactions with video games may lead young children to expect great excitement and entertainment associated with a strong sense of competitiveness when interacting with computers.

What implications does this have for preschool teachers and designers of educational software for young children?

# REFERENCES

Armstrong, T. (1987). *In their own way.* Los Angeles: Jeremy P. Tarcher.
Berhman, M. (Ed.). (1988). *Integrating computers into the curriculum: A handbook for special educators.* Boston, MA: College Hill Press.

Bialo, E., & Sivin, J. (1990). *Microcomputers and related learning technologies.* (unpublished report). New York: Interactive Educational Systems Design, Inc.

Bredekamp, S. (Ed.). (1987). *Developmentally Appropriate Practice in Early Childhood Programs Serving Children from Birth Through Age 8.* Washington, D.C. NAEYC.

Brown, J. S. (1985). Process versus product—A perspective on tools for communal and informal electronic learning. *Journal of Educational Computing Research, 1,* 179–201.

Bruner, J. S. (1985). Vygotsky: A historical and conceptual perspective. In J. V. Wertsch (Ed.), *Culture, communication and cognition: Vygotskian perspectives* (pp. 21–34). Cambridge, England: Cambridge University Press.

Buscaglia, L. F. (1986). *Bus 9 to Paradise.* Hillboro, NJ: Slack.

Butzin, S. M. (1990). Project CHILD: Not boring school, but work that's fun and neat. *The Computing Teacher,* March.

Clements, D. H. (1985). *Computers in early and primary education.* Englewood Cliffs, NJ: Prentice Hall.

Clements, D. H. (1987). Computers and young children: A review of research. *Young Children,* November, 34–44.

Clements, D. H., & Gullo, D. F. (1984). Effects of computer programming on young children's cognition. *Journal of Educational Psychology, 76,* 1051–1058.

Clements, D. H., & Nastasi, B. (1991). Research on Logo. In Gettinger et al. (Eds.), *Advances in school psychology, preschool and early childhood treatment directions.* Hillsdale, NJ: Lawrence Erlbaum Associates.

Cohen, I. B. (1985). *The birth of a new physics.* New York: Norton.

Comer, J. P. (1980). *School power.* New York: The Free Press.

Csikszentmihalyi, M. (1975). *Beyond boredom and anxiety.* San Francisco: Jossey-Bass.

Csikszentmihalyi, M., & Csikszentmihalyi, I. S. (Eds.). (1988). *Optimal experience: Psychological studies of flow in consciousness.* New York: Cambridge University Press.

Donahue, W. A., Bough, K., & Dickson, W. (1987). Computers in early childhood education. *Journal of Research in Childhood Education, 2*(1), 6–16.

*Electronic Builder* (1988). Computer software. Alexandria, VA: Mobius Corporation.

*Exploring Measurement, Time, and Money* (1988). Computer software. Atlanta, GA: IBM Corporation.

Fein, G., et al. (1988). Computing space, a conceptual and developmental analysis of LOGO. In G. Forman & P. Pufall (Eds.), *Constructivism in the computer age* (pp. 117–119). Hillsdale, NJ: Lawrence Erlbaum Associates.

Gardner, H. (1984). *Frames of mind—The theory of multiple intelligences.* New York: Basic Books.

Gardner, H., & Hatch, T. (1989). Multiple intelligences go to school. *Educational Researcher, 18*(8), 6.

Gardner, H., & Wolf, D. (Eds.). (1979). *New directions for child development: Early symbolization.* San Francisco: Jossey-Bass.

Greenfield, P. M. (1984). *Mind and media: The effects of television, video games, and computers.* Cambridge, MA: Harvard University Press.

Haugland, S., & Shade, D. (1985). Developmentally appropriate software for young children. *Young Children, 43*(4), 37–43.

Haugland, S., & Shade, D. (1990). *Developmental evaluations of software for young children.* Albany, NY: Delmar.

Hofman, R. (1986). Microcomputers, productive thinking, and children. In P. Campbell & G. Fein (Eds.), *Young children and microcomputers.* Englewood Cliffs, NJ: Prentice Hall.

*I Can Count the Petals of a Flower—KidWare.* (1989). Computer software. Alexandria, VA: Mobius Corporation.

Labelle, M., & Gelinas, C. (1989). *Educational computer activities and problem solving at the kindergarten level.* Quebec: Ministry of Education.

*Lapware.* (1986). Computer software. Cambridge, M.A.: Tom Snyder Productions.

Lepper, M. R., & Gurtner, J. (1989). Children and computers: Approaching the twenty-first century. *American Psychologist, 44*(2), 170–178.

Lepper, M. R., & Milojkovic, J. (1986). The "computer revolution" in education: A research perspective. In P. F. Campbell & G. Fein (Eds.), *Young children and microcomputers* (pp. 11–24). Englewood Cliffs, NJ: Prentice Hall.

*Listen to Learn* (1985). Computer software. Atlanta, GA: IBM Corporation.

*Mandala.* (1988). Computer software. Toronto, Canada: Vivid Effects, Ltd.

Massimini, F., & Carli, M. (1988). Figure 16.1 in Csikszentmihalyi, M. and Csikszentmihalyi, I. (Eds.), *Optimal experience: psychological studies of flow in consciousness* (p. 270). New York: Cambridge University Press.

Merl, J. (1990). Preschoolers find computer user-friendly. *Los Angeles Times,* June 6, B-1,4.

Morrison, G. S. (1988). *Early childhood education today.* Columbus, OH: Merrill.

NASBE (1988). *Right from the start.* Alexandria, VA: National Association of State Boards of Education.

Ornstein, R., & Ehrlich, P. (1989). *New worlds new minds.* New York: Doubleday.

Papert, S. (1980). *Mind-storms: Children, computers, and powerful ideas.* New York: Basic Books.

Pea, R. D. (1985). Beyond amplification: Using the computer to reorganize human mental functioning. *Educational Psychologist, 20,* 167–182.

Pea, R., & Soloway, E. (1987). *Mechanisms for facilitating a vital and dynamic education system: Fundamental roles for education science and technology.* Final report for the Office of Technology Assessment. Washington, DC: U.S. Congress.

Perl, T. (1990). Manipulatives and the computer. A powerful partnership for learning. *Classroom Computer Learning, 10*(6), 20–29.

*Primary Editor Plus.* (1988). Computer software. Atlanta, GA: IBM Corp.

Sanders, J. S., & Stone, A. (1986). *The neuter computer: Computers for girls and boys.* New York: Neal Schuman.

Shade, D. D., & Watson, J. A. (1987). Microworlds, mother teaching behavior and concept formation in the very young child. *Early Child Development and Care, 28*(2), 97–114.

Schank, R. C. (1984). *The cognitive computer: On language, learning, and artificial intelligence.* Meno Park, CA: Addison-Wesley.

Shneiderman, B. (1990). Future directions for human-computer interaction. *International Journal of Human-Computer Interaction, 2*(1), 73–90.

Schorr, L. B., & Schorr, D. (1988). *Within our reach: Breaking the cycle of disadvantage.* New York: Doubleday.

Solomon, C. (1983). *Computer environments for children.* Cambridge, MA: MIT Press.

Sternberg, R. J. (1988). *The triarchic mind.* New York: Viking Press.

Swick, K. J., & Robinson, S. (1988, Summer). Technology, children, and families: Confronting the challenge. *SACUS Public Policy Institute Report.* Southern Association for Children Under Six.

Tsantis, L. A., & Keefe, D. D. (1989, November). *An intergenerational literacy program.* Presented at the North American Forum, World Conference on Education for All, Boston.

Tsantis, L. A., Wright, J. L., & Thouvenelle, S. (1989). Computers and preschoolers—Head Start/IBM partnership. *Children Today.* January–February, (pp. 21–23).

Vygotsky, L. (1978). *Mind in society: The development of higher psychological processes.* Cambridge, MA: Harvard University Press.

Walker, D. F. (1983). Reflections on the educational potential and limitations of microcomputers. *Phi Delta Kappan, 65,* 103–107.

Weikart, D. (1987, September 9). *Testimony before the Committee on Labor and Human Resources and the Committee on Education and Labor, 100th Congress.* Washington, D.C.: U.S. House of Representatives.

White, M. A. (1987). *Curriculum for the information age?* Hillsdale, NJ: Lawrence Erlbaum Associates.

Wood, D., Bruner, J. S., & Ross, G. (1976). The role of tutoring in problem solving. *Journal of Child Psychology and Psychiatry, 17,* 89–100.

Wright, J. L. (1985). *Informatics in the education of young children.* Presented at IFIP Conference on Informatics and Teacher Training, July, 1984.

Wright, J. L. (1990a, April). *The use of digitized images in developing software for young children.* Presentation at symposium: "Crayons, Cartwheels, and Computers," AERA.

Wright, J. L. (1990b). *Transferrence of thinking skills.* Unpublished correspondence with Dr. Linda Tsantis, July, 1990.

Wright, J. L. (1990c). *Thinking skills development in preschoolers.* Unpublished correspondence with Dr. Linda Tsantis, July, 1990.

Wright, J. L., & Samaras, A. (1986). Play worlds and microworlds. In P. F. Campbell & G. Fein (Eds.), *Young children and microcomputers* (pp. 73–86). Englewood Cliffs, NJ: Prentice Hall.

Wright, J. L., Shade, D. D., Thouvenelle, S., & Davidson, J. (1989). New directions in software development for young children. *Journal of Computing in Childhood Education, 1*(1), 45–58.

Zurn, M. R. (1987). *A comparison of kindergartners' handwritten and word processor generated writing.* Unpublished dissertation, Georgia State University, Atlanta, GA.

# Introduction to
# Chapter 15

*Robert Glaser, University Professor of
Psychology and Education, and Director,
Learning Research and Development Center,
University of Pittsburgh*

Modern research on cognitive development and on the
nature of competence in domains of knowledge and skill has
reinforced the view that learning is essentially a process of
knowledge construction in which the learner must play an
active role. As a consequence, environments for learning
should assist an ongoing knowledge-building process and
the sharpen abilities that enable it. Palincsar and Klenk's
report, in this chapter, of an important case study of the
implementation of a innovative model of literacy instruction
clarifies the extent to which classroom programs of intentional, self-regulated learning are congruent with this theoretical perspective. The reported gains in reading and writing competence made by children identified as learning
disabled who were afforded the opportunities of the Reciprocal Teaching procedure can be seen as confirming that
students attain higher levels of competency where the environment is conducive to their directing and being
"accountable" for their progress. Palincsar and Klenk emphasize "the tenet that every child has the right to a level of
literacy . . . that equip(s) individuals with the tools to engage not only in the cognitive activity of thinking, reasoning, and problem solving but also in the uniquely human
activity of reflection, creation, and enjoyment." The outcomes, moreover, of their study are a very pointed assault
on an idea that recent research makes untenable: the view
that basic skills should be taught first—and probably represent the sole reasonable aim for students who can be expected to attain only limited levels of literacy—while the
higher levels of engagement required for reasoning, inquiry,

293

and problem solving should be demanded only of able children, and at later stages of instruction.

Changes in educational practice of the kind described in this case study will be the heart of the matter, if we are to meet the challenge of making our educational system responsive to advancing knowledge of the learning process. Many traditional teaching methodologies are not adequately responsive to our best understandings of how thinking and learning proceed. Modern knowledge of cognition makes it clear that diadatic, academically decontextualized, classroom objectives must be reconsidered. Successful teaching takes as its objective fostering constructive reasoning on part of the learner. All reading, even of very simple and elementary texts, as Palincsar and Klenk show, requires that the reader engage in processes of inference and elaboration. The same is true of writing. Successful learning of mathematics and science as well, even of facts and standard procedures, depends upon students' formation of ideas which link and integrate information. Good learners of all levels of ability and achievement do not just absorb information, they pose questions and build trial explanations for themselves, seeking to construct a coherent account of why a particular problem solution works or why a series of events turned out as it did. This knowledge manipulation activity of children and adults disallows the assumption that effective learning proceeds from acquiring lower level knowledge and skills through practice, with little thought, to engagement in the higher levels in which thinking and reasoning finally play a role. Reasoning and thinking to attain knowledge and skill should be central to school learning from its outset—as this study indicates—from kindergarten through high school and with children of all ability levels.

As we move toward a new conception of schooling, instruction should be grounded in the notion that thinking is a generative activity—a means for continued growth of knowledge and skill. What is required in school must be viewed by the student and the teacher as competencies of enablement. The subject areas of schooling should give equal attention to skills, knowledge, and the dispositions to learning that are essential to future learning. The purpose of students' learning to read is to enable them to learn from reading. Mastery of reading creates a new tool for learning and thinking. Reading, as an enabling skill, should make students aware that they can use what they know, as they read, to comprehend the meaning of the text and, then, can extend their knowledge by organizing and communicating their thoughts in discussions and through writing. The essence of enabling competencies is their providing entry into new ways of knowing.

Given these possibilities, Palincsar and Klenk's study takes on the central task of schooling in the 1990s—that is, challenging traditional practices with conceptions that are grounded in current knowledge of learning so that students have the benefit of new instructional approaches. In their instructional program, Palincsar and Klenk have considered how: learning to read can be presented as a task with meaningful outcomes; students can develop learning strategies; children can be assisted in performing cognitively complex activities before they are skilled at them, so that they can model and practice them; they can engage in opportunities in which they are motivated to reason in order to build their own knowledge. Their program of research is an outstanding example of the reconceptualization of classroom activity which will be necessary to fostering the levels of literacy that recent advances in our scientific understanding of learning and thinking now bring within reach.

# 15

# Examining and Influencing Contexts for Intentional Literacy Learning

Annemarie Sullivan Palincsar
Laura Klenk
*University of Michigan*

As we teeter on the edge of the 21st century, "the quality of thinking," which is the centerpiece of this volume, has become the centerpiece of school-reform dialogue. The literacy domain is a fitting one in which to illustrate the prominent issues and nature of this dialogue. Literacy has typically been associated with the ability to read and write; in fact, reading was initially valued principally for mastery of a very limited set of prescribed religious texts (Resnick & Resnick, 1977). It was not until the 1920s that the emphasis on reading for the purpose of deriving meaning from text emerged as an aspiration for reading instruction. With each decade since, the agenda attending literacy instruction has been re-defined to include increasingly lofty goals. Today, the goals of reading and writing instruction include: "high literacy" or the pursuit of learning that is beyond that of adapting to the goals of the prevailing culture (Bereiter & Scardamalia, 1987) and "critical literacy" or the ability to use reading and writing to exceed the demands that are associated with minimum competency (McGinley & Tierney, 1989).

At the heart of these discussions is the conception that the purpose of literacy instruction is to equip individuals with the tools to engage not only in the cognitive activity of thinking, reasoning, and problem solving but also in the uniquely human activity of reflection, creation, and enjoyment. Integral to the dialogue regarding the goals of literacy instruction is the tenet that every child has the right to this level of literacy, not simply "bright children," "normally achieving children," or the children of majority culture or middle class families.

In this chapter, we assume the position that essential to the attainment of the quality of thinking inherent in critical literacy is the ability to engage in intentional self-regulated learning with an awareness of the variables that influence learning and an ability to assume control of one's learning activity (Bereiter & Scardamalia, 1989). It is not the teaching of specific knowledge alone but rather the cultivation of general abilities that will facilitate learning throughout life and in an array of settings. Furthermore, these skills and knowledge cannot be taught independently of the contexts in which they are used; but rather, it is not until one attends to contextualized practice that learners can tune these skills to the situations in which they are useful and find the motivation to practice them (Resnick, 1989).

Soltis (1981) has argued that a different view of knowledge will underwrite a different view of educating. In the first portion of this chapter, we discuss the values and modes of traditional schooling. In the second section, we present some of our past research exploring an alternative context for teaching students to engage in intentional learning from text, and in the final section, we discuss our current research in which we are attempting to introduce a different view of educating into a system firmly entrenched in traditional views of schooling.

## TRADITIONAL SCHOOLING IN THE ELEMENTARY GRADES

At the preschool level, learning is primarily incidental in nature—the young child is not generally expected to learn for the express purpose of recalling and using information. Rather, it is assumed that learning is the naturally occurring product of the child's interaction with his or her environment. In fact, throughout our lives, learning occurs naturally as we attempt to make sense of new experiences and the new information that we encounter. With the shift into the elementary grades, however, there are new demands for the child to organize and structure his or her learning for the purpose of recalling what has been learned (Vygotsky, 1978). Ideally, schooling should serve to bring knowledge and the processes by which it is acquired under the control of the learner; to promote the intentional learning that enables the learner to make connections between knowledge acquired in and out of school.

To the extent that we define this learning in terms of the basic skills of reading, writing, and mathematics, there is considerable evidence that elementary schools are successful. However, to the extent that we define this learning in terms of conceptual understanding and the ability and inclination to use reading, writing, and mathematics for the purpose of problem-solving activity, both in and out of school, the picture is less encouraging. The most recent reports from the National Assessment of Educational Progress provide an overview of this picture (Applebee, Langer, & Mullis, 1985, 1986). The NAEP findings indicate that in both reading and writing, the achievement of language minority students has increased over the past 15 years; while White students were still performing better, the gap has been substantially narrowed between White and minority students. However, the results also suggest that in reading and writing, neither of the groups is performing well. The improvement reflected in the results is a consequence of greater numbers of students doing well at the lower levels of competence in reading and writing. As the texts become more complex and as the questions require more thoughtful literate thinking, comprehension plummets. For example, the 1988 NAEP results indicated that only 42% of the 17 year-olds tested could locate, summarize, and explain relatively complicated materials, while only 5% could synthesize specialized material. Similarly, in writing, while students can write simple stories and reports, they seem unable to explain and defend a position or mount a persuasive argument.

To understand this phenomenon, it is useful to consider the features of grade school education that might contribute to this profile. We will discuss: (1) the traditional views of teacher and student roles; (2) the instruction of basic skills before understanding; (3) the emphasis on the products vs. the processes of learning; and, (4) differential instruction.

## Traditional Views of Teacher and Student Roles

In many respects there is a sameness depicted by observational classroom studies conducted throughout the 70s and 80s. Whether observing in mathematics (e.g., Peterson & Fennema, 1985; Stodolsky, 1988) reading (e.g., Anderson, Evertson, & Brophy, 1979), or writing (Freedman, 1987), researchers portray classrooms in which children work alone, seldom interacting with their peers, seldom initiating learning activity. Learning is directed almost exclusively by the teacher. Cohen (1987) has referred to this practice as "ancient instructional inheritance"; while teachers are active, students are passive; and while teachers are the purveyors of truth, learners are the accumulators of a body of knowledge that is objective and stable.

This view of teaching and learning stands in direct contrast to the experiences hypothesized to lead to intentional learning. Implicit in the model of intentional learning is recognition that knowledge exists only in the mind of the knower and is the result of construction or reconstruction through a process of making sense of new information in terms of what one already knows. The intentional learner is one who feels in charge of learning rather than one who expects to be directed by teachers or others.

## Basic Skills Before Understanding

A second powerful trend observed in grade schools is the focus on basic skills before attending to higher level understanding. In reading, this is manifested by an emphasis on decoding before comprehension; in mathematics, it leads to an emphasis on automaticity in the application of algorithms before a focus on conceptual understanding of number; in writing, it is illustrated in the attention paid to the mechanics of handwriting and spelling before communication, rather than in the service of communication.

What is particularly disconcerting with regard to this trend is the impoverished understanding of knowledge and competence to which it can lead, from the perspective of the teacher as well as the learner. For example, teachers who believe that basic skills are prerequisite to meaningful experiences with literacy are unlikely to plan these experiences for their students and may also be unlikely to evaluate the extent to which the child is able to use the basic skills to achieve meaningful ends. In turn, students begin to acquire unusual notions about the means and ends of literacy instruction. An 8-year-old student recently explained to us that to become a good writer one should, "hope and hold your pencil right."

## Emphasis on the Products Rather Than Processes of Learning

Perhaps as a consequence of the emphasis on decontextualized learning of basic skills, there is little evidence that students receive explicit instruction regarding the strategies or heuristics that promote intentional learning (cf. Duffy, Roehler et al., 1987). Yet, there is considerable evidence that even capable students do not acquire a repertoire of strategies that they can engage opportunistically and flexibly without considerable instruction and guided practice (Brown, Bransford, Ferrara, & Campione, 1983; Schoenfeld, 1985).

For example, one hallmark of the critical reader is a repertoire of strategies for gaining knowledge from text and simultaneously monitoring levels of understanding (Brown, 1980; Paris, Wasik, & Turner, in press). These "metacognitive skills of reading" enable students to: (a) clarify the purposes of reading; (b) make use of relevant background knowledge; (c) allocate attention to focus on major content at the expense of trivia; (d) critically evaluate content for internal consistency and compatibility with prior knowledge and common sense; (e) monitor to ensure that comprehension is occurring; and, (f) draw and test inferences.

These complex problem-solving strategies do not emerge through the teaching of constituent subskills. For example, Brown and Palincsar (1987) conducted a study in which children were taught in an explicit and carefully sequenced manner, the rules for summarization: locating topic sentences, deleting what was redundant or trivial, naming lists, steps, or categories of information, and inventing topic sentences (Kintsch & VanDijk, 1978). While these 7th graders successfully learned these rules and were able to apply them in isolation, this learning did not make a difference in the children's independent comprehension of text. It is actually not that difficult to teach students strategies; what is difficult is teaching strategies so that they make a difference; and such that students will enlist the strategies for the purpose of enhancing their understanding of text in an array of situations. This brings us to the thorny issue of transfer.

To achieve transfer it is necessary to attend to the context in which instruction and practice of the strategies occur; transfer is likely to the extent that there are common elements between the situation in which students are learning strategies and the situations in which these strategies would be useful (Brown et al., 1983); for example, in the case of summarizing, the reading of coherent and extended text for authentic purposes of retelling what one learned in the reading.

## Differential Instruction

Observational research indicates that the fragmentation and incoherence discussed in the preceding sections are particularly characteristic of practice in special education and remedial settings, as well as in the instruction of children at risk for academic difficulty (also see Pogrow, Chapter 5 of this volume). In fact, it would appear that the artificial distinction drawn between basic skills and higher-order skills, may lead to targeting basic skill instruction for younger and disadvantaged learners while reserving the higher-order or reasoning skills for older and more successful students.

Allington (1986), Hiebert (1983), and McGill-Franzen and Allington (1990), among others, have demonstrated that: (1) "individualized instruction" often translates into children working alone on low-level skill tasks; (2) remedial materials are not comprised of interrelated activities; and (3) the reading and writing of extended texts for purposes of achieving or conveying meaning rarely appear in the lessons of these learners. Thus, there is a sense in which the problems of children who arrive at school without the skills of conventional reading and writing, and who experience difficulty attaining these skills, are exacerbated by the nature of the instruction they receive.

## RECONCEPTUALIZATIONS OF SCHOOLING

Theoretical and empirical explorations of the last two decades have led to alternative conceptions of environments that foster intentional learning. Features of these environments include: (1) the presentation of tasks in goal-embedded contexts; (2) instruction for the purpose of developing strategic conceptions of reading, writing, and mathematics, rather than mastery of isolated steps of a strategy; and, (3) situations where social interactions have a prominent role to play. One model of instruction whose development was guided by these features is Reciprocal Teaching (Brown & Palincsar, 1989; Palincsar & Brown, 1984, 1989).

### Reciprocal Teaching

Reciprocal Teaching is a procedure featuring guided practice in the application of four concrete strategies for the purposes of understanding text. Students and teachers take turns leading discussions about shared text, which they have read silently or aloud, or have listened to (depending upon their decoding ability).

These are not, however, open-ended discussions. The dialogue leader (adult or child) begins the discussion by *asking questions* about the content of the text. The group discusses these questions, raises additional questions, and, in the case of disagreement or misunderstanding, rereads the text. While questions are used to stimulate discussion, *summarizing* is used to identify the gist of what has been read and discussed, and to prepare students to proceed to the next portion of the text. Once again, there is discussion for the purpose of achieving consensus regarding the summary. The third strategy, *clarification,* is used opportunistically for the purpose of restoring meaning when a concept, word, or phrase has been misunderstood or is unfamiliar to someone in the group. Finally, the discussion leader provides the opportunity for *predictions* regarding upcoming content. Group members generate their predictions based on their prior knowledge of the text as well as clues that are provided in the text itself (e.g., embedded questions, headings).

These particular strategies were selected based on research suggesting that they are the kinds of strategic activities in which successful readers routinely engage when learning from text (Bereiter & Bird, 1985), but poor readers fail to use (Garner, 1987). The strategies provide the occasion for making explicit and visible the mental processes useful to constructing meaning for text. In addition, these strategies improve comprehension and provide the alert reader with the opportunity to monitor for understanding. Finally, these strategies support a discussion—providing an interactive and socially supportive context in which to learn about intentional learning from text.

The role of the teacher in reciprocal teaching is to scaffold the involvement of the learners in the discussion by providing the explanation, modeling, support, and feedback that will—in time—enable the full participation of the students in the dialogue (Palincsar, 1986).

The majority of the research on reciprocal teaching has been conducted in reading and listening comprehension instruction, by general, remedial, and special educators. Since 1981, when the research program began, 287 middle school students and 366 1st- to 3rd-grade children have taken part. Generally, the instruction has been conducted in small groups (averaging 6 to 8). Students entering the studies scored approximately 30% correct on independent measures of text comprehension and participated in the intervention for a minimum of 25 instructional days. The criterion used to determine success was the attainment of an independent score of 75–80% correct on four out of five consecutively administered measures of comprehension, assessing recall of text, ability to draw inferences, ability to state the gist of material read, and application of knowledge acquired from the text to a novel situation. Using this criterion, approximately 80% of both the primary and middle school students were judged successful. Furthermore, these gains have been observed to maintain for up to 6 months to a year following instruction (Brown & Palincsar, 1982; Palincsar & Brown, 1984, 1989).

In typical reciprocal teaching research, children have read an array of unrelated texts, drawn largely from readers and trade magazines for children. This selection of text provided little opportunity for cumulative reference and the acquisition and use of knowledge over time. In the most recent studies of reciprocal teaching (Brown, Palincsar, Ryan, & Slattery, work in progress), the dialogues were used to learn simple science concepts related to animal survival themes such as camouflage, mimicry, protection from the elements, extinction, etc. These themes were represented across the texts with which the groups were working. The students explained and justified their understandings of these themes during the course of the reciprocal teaching discussions. Twenty days of such discussions led to dramatic improvement in both comprehension processes (as assessed by the independent comprehension measures), as well as thematic understanding (as assessed by the content of the discussions, as well as independent measures of the content). The children were asked to sort pictures of animals into the six themes. While their initial sorting was based on physical characteristics of the animals, following the dialogues, the students sorted the animals correctly, by theme, 85% of the time. In addition, when presented novel examples, they could identify the theme and justify why the animal was an exemplar of that theme. Reciprocal teaching enabled the children both to learn a body of coherent and useful knowledge as well as a repertoire of strategies useful to learning content on their own.

In this section, we reviewed the reciprocal teaching research program for the purpose of illustrating an instructional procedure that provides a social and supportive context in which children learn the use of strategies for the purpose of constructing meaning and monitoring comprehension of text. In the next section, we present a case study taken from our current research program, in which we are exploring the literacy instruction of primary grade students in a self-contained classroom for students identified as learning disabled.

## IMPLEMENTING A DIFFERENT MODEL OF LITERACY INSTRUCTION IN A TRADITIONAL SETTING: A CASE STUDY[1]

In this case study, we report on the process of introducing meaningful and strategic literacy instruction in a special education primary-grade classroom where the majority of students had yet to acquire conventional literacy, despite

[1]This case study is drawn from a larger project entitled, Transforming the Learning Disabled into Self-Regulated Learners: The Development and Implementation of a Sustainable Early Literacy Curriculum, that is funded by a grant from the Office of Special Education Programs (#H023C90076). This grant has been awarded to the first author and Carol Sue Englert (co-principal investigator), Taffy Raphael, and James Gavelek.

their ages. The purpose of the study was to examine the teacher's and childrens' responses to instruction designed to promote intentional learning by: (1) presenting literacy tasks in goal-embedded contexts; (2) developing strategic conceptions of reading and writing; and, (3) designing activities that fostered social interactions among the students. A description of the setting and participants is followed by the presentation of a subset of events and a discussion regarding selected outcomes.

## The Setting

*The School.*    This study was conducted in a school district located on the outskirts of Detroit, where the local economy is still reeling from setbacks suffered by the auto industry in the early 1980s. Of the children who were enrolled in the Chapter I elementary (K–5) school, 74% were White and 26% were African-American.

The school climate is best captured by describing the qualities of its leadership. The principal promoted a nurturing, familial environment in the school. She was frequently observed in classrooms, sitting beside children and assisting them with seatwork, making inquiries about their academic progress, or giving them recognition for their accomplishments. She was supportive of her teachers and appeared to approach her role as an advocate for children and teachers.

*The Classroom.*    The classroom in which we conducted this case study was selected due to the teacher's willingness to participate as well as for its representativeness as a setting for children having school-related difficulty. Twelve children were assigned to this class, and all were eligible, according to state criteria (emphasizing a disparity between projected success in school and actual academic achievement) to receive special education services for the learning disabled.

The children in this class represented a heterogeneous group whose school-related difficulties reflected an interaction among learner characteristics (physical and medical conditions, behavioral difficulties), familial background (economically disadvantaged, single-parent homes), and school history (poor attendance). These interactions are commonly noted in special education populations (Mehan, Hertwich, & Miehls, 1985). Specific problems for which the children were referred included emotional and/or behavioral difficulty, language delay and speech impairments due to temporary hearing loss, and poor academic achievement in kindergarten and 1st grade.

The children ranged in age from 6 to 8 years. There were 7 White and 5 African-American children in the class. As is typical of special education settings, boys outnumbered girls; in this case, 9 to 3. Eight of the children remained in this setting for the entire school day, joining age appropriate peers in general education programs for physical education, music, art, and recess. The remaining four children were mainstreamed into general education classes for varying amounts of time, and did not participate in this study.

The children were assessed to determine reading and writing achievement at the outset of the study. Two of the 7 children were able to recognize almost all the letters of the alphabet. Four of the children could read a few sight words, and were reading from a preprimer. The writing assessment showed that three of the children could write in sentences with some conventional spellings. Three of the children used preconventional forms of of writing such as random letter strings, patterned letter strings, and invented spellings. One child refused to do anything but copy environmental print during the initial assessment.

Their teacher was a White male whose 8 years in education have been spent teaching in this self-contained setting. The teacher considered himself a behavioral specialist, and his overriding concerns in the classroom were for behavior management and classroom control. Instructional concerns were rarely addressed by the teacher either in his daily routines or in the remarks he shared with the researchers. He believed that his students benefited most from a highly structured classroom environment and adherence to strict routine. The emphasis on structure and routine was clearly noted in the daily class program. The teacher began each school day with an activity called, "Morning News." He would begin the story by identifying a topic for the day related to some event of interest to the children (e.g., birthdays, sporting events, special school activities, etc.) and solicited the children's help to complete several sentences about the topic. The teacher printed these sentences on the chalkboard, where they remained for the children to copy later in the day. The teacher justified the Morning News activity with both behavioral and academic objectives. In line with his concern for behavior management, he felt that Morning News was a constructive way to settle the children into the class routine and provide an "emotional outlet." Academically, it was useful for instruction in spelling, capitalization, punctuation, and it provided the children with opportunities to generate and recognize complete sentences, all skills which the teacher espoused to be important prerequisites to learning to write.

Although he identified instructional objectives for the Morning News activity and faithfully included it in the daily schedule, little instruction was ever observed during this activity. The teacher never questioned the effectiveness of this routine, even though he indicated that, in his 8 years as a special education teacher, none of his students had ever mastered these prerequisite skills well enough to benefit from writing instruction beyond copying from the board.

Following the morning news and flag pledge, the rest of the morning was devoted to reading instruction and seatwork. The teacher met with the children individually or in small groups to work from their basal readers and a special phonics curriculum (Explode the Code, Hall & Price, 1976–78). Children not called to the reading group worked on their own to complete a set of duplicated language arts and mathematics worksheets. In a fashion that is typical of special education and remedial settings (McGill-Franzen & Allington, 1990), the content of these folders was generally identical for each child. An aide in the room was available to respond to children's requests for help. Since there was little instruction regarding the worksheets, and the level of reading required in the worksheets exceeded the decoding skills of the children, they frequently requested assistance, principally regarding the directions to follow in completing these worksheets. The children were rewarded for completing their worksheets with stickers, which they placed on a chart to display their daily accomplishments.

The children were grouped according to their placement in a basal series reader. Levels ranged from pre-primer to the grade 1 reader. A significant part of the children's instruction was drawn from the phonics program that had been adopted for use in the special education classrooms of this district. Phonics instruction was followed by round-robin reading during which the children took turns reading aloud and, following each page of reading, responded to the teacher's questions. Discussions with the teacher suggested that his aspirations in reading were generally at the performative level.

Afternoons in this class were less predictable than were the mornings. Lunch was generally followed by a whole group activity, such as watching a filmstrip, listening to a story, or handwriting instruction. Mathematics instruction occurred in the afternoon and some amount of time was usually reserved for children to complete their morning board or seat work.

The teacher recognized the considerable routine and "sameness" in his class, causing him a degree of ambivalence. On the one hand, he believed, without reservation, that the high degree of structure and routine were essential ingredients for successful classroom management and learning. On the other hand, he recognized shortcomings in both of these areas. He was perplexed, for example, that the children were less compliant for visitors (such as the counselor, special teachers, or researchers) who attempted to work with the class. He expressed his personal dissatisfaction with the tedium of the routine, even remarking, "Boredom is a deadly enemy in this classroom." Indeed, this routine and "sameness" became our serious enemies as we attempted to introduce a different model of literacy instruction in this classroom. The children, accustomed to the comfort and security of these predictable routines, reacted with reluctance and even outright resistance as we introduced change.

The teacher's conceptions of writing and reading were reflected in his students' responses to questions about reading and writing. For example, when his students were interviewed regarding the purposes of reading and writing, they were unable to identify any reasons beyond completing the work in class (e.g., "We do math work with a pencil"; "Writing is when we copy the morning news."). Occasions the students identified for using reading and writing were confined to the completion of worksheets and board work. When asked to characterized "good" readers and writers, representative responses included: "Good writers go fast;" "Good writers have strong muscles so that they can do cursive' " "Good readers don't make too many mistakes"; and, "Good readers read fast and loud."

Following 3 months of observations and interviews with the teacher and children, we were permitted to teach the 8 children who were in the classroom during the afternoon, two afternoons a week, 1 hour each session, for the remainder of the school year. In our initial discussions with the teacher, we enlisted his assistance observing the children's responses to the instruction, critiquing the lessons, and helping to refine them to better meet the needs of his students. Since this particular teacher placed considerable emphasis on his students "gaining control of themselves" (used exclusively in a behavioral sense), we identified the overarching goal of this instruction to be placing the students in control of their learning as well as their behavior. The teacher agreed to remain in the room during instruction, observe and comment on the instruction, and suggest how it could be adapted or modified.

We used the following characteristics as a template for designing the lessons that we would implement. First, we wanted the children to experience four levels of literacy: (cf. Wells, Chang, & Maher, in press): (1) performative (decoding, printing); (2) functional (interpersonal exchange); (3) informational (communication of knowledge); and, (4) epistemic (creative, exploratory, and evaluative). We planned experiences in which these levels of literacy would be experienced simultaneously to enrich the children's conceptions of literacy and to provide a broader range of thinking and reasons for wanting to learn to read and write. Second, we wanted to instruct, model, and guide students in the use of specific thinking strategies that would enable them to engage in these levels of literacy. Third, we wanted to select themes and topics that, in addition to capturing the interest and attention of the children, would provide occasions for children to acquire, organize, and use knowledge in and out of school over time. Finally, we wanted to plan occasions for the children to think and collaborate with the teacher and with one another in meaningful uses of literacy. We have selected several events to illustrate how these goals translated into activities and to discuss the outcomes of these activities.

*Getting Started.*    We chose to initiate our instructional encounters by focusing on the topic, Animals, specifically Pets, since this would personalize the topic for most of the children and promote their use of background knowledge. An important goal was to convince the children to recognize themselves and others as sources of knowledge and to teach them how to use this knowledge. Therefore, in our introduction of *Pets* as a topic, we explained that we knew the children already knew a great deal about pets, information that would be helpful to them in their reading and writing. The teacher[2] recorded the children's ideas on the board: "dogs bite," "cats lick," "cats stink," "dogs bark," "bears growl," "lions growl" . . . While few of the children could read these ideas, they were excellent at recalling them and remembering whose idea each was.

Because the children had not distinguished pets from other animals, we returned to the issue of "pets" and "not pets" in a subsequent lesson. The teacher

---

[2]In discussions of the instruction, the "teacher" refers to one of the two researchers rather than the classroom teacher.

made two columns on a chart and asked the children to suggest animals that were pets and those that were not pets. The children quickly generated a list of animals, all of which they identified as pets. Finally, "snake" came up. There was controversy over the proper classification for snake, so the teacher placed it in both columns, and suggested that we would return to discuss snake. After identifying a few examples of "not pets," we returned to the two lists. Several animals showed up on both lists, leading to a discussion of the characteristics that determine whether an animal makes a good pet. The children generated the following list to help make decisions about what makes a good pet: "You can keep it." "It will not hurt you." "It is the right size." For these children, the experience of sustaining a discussion about one topic and using their knowledge in a disciplined manner was a challenge to which we returned repeatedly.

*Integrating Oral Language, Reading, and Writing Experiences.*    In each lesson we attempted to incorporate opportunities for the students to integrate the topic-related discussions with reading and writing about the theme. For example, following the discussion about the characteristics of pets, the children heard the story, *Clifford, the Big Red Dog* (Bridwell, 1985). To enhance the children's concepts about print (Clay, 1975; Mason & Allen, 1986), we began the reading by calling the children's attention to features of text and stories (e.g., identifying the genre, author, illustrator, etc.). In addition, we modeled identifying a purpose for reading, with the intention that, in time, the children would identify their own reasons for reading text. In the case of *Clifford,* the class was listening to identify the various ways in which Emily Elizabeth cared for her pet, Clifford. The teacher began to model making predictions regarding upcoming events in the story and the children readily joined in. The problems created by Clifford's unwieldy size render the *Clifford* stories highly predictable. The children's familiarity with this character drew an enthusiastic response during the reading. At the conclusion of the reading, the group summarized orally, via a short list, the various ways in which Elizabeth cared for her dog. *Clifford* was such a success that we decided to try a shared-book experience using other books in the *Clifford* series. Each pair of children was given a new *Clifford* book and, following a discussion about the usefulness of pictures for telling a story (even if one does not know all the words), the children practiced telling the story to one another in preparation for assuming the "reader's chair" and sharing their story with the remainder of the class.

To achieve the kinds of social interactions we had deemed important for these children's literacy learning, it was necessary for them to experience a number of participation structures with which they were unfamiliar. For these children, the peer collaboration and reader's chair represented novel participation structures (Cazden, 1986) and, as might be anticipated, led to conflicts over sharing the book with one another, deciding how to divide the retelling and sustaining the attention of peers during the retelling (accomplished by some children through voice control and showing the pictures). While these discussions met the objective of increasing "problem-solving," recalling the importance the teacher attached to order in the classroom, the behavior problems that sometimes arose in conjunction with these activities had the unfortunate effect of clouding his perception of the value of the activity itself. This effect could have contributed to the fact that the teacher, for the remainder of the school year, regarded the lessons as interesting and useful supplements to his curriculum but not as something likely to supplant his curriculum.

The *Clifford* stories also provided the basis for the children's first writing experience in which they generated their own text. The children were asked to write letters to Emily Elizabeth about their favorite Clifford story. The teacher explained that she was going to show them how she would write her letter and that she wanted the children to help her. We used this opportunity to model the process of spelling words from recall as well as using invented spellings. When it was time to hand the writing activity over to the children, there was a palpable sense of anxiety; one child began crying, several others became angry when they realized that the Clifford books would not be returned to them, rendering it impossible for them to copy. However, with our assistance, each child, using either letter strings or patterns, sometimes in combination with words they knew, generated some text and an illustration. One child refused our aid and insisted on copying from environmental print.

On this occasion, and every subsequent time when the children wrote, we collected their writings, typed them—editing for spelling—and returned them with the edited copies attached to their original sheets. This proved to be a very successful means of scaffolding both the children's reading and writing efforts. There was an intense interest on the part of children to learn the words that they had written in their stories. They engaged in repeated readings of their own text in preparation for coming to the front of the room and assuming the author's chair to share their text with the class. Opportunities to read their own writing became the highlight of our sessions with the children and soon they expected to have sharing time during each session. In addition, words that appeared frequently in their writings (e.g., "like") became part of their spelling vocabulary.

*Providing Occasions for Intentional Learning.* One of the striking characteristics of this classroom was the scarcity of opportunities for the children to engage in intentional learning and learning how to learn. In our experiences, informational text provided multiple opportunities to teach and guide intentional learning. For example, when using a book about frogs, we began by reminding the children that they had recently read a book about rabbits and asking them what kinds of information they would expect to learn about frogs. This was not a fruitful question, so we asked the children what they already knew about frogs. This led to a smattering of ideas (frogs swim and like water). Shown the cover of the book, with a photograph of a frog, the children had numerous ideas related to the color, size, and eyes of the frog, and where frogs are found. The teacher then began reading, a page at a time, stopping occasionally to remark on what she was learning from this book and relating the new information to knowledge she already had regarding frogs. By the third page, the children began joining in, extracting and paraphrasing information from these brief segments of text. At the conclusion of the story, the students were asked to help recall what we had learned about frogs, so that we could add to the list of information we already knew about frogs. As the children raised various points, many of them prompted by returning to photos that accompanied the text, the teacher began to map their ideas (e.g., placing descriptors of the frogs' eggs under the children's sentence, "Frogs lay eggs").

We placed considerable emphasis on communicating to the children that they were capable of learning from print—even though they were not yet conventional readers—by listening to text, studying the pictures from children's nature magazines and trade books, and sharing newspapers covering familiar topics (e.g., coverage of local sports events, Isaah Thomas delivering a slam-dunk). From our observations, these were the first school experiences in which these students were assumed to be learning and for which they were held accountable.

*Cognitive Bootstrapping.*    Cognitive bootstrapping refers to the practice of approaching an instructional activity as though the children had a firm grasp of prerequisite skills or knowledge to engage in that activity when, indeed, the skills and knowledge may be quite limited. Cognitive bootstrapping with these primary children can be illustrated in the writing instruction we conducted. As we have mentioned, writing for these children required a degree of risk-taking that some children found uncomfortable while others found downright frightening. We first asked each child to talk about what they wanted to write. When the child reached a decision, we would ask, "How will you begin?" We proceeded to repeat the child's own words, encouraging him or her to "write what you hear." For some children, it was enough to get one sound per word. With others, who demonstrated greater phonemic awareness and letter knowledge, we would continue, "What else do you hear?" As the children became accustomed to writing on their own, our prompts decreased and the nature of support we provided changed. When children asked, "How do you spell ———?", our response, instead of "What do you hear?" might be, "What do you have so far?" In this way, the children learned that we anticipated their private efforts to solve the sounding out of words. In this manner, children, who did not yet even recognize all the letters of the alphabet were using written language to convey their opinions, important ideas, and requests for information. By conceptualizing instruction as cognitive bootstrapping and the teaching process as scaffolding, these children were able to experience the performative, functional, informational, and epistemic[3] levels of literacy concurrently.

---

[3]Even with the brief, one or two sentence, writing that these children generated, they were observed to engage in criticism of their own work. One child, realizing that he had repeated a statement in his composition decided, "That's stupid!" and erased the repetitious line.

*Contextualized Practice.*   We mentioned earlier that the routines represented in the mindless completion of seatwork frequently threatened our attempts to help the children reconceptualize literacy learning. Their single-minded pursuits to *finish* their folder meant that our activities were often regarded as intrusions. We were, after all, coming during a time of the day that was generally designated for completing seatwork. Furthermore, we were striving to create a culture of sense-making (cf. Lampert, 1986) in a classroom where previously sense-making assumed little prominence. This meant that the contexts in which we presented this literacy learning assumed particular importance. Rogoff (1984) has suggested that the context of cognitive functioning includes, not only the physical objects, task characteristics and people present, but also the less immediate social context in which the task and problem solver are embedded. Each of these features were considered when planning the contextualized practice.

Interestingly, while the children found the animal theme to be somewhat interesting, their preferred topic was people—themselves, their families, other people in the school. This led us to design activities that would accommodate this interest. For example, the children assembled a class book entitled "Our School," for the purpose of informing new students about life at their school. To prepare the book, they wrote a chapter on the school rules, took photos of their favorite people/places in the school, and wrote about these people and places. They wrote letters to family members and designed interviews, providing an authentic occasion for teaching question-generating as a strategy.

## The Outcomes

Space precludes a lengthy description of the outcomes of our 34 lessons (over 4 months). Indeed, these lessons represented only a modest beginning to our goal of introducing an alternative conception of literacy learning that focused on teaching for generative thinking and intentional learning by: presenting tasks in goal-embedded contexts, instructing for the purpose of developing strategic conceptions of reading and writing, and elevating the role of social interactions in learning.

It is honest to suggest that we ended the school year with the "emergence" of outcomes; we saw a shift from procedural to epistemic questioning, an increase in the children's willingness to take risks with the content, a more intense interest in learning to read for self-generated text, the use of unsolicited writing for personal expression [Scot, returning from a trip to the office for disciplinary reasons, wrote "I hate [this] school." It was the most he had written in weeks!], and an interest in sharing and displaying their knowledge.

The most concrete illustrations of the changes we observed are found in the children's writing. Reproduced here are the beginning and end of year writing assessments completed by David. In each instance, David was asked to "write about something you like to do." In the first piece, David displayed age-appropriate, emergent knowledge of print (see Fig. 15.1). He used patterned letter strings to represent his message. The length of these letter strings corresponds to the length of the accompanying message. The sheer amount of writing indicates David's confidence in himself as a writer.

Over time, we witnessed a decrease in this confidence, as David came to regard accurate copying as a more legitimate form of writing. By the end of the school year, however, David demonstrated a more conventional knowledge of writing. His message is now expressed in a complete sentence (see Fig. 15.2). The patterned letter strings have been replaced by words. David's memory of conventional spellings, though not entirely accurate, is present (liek for like, two for to), and his confidence for inventing spellings for less common words is noted (fosentag for frozen tag).

These changes in David's writing are not significant in and of themselves. In fact, they suggest a pattern of development not unlike that observed in general education classes where children have opportunities to write. Rather, these observations are significant given the teacher's limited and limiting assumptions regarding his students' abilities to meet the "prerequisites" to meaningful writing.

Perhaps our greatest disappointment in this endeavor was how little we affected the beliefs and practices of the classroom teacher. When asked to describe the activities that we had conducted in his classroom, the teacher was most astute; he commented on the relationships that we were drawing between written and spoken language, on writing as a means of teaching reading, on the "child-

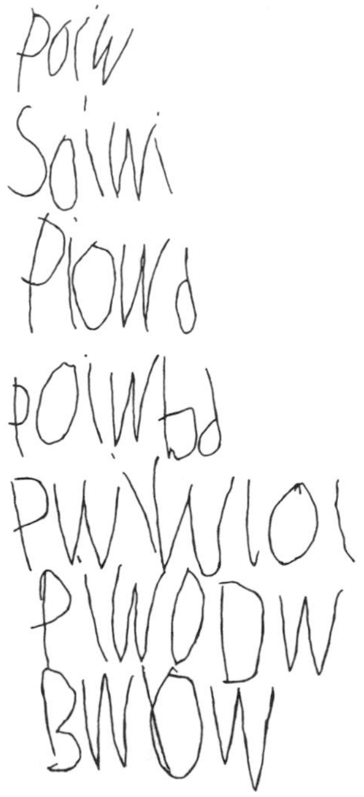

FIG. 15.1. David's writing sample from the fall of the year demonstrates emergent knowledge of writing as he uses patterned letter strings to represent his message. For each string of letters, David verbalized an activity that he enjoyed on the playground (e.g., "play with your friends," "play on the swings").

focused" nature of the activities, and on "project oriented" instruction. At the same time, he was hard-pressed to see how these activities might supplant his instructional program, commenting that—at best—they might supplement the curriculum ("They haven't been taught phonics yet.") He continued to maintain that we "ought to break it down into smaller chunks to make concepts functional for these children," and he expressed unease with the amount of "novelty" being introduced into the classroom; an unease which might be best interpreted in light of his concern with classroom and behavior management.

### Conclusion

There is little question that social change, the kind that will be necessary to reorient schools to valuing and teaching quality thinking, will require some combination of the technical and the political. In our own research program, we will continue to pursue the technical—asking questions about alternative ways of achieving cognitive bootstrapping, inquiring into the adaptation of an emergent literacy perspective (Teale & Sulzby, 1986) with children who have exceeded the chronological age typically associated with emergent literacy, exploring the role of teacher-researcher collaboration to find ways in which teachers can be better prepared to take an active role in promoting thinking and supporting intentional learning.

At the same time, we are convinced that these "technical" exploits will lead us into the political arena as well, examining the ways in which teachers and children are held accountable for the activities of classrooms, exploring the processes by which some children are deemed "different" and subsequently denied certain opportunities, and confronting the impediments and seeking the facilitators to change.

FIG. 15.2.   David's writing sample from the spring of the year demonstrates more conventional knowledge of writing; his message ("I like to play frozen tag") is now expressed in a complete sentence. The patterned letter strings have been replaced by words. He uses a combination of conventional and invented spellings.

# REFERENCES

Allington, R. (1986). Policy constraints and effective compensatory reading instruction: A review. In J. Hoffman (Ed.), *The effective teaching of reading: From research to practice* (pp. 261–289). Newark, DE: International Reading Association.

Anderson, L. M., Evertson, C., & Brophy, J. (1979). An experimental study of effective teaching in first-grade reading groups. *Elementary School Journal, 79,* 193–223.

Applebee, A. N., Langer, J. A., & Mullis, I. V. S. (1985). *The reading report card.* Princeton, NJ: Educational Testing Service.

Applebee, A. N., Langer, J. A., & Mullis, I. V. S. (1986). *Crossroads in American Education.* Princeton, NJ: Educational Testing Service.

Bereiter, C., & Bird, M. (1985). Use of thinking aloud in identification and teaching of reading comprehension strategies. *Cognition and Instruction, 2,* 131–156.

Bereiter, C., & Scardamalia, M. (1987). An attainable version of high literacy: Approaches to teaching higher-order skills in reading and writing. *Curriculum Inquiry, 17*(1), 9–30.

Bereiter, C. & Scardamalia, M. (1989). Intentional learning as a goal of instruction. In L. B. Resnick (Ed.), *Knowing, learning, and instruction: Essays in honor of Robert Glaser* (pp. 361–392), Hillsdale, NJ: Lawrence Erlbaum Associates.

Bridwell, N. (1985). *Clifford the Big Red Dog.* New York: Scholastic, Inc.

Brown, A. L. (1980). Metacognitive development and reading. In R. J. Spiro, B. C. Bruce, & W. Brewer (Eds.), *Theoretical issues in reading comprehension* (pp. 453–481). Hillsdale, NJ: Lawrence Erlbaum Associates.

Brown, A. L., Bransford, J. D., Ferrara, R. A., & Campione, J. C. (1983). Learning, remembering, and understanding. In J. Flavell & E. Markman (Eds.), *Handbook of child psychology* (4th ed.). *Cognitive development* (Vol. 3, pp. 515–629). New York: Wiley.

Brown, A. L., & Palincsar, A. S. (1982). Inducing strategic learning from texts by means of informed, self-control training. *Topics in Learning and Learning Disabilities, 2,*(1), 1–17.

Brown, A. L., & Palincsar, A. S. (1987). Reciprocal teaching of comprehension strategies: A natural history of one program for enhancing learning. In J. D. Day & J. Borkowski (Eds.), *Intelligence and exceptionality: New directions for theory, assessment and instructional practice* (pp. 81–132), Norwood, NJ: Ablex.

Brown, A. L., & Palincsar, A. S. (1989). Guided cooperative learning and individual knowledge acquisition. In L. Resnick (Ed.), *Knowing and Learning: Issues for a Cognitive Psychology of Learning. Essays in honor of Robert Glaser.* Hillsdale, NJ: Lawrence Erlbaum Associates.

Cazden, C. (1986). Classroom discourse. In M. Wittrock (Ed.), *Handbook of Research on Teaching.* New York: Macmillan.

Cohen, D. (1987, December). *Teaching practice: Plus que ca change . . .* Essay prepared for a Conference on Curriculum and Instruction, University of Chicago.

Clay, M. (1975). *What did I write?* Portsmouth, NH: Heinemann.

Duffy, G. G., Roehler, L. R., Sivan, E., Rackliffe, G., Book, C., Meloth, M. S., Vavrus, L. G., Wesselman, R., Putnam, J., & Bassiri, D. (1987). Effects of explaining the reasoning associated with using reading strategies. *Reading Research Quarterly, 22*(3), 347–368.

Freedman, S. W. (1987). *Response to student writing.* Research report no. 23. Urbana, IL: National Council of Teachers of English.

Garner, R. (1987). *Metacognition and reading comprehension.* Norwood: Ablex.

Hiebert, E. (1983). An examination of ability grouping for reading instruction. *Reading Research Quarterly, 18,* 231–255.

Kintch, W., & VanDijk, T. A. (1978). Toward a model of text comprehension and production. *Psychological Review, 85,* 363–394.

Lampert, M. (1986). Knowing, doing, and teaching multiplication. *Cognition and Instruction, 3*(4), 305–342.

Mason, J., & Allen, J. (1986). A review of emergent literacy with implications for research and practice in reading. In E. Rothkopf (Ed.), *Review of Research in Education* (Vol. 13). Washington, D.C.: American Education Research Association.

McGill-Franzen, A. M., & Allington, R. L. (1990). Comprehension and coherence: Neglected elements of literacy instruction in remedial and resource room services. *Journal of Reading, Writing, and Learning Disabilities, 6,* 149–180.

McGinley, W., & Tierney, R. J. (1989). Traversing the topical landscape. *Written Communication, 6*(3), 243–269.

Mehan, H., Hertweck, J. H., & Meihls, M. M. (1985). Handicapping the handicapped: Decision making in students' educational careers. New York: Academic Press.

Palincsar, A. S. (1986). The role of dialogue in providing scaffolded instruction. *Educational Psychologist, 21,* 73–98.

Palincsar, A. S., & Brown, A. L. (1984). Reciprocal teaching of comprehension-fostering and comprehension-monitoring activities. *Cognition and Instruction, 1*(2), 117–175.

Palincsar, A. A., & Brown, A. L. (1989). Instruction for self-regulated reading. In Resnick, L. B. & Klopfer, L. E. (Eds.), *Toward the thinking curriculum: Current cognitive research.* Alexandria, VA: ASCD.

Paris, S. G., Wasik, B. A., & Turner, J. C. (in press). The development of strategic readers. In P. D. Pearson (Ed.), *Handbook of reading research* (second edition). New York: Longman.

Peterson, P. L., & Fennema, E. (1985). Effective teaching, student engagement in classroom activities, and sex-related differences in learning mathematics. *American Educational Research Journal, 22,* 309–335.

Resnick, L. B. (1989). Introduction. In L. B. Resnick (Ed.), *Knowing, learning and instruction: Essays in honor of Robert Glaser* (pp. 1–14), Hillsdale, NJ: Lawrence Erlbaum Associates.

Resnick, D. P., & Resnick, L. B. (1977). The nature of literacy: An historical exploration. *Harvard Educational Review, 47*(3), 370–385.

Rogoff, B. (1984). Introduction: Thinking and learning in social context. In B. Rogoff & J. Lave (Eds.), *Everyday cognition: Its development in social context.* Cambridge, MA: Harvard University Press.

Schoenfeld, A. H. (1985). *Mathematical problem solving.* New York: Academic Press.

Soltis, J. F. (1981). Education and the concept of knowledge. In J. F. Soltis (Ed.), *Philosophy and education.* Eightieth Yearbook of the National Society for the Study of Education, Part I. Chicago, IL: University of Chicago Press.

Stodolsky, S. (1988). *The subject matter: Classroom activity in math and social studies.* Chicago: University of Chicago Press.

Teale, W., & Sulzby, E. (1986). Emergent literacy as a perspective for examining how young children become writers and readers. In W. Teale & E. Sulzby (Eds.), *Emergent literacy in writing and reading,* Norwood, NJ: Albex.

Vygotsky, L. S. (1978). *Mind in society: The development of higher psychological processes.* Cambridge, MA: Harvard University Press.

Wells, G., Chang, G. L., & Maher, A. (in press). Creating classroom communities of literate thinkers. In S. Sharan (Ed.), *Cooperative learning: Theory and Research.* New York: Praeger.

# Introduction to
# Chapter 16

*William H. Teale, The University of Texas at San Antonio, Co-editor,* Emergent Literacy: Writing and Reading, *and Editor,* Language Arts.

The past decade and a half has been a time of great activity in the area of early childhood literacy learning. The activity has taken two, often complementary, forms: basic research on early literacy development; and, study of innovative reading and writing curriculum and teaching practices for the early childhood classroom. From this work, we have seen that legitimate literacy learning begins very early for children in a society like ours. It has also become clear that, like oral language development, literacy learning is a constructive process. This constructive process results from the child's own independent explorations of written language and its uses (e.g., the child's invented spellings or attempts to read books before he or she is conventionally literate) and from social interaction with others in activities that involve literacy (e.g., helping mom or dad make the shopping list, listening to a storybook being read aloud). The better parents and educators can understand what is at work in early childhood literacy development, the better we can help foster this learning by creating conditions that allow children to build quality literacy, thinking, and literacy use, in and out of school.

In this chapter, Terry Salinger makes many good suggestions about how children's knowledge of written language, their reading and writing behaviors, and their attitudes toward literacy can be enhanced. Literacy is thinking. It's not all there is to thinking, but it is thinking. This chapter helps us see more clearly how we can support the development of young children's thinking as well as their thinking about and through written language.

317

# 16 Critical Thinking and Young Literacy Learners

Terry Salinger
*Educational Testing Service*

Children like to play, to listen, and to mimic. They play in many ways—with things, situations, roles, behaviors, and also with ideas. They listen to and observe and then "try out" the behaviors, speech patterns, and interactions they see within their worlds. They think about and integrate what they see and hear into their play and give those around them opportunities to view their emerging hypotheses about the environment, their thinking patterns, and their efforts to construct meaningful explanations of their surroundings. Doing so, they manipulate ideas and concepts, form hypotheses, and alter existing constructs to accommodate new learning.

In actuality, because children are thinkers—and critical ones at that—they develop their own "curricula" to find out about the world. As part of their striving for personal constructs, children want to work and to have help in working toward mastery of what they perceive as adult activities, including acquisition of beginning concepts of reading, writing, literacy and numeracy (Bussis, Chittenden, Amarel, & Klausner, 1985; Kamii, 1982; Kelly, 1955; Wells, 1986). Identifying and then building and extending on this innate "curricula" is a major responsibility of early childhood educators who recognize that children attempt to develop personal constructs to explain how the world "works."

This chapter discusses young children's thinking and uses their thinking about literacy as an exemplar. Children's explorations of literacy fit the definition of critical thinking as "purposeful, reasonable, and goal directed" (Halpern, 1989, p. 38), in that children address a specific phenomena in their worlds—how the graphic symbol system works—and view the phenomena as a problem they wish to investigate and solve. It also discusses preschool, kindergarten, and early primary curricula that can nurture and refine learners' active explorations of their world and thereby enhance their thinking skills.

## HOW CHILDREN CONSTRUCT UNDERSTANDINGS
## ABOUT LITERACY: A PARADIGM

Before they can actually read the simplest signs or package labels or even their own names, children experiment with written communication: they write letters, signs, stories, or annotations on their art work. With time, children also perceive that specific letters (graphemes) are used to express specific sounds (phonemes) within oral utterances, and they begin to map "sounds" and letters in an attempt to unravel the puzzle of traditional spelling. Researchers have documented specific stages through which children progress (Gentry, 1981) and agree that "[b]eginning writers of English seem to proceed like this: they first discover the unit of language the symbols are to represent (word, syllable, or phoneme); they invent a plausible way for the symbols to represent language units; then they revise their invented spelling in favor of the standard spelling used around them" (Temple, Nathan, & Burris, 1988, p. 58). The salient words here are "discover" and "invent," for they capture the depth of thinking young learners exert toward this end.

Children also retell stories they have heard and make up new ones to accompany illustrations in books. Through these storybook reenactments, children become familiar with book format and handling, as they attend to pictures closely enough to label pictures and weave stories. These stories are often offered in a specific, formal *book* language that differs markedly from normal, conversational speech (Purcell-Gates, 1988). That prereaders shift into this second register as they reenact stories again attests to the depth of their analysis of conversational versus book reading situations.

Children ask questions about reading and writing and submit their *products* for adult *review* and comment. In essence, they are seeking information about literacy and affirmation of what they have thought about themselves. These beginning efforts indicate that children have learned that squiggles on paper communicate messages with the same intentionality as oral communication (Clay, 1976; Ferreiro, 1990). Table 16.1 summarizes the cognitive understandings children gain about beginning literacy.

This progression toward literacy takes place without direct instruction, motivated by children's curiosity and quest for mastery of an adult mode of communication. It appears that preschool students conceive an ideal goal and indiscriminantly work toward it. Children seek out, collate, compare and contrast, evaluate, and use information that will build emerging knowledge structures, and systematically discard what does not seem relevant to their pursuit.

Early childhood learning environments—preschools, daycares, kindergartens, and early primary grades—should support children's efforts to experiment and refine their knowledge. When children know that their efforts are validated by their care givers or teachers, they will feel freer to ask questions, to share their experiments, and to take the risks needed for growth—in all learning areas.

TABLE 16.1
Cognitive Understandings Children Gain About Literacy

Children actively gather data about print as they observe environmental print and people using print around them. Data gathering yields this information:

Print communicates a message, that is, it stands for something that can be spoken.

Thre is a difference between writing and drawing.

Some print provides information; some provides pleasure.

As they analyze data about print, young learners form, test, and refine hypotheses. They realize the following:

Print is formed by only a few strokes, both circular and straight.

In order to be print, the few strokes must be combined in a somewhat varied pattern; Thus:

O\ P 2 m m           can be print, but

O OOO m m           cannot be print.

Printed communication does not look at all like what it symbolizes; thus:

dog, Dog, DOG, *dog*           do not look like a dog.

But there are some exceptions, as in:

Print can be of many different forms, both cursive and manuscript, with many variations among the two basic styles.

Print follows definite directional principles, even though young learners do not necessarily recognize the direction to be left to right.

Print is equivalent to talk written down, so a long string of letters should be used to recored a long verbal utterance and only a few letteers can stand for short statements.

STAGES IN INVENTED SPELLING

Children practice using print to communicate by writing messages and stories on their drawings, incorporating writing and reading into their play, and by engaging in endless efforts to master the strokes and circles needed for writing. They ask adults questions and gather more data about literacy. By synthesizing and evaluating the information they gain from conversations with others, from answers to specific questions about "What does it say?," from listening to others read to them, and from television programs and other instruction, children figure out--or invent— rudimentary spelling rules.

Stage I,  Prephonemic or Deviant Spelling:
                 no correspondence between letters use in writing and their sounds

(*continued*)

TABLE 16.1 *(Continued)*

Stage II, Early Phonemic Spelling:
some few examples of correspondence, as in clear consonantal sounds, some long vowels

Stage III, Letter-Name Spelling:
an almost perfect match of some letters and sound, usually without consonant blants or digraphs or correct vowel digraphs or dipthongs

Stage IV, Transitional Invented Spelling:
spelling looks very much like traditional orthography, with children's attempts to apply spelling rules sprinkled throughout

Stage V, Correct Spelling:
The basic rules of spelling have been mastered and children have learned strategies to figure out how to spell unfamiliar words.

Children also analyze data they gather about book reading and book handling strategies. They realize the following:

Books must be read in a specific direction; eventually they recognize that the direction is from front to back.

Print itself on each page must be read in a particular direction, eventually recognized as left to right.

There is a connection between the pictures in a book and the story it tells; at first, they think that "reading" involves making up a story from the picture but gradually they recognize the importance and stability of print.

Different books have different arrangement schema: picture books are usually intact, some books have stories or chapters, some books depend on many pictures and other graphics.

Books are of many types, not just story books; and accomplished readers use the different kinds for different purposes.

Young children make many observations about the print they see displayed and used in their environments. From increasingly sophicticated and focused data collection, they are able to form and test hypotheses about how reading and writing work. Their analyses should become the foundation of their initial rading and writing instruction.

## NECESSARY ASSUMPTIONS

Seeking to develop classroom environments that encourage young children's critical thinking means accepting certain assumptions. The strong empirical and ethnographic proof that children do indeed construct knowledge about the conventions of school-related subjects supports the first assumption: Children are interested in knowing long before they enter school and strive to understand abstractions about numeracy and literacy as part of their explorations of the world (Ferreiro & Teberosky, 1982; Kamii, 1982). The second assumption is almost a bromide: Young children are active thinkers and respond enthusiastically to challenges that require them to stretch and expand their existing knowledge structures.

The third assumption is more complex: Developmentally appropriate instructional experiences for young children do not necessarily preclude opportunities for them to encounter, use, and master beginning critical thinking skills. Such opportunities build on the curiosity and cognitive energy which all children bring to new situations and support young learners' attempts to reflect upon, construct, and refine hypotheses. This assumption does not mean that children should be unrealistically pushed beyond their capabilities, that there is one curriculum that "infuses" critical thinking into a reading and writing readiness program; but it does mean that *all* children should be considered active thinkers and given opportunities to use their experiential knowledge and to follow their interests and inclinations in learning the functions and forms of abstract thinking. For example, their acquisition of literacy should not be stymied by teachers' withholding information, materials, or opportunities to explore reading and writing, nor by incorrect assumptions about what children bring to their learning. Incorrect assumptions can result in teachers failing to recognize the depth and breadth of both procedural and declarative knowledge children have actually acquired. An example would be the teacher who acknowledged that children could sing jump rope and other street rhymes fluently while decrying the inability of the same students to *rhyme* in an instructional context such as initial consonant substitution (Purcell-Gates & Salinger, 1991).

## NECESSARY COMPONENTS

Classrooms where young learners are encouraged to use their emerging critical thinking skills to best advantage are places in which three components are carefully considered, planned, and orchestrated. They are:

1. Teachers' theoretical stance as evidenced in the classroom, including the definition of learning underlying classroom decisions;

2. Teachers' behaviors as a model of thinking strategies and poser and answerer of questions;

3. Activities and opportunities provided for the children, which are discussed in the section on curriculum.

### Theoretical Stance

What teachers believe about how children learn influences what and how they teach, how they structure their classrooms, and what they expect from their students. Teachers of young children who believe that early learning means learning to construct meaning recognize the depth and breadth of children's thinking. Accepting this theoretical stance is teachers' first, necessary step toward an environment that supports young learners' critical thinking.

## Teachers Providing Models, Scaffolds, and Questions

Teachers are models. In addition to demonstrating how to do certain things, they model values, appreciation, and attitudes. They also can become models for thinking processes.

The concept of *scaffolding* has its roots in the interaction between infants and parents as the parents strive to establish some kind of "conversation" between preverbal offspring or structure a game such as peekaboo so that the child learns to participate. As an infant learns the desired procedure or verbalization, parents withdraw the scaffold and prompt the child to independent action. The term has become common in early childhood instruction, where it refers to teachers' attempts to provide a verbal framework or *scaffold* to help children understand processes they are attempting to master. Teachers lead children to figure out the next step or idea or procedure or concept necessary for new understandings and support them in assimilating new knowledge into existing schema (see also Vygotsky, 1962/1979).

The stages are simple. At first teachers must assume entire responsibility for instruction and guidance of learning, then students gradually accept more responsibility, and finally students must assume entire responsibility for independent completion of tasks and demonstration of skills. Teachers' role throughout is to gauge the extent to which and the points at which to release responsibility, that is, to remove components of the initial scaffold.

Instructional use of scaffolds frequently stresses the mastery of skills; what this chapter proposes for preschoolers, kindergartners, and 1st graders who are grappling with varying levels of understanding are *thinking scaffolds*. This use of the principle of scaffolding would involve two teacher behaviors, often used in concert: (1) offering explanations, and (2) asking questions. The purposes of thinking scaffolds for young learners would be:

- to help young learners refine emerging hypotheses;
- to clarify misconceptions before they become habituated;
- to provide new information when it is needed to clarify and extend emerging hypotheses; and
- to motivate children to extend their thinking and stretch to new understandings and mastery of skills.

To be most beneficial, thinking scaffolds should be embedded within the fabric of instruction and learning activities and should become a way of interacting between teachers, learners, and the concepts and skills learners are attempting to master. Scaffolds are not pat phrases to be used at predetermined times, nor are they a sequence of scripted statements offered in instructional language. In discussing instructional scaffolding, Cazden (1988) pointed out, "As with children's language development, the models provided are samples to learn from, not examples to learn" (p. 108).

Verbalizing their own thinking strategies, demonstrating self-questioning, and suggesting other methods they use to monitor and clarify their own thought processes are among the ways teachers provide thinking scaffolds. During story-time, for example, a teacher might pose a question about an ambiguous passage, make a prediction about what the section means, and state, "Well, I'll keep reading and find out." When clarification emerges within the text, the teacher again comments to indicate a successful solution to the cognitive puzzle.

Teachers also need to respond to students in cognitive as well as affective ways. For example, teachers who might simply say "Good writing" in response to a child's story can elaborate by saying "Your story tells me that you understand that stories begin with 'Once upon a time' " or "Look how you have used *m* at the beginning of the word 'monkey.' You heard the right sound!" Such comments affirm that children's thinking has been accurate and encourage them to use the same strategies again.

*Questioning* can be a constructive part of the interactions between teachers and young learners, another important part of the scaffolds which teachers provide. Unfortunately, this is not always the case. In the best of circumstances, questions should contribute to thinking scaffolds and be interjected at significant times during instructional interactions. Children must not perceive teachers' questioning as interruptions to their thinking or negative evaluation. Cazden (1988) reminds us, "There is a critical difference between helping a child somehow get a particular answer and helping a child gain some conceptual understanding from which answers to similar questions can be constructed at a future time" (p. 108). Questions that help children gain conceptual understanding and that can be generalized to other situations are crucial to encourage young learners to become critical thinkers.

Questions to stimulate critical thinking about literacy are of two distinct types: (1) those that target the concepts and skills children must draw upon, and (2) those that address specific pieces of the text which children encounter. "Can you tell me how you figured out that word?" illustrates the first type, and "What do you think the boy in the story might do next?" addresses text. Worthwhile, critical thinking questions about concepts and skills are invariably coupled with explanations and expansions. Using them as appropriate scaffolding statements, teachers attempt to gain insight into children's cognitive processes without implying that the processes children are using are wrong, inadequate, or somehow deficient. They also can provide corrective and elaborative feedback on what children are trying to do as they develop and refine procedural and declarative knowledge about literacy. Questions help children reconceptualize learning through critical thinking. As such, they constitute much of schooling: "A great deal of education is devoted to teaching students to see phenomena in a new way, to reconceptualize circles as wheels or wheels as circles" (Cazden, 1988, p. 112). Reconceptualization also means elaborating emerging concepts and expanding the ways in which skills are used. A succinct and useful way of labeling such teacher/student interaction is "cognition in context" (Newman, Griffin, & Cole, 1984), with the teacher attempting to shape and expand the cognition demonstrated so that it will be applied in new, diverse contexts.

To use questions effectively to spur "cognition in context," teachers must learn first to be good listeners. They must listen both to what students are saying lexically (what words are uttered) and what their words imply about their thinking. Grossi (1990, p. 104) cited two illustrative examples of situations meriting close teacher listening: "[A] girl named Lize said, 'My name has 4 letters because I'm very young. My mommy's name must have 10 letters and my daddy's 15 because he is even older than Mommy.' " Her second example is a boy "who was asked how many letters were needed to write the word *bread*. He said, 'It depends on the size of it. Bread [meaning the written word] standing for a loaf of bread is written with more letters than bread standing for rolls.' " Appropriate questions about either statement should seek to shape and refocus the ideas presented and help students refine their thinking, without belittling the critical and creative thinking the children have most obviously exercised.

In responding to children, teachers must rely on their own knowledge about the structure and underpinnings of the skills and concepts children are attempting to learn. Sequences of verbal interactions between children and teachers should affirm accurate thinking and avert habituation of incorrect ideas or inefficient strategies (as could easily happen if the statements quoted above were not addressed). Indeed, problems in beginning literacy are often the result of critical thinking gone awry, of naive and incorrect hypotheses which children actively developed and tested but which were never appropriately refined and corrected. Attempting to construct a workable understanding of literacy behaviors, children may have "tried to do [their] work . . . practised [sic] [their] primitive skills and . . . habituated, daily, the wrong responses" (Clay, 1979, p. 11). In literacy and in all learning areas, teachers who look primarily at children's products, for example, written work and oral reading, miss the more complex, underlying cognition that is driving children's efforts toward success or failure as learners and thinkers.

## CURRICULUM TO ENCOURAGE CRITICAL THINKING ABOUT BEGINNING LITERACY

While maintaining the illustrative example of literacy learning, three major components of an early childhood curriculum can be identified as especially important for encouraging children's critical thinking. These are:

1. Drawing for its own sake and as a precursor to, and support for, writing;

2. Shared literacy experiences and supportive group discussions of learning;
3. Extensive experience with the writing process.

These exist on a continuum. Each component has a place in the curriculum from preschool to early primary grades; the nature and shape of the experiences change as children gain knowledge and competence, but the basic approaches—and their theoretical underpinnings—remain essentially the same.

## Drawing

Drawing is a vital part of early childhood classes because it allows children to experiment with methods to represent things in symbols, to experiment with the conventions of print, and also to communicate with others through nonverbal means. Drawing may also give teachers and children their first opportunities to share discussion about the processes of thinking and communicating on paper with abstract symbols in the forms of pictures and pseudoletters. Dyson (1986, 1988) has written persuasively about the role of drawing in young learners' efforts to create "text worlds." Her detailed transcriptions of children's talk while drawing, writing, *and thinking* testify to the critical thinking and thoughtful decision making that children engage in when they are in a classroom that invites them to experiment as authors.

As children draw, they think about what they want to do, are doing, and need to do to accomplish their goals. They make important decisions about the marks they put on paper, even if they appear as little more than scribbles. Children consider the pictorial and verbal representations of what they want to communicate in their drawing, and figure ways to represent their ideas in a two-dimensional format. As children strive to master invented spelling, these pictorial representations stimulate memories about content and help them stay on task. In similar fashion, drawing may sometimes replace writing, as when children convey the emotions of characters in a story by giving them all smiling faces. Additionally, drawing can motivate children to produce elaborated stories as they attempt to write, draw a little to help them think, and then write some more. Because drawing is important, teachers should provide ample paper of many sizes and a variety of writing/drawing tools.

Even preschoolers should be encouraged to "write something" on their drawings; this serves as an introduction to authoring. At first, children may only label aspects of a drawing but gradually they begin to create verbal text worlds to comment on or describe the world they have drawn. Teachers may or may not transcribe the "stories" into traditional orthography but should take every opportunity to discuss both process and product with young learners and provide scaffolds for further experimentation. Discussions about the origin of the story/drawing itself and the decisions behind its production let teachers view children's emerging sense of how to orchestrate diverse aspects of text production.

Correct hypotheses can be affirmed; and incorrect, inefficient strategies can be remediated before they become habituated.

## Shared Literacy Experiences and Discussions of Learning

There are many appropriate methodologies for sharing learning/thinking experiences and providing scaffolds for students' emerging thinking skills. For literacy learning, these include storybook reading, shared book experiences, especially with big books, and the language experience approach.

While stories can be read to students as a purely pleasurable experience, teachers should also consider using the *Directed Listening Thinking Activity* (DLTA). The DLTA is an elaborated scaffold to help youngsters shape their thinking about stories they hear, almost a "conversation" about many aspects of the story being shared (Saul, 1989); teachers and students talk about what they have shared, with the teacher controlling and structuring the conversation to provide a model for thinking. Encouraging children to draw upon their own knowledge bases as they interact with stories gives them an additional and very powerful strategy which they should readily extend as they begin to read themselves. Through teacher-guided discussion, they learn to draw inferences, compare and contrast material, analyze what they hear, and make predictions based on evidence in the stories they hear.

Introducing nonnarrative materials—beginning content area books—expands students' thinking strategies even further because teachers can provide scaffolds for children to use in thinking about science, social studies, and other areas.

Teachers reading a small, traditional-sized book to a group of children is the standard method of sharing books; but using books with enlarged print can be a good alternative presentation method and a successful introduction to more "formal" thinking about instruction. So-called *big books* allow small groups of children sitting in a circle in front of the teacher to approximate the visual intimacy of parent/child book sharing (Holdaway, 1979). Big books are available commercially or can be teacher-made (Salinger, 1988).

Familiarity with big books is a first step to students engaging in *supportive reading groups* (Holdaway, 1979). The objective of such groups is movement from teacher direction to student independent reading with no sacrifice of the support and scaffolding that teachers have provided. Although teachers are constantly assessing children's emerging skills, instruction should remain low-keyed, almost submerged in the "conversation" about text. Teachers never really withdraw support from beginning readers: They continue to challenge children to exercise skills, stretch what they know, and apply knowledge in new situations. Questions that teachers ask should be balanced between attention to the mechanics of reading (letter/sound correspondences, context clues, expectations of what words would be right in particular situations) and higher order thinking questions similar to those asked during a Directed Listening Thinking Activity.

For beginning and advanced supportive reading groups, repetition and review are essential. Going over stories that have been well received and reviewing discussions about skills help children reach for independence and give them opportunities to revisit their initial impressions about text, to revise opinions, and to expand on their initial thinking. During the lag time, they may have thought differently, reached new conclusions, made new connections—essentially, exercised their critical thinking. Opportunities to discuss stories a second or third time allows children to air their views and refine and affirm their ideas.

## Extensive Writing Experience

Young learners need to be given extensive opportunities to take part in writing activities and to write on their own.

The *language experience approach* (LEA) to beginning literacy draws upon children's initial hypotheses about literacy and helps to scaffold emerging ideas about print production. The basic application of language experience involves teachers transcribing children's ideas about a shared experience or question posed to activate background knowledge and prompt discussion. LEA sessions can also model processes of review, revision, and editing early enough in students' experiences as authors that they realize that these steps equate to much more than "copying over." Even as children dictate, teachers could ask for "other ways of stating that" to stress the importance of careful word choice; they could delay transcription to illustrate how several ideas can be combined or sequenced; or they can insert and delete words and ideas while guiding children to reread their dictation. Essentially, teachers act as verbal models of the processes for transforming ideas to text and stress the junctures in the process at which evaluation is necessary. Asking children to participate in the decision making and shaping discussion about the decisions and evaluation points provide the scaffold for independent application of critical thinking in children's own writing. Young learners must be encouraged to write and to discuss the thinking that undergirds their efforts to become authors. Writing provides opportunities for children to take risks; and to advance thinking, student writers must take risks. Harste, Woodward, and Burke (1984) commented:

> Counter to current instructional folklore, recent insights into risk-taking and its relationship to literacy and literacy learning suggest that literacy programs which emphasize correct responses and attempt to eliminate error fail to best serve literacy learning. It is only when language users get themselves in trouble within what was perceived to be a moderately predictable setting that growth occurs. . . . [Children's] latest language discoveries are always more fun to think about than those which [they] already think [they] have sorted out. (pp. 136, 192)

For young literacy learners, risk taking and their own critical analysis of both how to apply skills and how to decide upon topics about which to write are intertwined. For example, selecting a topic for drawing is one form of risk: What if it is silly or inappropriate? Actual composition requires even more risks as children think about and coordinate what they know about letter formation, spelling, the conventions of print (e.g., spacing or punctuation), grammar and sentence structure, and vocabulary.

In addition to environmental supports such as ample writing supplies and a general tone of acceptance for risk taking and making mistakes, teachers provide scaffolds for beginning writers through student/teacher conferences. Talking to children about what they are trying to do—that is, about cognitive processes rather than mechanics—helps young learners figure out the complexities of expressing their ideas on paper. Discussion encourages them to reach for original thoughts, unique expressions of their worlds, and playful experimentations with the creation of text worlds—to achieve what Dyson (1988) has called the "controlled meshing of the experienced and the imaginary world" in texts (p. 376). Discussions between students and teachers and eventually between pairs and small groups of students also help children learn important strategies for evaluating writing. In this case, evaluation leads not to assigning grades or qualitative labels but to refining process, increasing competency, and gaining insight into written expression. Children's evaluation is truly critical thinking. Dyson (1988) wrote of one student:

> [I]n the kindergarten, Maggie had often been silly with her texts (e.g., reading them in a falsetto voice), but her texts themselves had not been funny. Late in the first grade, though, she began to find them quite funny ('I can't believe what I'm writing. This is so funny.')
>
> One funny text was a story about two friends, Alice and Lacey. Maggie orally elaborated upon her written characters: 'Alice and Lacey are the real people. They're real names. Anyone could be them.' The 'anyones' had a common experiences, particularly common for Maggie—they were consistently late to school: as she put it in her text, 'as usual they Got a tarDy tag again.' The 'as usual' reflects the resigned but slightly amused stance Maggie herself often adopted. (pp. 375–376)

Environmental, attitudinal supports and teachers' thoughtful scaffolding and questioning help children learn to reflect on their work meaningfully and comfortably. Also, time and experience contribute to young learners emergence as evaluators of their own work. Growth in these important thinking skills quickly extends beyond literacy acquisition to other learning areas, and students learn to monitor their progress reflectively and realistically.

As children gain skills, confidence, and independence, writing should be required in all relevant content areas, and time should be set aside several times a week for independent creative writing. To the extent possible, all children should keep logs and be expected to write about what they have read or have heard read to them. Instruction in writing strategies must focus on decision making rather than mastery of specific mechanics. Essentially, children are taught that authors make many decisions and select from a range of mechanical and rhetorical options available to express themselves. For example, a lesson on quotation marks that leads to rote memorization of rules for their use will not encourage children to integrate dialogue into their individual repertoire of useful rhetorical devises. A lesson couched as decision making, on the other hand, teaches children that they have a choice in how to express dialogue (quoting directly or embedding in text) and that they must think critically about which to use within each attempt to construct a text world.

Children must also learn that the process of revision involves critical thinking, not merely copying papers over with correct spelling and neater handwriting. Interactive LEA sessions, in which teachers have elicited revisions and stated reasons for changes, are the first models of this process for young learners. As they write independently, children should be encouraged to revise their own work, to discuss it with others and with their teacher, and to make and defend changes that improve their ability to communicate their ideas. Teachers' discussions of revision strategies and decision making provide scaffold for these behaviors through direct instruction, teacher-child conferences, LEA sessions, and peer conferencing.

It is essential that the inclination to revise stem from each child's own sense of authoring and from the realization that the major purpose of revision is to communicate more effectively what one's thoughts actually are. First of all, then, revision involves critical thinking about content, with secondary consideration to mechanics and neatness. This does not mean that technical aspects of writing can be ignored but that introductions to revision that seem to privilege rote application of rules and neatness over critical interaction with text (however brief it may be for beginners) conveys entirely the wrong message to young authors. As children learn the cognitive processes involved in revision, they acquire the inclination to monitor and revise their work in all areas.

## SUMMARY

Gathering evidence, forming initial hypotheses, and trying out their ideas are behaviors which young learners exert in their attempts to make sense of what they see in their world. Their efforts to understand literacy are illustrative of the depth and breadth of thinking they can exert toward desired goals.

To capitalize on children's search for understanding, teachers can provide verbal scaffolds of the kinds of thinking children should use. Teachers can verbalize cognitive processes, model tactics for seeking clarification, and question children to encourage their own mastery of self-questioning and self-monitoring strategies of the kinds of thinking in which young learners engage as they attempt to construct meaning about phenomena in their world.

That young learners engage in this search for understanding of literacy behaviors should guide early childhood caregivers and teachers to structure their learning environments in the ways discussed in this chapter and to offer young learners opportunities to build on their thinking. To ignore the power of children's critical thinking, to relegate their curious investigations of the world to areas other than literacy, minimizes the importance of their inquiry for immediate and future learning.

## REFERENCES

Bussis, A. M., Chittenden, E. A., Amarel, M., & Klausner, E. (1985). *Inquiry into meaning: An investigation of learning to read*. Hillsdale, NJ: Lawrence Erlbaum Associates.

Cazden, C. B. (1988). *Classroom discourse: The language of teaching and learning*. Portsmouth, NH: Heinemann Educational Books.

Clay, M. M. (1976). *What did I write?* Portsmouth, NH: Heinemann Educational Books.

Clay, M. M. (1979). *Reading: The patterning of complex behaviour*. Portsmouth, NH: Heinemann Educational Books.

Dyson, A. H. (1986). Transitions and tensions: Interrelationships between the drawing, talking, and dictating of young children. *Research in the Teaching of English, 20,* 379–409.

Dyson, A. H. (1988). Negotiating among multiple worlds: The space/time dimension of young children's composing. *Research in the Teaching of English, 22,* 355–390.

Ferreiro, E. (1990). Literacy development: Psychogenesis. In Y. Goodman (Ed.), *How children construct literacy*. Newark, DE: International Reading Association.

Ferreiro, E., & Teberosky, A. (1982). *Literacy before schooling*. Portsmouth, NH: Heinemann Educational Books.

Gentry, J. R. (1981). Learning to spell developmentally. *The Reading Teacher, 34,* 378–381.

Grossi, E. P. (1990). Applying psychogenesis principles to literacy instruction of lower-class children in Brazil. In Y. Goodman (Ed.), *How children construct literacy*. Newark, DE: International Reading Association.

Halpern, D. F. (1989). *Thought and knowledge: An introduction to critical thinking* (2nd Edition). Hillsdale, NJ: Lawrence Erlbaum Associates.

Harste, J. C., Woodward, V. A., & Burke, C. L. (1984). *Language stories and literacy lessons*. Portsmouth, NH: Heinemann Educational Books.

Holdaway, D. (1979). *The foundations of literacy*. Sydney: Ashton-Scholastic.

Kamii, C. (1982). *Number in preschool and kindergarten*. Washington: National Association for the Education of Young Children.

Kelly, G. A. (1955). *The psychology of personal constructs*. New York: W. W. Norton.

Newman, D., Griffin, P., & Cole, M. (1984). Laboratory and classroom tasks: Social constraints and the evaluation of children's performance. In B. Rogoff & J. Lave (Eds.) *Everyday cognition: Its development in social contexts*. Cambridge, MA: Harvard University Press.

Purcell-Gates, V. (1988). Lexical and syntactic knowledge of written narratives held by well-read-to kindergartners and second graders. *Research in the Teaching of English, 22,* 128–160.

Purcell-Gates, V., & Salinger, T. (1991). Access to literacy for young learners. In K. H. Borman, P. Swami, & L. D. Wagstaff (Eds.), *Contemporary issues in U.S. education*. Norwood, NJ: Ablex.

Salinger, T. (1988). *Language arts and literacy for young children*. Columbus: Merrill.

Saul, E. W. (1989). "What did Leo feed the turtle?" And other nonliterary questions. *Language Arts, 66,* 295–303.

Temple, C., Nathan, R., & Burris, N. A. (1988). *The beginnings of writing*, 2nd Ed. Boston: Allyn and Bacon.

Vygotsky, L. S. (1962/1979). *Thought and language*. Cambridge, MA: MIT Press.

Wells, G. (1986). *The meaning makers: Children learning language and using language to learn*. Portsmouth, NH.

# 17

## Discussion: Fatal Vision—The Failure of the Schools in Teaching Children to Think

Patricia A. McGrane
Robert J. Sternberg
*Yale University*

Throughout this book, the authors have offered us a vision of what education could and should be like in the 21st century. They suggest that the primary purpose of education should be to develop students' abilities to think and to encourage a disposition toward thoughtfulness. This vision of education is not new; similar ideas have been around since before we last entered a new century. Unfortunately, in the past 100 years little real progress has been made toward achieving these goals. Hundreds of reports from numerous committees and researchers point to the fact that our nation's children still cannot think well and that our schools are not yet teaching students to think. Sadly, many of the calls for teaching thinking that were made over 100 years ago, rather than sounding archaic, are still pertinent today.

The lack of progress in improving thinking skills in our schools over the past century is rather depressing and forces us to ask the question: Will this book sound archaic and dated, of historical interest only, in another 100 years or will it *still* be necessary to make the same points then? As we enter a new century, it seems appropriate to question why, if the ideas are all there, our nation's schools are not yet teaching children to think. Although one could maintain that never before have we had the impetus, motivation, support, and societal recognition of the need for change, it may also be that the same fundamental problems that have stymied programs for the last 100 years will continue to plague us during the next century.

This chapter offers no obvious solutions but instead highlights and brings to the forefront some of the issues and paradoxes in teaching thinking skills. In particular, we first focus on our nation's vision of the purpose of education and the accepted view of how this purpose is best accomplished. We then suggest that this vision has been institutionalized into a self-correcting system that works to keep the vision in place, making incremental changes virtually impossible. Next, we discuss the self-correcting mechanisms that have developed in our education system that present a roadblock to teaching thinking skills. Finally, we address the question of whether a nation's vision can be changed.

## OUR NATION'S VISION

What is our nation's vision of the purpose of education? When we speak of our vision of education, we are not referring to trends and ongoing debates in academic circles that sometimes surface in the popular press, nor are we talking about fads in education that come and go. Instead, we are referring to the stable, underlying view that most Americans share, based on our common history and shared values. This underlying vision is not difficult to discover. It becomes clear when you talk with parents, students, and teachers, if you visit a classroom, or when you simply introspect upon your own experience with education. Simply stated, the goal of education is to provide children, by the time they are 18, with all of the facts and "basic" skills they will need throughout their lives in order to succeed in our society. This view has been discussed in many other papers, including several chapters of this book. It is what Tinzmann, Jones, and Pierce, in Chapter 10, refer to as the "basic skills model" or the "assembly line model." In Chapter 7, Gross refers to it as "innoculation theory" or the "front-end load" concept of education. This institutionalized vision pervades every aspect of education today. Teachers, parents, and administrators were educated in schools with this ideal and the pedagogical techniques most teachers are taught stem from this vision. Testing and evaluation at every level reflects this goal, as do our curriculum guidelines and textbooks. If you visit virtually any classroom in the United States, you will find teaching styles based on this vision.

How is this vision incorporated into the average classroom? Typically, in order to provide children with the basic information and skills they need, the teacher must maintain control of the class so students can hear the lectures and absorb the isolated facts. Teachers frequently ask children questions to determine whether they understand and have absorbed the material. At other times, the children work alone at their desks. The children's goal is to learn the material well enough to do well on the regular tests which evaluate how well they have mastered the materials. Frequently, the students will take a standardized test to determine whether they are learning these facts at an appropriate speed. These tests assess the important things—the basics—reading, writing, and arithmetic. This is the accepted means to achieve the goals established by our implicit vision.

Is there anything inherently wrong with this vision of education? Certainly our schools are in trouble today, but this may be a problem of implementation, not vision as such. Schooling can only be evaluated by looking at the goals we are trying to achieve. As many authors have mentioned (see Gross and Tinzmann et al.), if our goal was to train factory workers for the year 1920, our current vision might be very effective. In contrast, if our goal is to prepare our children for employment in the year 2000, this vision seems inappropriate. Our current vision assumes that children can learn essentially all of the facts they will need by the time they are eighteen. In this rapidly changing society where new information is generated and old information is made obsolete every day, this assumption is patently unwarranted. As Gross notes in Chapter 7, and Duffy in Chapter 12, formal schooling simply will not be enough learning for a lifetime in this day and age. Children today will need more than facts to succeed; they will need to know how to, and have the motivation to, continue learning throughout their lives. In addition, the changes in our economy require more than a knowledge of unconnected facts and a minimal grasp of basic skills for success. The occupations of the future will not require workers who can merely add, subtract, read, and write. People will need to be able to think problems through, reason well, and come up with creative solutions.

Alternatively, if the purpose of our education system should be to prepare our children for participation in a democracy, this current vision has probably never been appropriate. Active participation in a democracy calls for higher order thinking skills, such as the ability to analyze politicians' statements critically. Our current vision, although requiring that our children be literate, has never emphasized the necessary higher order thinking skills.

Yet another possibility is that the goal of our school system should be to provide people with the tools for lifelong learning and an appreciation for literature, art, etc. As Tsantis and Keefe note in Chapter 14, there can be little argument that our current vision fails miserably in this respect. It destroys intrinsic motivation and encourages students to learn only that on which they will be tested. Hence, while our current vision appears adequate to provide factory workers for the year 1920, it is obviously ill-equipped to create workers for today's economy, active citizens in a democracy, or well-rounded adults.

There are numerous alternative visions that have been proposed throughout history, emphasizing various purposes of education. In this book, the authors have provided us with a vision of education that focuses on thinking as the centerpiece. Calfee emphasizes "critical literacy," whereas Costa emphasizes "an environment for thinking" but the visions share many similarities. From this perspective, the goal of education is to teach our children to use higher order thinking skills and to create in them the disposition and motivation to think. Children learn not isolated facts, but instead learn to think and learn to learn. Facts are acquired almost incidentally. Teachers are not simply lecturers, but are instead coaches, facilitators, and accomplished, skilled professionals. Students work together to solve real-world problems and learn to satisfy their own curiosity, not merely to perform well on tests. Process is emphasized over product.

This vision is not particularly novel. Historically, researchers, educators, and policy makers have often been inspired by such goals and have attempted to make changes in our education system in accordance with this vision. What has happened when such changes were implemented? Generally, although sometimes producing excellent short-term results, they have had no long-term impact. To understand why this is, it is necessary to view our education system as the homeostatic (self-correcting) system that it is.

## EDUCATION AS A HOMEOSTATIC SYSTEM

Webster's New World Dictionary defines homeostasis as:

> **1** the tendency to maintain, or the maintenance of, normal, internal stability in an organism by coordinated responses of the organ systems that automatically compensate for environmental changes **2** any analogous maintenance of stability or equilibrium, as within a social group.

Our educational system has developed so that when any attempt at change is made that is not in accordance with the underlying vision, different structures within the system will work to force the reformed program back in line with the traditional vision. What are these corrective mechanisms? They include teachers, parents, administrators, teacher education programs, standardized evaluation, and the students themselves. For example, a thinking skills program may be abandoned because it fails to produce short-term results, it produces no measurable improvement on standardized tests, or because the teachers cannot implement it correctly.

This is not to suggest that change is not possible within the educational system. Many current proposals for reform fit in with our current vision: calls for greater accountability, a return to the "basics," increasing choice for parents, giving teachers more voice in decision making, etc. These reforms will not run up against the type of corrective mechanisms described here because all can be incorporated within our current vision. But precisely for this reason, these types of reforms will also fail to promote classroom thoughtfulness. As Newmann noted in Chapter 6, restructured programs do not lead to greater thoughtfulness unless the school has set forth improving thinking skills as a goal and has developed specific and comprehensive programs. On the other hand, if a researcher or teacher tries to implement many of the programs and approaches discussed in this book, he/she *will* run up against these corrective mechanisms.

It is because our educational system is homeostatic (self-correcting) that incremental changes that are not in line with the current vision inevitably fail. Although many authors emphasize different roadblocks to teaching thinking, they do not fully acknowledge the fundamental problem—the vision that underlies our education system. The various corrective mechanisms all work in concert to maintain this vision, so that in order to accomplish any real change, the system and the vision upon which it is based must be changed.

Changing a nation's vision is not a simple task, however. Our current vision has been institutionalized to the extent that change is made virtually impossible. What we teach our children is a good indication of what we value as a nation, and there are no ready-made solutions to changing a nation's values. We take up this issue of changing a vision in the last section of this chapter.

## CORRECTIVE MECHANISMS

What are the corrective mechanisms that make thinking skills programs so difficult to implement? In this section we will discuss some of the most important corrective mechanisms that work in concert to preserve the current vision. One of the most important of these mechanisms is our nation's teachers.

*Teachers.* Even the most perfect techniques for teaching thinking are of little value when there are few teachers who can use them effectively. Like the majority of students today, most teachers were not taught thinking skills when they were children. Yet, it is assumed that either (1) somewhere along the way to adulthood, our nation's teachers have learned to think (perhaps it just comes with the teaching certificate), or (2) being able to think is not a prerequisite for teaching thinking. There are problems with either of these assumptions.

First, if the teachers have somehow mysteriously learned to think along the way, there is no reason to think the average student today cannot learn to think in adulthood on her own, and indeed reach a high enough level of mastery to teach someone else to think. If so, why waste precious time teaching thinking in school?

Alternatively, if teachers have *not* somehow picked up the thinking skills we want our children to develop, maybe we can teach them. We can give our teachers a quick seminar on thinking skills so they understand thinking and can then teach it. The problem with this approach is that if teaching thinking was this easy, we could just give each student a week-long seminar in thinking skills when he/she turns eighteen and spend the rest of our time teaching the basics, once again rendering a curriculum for teaching thinking skills unnecessary.

The final possibility is that our teachers can perhaps teach thinking without necessarily having mastered all of the skills themselves—"Those who can, do. Those who can't, teach." This is a point that deserves closer examination. There are many skills that teachers can learn and apply mindlessly that will probably improve student thinking. Several chapters in this book mention skills that teachers could learn that would improve student thinking, such as appropriate questioning techniques. In fact, there are many programs currently available that lay out lessons plans and materials, and that specify exactly what the teacher needs to say and do to effectively implement the program. These programs appear to produce results, often significant, in the short run. But, as already noted in this volume, it is important for children to develop a thinking disposition and a tendency to engage with materials. It may be very difficult to instill a disposition to think and a desire to learn by merely applying techniques. Virtually all of the programs discussed in this book require more than the mindless application of methods by the teacher. Teachers in programs such as those described by Collins, Ogle, Tsantis and Keefe, Salinger, and Palincsar and Klenk, are expected to guide, coach, facilitate, question, and listen. Perhaps more importantly, teachers are expected to understand their own thinking processes and to be able to model intrinsic motivation and metacognition and to explain and discuss other thinking processes. Hence, it appears that the ability to think and a disposition toward thoughtfulness are necessary to be able to teach thinking effectively.

Where does this leave us? In order for teachers to be able to teach thinking, they need not only pedagogical skills—they need to be able to think themselves. Therefore, teachers unintentionally work to maintain the current vision. Like much of the rest of the population, they were not taught to think in school, nor to recognize the importance and necessity of teaching good thinking. They therefore may lack many of the skills and dispositions necessary to effectively teach thinking.

In addition, teachers cannot step outside of our societal view of knowledge and the purpose of education. Most have spent over 16 years in our education system and have learned its lessons well. As Romberg notes in Chapter 3, teachers are generally teaching in the way they were taught in school; the role of teachers is to transmit knowledge, often merely covering pages of a prepackaged program. As he mentions, maintaining order and control is essential and highly efficient for this type of education. Due to this indoctrination, teachers often have difficulty envisioning education in any different way, and even when shown new possibilities, they cannot leave behind these deeply engrained beliefs. An excellent example of this is the teacher discussed in Palincsar and Klenk's chapter, who, after witnessing the authors' program and its results, could still only regard it as supplementary. Entrapped in a societal view, acquired during his/her own education and strengthened by years in the current system, a teacher often cannot conceive of other ways of educating students and fails to recognize the value of alternative programs, even when they produce impressive results.

Our teacher education system could help teachers to overcome this indoctrination, but instead, it supports the current vision. Teachers are often taught how to manage a classroom instead of how to facilitate a discussion and how to lecture properly rather than how to think well. Few teacher training programs work to instill teachers with a lifelong love of learning and a disposition toward thinking. In addition, it takes a highly skilled professional to teach thinking effectively. To teach thinking, you must not only be able to think but also to nurture thinking in others. As Pogrow notes, only a small number of teachers are able to use the sophisticated techniques required for programs such as his Higher Order Thinking Skills program. Whereas simply reciting facts to a classroom and keeping control may not require a highly intelligent, motivated group of teachers, teaching thinking certainly does. Yet, in this country, teaching is a poorly regarded and poorly paid profession. As in so many other areas of life, you get what you pay for. Hence, due to their own educational experience, lack of education in thinking skills, the emphasis of teacher training programs, and the societal view of teaching as a profession, teachers generally serve as a corrective mechanism to maintain the current system.

We are not suggesting that there are no teachers capable of teaching thinking. Rather, we suggest that it is extremely difficult for a teacher to survive his or her years in our current system and retain a desire to learn and to think, and to communicate this desire to others. Regretably, even when the rare teacher has all of the abilities needed and the motivation to teach thinking, the education system still works to straitjacket the teacher.

*Fellow Teachers.* Fellow teachers can also work as a correcting mechanism. While Collins, in Chapter 4, emphasizes the importance of interdisciplinary teaching teams working together to emphasize certain thinking skills, this is generally not the case. Instead, many teachers receive little support from administration or fellow teachers. It is a rare school where innovation is truly appreciated, so teachers who attempt to change teaching style, curriculum, etc., usually are regarded as a threat and face hostility and suspicion, receiving little support. In addition, because each teacher only teaches certain grade levels and certain courses, a teacher may have only one year with any given group of students. One year is not much time to teach thinking or to instill a love of learning, especially when other teachers essentially indoctrinate children into the current vision or inadvertently work to sabotage the teacher's efforts. In fact, teachers who teach these same students the next year or in other classes may find them difficult to "manage" and lacking in knowledge in certain content areas. Just as parents do not always appreciate critical thinking on the part of their children, many teachers will fail to appreciate "problem" children who are continually asking, "Why?".

*Students.* Students are quickly socialized into our nation's vision and also into their role in the education system. As Salinger describes in Chapter 16, although children enter the school system with an innate desire to learn and with natural curiosity, intrinsic motivation is quickly destroyed and children become primarily motivated by grades. Very early on, they realize that their job is to memorize isolated facts, and, as Romberg explains, to store them in separate schemas where they can be recalled for the test. The information they learn is not for the enrichment of their daily lives but merely for class. In addition, as Collins notes in Chapter 4, children are rapidly taught that there is only one "right" answer and seldom search for, or consider, alternatives. Students thus resist any change in their role and regard requests to think problems through as unreasonable and out of line. Many teachers attempting to stimulate thought are frustrated by silence in response to questions or by the question, "Will this be on the test?". Hence, the students themselves can act as a correcting mechanism. They are quickly indoctrinated into the values and underlying vision of our education system, and they work to maintain the vision as well as their role within it.

*Parents.*    Parents can also act as a roadblock to change. Just as teachers have been socialized within our education system, parents have also absorbed the current vision and may fail to understand why their children are being taught differently from the way they were. Also, if their children or their children's school is below the nation's average on standardized tests, which is possible if the tests emphasize materials and skills that the school or teacher does not regard as important, they will certainly take action. Parents can complain to principals and administrators to force change. Finally, one goal of teaching thinking skills is to teach children to think not just in the classroom, but in their daily lives. Yet, parents who believe "Children are to be seen and not heard" may not appreciate their child's newly developed thinking skills, particularly critical thinking skills. Parents can directly sabotage a teacher's efforts by biasing their child's attitudes toward the teacher and education and by squelching their child's motivation to learn and disposition toward thoughtfulness.

*Administrators.*    School administrators can also act to limit the teaching of thinking skills. Because they are dependent on standardized test scores for evaluations of their performance, they will often encourage teachers to teach to the test, which makes teaching thinking almost impossible. They also often may require short-term results, whereas teaching thinking skills may take years to yield results. Hence, many programs are not given a fair trial. Like everyone else, administrators generally grew up and were indoctrinated into the current vision. It can be very difficult to appreciate the value of other alternatives and innovations when they are turning your school upside down. In addition, administrators often establish curricula that leave little time to teach thinking and impose class-loads which give teachers little time to prepare for lessons. Finally, as Costa notes in Chapter 9, it is difficult to teach thinking in an atmosphere where thought is discouraged. Only when teachers are free to think and their thoughts are respected, and their students are encouraged to do the same, will teaching thinking be effective.

*Federal and State Policies.*    Federal and state policies can also act as a correcting mechanism. States often establish curriculum guidelines that are not conducive to thinking and also require standardized tests. As long as such mandates are handed down from above, it is extremely difficult to make real changes or implement thinking skills programs effectively. There is also poor communication from the statehouse, where decisions and rules are made, and the schools, where curriculum and testing changes must be implemented. The federal and state governments also poorly fund education and education research, causing teachers to be underpaid and overworked, with little time left to continue their own learning or to invest in teaching thinking well. Finally, calls by politicians for returning to the basics and for further accountability act to silence the cries for reform without addressing the real problem—our underlying vision.

*Text Book Publishers.*    Yet another corrective mechanism is our nation's text book publishers. In Chapter 1, Beck and Dole discuss problems with our nation's texts in depth. Publishers often make teaching thinking difficult by publishing texts that fail to incorporate thinking skills and that are lacking in the coherence and structure necessary to allow the students to be able to use and elaborate upon, or become engaged with, the materials.

*Evaluation and Testing.*    Finally, perhaps the greatest corrective mechanism is our institutionalized evaluation system. The fact that we have such evaluation mechanisms in place is an illustration of the power wielded by the current vision. With this view, grades are necessary in order to motivate students to learn and as a method for grouping and categorizing them. Because students must acquire a certain number of facts by the time they reach a certain grade, it is important to know how well schools, teachers, and individual students are succeeding. It can be very difficult for us to step back and acknowledge that our belief in the need for testing is a product of our current vision and to seriously question the necessity of this type of evaluation.

As many authors in this book have noted, the current evaluations were all created with the current vision of education in mind and therefore are contradictory to teaching thinking under a vision that emphasizes thinking skills. Paris, Lawton, and Turner, in Chapter 11, discuss how our current testing system can sabotage efforts to improve thinking skills. The tests encourage low level thinking, misdirect students' motivation, and distort the educational agenda. Paris et al. also note the profoundly negative effects testing has on students, causing lack of motivation, resentment, cynicism, and mistrust. Hence, it is obvious that the current testing system makes it virtually impossible to teach thinking skills well.

## CORRECTIVE MECHANISMS AS A SYSTEM

Although we have discussed each of these corrective mechanisms alone, it is necessary to consider them as a system. All of these mechanisms work in unison to maintain the current institutionalized vision, making genuine change extremely difficult. Incremental changes at virtually any level that are not in line with our common vision will be obstructed. Therefore, educators and researchers must recognize the homeostatic nature of our educational system. Generally, they will discuss a specific problem (e.g., teachers or testing), suggest solutions, and then go on and propose their incremental changes. These incremental changes will not be effective in the long run, because they will run up against the corrective mechanisms. Any mechanism alone is not the problem. Instead of treating the symptoms, we need to address the problem itself—our underlying vision.

Several chapters in this book, for example, those of Costa and Calfee, discuss schools where attempts are made to change administrators, students, teachers, and the staff's vision of education at the school or district level. We would still predict that somewhere along the way, these programs will run up against the typical roadblocks, whether it be parents, required testing, or the lack of measurable results. It may be possible that some prototype programs can survive, but, due to the corrective mechanisms described above, it is doubtful they will spread throughout the nation. The message is not one of pessimism and negativity, but a reminder that before we can overcome the fundamental problem of changing our nation's vision, we need to recognize the problem and come to grips with it.

## CAN A NATION'S VISION BE CHANGED?

Due to the corrective mechanisms described earlier, incremental change is ineffective. Attempts to teach thinking ultimately fail when they run up against our institutionalized vision of education. Hence, it is time to face the question of how we can change our nation's vision of education. Any other reforms are simply treating the symptoms, not the actual cause.

As previously noted, it is extremely difficult to change a vision, because it is based on our basic societal values. It may take a radical societal change. Although such change is possible in countries where revolution is a tradition and ideology changes overnight, it is more difficult in our country, because we are lacking the centralization in government and tradition to make such sweeping changes possible.

Is there any basis for hope? Yes, for several reasons. As authors have noted, the timing may be right. First of all, there is a widespread discontent with our current educational system. There are many calls for change, and people seem willing to consider more radical changes. Regretably, there is little sign that these changes will involve any change in our current vision of education. As previously noted, people appear to be looking for solutions within the current vision.

Another hopeful sign is that there appear to be some changes occurring in our view of education. Several chapters in this book have noted trends in our society that seem to be pointing to an alternative vision of education. For example, Gross discusses ways adults appear to be propelled into a new way of thinking about education. He notes that adults are beginning to attend continued and nontraditional education programs and that more adults are gaining and using knowledge about their own thinking processes and learning. Duffy discusses the ways schools and businesses are working together in cooperative programs and Decker discusses the potential of community education.

Why are such changes occurring? Perhaps our greatest hope for change is the change in the requirements of our economic system, particularly, the decline of the United States as an economic world power and the current change to a postindustrial economy. Several authors have suggested that our changing economy may force a change in education (e.g., Tinzmann et al. in Chapter 10). It may be that as our economic system changes, our nation's vision of education will change accordingly. Why is this possible?

Our nation's educational system has previously changed its purposes in response to external economic factors. When the industrial revolution and flood of immigrants occurred earlier in our nation's history, the purpose of our education system changed from creating educated moral citizens to indoctrinating immigrants into our national culture and educating them to work in our factories. Therefore, our current vision is due in a large part to the economic system in this country.

In addition, other necessary changes in our society have been ignored (e.g., daycare and health insurance), until they became issues that affected our nation's businesses. Suddenly, the issues then came to the forefront and were seriously addressed and real attempts at change were made. Why is big business suddenly becoming involved in education? As we are approaching the 21st century, in order to compete in a world economy, we no longer need factory workers, but workers who can handle complex information and think. Business leaders are forced to pay considerable sums of money to retrain their workers and still have problems finding workers who can do the job. For this reason, business leaders are getting involved in the education system and calling for change. We can only hope that with this sudden change in demand, supply will also change accordingly. How might this happen?

As the changing needs of our nation's businesses are widely discussed, it may be that although the topic of our nation's underlying vision will not be addressed, people's assumptions about the purpose of education will be questioned and changed. Generally, parents want their children to succeed in life and count on schools to give them the skills they will need. Hence, when experience with a computer became a prerequisite for many jobs, schools obtained and began to teach computers to provide children with a valuable skill they would need in the future. It is now not unusual to see fifth graders receiving keyboard training and learning text processing. Similarly, if parents realize their children will need to be able to think in the future, they will begin to ask for thinking skills programs in the schools. They may realize that the traditional approach will not provide their child with the skills necessary to compete in the marketplace. Of course, another very real possibility is that instead of questioning basic assumptions, parents, teachers, and administrators will try to graft thinking skills training onto the current system. As we have established, as long as the current vision is firmly in place, there is little hope for the success of such attempts.

Therefore, while changes in our economic system offer some hope for change, we cannot depend on these economic changes to take care of this problem and simply assume that if we do not think about it, it will go away. We must confront the fact that our educational system is homeostatic and deal with it as such. We can begin by implementing ideas in this book. Otherwise, 100 years from now, another group of authors will need to write another book, entitled "Thinking Development: An Agenda for the *Twenty-Second* Century," and little will have changed.

## ACKNOWLEDGMENTS

Preparation of this manuscript was supported by a National Science Foundation fellowship to the first author and by the Javits Act Program as administered by the Office of Educational Research and Improvement, U.S. Department of Education, through a grant to the National Research Center on the Gifted and Talented. The findings and opinions expressed in this report do not reflect the position or policies of the Office of Educational Research and Improvement or the U.S. Department of Education.

## REFERENCES

*Webster's New World Dictionary* (3rd ed.). 1988. New York: Simon & Schuster, Inc.

# Author Index

# Subject Index